DIAGNOSIS BUDDY

A symptom tracking journal

WELLNESS WARRIOR PRESS
WWW.WELLNESSWARRIORPRESS.COM

ISBN: 978-1-990775-02-4

This journal belongs to…

Doctor / Specialist Information

Name	Address	Contact

Daily Medication / Supplements

Medication / Supplement	Dosage

Appointments / Surgeries

Details	Time / Location	Notes

Summary

For each journal entry, return to this summary page and rate your overall pain / discomfort level (1 being no pain / discomfort and 10 being unbearable)

Entry #	Rating	Entry #	Rating	Entry #	Rating
1		31		61	
2		32		62	
3		33		63	
4		34		64	
5		35		65	
6		36		66	
7		37		67	
8		38		68	
9		39		69	
10		40		70	
11		41		71	
12		42		72	
13		43		73	
14		44		74	
15		45		75	
16		46		76	
17		47		77	
18		48		78	
19		49		79	
20		50		80	
21		51		81	
22		52		82	
23		53		83	
24		54		84	
25		55		85	
26		56		86	
27		57		87	
28		58		88	
29		59		89	
30		60		90	

Weekly Analysis

After completing 7 daily entries, return to your weekly analysis page and try to understand what might have triggered some of your symptoms. Look for reoccurring patterns and trends, or maybe something new that was introduced into your life (whether it be food, stress, poor sleep, etc.).

Week 1 (entries 1 – 7)

Average pain rating ① ② ③ ④ ⑤
Average wellness rating ① ② ③ ④ ⑤
Average mood rating ① ② ③ ④ ⑤

Patterns

Events/ Changes

Week 2 (entries 8 – 14)

Average pain rating ① ② ③ ④ ⑤
Average wellness rating ① ② ③ ④ ⑤
Average mood rating ① ② ③ ④ ⑤

Patterns

Events/ Changes

Week 3 (entries 15 – 21)

Average pain rating ① ② ③ ④ ⑤
Average wellness rating ① ② ③ ④ ⑤
Average mood rating ① ② ③ ④ ⑤

Patterns

Events/ Changes

Week 4 (entries 22 – 28)

Average pain rating ① ② ③ ④ ⑤
Average wellness rating ① ② ③ ④ ⑤
Average mood rating ① ② ③ ④ ⑤

Patterns

Events/ Changes

Weekly Analysis – cont'd

After completing 7 daily entries, return to your weekly analysis page and try to understand what might have caused / triggered some of your symptoms. Look for reoccurring patterns and trends, or maybe something new that was introduced into your life (whether it be food, stress, poor sleep, etc.).

Week 5
(entries 29 – 35)

Average pain rating ① ② ③ ④ ⑤ Average wellness rating ① ② ③ ④ ⑤ Average mood rating ① ② ③ ④ ⑤

Patterns

Events/ Changes

Week 6
(entries 36 – 42)

Average pain rating ① ② ③ ④ ⑤ Average wellness rating ① ② ③ ④ ⑤ Average mood rating ① ② ③ ④ ⑤

Patterns

Events/ Changes

Week 7
(entries 43 – 49)

Average pain rating ① ② ③ ④ ⑤ Average wellness rating ① ② ③ ④ ⑤ Average mood rating ① ② ③ ④ ⑤

Patterns

Events/ Changes

Week 8
(entries 50 – 56)

Average pain rating ① ② ③ ④ ⑤ Average wellness rating ① ② ③ ④ ⑤ Average mood rating ① ② ③ ④ ⑤

Patterns

Events/ Changes

Week 9
(entries 57 – 63)

Average pain rating ① ② ③ ④ ⑤

Average wellness rating ① ② ③ ④ ⑤

Average mood rating ① ② ③ ④ ⑤

Patterns

Events/ Changes

Week 10
(entries 64 – 70)

Average pain rating ① ② ③ ④ ⑤

Average wellness rating ① ② ③ ④ ⑤

Average mood rating ① ② ③ ④ ⑤

Patterns

Events/ Changes

Week 11
(entries 71– 77)

Average pain rating ① ② ③ ④ ⑤

Average wellness rating ① ② ③ ④ ⑤

Average mood rating ① ② ③ ④ ⑤

Patterns

Events/ Changes

Week 12
(entries 78 – 84)

Average pain rating ① ② ③ ④ ⑤

Average wellness rating ① ② ③ ④ ⑤

Average mood rating ① ② ③ ④ ⑤

Patterns

Events/ Changes

Week 13
(entries 85 – 90)

Average pain rating ① ② ③ ④ ⑤

Average wellness rating ① ② ③ ④ ⑤

Average mood rating ① ② ③ ④ ⑤

Patterns

Events/ Changes

Detailed Symptom Analysis

Symptom	Avg. severity	Avg. times per week	Total count in last 90 days
	① ② ③ ④ ⑤		
	① ② ③ ④ ⑤		
	① ② ③ ④ ⑤		
	① ② ③ ④ ⑤		
	① ② ③ ④ ⑤		
	① ② ③ ④ ⑤		
	① ② ③ ④ ⑤		
	① ② ③ ④ ⑤		
	① ② ③ ④ ⑤		
	① ② ③ ④ ⑤		
	① ② ③ ④ ⑤		
	① ② ③ ④ ⑤		
	① ② ③ ④ ⑤		
	① ② ③ ④ ⑤		
	① ② ③ ④ ⑤		
	① ② ③ ④ ⑤		
	① ② ③ ④ ⑤		
	① ② ③ ④ ⑤		
	① ② ③ ④ ⑤		
	① ② ③ ④ ⑤		
	① ② ③ ④ ⑤		
	① ② ③ ④ ⑤		
	① ② ③ ④ ⑤		
	① ② ③ ④ ⑤		
	① ② ③ ④ ⑤		
	① ② ③ ④ ⑤		
	① ② ③ ④ ⑤		
	① ② ③ ④ ⑤		
	① ② ③ ④ ⑤		

Detailed Trigger Analysis

Symptom	Cause / Trigger		Treatment Method	
	☐ Suspected	☐ Confirmed	☐ Natural	☐ Medical

Details / notes

Symptom	Cause / Trigger		Treatment Method	
	☐ Suspected	☐ Confirmed	☐ Natural	☐ Medical

Details / notes

Symptom	Cause / Trigger		Treatment Method	
	☐ Suspected	☐ Confirmed	☐ Natural	☐ Medical

Details / notes

Symptom	Cause / Trigger		Treatment Method	
	☐ Suspected	☐ Confirmed	☐ Natural	☐ Medical

Details / notes

Symptom	Cause / Trigger		Treatment Method	
	☐ Suspected	☐ Confirmed	☐ Natural	☐ Medical

Details / notes

Detailed Trigger Analysis

Symptom	Cause / Trigger		Treatment Method	
	☐ Suspected	☐ Confirmed	☐ Natural	☐ Medical

Details / notes

Symptom	Cause / Trigger		Treatment Method	
	☐ Suspected	☐ Confirmed	☐ Natural	☐ Medical

Details / notes

Symptom	Cause / Trigger		Treatment Method	
	☐ Suspected	☐ Confirmed	☐ Natural	☐ Medical

Details / notes

Symptom	Cause / Trigger		Treatment Method	
	☐ Suspected	☐ Confirmed	☐ Natural	☐ Medical

Details / notes

Symptom	Cause / Trigger		Treatment Method	
	☐ Suspected	☐ Confirmed	☐ Natural	☐ Medical

Details / notes

Detailed Trigger Analysis

Symptom	Cause / Trigger		Treatment Method	
	☐ Suspected	☐ Confirmed	☐ Natural	☐ Medical

Details / notes

Symptom	Cause / Trigger		Treatment Method	
	☐ Suspected	☐ Confirmed	☐ Natural	☐ Medical

Details / notes

Symptom	Cause / Trigger		Treatment Method	
	☐ Suspected	☐ Confirmed	☐ Natural	☐ Medical

Details / notes

Symptom	Cause / Trigger		Treatment Method	
	☐ Suspected	☐ Confirmed	☐ Natural	☐ Medical

Details / notes

Symptom	Cause / Trigger		Treatment Method	
	☐ Suspected	☐ Confirmed	☐ Natural	☐ Medical

Details / notes

ENTRY #1 | M T W T F S S | DATE:

HOW ARE YOU *Feeling today?*

Amazing!	Meh
Great	Not good
Good	Terrible!

RATE YOUR PAIN LEVEL

① ② ③ ④ ⑤ ⑥ ⑦ ⑧ ⑨ ⑩

WHAT ABOUT YOUR...?

Mood	① ② ③ ④ ⑤ ⑥ ⑦ ⑧ ⑨ ⑩
Energy Levels	① ② ③ ④ ⑤ ⑥ ⑦ ⑧ ⑨ ⑩
Mental Clarity	① ② ③ ④ ⑤ ⑥ ⑦ ⑧ ⑨ ⑩

PAIN & PHYSICAL SYMPTOMS

Symptom	Severity	am	pm
	① ② ③ ④ ⑤	☐	☐
	① ② ③ ④ ⑤	☐	☐
	① ② ③ ④ ⑤	☐	☐
	① ② ③ ④ ⑤	☐	☐
	① ② ③ ④ ⑤	☐	☐
	① ② ③ ④ ⑤	☐	☐
	① ② ③ ④ ⑤	☐	☐
	① ② ③ ④ ⑤	☐	☐

front ***back***

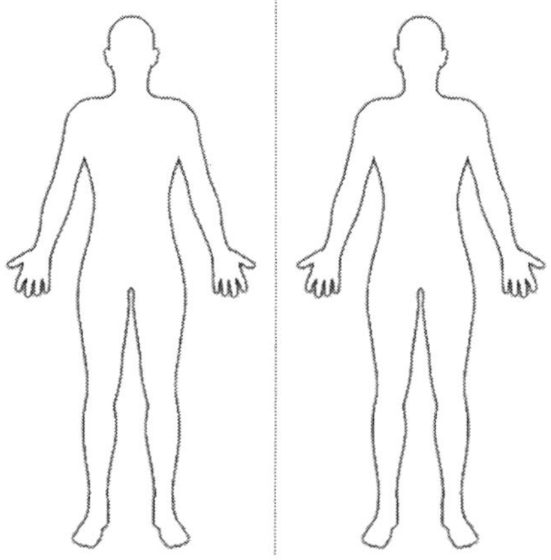

OTHER SYMPTOMS

general

Symptom	Severity	Time	
☐ Fatigue	① ② ③ ④ ⑤	☐ a.m.	☐ p.m.
☐ Lethargy	① ② ③ ④ ⑤	☐ a.m.	☐ p.m.
☐ Malaise	① ② ③ ④ ⑤	☐ a.m.	☐ p.m.
☐ Weakness	① ② ③ ④ ⑤	☐ a.m.	☐ p.m.
☐ Dizziness	① ② ③ ④ ⑤	☐ a.m.	☐ p.m.
☐ Trembling	① ② ③ ④ ⑤	☐ a.m.	☐ p.m.
☐ Twitching	① ② ③ ④ ⑤	☐ a.m.	☐ p.m.
☐ Insomnia	① ② ③ ④ ⑤	☐ a.m.	☐ p.m.

illness

Symptom	Severity	Time	
☐ Nausea	① ② ③ ④ ⑤	☐ a.m.	☐ p.m.
☐ Vomiting	① ② ③ ④ ⑤	☐ a.m.	☐ p.m.
☐ Constipation	① ② ③ ④ ⑤	☐ a.m.	☐ p.m.
☐ Diarrhea	① ② ③ ④ ⑤	☐ a.m.	☐ p.m.
☐ Sore throat	① ② ③ ④ ⑤	☐ a.m.	☐ p.m.
☐ Congestion	① ② ③ ④ ⑤	☐ a.m.	☐ p.m.
☐ Coughing	① ② ③ ④ ⑤	☐ a.m.	☐ p.m.
☐ Acid reflux	① ② ③ ④ ⑤	☐ a.m.	☐ p.m.

psychological

Symptom	Severity	Time	
☐ Anxiety	① ② ③ ④ ⑤	☐ a.m.	☐ p.m.
☐ Depression	① ② ③ ④ ⑤	☐ a.m.	☐ p.m.
☐ Memory loss	① ② ③ ④ ⑤	☐ a.m.	☐ p.m.
☐ Confusion	① ② ③ ④ ⑤	☐ a.m.	☐ p.m.
☐ Poor focus	① ② ③ ④ ⑤	☐ a.m.	☐ p.m.
☐ Mood swings	① ② ③ ④ ⑤	☐ a.m.	☐ p.m.
☐ Suicidal	① ② ③ ④ ⑤	☐ a.m.	☐ p.m.

other

Symptom	Severity	Time	
	① ② ③ ④ ⑤	☐ a.m.	☐ p.m.
	① ② ③ ④ ⑤	☐ a.m.	☐ p.m.
	① ② ③ ④ ⑤	☐ a.m.	☐ p.m.
	① ② ③ ④ ⑤	☐ a.m.	☐ p.m.
	① ② ③ ④ ⑤	☐ a.m.	☐ p.m.
	① ② ③ ④ ⑤	☐ a.m.	☐ p.m.
	① ② ③ ④ ⑤	☐ a.m.	☐ p.m.

SLEEP

hours ________ *quality* ① ② ③ ④ ⑤

STRESS LEVELS

None	Low	Medium	High	Max	@$#%!

WEATHER

☐ Cold ☐ Mild ☐ Hot
☐ Dry ☐ Humid ☐ Wet

Allergen Levels: ________
BM Pressure: ________

EXERCISE

☐ Heck yes, I worked out.
☐ I managed to exercise a bit.
☐ No, I haven't exercised at all.
☐ I did some stuff, and that counts.

DETAILS

FOOD / MEDICATION

Food / Drinks

Meds / Supplements	Time	Dose
☐ usual daily medication		

Water *Caffeine* *Alcohol*

x ________ x ________

FOOD ANALYSIS

New food introduced?
☐ Yes ☐ No
Food reintroduction?
☐ Yes ☐ No

Details

MEDICATION ANALYSIS

New med/dose introduced?
☐ Yes ☐ No
Medication stopped?
☐ Yes ☐ No

Details

ACTIVITY ANALYSIS

Heightened exertion levels?
☐ Yes ☐ No
Lowered exertion levels?
☐ Yes ☐ No

Details

SLEEP ANALYSIS

When you woke up this morning, did you feel well-rested?	☐ Yes	☐ No	☐ A bit
Did you snore or stop breathing throughout the night?	☐ Yes	☐ No	☐ Not sure
Roughly how many times did you wake up throughout the night?			

Notes / Suspected Triggers

ENTRY #2 | M T W T F S S | DATE:

HOW ARE YOU *Feeling today?*

Amazing!	Meh
Great	Not good
Good	Terrible!

RATE YOUR PAIN LEVEL

① ② ③ ④ ⑤ ⑥ ⑦ ⑧ ⑨ ⑩

WHAT ABOUT YOUR...?

Mood	① ② ③ ④ ⑤ ⑥ ⑦ ⑧ ⑨ ⑩
Energy Levels	① ② ③ ④ ⑤ ⑥ ⑦ ⑧ ⑨ ⑩
Mental Clarity	① ② ③ ④ ⑤ ⑥ ⑦ ⑧ ⑨ ⑩

PAIN & PHYSICAL SYMPTOMS

Symptom	Severity	am	pm
	① ② ③ ④ ⑤	☐	☐
	① ② ③ ④ ⑤	☐	☐
	① ② ③ ④ ⑤	☐	☐
	① ② ③ ④ ⑤	☐	☐
	① ② ③ ④ ⑤	☐	☐
	① ② ③ ④ ⑤	☐	☐
	① ② ③ ④ ⑤	☐	☐
	① ② ③ ④ ⑤	☐	☐

front ***back***

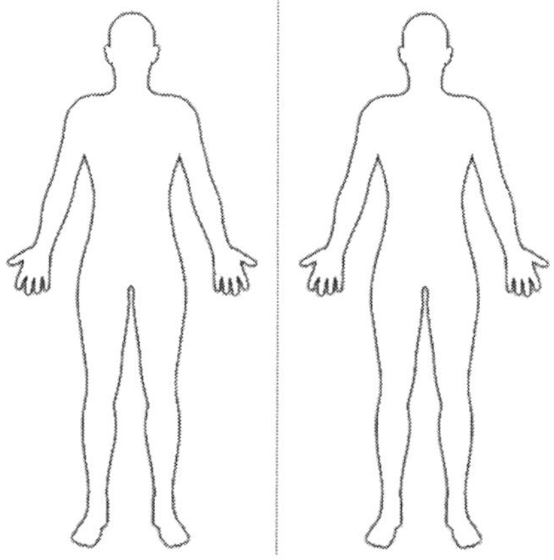

OTHER SYMPTOMS

general

Symptom	Severity	Time	
☐ Fatigue	① ② ③ ④ ⑤	☐ a.m.	☐ p.m.
☐ Lethargy	① ② ③ ④ ⑤	☐ a.m.	☐ p.m.
☐ Malaise	① ② ③ ④ ⑤	☐ a.m.	☐ p.m.
☐ Weakness	① ② ③ ④ ⑤	☐ a.m.	☐ p.m.
☐ Dizziness	① ② ③ ④ ⑤	☐ a.m.	☐ p.m.
☐ Trembling	① ② ③ ④ ⑤	☐ a.m.	☐ p.m.
☐ Twitching	① ② ③ ④ ⑤	☐ a.m.	☐ p.m.
☐ Insomnia	① ② ③ ④ ⑤	☐ a.m.	☐ p.m.

illness

Symptom	Severity	Time	
☐ Nausea	① ② ③ ④ ⑤	☐ a.m.	☐ p.m.
☐ Vomiting	① ② ③ ④ ⑤	☐ a.m.	☐ p.m.
☐ Constipation	① ② ③ ④ ⑤	☐ a.m.	☐ p.m.
☐ Diarrhea	① ② ③ ④ ⑤	☐ a.m.	☐ p.m.
☐ Sore throat	① ② ③ ④ ⑤	☐ a.m.	☐ p.m.
☐ Congestion	① ② ③ ④ ⑤	☐ a.m.	☐ p.m.
☐ Coughing	① ② ③ ④ ⑤	☐ a.m.	☐ p.m.
☐ Acid reflux	① ② ③ ④ ⑤	☐ a.m.	☐ p.m.

psychological

Symptom	Severity	Time	
☐ Anxiety	① ② ③ ④ ⑤	☐ a.m.	☐ p.m.
☐ Depression	① ② ③ ④ ⑤	☐ a.m.	☐ p.m.
☐ Memory loss	① ② ③ ④ ⑤	☐ a.m.	☐ p.m.
☐ Confusion	① ② ③ ④ ⑤	☐ a.m.	☐ p.m.
☐ Poor focus	① ② ③ ④ ⑤	☐ a.m.	☐ p.m.
☐ Mood swings	① ② ③ ④ ⑤	☐ a.m.	☐ p.m.
☐ Suicidal	① ② ③ ④ ⑤	☐ a.m.	☐ p.m.

other

Symptom	Severity	Time	
	① ② ③ ④ ⑤	☐ a.m.	☐ p.m.
	① ② ③ ④ ⑤	☐ a.m.	☐ p.m.
	① ② ③ ④ ⑤	☐ a.m.	☐ p.m.
	① ② ③ ④ ⑤	☐ a.m.	☐ p.m.
	① ② ③ ④ ⑤	☐ a.m.	☐ p.m.
	① ② ③ ④ ⑤	☐ a.m.	☐ p.m.
	① ② ③ ④ ⑤	☐ a.m.	☐ p.m.

SLEEP

hours ________ *quality* ① ② ③ ④ ⑤

STRESS LEVELS

None	Low	Medium	High	Max	@$#%!

WEATHER

☐ Cold ☐ Mild ☐ Hot
☐ Dry ☐ Humid ☐ Wet

Allergen Levels: ________
BM Pressure: ________

EXERCISE

☐ Heck yes, I worked out.
☐ I managed to exercise a bit.
☐ No, I haven't exercised at all.
☐ I did some stuff, and that counts.

DETAILS

FOOD / MEDICATION

Food / Drinks

Meds / Supplements	Time	Dose

☐ usual daily medication

Water *Caffeine* *Alcohol*

x ________ x ________

FOOD ANALYSIS

New food introduced?
☐ Yes ☐ No
Food reintroduction?
☐ Yes ☐ No

Details

MEDICATION ANALYSIS

New med/dose introduced?
☐ Yes ☐ No
Medication stopped?
☐ Yes ☐ No

Details

ACTIVITY ANALYSIS

Heightened exertion levels?
☐ Yes ☐ No
Lowered exertion levels?
☐ Yes ☐ No

Details

SLEEP ANALYSIS

When you woke up this morning, did you feel well-rested?	☐ Yes	☐ No	☐ A bit
Did you snore or stop breathing throughout the night?	☐ Yes	☐ No	☐ Not sure
Roughly how many times did you wake up throughout the night?			

Notes / Suspected Triggers

ENTRY #3 | M T W T F S S | DATE:

HOW ARE YOU *Feeling today?*

Amazing!	Meh
Great	Not good
Good	Terrible!

RATE YOUR PAIN LEVEL

① ② ③ ④ ⑤ ⑥ ⑦ ⑧ ⑨ ⑩

WHAT ABOUT YOUR...?

Mood	① ② ③ ④ ⑤ ⑥ ⑦ ⑧ ⑨ ⑩
Energy Levels	① ② ③ ④ ⑤ ⑥ ⑦ ⑧ ⑨ ⑩
Mental Clarity	① ② ③ ④ ⑤ ⑥ ⑦ ⑧ ⑨ ⑩

PAIN & PHYSICAL SYMPTOMS

Symptom	Severity	am	pm
	① ② ③ ④ ⑤	☐	☐
	① ② ③ ④ ⑤	☐	☐
	① ② ③ ④ ⑤	☐	☐
	① ② ③ ④ ⑤	☐	☐
	① ② ③ ④ ⑤	☐	☐
	① ② ③ ④ ⑤	☐	☐
	① ② ③ ④ ⑤	☐	☐
	① ② ③ ④ ⑤	☐	☐

front ***back***

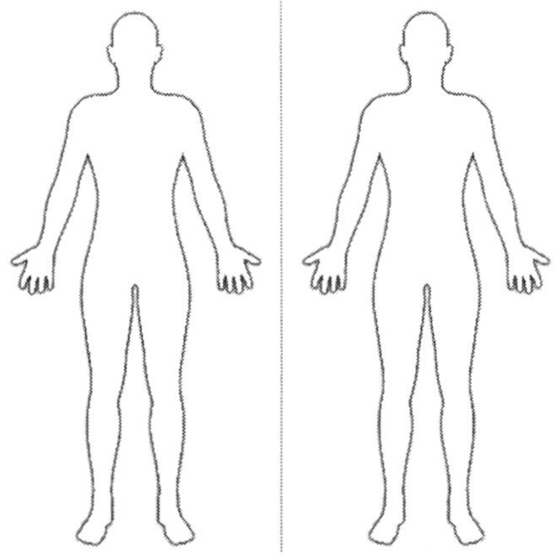

OTHER SYMPTOMS

general

Symptom	Severity	Time	
☐ Fatigue	① ② ③ ④ ⑤	☐ a.m.	☐ p.m.
☐ Lethargy	① ② ③ ④ ⑤	☐ a.m.	☐ p.m.
☐ Malaise	① ② ③ ④ ⑤	☐ a.m.	☐ p.m.
☐ Weakness	① ② ③ ④ ⑤	☐ a.m.	☐ p.m.
☐ Dizziness	① ② ③ ④ ⑤	☐ a.m.	☐ p.m.
☐ Trembling	① ② ③ ④ ⑤	☐ a.m.	☐ p.m.
☐ Twitching	① ② ③ ④ ⑤	☐ a.m.	☐ p.m.
☐ Insomnia	① ② ③ ④ ⑤	☐ a.m.	☐ p.m.

illness

Symptom	Severity	Time	
☐ Nausea	① ② ③ ④ ⑤	☐ a.m.	☐ p.m.
☐ Vomiting	① ② ③ ④ ⑤	☐ a.m.	☐ p.m.
☐ Constipation	① ② ③ ④ ⑤	☐ a.m.	☐ p.m.
☐ Diarrhea	① ② ③ ④ ⑤	☐ a.m.	☐ p.m.
☐ Sore throat	① ② ③ ④ ⑤	☐ a.m.	☐ p.m.
☐ Congestion	① ② ③ ④ ⑤	☐ a.m.	☐ p.m.
☐ Coughing	① ② ③ ④ ⑤	☐ a.m.	☐ p.m.
☐ Acid reflux	① ② ③ ④ ⑤	☐ a.m.	☐ p.m.

psychological

Symptom	Severity	Time	
☐ Anxiety	① ② ③ ④ ⑤	☐ a.m.	☐ p.m.
☐ Depression	① ② ③ ④ ⑤	☐ a.m.	☐ p.m.
☐ Memory loss	① ② ③ ④ ⑤	☐ a.m.	☐ p.m.
☐ Confusion	① ② ③ ④ ⑤	☐ a.m.	☐ p.m.
☐ Poor focus	① ② ③ ④ ⑤	☐ a.m.	☐ p.m.
☐ Mood swings	① ② ③ ④ ⑤	☐ a.m.	☐ p.m.
☐ Suicidal	① ② ③ ④ ⑤	☐ a.m.	☐ p.m.

other

Symptom	Severity	Time	
	① ② ③ ④ ⑤	☐ a.m.	☐ p.m.
	① ② ③ ④ ⑤	☐ a.m.	☐ p.m.
	① ② ③ ④ ⑤	☐ a.m.	☐ p.m.
	① ② ③ ④ ⑤	☐ a.m.	☐ p.m.
	① ② ③ ④ ⑤	☐ a.m.	☐ p.m.
	① ② ③ ④ ⑤	☐ a.m.	☐ p.m.
	① ② ③ ④ ⑤	☐ a.m.	☐ p.m.

SLEEP

hours ________

quality ① ② ③ ④ ⑤

STRESS LEVELS

None	Low	Medium	High	Max	@$#%!

WEATHER

☐ Cold ☐ Mild ☐ Hot

☐ Dry ☐ Humid ☐ Wet

Allergen Levels: ________

BM Pressure: ________

EXERCISE

☐ Heck yes, I worked out.

☐ I managed to exercise a bit.

☐ No, I haven't exercised at all.

☐ I did some stuff, and that counts.

DETAILS

FOOD / MEDICATION

Food / Drinks

Meds / Supplements	Time	Dose
☐ usual daily medication		

Water *Caffeine* *Alcohol*

x ________ x ________

FOOD ANALYSIS

New food introduced?

☐ Yes ☐ No

Food reintroduction?

☐ Yes ☐ No

Details

MEDICATION ANALYSIS

New med/dose introduced?

☐ Yes ☐ No

Medication stopped?

☐ Yes ☐ No

Details

ACTIVITY ANALYSIS

Heightened exertion levels?

☐ Yes ☐ No

Lowered exertion levels?

☐ Yes ☐ No

Details

SLEEP ANALYSIS

When you woke up this morning, did you feel well-rested?	☐ Yes	☐ No	☐ A bit
Did you snore or stop breathing throughout the night?	☐ Yes	☐ No	☐ Not sure
Roughly how many times did you wake up throughout the night?			

Notes / Suspected Triggers

ENTRY #4 | M T W T F S S | DATE:

HOW ARE YOU *Feeling today?*

Amazing!	Meh
Great	Not good
Good	Terrible!

RATE YOUR PAIN LEVEL

① ② ③ ④ ⑤ ⑥ ⑦ ⑧ ⑨ ⑩

WHAT ABOUT YOUR...?

Mood	① ② ③ ④ ⑤ ⑥ ⑦ ⑧ ⑨ ⑩
Energy Levels	① ② ③ ④ ⑤ ⑥ ⑦ ⑧ ⑨ ⑩
Mental Clarity	① ② ③ ④ ⑤ ⑥ ⑦ ⑧ ⑨ ⑩

PAIN & PHYSICAL SYMPTOMS

Symptom	Severity	am	pm
	① ② ③ ④ ⑤	☐	☐
	① ② ③ ④ ⑤	☐	☐
	① ② ③ ④ ⑤	☐	☐
	① ② ③ ④ ⑤	☐	☐
	① ② ③ ④ ⑤	☐	☐
	① ② ③ ④ ⑤	☐	☐
	① ② ③ ④ ⑤	☐	☐
	① ② ③ ④ ⑤	☐	☐

front ***back***

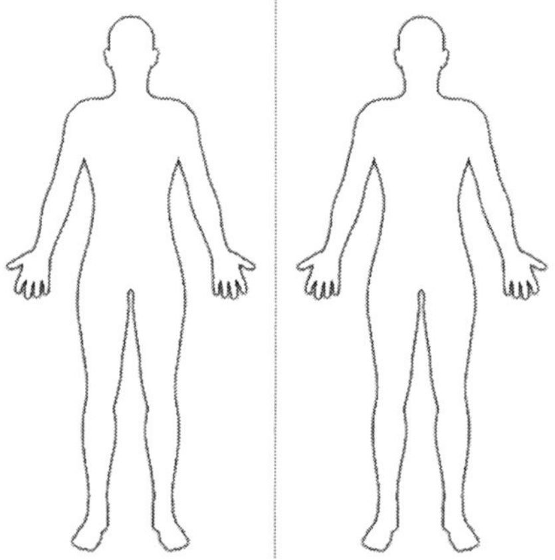

OTHER SYMPTOMS

general

Symptom	Severity	Time	
☐ Fatigue	① ② ③ ④ ⑤	☐ a.m.	☐ p.m.
☐ Lethargy	① ② ③ ④ ⑤	☐ a.m.	☐ p.m.
☐ Malaise	① ② ③ ④ ⑤	☐ a.m.	☐ p.m.
☐ Weakness	① ② ③ ④ ⑤	☐ a.m.	☐ p.m.
☐ Dizziness	① ② ③ ④ ⑤	☐ a.m.	☐ p.m.
☐ Trembling	① ② ③ ④ ⑤	☐ a.m.	☐ p.m.
☐ Twitching	① ② ③ ④ ⑤	☐ a.m.	☐ p.m.
☐ Insomnia	① ② ③ ④ ⑤	☐ a.m.	☐ p.m.

illness

Symptom	Severity	Time	
☐ Nausea	① ② ③ ④ ⑤	☐ a.m.	☐ p.m.
☐ Vomiting	① ② ③ ④ ⑤	☐ a.m.	☐ p.m.
☐ Constipation	① ② ③ ④ ⑤	☐ a.m.	☐ p.m.
☐ Diarrhea	① ② ③ ④ ⑤	☐ a.m.	☐ p.m.
☐ Sore throat	① ② ③ ④ ⑤	☐ a.m.	☐ p.m.
☐ Congestion	① ② ③ ④ ⑤	☐ a.m.	☐ p.m.
☐ Coughing	① ② ③ ④ ⑤	☐ a.m.	☐ p.m.
☐ Acid reflux	① ② ③ ④ ⑤	☐ a.m.	☐ p.m.

psychological

Symptom	Severity	Time	
☐ Anxiety	① ② ③ ④ ⑤	☐ a.m.	☐ p.m.
☐ Depression	① ② ③ ④ ⑤	☐ a.m.	☐ p.m.
☐ Memory loss	① ② ③ ④ ⑤	☐ a.m.	☐ p.m.
☐ Confusion	① ② ③ ④ ⑤	☐ a.m.	☐ p.m.
☐ Poor focus	① ② ③ ④ ⑤	☐ a.m.	☐ p.m.
☐ Mood swings	① ② ③ ④ ⑤	☐ a.m.	☐ p.m.
☐ Suicidal	① ② ③ ④ ⑤	☐ a.m.	☐ p.m.

other

Symptom	Severity	Time	
	① ② ③ ④ ⑤	☐ a.m.	☐ p.m.
	① ② ③ ④ ⑤	☐ a.m.	☐ p.m.
	① ② ③ ④ ⑤	☐ a.m.	☐ p.m.
	① ② ③ ④ ⑤	☐ a.m.	☐ p.m.
	① ② ③ ④ ⑤	☐ a.m.	☐ p.m.
	① ② ③ ④ ⑤	☐ a.m.	☐ p.m.
	① ② ③ ④ ⑤	☐ a.m.	☐ p.m.

SLEEP

hours ________ *quality* ① ② ③ ④ ⑤

STRESS LEVELS

None	Low	Medium	High	Max	@$#%!

WEATHER

☐ Cold ☐ Mild ☐ Hot
☐ Dry ☐ Humid ☐ Wet

Allergen Levels: ________

BM Pressure: ________

EXERCISE

☐ Heck yes, I worked out.
☐ I managed to exercise a bit.
☐ No, I haven't exercised at all.
☐ I did some stuff, and that counts.

DETAILS

FOOD / MEDICATION

Food / Drinks

Meds / Supplements	Time	Dose

☐ usual daily medication

Water	Caffeine	Alcohol
	x ________	x ________

FOOD ANALYSIS

New food introduced?
☐ Yes ☐ No

Food reintroduction?
☐ Yes ☐ No

Details

MEDICATION ANALYSIS

New med/dose introduced?
☐ Yes ☐ No

Medication stopped?
☐ Yes ☐ No

Details

ACTIVITY ANALYSIS

Heightened exertion levels?
☐ Yes ☐ No

Lowered exertion levels?
☐ Yes ☐ No

Details

SLEEP ANALYSIS

When you woke up this morning, did you feel well-rested?	☐ Yes	☐ No	☐ A bit
Did you snore or stop breathing throughout the night?	☐ Yes	☐ No	☐ Not sure
Roughly how many times did you wake up throughout the night?			

Notes / Suspected Triggers

ENTRY #5 | M T W T F S S | DATE:

HOW ARE YOU *Feeling today?*

Amazing!	Meh
Great	Not good
Good	Terrible!

RATE YOUR PAIN LEVEL

① ② ③ ④ ⑤ ⑥ ⑦ ⑧ ⑨ ⑩

WHAT ABOUT YOUR...?

Mood	① ② ③ ④ ⑤ ⑥ ⑦ ⑧ ⑨ ⑩
Energy Levels	① ② ③ ④ ⑤ ⑥ ⑦ ⑧ ⑨ ⑩
Mental Clarity	① ② ③ ④ ⑤ ⑥ ⑦ ⑧ ⑨ ⑩

PAIN & PHYSICAL SYMPTOMS

Symptom	Severity	am	pm
	① ② ③ ④ ⑤	☐	☐
	① ② ③ ④ ⑤	☐	☐
	① ② ③ ④ ⑤	☐	☐
	① ② ③ ④ ⑤	☐	☐
	① ② ③ ④ ⑤	☐	☐
	① ② ③ ④ ⑤	☐	☐
	① ② ③ ④ ⑤	☐	☐
	① ② ③ ④ ⑤	☐	☐

front ***back***

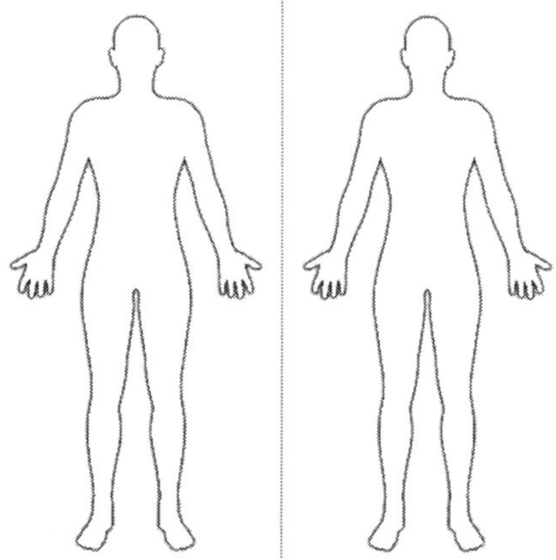

OTHER SYMPTOMS

general

Symptom	Severity	Time	
☐ Fatigue	① ② ③ ④ ⑤	☐ a.m.	☐ p.m.
☐ Lethargy	① ② ③ ④ ⑤	☐ a.m.	☐ p.m.
☐ Malaise	① ② ③ ④ ⑤	☐ a.m.	☐ p.m.
☐ Weakness	① ② ③ ④ ⑤	☐ a.m.	☐ p.m.
☐ Dizziness	① ② ③ ④ ⑤	☐ a.m.	☐ p.m.
☐ Trembling	① ② ③ ④ ⑤	☐ a.m.	☐ p.m.
☐ Twitching	① ② ③ ④ ⑤	☐ a.m.	☐ p.m.
☐ Insomnia	① ② ③ ④ ⑤	☐ a.m.	☐ p.m.

illness

Symptom	Severity	Time	
☐ Nausea	① ② ③ ④ ⑤	☐ a.m.	☐ p.m.
☐ Vomiting	① ② ③ ④ ⑤	☐ a.m.	☐ p.m.
☐ Constipation	① ② ③ ④ ⑤	☐ a.m.	☐ p.m.
☐ Diarrhea	① ② ③ ④ ⑤	☐ a.m.	☐ p.m.
☐ Sore throat	① ② ③ ④ ⑤	☐ a.m.	☐ p.m.
☐ Congestion	① ② ③ ④ ⑤	☐ a.m.	☐ p.m.
☐ Coughing	① ② ③ ④ ⑤	☐ a.m.	☐ p.m.
☐ Acid reflux	① ② ③ ④ ⑤	☐ a.m.	☐ p.m.

psychological

Symptom	Severity	Time	
☐ Anxiety	① ② ③ ④ ⑤	☐ a.m.	☐ p.m.
☐ Depression	① ② ③ ④ ⑤	☐ a.m.	☐ p.m.
☐ Memory loss	① ② ③ ④ ⑤	☐ a.m.	☐ p.m.
☐ Confusion	① ② ③ ④ ⑤	☐ a.m.	☐ p.m.
☐ Poor focus	① ② ③ ④ ⑤	☐ a.m.	☐ p.m.
☐ Mood swings	① ② ③ ④ ⑤	☐ a.m.	☐ p.m.
☐ Suicidal	① ② ③ ④ ⑤	☐ a.m.	☐ p.m.

other

Symptom	Severity	Time	
	① ② ③ ④ ⑤	☐ a.m.	☐ p.m.
	① ② ③ ④ ⑤	☐ a.m.	☐ p.m.
	① ② ③ ④ ⑤	☐ a.m.	☐ p.m.
	① ② ③ ④ ⑤	☐ a.m.	☐ p.m.
	① ② ③ ④ ⑤	☐ a.m.	☐ p.m.
	① ② ③ ④ ⑤	☐ a.m.	☐ p.m.
	① ② ③ ④ ⑤	☐ a.m.	☐ p.m.

SLEEP

hours ________ quality ① ② ③ ④ ⑤

STRESS LEVELS

None	Low	Medium	High	Max	@$#%!

WEATHER

☐ Cold ☐ Mild ☐ Hot
☐ Dry ☐ Humid ☐ Wet

Allergen Levels: ________

BM Pressure: ________

EXERCISE

☐ Heck yes, I worked out.
☐ I managed to exercise a bit.
☐ No, I haven't exercised at all.
☐ I did some stuff, and that counts.

DETAILS

FOOD / MEDICATION

Food / Drinks

Meds / Supplements	Time	Dose
☐ usual daily medication		

Water	Caffeine	Alcohol
☐☐☐☐☐☐☐☐☐☐	x ________	x ________

FOOD ANALYSIS

New food introduced?
☐ Yes ☐ No

Food reintroduction?
☐ Yes ☐ No

Details

MEDICATION ANALYSIS

New med/dose introduced?
☐ Yes ☐ No

Medication stopped?
☐ Yes ☐ No

Details

ACTIVITY ANALYSIS

Heightened exertion levels?
☐ Yes ☐ No

Lowered exertion levels?
☐ Yes ☐ No

Details

SLEEP ANALYSIS

When you woke up this morning, did you feel well-rested?	☐ Yes	☐ No	☐ A bit
Did you snore or stop breathing throughout the night?	☐ Yes	☐ No	☐ Not sure
Roughly how many times did you wake up throughout the night?			

Notes / Suspected Triggers

ENTRY #6 | M T W T F S S | DATE:

HOW ARE YOU *Feeling today?*

Amazing!	Meh
Great	Not good
Good	Terrible!

RATE YOUR PAIN LEVEL

① ② ③ ④ ⑤ ⑥ ⑦ ⑧ ⑨ ⑩

WHAT ABOUT YOUR...?

Mood	① ② ③ ④ ⑤ ⑥ ⑦ ⑧ ⑨ ⑩
Energy Levels	① ② ③ ④ ⑤ ⑥ ⑦ ⑧ ⑨ ⑩
Mental Clarity	① ② ③ ④ ⑤ ⑥ ⑦ ⑧ ⑨ ⑩

PAIN & PHYSICAL SYMPTOMS

Symptom	Severity	am	pm
	① ② ③ ④ ⑤	☐	☐
	① ② ③ ④ ⑤	☐	☐
	① ② ③ ④ ⑤	☐	☐
	① ② ③ ④ ⑤	☐	☐
	① ② ③ ④ ⑤	☐	☐
	① ② ③ ④ ⑤	☐	☐
	① ② ③ ④ ⑤	☐	☐
	① ② ③ ④ ⑤	☐	☐

front

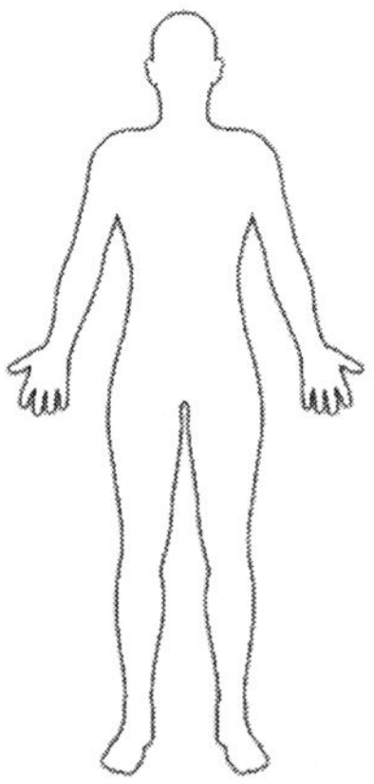

back

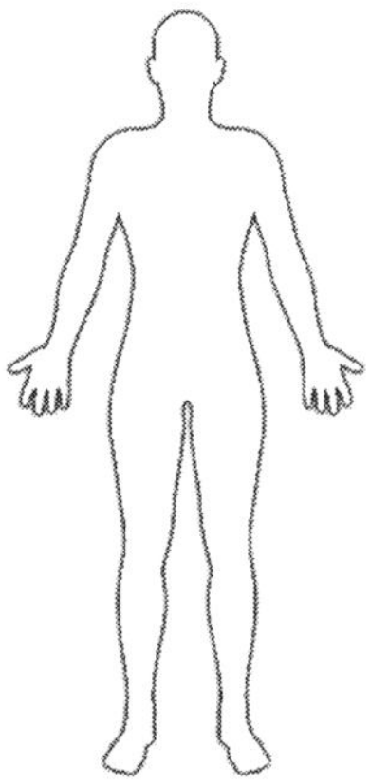

OTHER SYMPTOMS

general

Symptom	Severity	Time	
☐ Fatigue	① ② ③ ④ ⑤	☐ a.m.	☐ p.m.
☐ Lethargy	① ② ③ ④ ⑤	☐ a.m.	☐ p.m.
☐ Malaise	① ② ③ ④ ⑤	☐ a.m.	☐ p.m.
☐ Weakness	① ② ③ ④ ⑤	☐ a.m.	☐ p.m.
☐ Dizziness	① ② ③ ④ ⑤	☐ a.m.	☐ p.m.
☐ Trembling	① ② ③ ④ ⑤	☐ a.m.	☐ p.m.
☐ Twitching	① ② ③ ④ ⑤	☐ a.m.	☐ p.m.
☐ Insomnia	① ② ③ ④ ⑤	☐ a.m.	☐ p.m.

illness

Symptom	Severity	Time	
☐ Nausea	① ② ③ ④ ⑤	☐ a.m.	☐ p.m.
☐ Vomiting	① ② ③ ④ ⑤	☐ a.m.	☐ p.m.
☐ Constipation	① ② ③ ④ ⑤	☐ a.m.	☐ p.m.
☐ Diarrhea	① ② ③ ④ ⑤	☐ a.m.	☐ p.m.
☐ Sore throat	① ② ③ ④ ⑤	☐ a.m.	☐ p.m.
☐ Congestion	① ② ③ ④ ⑤	☐ a.m.	☐ p.m.
☐ Coughing	① ② ③ ④ ⑤	☐ a.m.	☐ p.m.
☐ Acid reflux	① ② ③ ④ ⑤	☐ a.m.	☐ p.m.

psychological

Symptom	Severity	Time	
☐ Anxiety	① ② ③ ④ ⑤	☐ a.m.	☐ p.m.
☐ Depression	① ② ③ ④ ⑤	☐ a.m.	☐ p.m.
☐ Memory loss	① ② ③ ④ ⑤	☐ a.m.	☐ p.m.
☐ Confusion	① ② ③ ④ ⑤	☐ a.m.	☐ p.m.
☐ Poor focus	① ② ③ ④ ⑤	☐ a.m.	☐ p.m.
☐ Mood swings	① ② ③ ④ ⑤	☐ a.m.	☐ p.m.
☐ Suicidal	① ② ③ ④ ⑤	☐ a.m.	☐ p.m.

other

Symptom	Severity	Time	
	① ② ③ ④ ⑤	☐ a.m.	☐ p.m.
	① ② ③ ④ ⑤	☐ a.m.	☐ p.m.
	① ② ③ ④ ⑤	☐ a.m.	☐ p.m.
	① ② ③ ④ ⑤	☐ a.m.	☐ p.m.
	① ② ③ ④ ⑤	☐ a.m.	☐ p.m.
	① ② ③ ④ ⑤	☐ a.m.	☐ p.m.
	① ② ③ ④ ⑤	☐ a.m.	☐ p.m.

SLEEP

hours ______

quality ① ② ③ ④ ⑤

STRESS LEVELS

None	Low	Medium	High	Max	@$#%!

WEATHER

☐ Cold ☐ Mild ☐ Hot

☐ Dry ☐ Humid ☐ Wet

Allergen Levels: ______

BM Pressure: ______

EXERCISE

☐ Heck yes, I worked out.

☐ I managed to exercise a bit.

☐ No, I haven't exercised at all.

☐ I did some stuff, and that counts.

DETAILS

FOOD / MEDICATION

Food / Drinks

Meds / Supplements	Time	Dose

☐ usual daily medication

Water	Caffeine	Alcohol
☐☐☐☐☐☐☐☐☐☐	x ______	x ______

FOOD ANALYSIS

New food introduced?

☐ Yes ☐ No

Food reintroduction?

☐ Yes ☐ No

Details

MEDICATION ANALYSIS

New med/dose introduced?

☐ Yes ☐ No

Medication stopped?

☐ Yes ☐ No

Details

ACTIVITY ANALYSIS

Heightened exertion levels?

☐ Yes ☐ No

Lowered exertion levels?

☐ Yes ☐ No

Details

SLEEP ANALYSIS

When you woke up this morning, did you feel well-rested?	☐ Yes	☐ No	☐ A bit
Did you snore or stop breathing throughout the night?	☐ Yes	☐ No	☐ Not sure
Roughly how many times did you wake up throughout the night?			

Notes / Suspected Triggers

ENTRY #7 | M T W T F S S | DATE:

HOW ARE YOU *Feeling today?*

Amazing!	Meh
Great	Not good
Good	Terrible!

RATE YOUR PAIN LEVEL

① ② ③ ④ ⑤ ⑥ ⑦ ⑧ ⑨ ⑩

WHAT ABOUT YOUR...?

Mood	① ② ③ ④ ⑤ ⑥ ⑦ ⑧ ⑨ ⑩
Energy Levels	① ② ③ ④ ⑤ ⑥ ⑦ ⑧ ⑨ ⑩
Mental Clarity	① ② ③ ④ ⑤ ⑥ ⑦ ⑧ ⑨ ⑩

PAIN & PHYSICAL SYMPTOMS

Symptom	Severity	am	pm
	① ② ③ ④ ⑤	☐	☐
	① ② ③ ④ ⑤	☐	☐
	① ② ③ ④ ⑤	☐	☐
	① ② ③ ④ ⑤	☐	☐
	① ② ③ ④ ⑤	☐	☐
	① ② ③ ④ ⑤	☐	☐
	① ② ③ ④ ⑤	☐	☐
	① ② ③ ④ ⑤	☐	☐

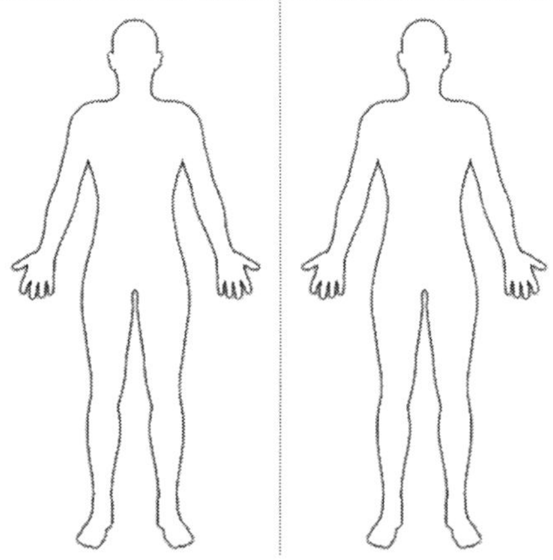

OTHER SYMPTOMS

general

Symptom	Severity	Time	
☐ Fatigue	① ② ③ ④ ⑤	☐ a.m.	☐ p.m.
☐ Lethargy	① ② ③ ④ ⑤	☐ a.m.	☐ p.m.
☐ Malaise	① ② ③ ④ ⑤	☐ a.m.	☐ p.m.
☐ Weakness	① ② ③ ④ ⑤	☐ a.m.	☐ p.m.
☐ Dizziness	① ② ③ ④ ⑤	☐ a.m.	☐ p.m.
☐ Trembling	① ② ③ ④ ⑤	☐ a.m.	☐ p.m.
☐ Twitching	① ② ③ ④ ⑤	☐ a.m.	☐ p.m.
☐ Insomnia	① ② ③ ④ ⑤	☐ a.m.	☐ p.m.

illness

Symptom	Severity	Time	
☐ Nausea	① ② ③ ④ ⑤	☐ a.m.	☐ p.m.
☐ Vomiting	① ② ③ ④ ⑤	☐ a.m.	☐ p.m.
☐ Constipation	① ② ③ ④ ⑤	☐ a.m.	☐ p.m.
☐ Diarrhea	① ② ③ ④ ⑤	☐ a.m.	☐ p.m.
☐ Sore throat	① ② ③ ④ ⑤	☐ a.m.	☐ p.m.
☐ Congestion	① ② ③ ④ ⑤	☐ a.m.	☐ p.m.
☐ Coughing	① ② ③ ④ ⑤	☐ a.m.	☐ p.m.
☐ Acid reflux	① ② ③ ④ ⑤	☐ a.m.	☐ p.m.

psychological

Symptom	Severity	Time	
☐ Anxiety	① ② ③ ④ ⑤	☐ a.m.	☐ p.m.
☐ Depression	① ② ③ ④ ⑤	☐ a.m.	☐ p.m.
☐ Memory loss	① ② ③ ④ ⑤	☐ a.m.	☐ p.m.
☐ Confusion	① ② ③ ④ ⑤	☐ a.m.	☐ p.m.
☐ Poor focus	① ② ③ ④ ⑤	☐ a.m.	☐ p.m.
☐ Mood swings	① ② ③ ④ ⑤	☐ a.m.	☐ p.m.
☐ Suicidal	① ② ③ ④ ⑤	☐ a.m.	☐ p.m.

other

Symptom	Severity	Time	
	① ② ③ ④ ⑤	☐ a.m.	☐ p.m.
	① ② ③ ④ ⑤	☐ a.m.	☐ p.m.
	① ② ③ ④ ⑤	☐ a.m.	☐ p.m.
	① ② ③ ④ ⑤	☐ a.m.	☐ p.m.
	① ② ③ ④ ⑤	☐ a.m.	☐ p.m.
	① ② ③ ④ ⑤	☐ a.m.	☐ p.m.
	① ② ③ ④ ⑤	☐ a.m.	☐ p.m.

SLEEP

hours ________ *quality* ① ② ③ ④ ⑤

STRESS LEVELS

None	Low	Medium	High	Max	@$#%!

WEATHER

☐ Cold ☐ Mild ☐ Hot
☐ Dry ☐ Humid ☐ Wet

Allergen Levels: ________

BM Pressure: ________

EXERCISE

☐ Heck yes, I worked out.
☐ I managed to exercise a bit.
☐ No, I haven't exercised at all.
☐ I did some stuff, and that counts.

DETAILS

FOOD / MEDICATION

Food / Drinks

Meds / Supplements	Time	Dose
☐ usual daily medication		

Water	*Caffeine*	*Alcohol*
☐ ☐ ☐ ☐ ☐ ☐ ☐ ☐ ☐ ☐	x ________	x ________

FOOD ANALYSIS

New food introduced?
☐ Yes ☐ No

Food reintroduction?
☐ Yes ☐ No

Details

MEDICATION ANALYSIS

New med/dose introduced?
☐ Yes ☐ No

Medication stopped?
☐ Yes ☐ No

Details

ACTIVITY ANALYSIS

Heightened exertion levels?
☐ Yes ☐ No

Lowered exertion levels?
☐ Yes ☐ No

Details

SLEEP ANALYSIS

When you woke up this morning, did you feel well-rested?	☐ Yes	☐ No	☐ A bit
Did you snore or stop breathing throughout the night?	☐ Yes	☐ No	☐ Not sure
Roughly how many times did you wake up throughout the night?			

Notes / Suspected Triggers

ENTRY #8 | M T W T F S S | DATE:

HOW ARE YOU *Feeling today?*

Amazing!	Meh
Great	Not good
Good	Terrible!

RATE YOUR PAIN LEVEL

① ② ③ ④ ⑤ ⑥ ⑦ ⑧ ⑨ ⑩

WHAT ABOUT YOUR...?

Mood	① ② ③ ④ ⑤ ⑥ ⑦ ⑧ ⑨ ⑩
Energy Levels	① ② ③ ④ ⑤ ⑥ ⑦ ⑧ ⑨ ⑩
Mental Clarity	① ② ③ ④ ⑤ ⑥ ⑦ ⑧ ⑨ ⑩

PAIN & PHYSICAL SYMPTOMS

Symptom	Severity	am	pm
	① ② ③ ④ ⑤	☐	☐
	① ② ③ ④ ⑤	☐	☐
	① ② ③ ④ ⑤	☐	☐
	① ② ③ ④ ⑤	☐	☐
	① ② ③ ④ ⑤	☐	☐
	① ② ③ ④ ⑤	☐	☐
	① ② ③ ④ ⑤	☐	☐
	① ② ③ ④ ⑤	☐	☐

front

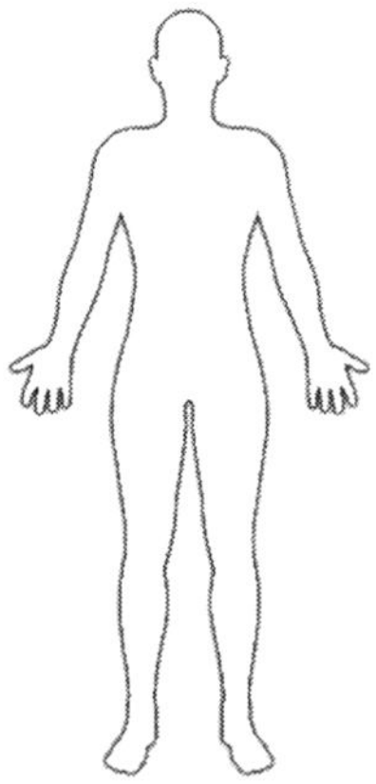

back

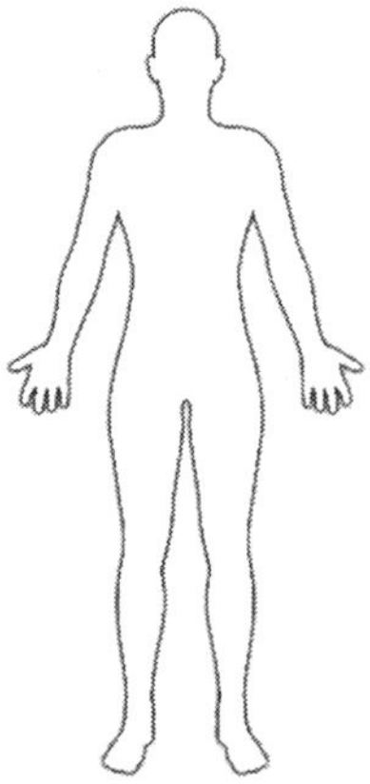

OTHER SYMPTOMS

general

Symptom	Severity	Time	
☐ Fatigue	① ② ③ ④ ⑤	☐ a.m.	☐ p.m.
☐ Lethargy	① ② ③ ④ ⑤	☐ a.m.	☐ p.m.
☐ Malaise	① ② ③ ④ ⑤	☐ a.m.	☐ p.m.
☐ Weakness	① ② ③ ④ ⑤	☐ a.m.	☐ p.m.
☐ Dizziness	① ② ③ ④ ⑤	☐ a.m.	☐ p.m.
☐ Trembling	① ② ③ ④ ⑤	☐ a.m.	☐ p.m.
☐ Twitching	① ② ③ ④ ⑤	☐ a.m.	☐ p.m.
☐ Insomnia	① ② ③ ④ ⑤	☐ a.m.	☐ p.m.

illness

Symptom	Severity	Time	
☐ Nausea	① ② ③ ④ ⑤	☐ a.m.	☐ p.m.
☐ Vomiting	① ② ③ ④ ⑤	☐ a.m.	☐ p.m.
☐ Constipation	① ② ③ ④ ⑤	☐ a.m.	☐ p.m.
☐ Diarrhea	① ② ③ ④ ⑤	☐ a.m.	☐ p.m.
☐ Sore throat	① ② ③ ④ ⑤	☐ a.m.	☐ p.m.
☐ Congestion	① ② ③ ④ ⑤	☐ a.m.	☐ p.m.
☐ Coughing	① ② ③ ④ ⑤	☐ a.m.	☐ p.m.
☐ Acid reflux	① ② ③ ④ ⑤	☐ a.m.	☐ p.m.

psychological

Symptom	Severity	Time	
☐ Anxiety	① ② ③ ④ ⑤	☐ a.m.	☐ p.m.
☐ Depression	① ② ③ ④ ⑤	☐ a.m.	☐ p.m.
☐ Memory loss	① ② ③ ④ ⑤	☐ a.m.	☐ p.m.
☐ Confusion	① ② ③ ④ ⑤	☐ a.m.	☐ p.m.
☐ Poor focus	① ② ③ ④ ⑤	☐ a.m.	☐ p.m.
☐ Mood swings	① ② ③ ④ ⑤	☐ a.m.	☐ p.m.
☐ Suicidal	① ② ③ ④ ⑤	☐ a.m.	☐ p.m.

other

Symptom	Severity	Time	
	① ② ③ ④ ⑤	☐ a.m.	☐ p.m.
	① ② ③ ④ ⑤	☐ a.m.	☐ p.m.
	① ② ③ ④ ⑤	☐ a.m.	☐ p.m.
	① ② ③ ④ ⑤	☐ a.m.	☐ p.m.
	① ② ③ ④ ⑤	☐ a.m.	☐ p.m.
	① ② ③ ④ ⑤	☐ a.m.	☐ p.m.
	① ② ③ ④ ⑤	☐ a.m.	☐ p.m.

SLEEP

hours ________ quality ① ② ③ ④ ⑤

STRESS LEVELS

None	Low	Medium	High	Max	@$#%!

WEATHER

☐ Cold ☐ Mild ☐ Hot
☐ Dry ☐ Humid ☐ Wet

Allergen Levels: ________

BM Pressure: ________

EXERCISE

☐ Heck yes, I worked out.
☐ I managed to exercise a bit.
☐ No, I haven't exercised at all.
☐ I did some stuff, and that counts.

DETAILS

FOOD / MEDICATION

Food / Drinks

Meds / Supplements	Time	Dose
☐ usual daily medication		

Water	Caffeine	Alcohol
	x ________	x ________

FOOD ANALYSIS

New food introduced?
☐ Yes ☐ No
Food reintroduction?
☐ Yes ☐ No

Details

MEDICATION ANALYSIS

New med/dose introduced?
☐ Yes ☐ No
Medication stopped?
☐ Yes ☐ No

Details

ACTIVITY ANALYSIS

Heightened exertion levels?
☐ Yes ☐ No
Lowered exertion levels?
☐ Yes ☐ No

Details

SLEEP ANALYSIS

When you woke up this morning, did you feel well-rested?	☐ Yes	☐ No	☐ A bit
Did you snore or stop breathing throughout the night?	☐ Yes	☐ No	☐ Not sure
Roughly how many times did you wake up throughout the night?			

Notes / Suspected Triggers

ENTRY #9 | M T W T F S S | DATE:

HOW ARE YOU *Feeling today?*

Amazing!	Meh
Great	Not good
Good	Terrible!

RATE YOUR PAIN LEVEL

① ② ③ ④ ⑤ ⑥ ⑦ ⑧ ⑨ ⑩

WHAT ABOUT YOUR...?

Mood	① ② ③ ④ ⑤ ⑥ ⑦ ⑧ ⑨ ⑩
Energy Levels	① ② ③ ④ ⑤ ⑥ ⑦ ⑧ ⑨ ⑩
Mental Clarity	① ② ③ ④ ⑤ ⑥ ⑦ ⑧ ⑨ ⑩

PAIN & PHYSICAL SYMPTOMS

Symptom	Severity	am	pm
	① ② ③ ④ ⑤	☐	☐
	① ② ③ ④ ⑤	☐	☐
	① ② ③ ④ ⑤	☐	☐
	① ② ③ ④ ⑤	☐	☐
	① ② ③ ④ ⑤	☐	☐
	① ② ③ ④ ⑤	☐	☐
	① ② ③ ④ ⑤	☐	☐
	① ② ③ ④ ⑤	☐	☐

front ***back***

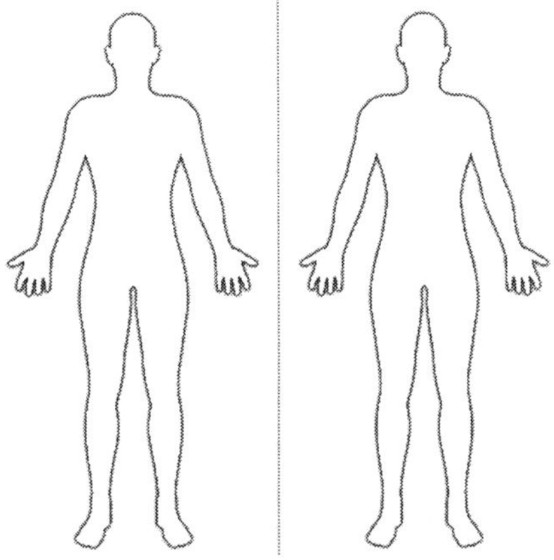

OTHER SYMPTOMS

general

Symptom	Severity	Time	
☐ Fatigue	① ② ③ ④ ⑤	☐ a.m.	☐ p.m.
☐ Lethargy	① ② ③ ④ ⑤	☐ a.m.	☐ p.m.
☐ Malaise	① ② ③ ④ ⑤	☐ a.m.	☐ p.m.
☐ Weakness	① ② ③ ④ ⑤	☐ a.m.	☐ p.m.
☐ Dizziness	① ② ③ ④ ⑤	☐ a.m.	☐ p.m.
☐ Trembling	① ② ③ ④ ⑤	☐ a.m.	☐ p.m.
☐ Twitching	① ② ③ ④ ⑤	☐ a.m.	☐ p.m.
☐ Insomnia	① ② ③ ④ ⑤	☐ a.m.	☐ p.m.

illness

Symptom	Severity	Time	
☐ Nausea	① ② ③ ④ ⑤	☐ a.m.	☐ p.m.
☐ Vomiting	① ② ③ ④ ⑤	☐ a.m.	☐ p.m.
☐ Constipation	① ② ③ ④ ⑤	☐ a.m.	☐ p.m.
☐ Diarrhea	① ② ③ ④ ⑤	☐ a.m.	☐ p.m.
☐ Sore throat	① ② ③ ④ ⑤	☐ a.m.	☐ p.m.
☐ Congestion	① ② ③ ④ ⑤	☐ a.m.	☐ p.m.
☐ Coughing	① ② ③ ④ ⑤	☐ a.m.	☐ p.m.
☐ Acid reflux	① ② ③ ④ ⑤	☐ a.m.	☐ p.m.

psychological

Symptom	Severity	Time	
☐ Anxiety	① ② ③ ④ ⑤	☐ a.m.	☐ p.m.
☐ Depression	① ② ③ ④ ⑤	☐ a.m.	☐ p.m.
☐ Memory loss	① ② ③ ④ ⑤	☐ a.m.	☐ p.m.
☐ Confusion	① ② ③ ④ ⑤	☐ a.m.	☐ p.m.
☐ Poor focus	① ② ③ ④ ⑤	☐ a.m.	☐ p.m.
☐ Mood swings	① ② ③ ④ ⑤	☐ a.m.	☐ p.m.
☐ Suicidal	① ② ③ ④ ⑤	☐ a.m.	☐ p.m.

other

Symptom	Severity	Time	
	① ② ③ ④ ⑤	☐ a.m.	☐ p.m.
	① ② ③ ④ ⑤	☐ a.m.	☐ p.m.
	① ② ③ ④ ⑤	☐ a.m.	☐ p.m.
	① ② ③ ④ ⑤	☐ a.m.	☐ p.m.
	① ② ③ ④ ⑤	☐ a.m.	☐ p.m.
	① ② ③ ④ ⑤	☐ a.m.	☐ p.m.
	① ② ③ ④ ⑤	☐ a.m.	☐ p.m.

SLEEP

hours ________ *quality* (1) (2) (3) (4) (5)

STRESS LEVELS

None	Low	Medium	High	Max	@$#%!

WEATHER

☐ Cold ☐ Mild ☐ Hot
☐ Dry ☐ Humid ☐ Wet

Allergen Levels: ________

BM Pressure: ________

EXERCISE

☐ Heck yes, I worked out.
☐ I managed to exercise a bit.
☐ No, I haven't exercised at all.
☐ I did some stuff, and that counts.

DETAILS

FOOD / MEDICATION

Food / Drinks

Meds / Supplements	Time	Dose
☐ usual daily medication		

Water *Caffeine* *Alcohol*

x ________ x ________

FOOD ANALYSIS

New food introduced?
☐ Yes ☐ No

Food reintroduction?
☐ Yes ☐ No

Details

MEDICATION ANALYSIS

New med/dose introduced?
☐ Yes ☐ No

Medication stopped?
☐ Yes ☐ No

Details

ACTIVITY ANALYSIS

Heightened exertion levels?
☐ Yes ☐ No

Lowered exertion levels?
☐ Yes ☐ No

Details

SLEEP ANALYSIS

When you woke up this morning, did you feel well-rested?	☐ Yes	☐ No	☐ A bit
Did you snore or stop breathing throughout the night?	☐ Yes	☐ No	☐ Not sure
Roughly how many times did you wake up throughout the night?			

Notes / Suspected Triggers

ENTRY #10	M T W T F S S	DATE:

HOW ARE YOU *Feeling today?*

Amazing!	Meh
Great	Not good
Good	Terrible!

RATE YOUR PAIN LEVEL

① ② ③ ④ ⑤ ⑥ ⑦ ⑧ ⑨ ⑩

WHAT ABOUT YOUR...?

Mood	① ② ③ ④ ⑤ ⑥ ⑦ ⑧ ⑨ ⑩
Energy Levels	① ② ③ ④ ⑤ ⑥ ⑦ ⑧ ⑨ ⑩
Mental Clarity	① ② ③ ④ ⑤ ⑥ ⑦ ⑧ ⑨ ⑩

PAIN & PHYSICAL SYMPTOMS

Symptom	Severity	am	pm
	① ② ③ ④ ⑤	☐	☐
	① ② ③ ④ ⑤	☐	☐
	① ② ③ ④ ⑤	☐	☐
	① ② ③ ④ ⑤	☐	☐
	① ② ③ ④ ⑤	☐	☐
	① ② ③ ④ ⑤	☐	☐
	① ② ③ ④ ⑤	☐	☐
	① ② ③ ④ ⑤	☐	☐

front ***back***

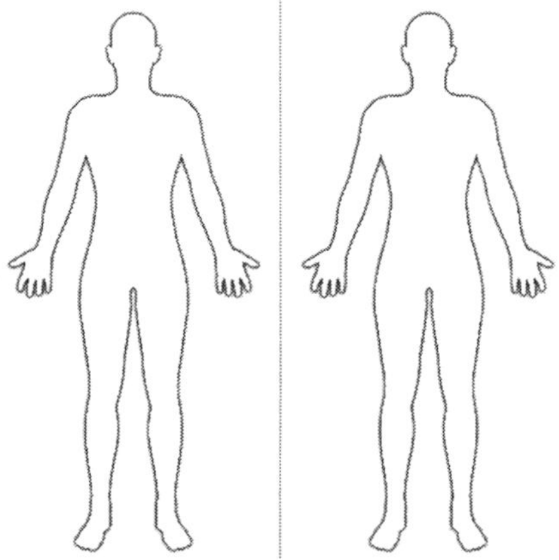

OTHER SYMPTOMS

general

Symptom	Severity	Time	
☐ Fatigue	① ② ③ ④ ⑤	☐ a.m.	☐ p.m.
☐ Lethargy	① ② ③ ④ ⑤	☐ a.m.	☐ p.m.
☐ Malaise	① ② ③ ④ ⑤	☐ a.m.	☐ p.m.
☐ Weakness	① ② ③ ④ ⑤	☐ a.m.	☐ p.m.
☐ Dizziness	① ② ③ ④ ⑤	☐ a.m.	☐ p.m.
☐ Trembling	① ② ③ ④ ⑤	☐ a.m.	☐ p.m.
☐ Twitching	① ② ③ ④ ⑤	☐ a.m.	☐ p.m.
☐ Insomnia	① ② ③ ④ ⑤	☐ a.m.	☐ p.m.

illness

Symptom	Severity	Time	
☐ Nausea	① ② ③ ④ ⑤	☐ a.m.	☐ p.m.
☐ Vomiting	① ② ③ ④ ⑤	☐ a.m.	☐ p.m.
☐ Constipation	① ② ③ ④ ⑤	☐ a.m.	☐ p.m.
☐ Diarrhea	① ② ③ ④ ⑤	☐ a.m.	☐ p.m.
☐ Sore throat	① ② ③ ④ ⑤	☐ a.m.	☐ p.m.
☐ Congestion	① ② ③ ④ ⑤	☐ a.m.	☐ p.m.
☐ Coughing	① ② ③ ④ ⑤	☐ a.m.	☐ p.m.
☐ Acid reflux	① ② ③ ④ ⑤	☐ a.m.	☐ p.m.

psychological

Symptom	Severity	Time	
☐ Anxiety	① ② ③ ④ ⑤	☐ a.m.	☐ p.m.
☐ Depression	① ② ③ ④ ⑤	☐ a.m.	☐ p.m.
☐ Memory loss	① ② ③ ④ ⑤	☐ a.m.	☐ p.m.
☐ Confusion	① ② ③ ④ ⑤	☐ a.m.	☐ p.m.
☐ Poor focus	① ② ③ ④ ⑤	☐ a.m.	☐ p.m.
☐ Mood swings	① ② ③ ④ ⑤	☐ a.m.	☐ p.m.
☐ Suicidal	① ② ③ ④ ⑤	☐ a.m.	☐ p.m.

other

Symptom	Severity	Time	
	① ② ③ ④ ⑤	☐ a.m.	☐ p.m.
	① ② ③ ④ ⑤	☐ a.m.	☐ p.m.
	① ② ③ ④ ⑤	☐ a.m.	☐ p.m.
	① ② ③ ④ ⑤	☐ a.m.	☐ p.m.
	① ② ③ ④ ⑤	☐ a.m.	☐ p.m.
	① ② ③ ④ ⑤	☐ a.m.	☐ p.m.
	① ② ③ ④ ⑤	☐ a.m.	☐ p.m.

SLEEP

hours ______ quality ① ② ③ ④ ⑤

STRESS LEVELS

None	Low	Medium	High	Max	@$#%!

WEATHER

☐ Cold ☐ Mild ☐ Hot
☐ Dry ☐ Humid ☐ Wet

Allergen Levels: ______

BM Pressure: ______

EXERCISE

☐ Heck yes, I worked out.
☐ I managed to exercise a bit.
☐ No, I haven't exercised at all.
☐ I did some stuff, and that counts.

DETAILS

FOOD / MEDICATION

Food / Drinks

Meds / Supplements	Time	Dose
☐ usual daily medication		

Water

Caffeine x ______

Allcohol x ______

FOOD ANALYSIS

New food introduced?

☐ Yes ☐ No

Food reintroduction?

☐ Yes ☐ No

Details

MEDICATION ANALYSIS

New med/dose introduced?

☐ Yes ☐ No

Medication stopped?

☐ Yes ☐ No

Details

ACTIVITY ANALYSIS

Heightened exertion levels?

☐ Yes ☐ No

Lowered exertion levels?

☐ Yes ☐ No

Details

SLEEP ANALYSIS

When you woke up this morning, did you feel well-rested?	☐ Yes	☐ No	☐ A bit
Did you snore or stop breathing throughout the night?	☐ Yes	☐ No	☐ Not sure
Roughly how many times did you wake up throughout the night?			

Notes / Suspected Triggers

ENTRY #11 | M T W T F S S | DATE:

HOW ARE YOU *Feeling today?*

Amazing!	Meh
Great	Not good
Good	Terrible!

RATE YOUR PAIN LEVEL

① ② ③ ④ ⑤ ⑥ ⑦ ⑧ ⑨ ⑩

WHAT ABOUT YOUR...?

Mood	① ② ③ ④ ⑤ ⑥ ⑦ ⑧ ⑨ ⑩
Energy Levels	① ② ③ ④ ⑤ ⑥ ⑦ ⑧ ⑨ ⑩
Mental Clarity	① ② ③ ④ ⑤ ⑥ ⑦ ⑧ ⑨ ⑩

PAIN & PHYSICAL SYMPTOMS

Symptom	Severity	am	pm
	① ② ③ ④ ⑤	☐	☐
	① ② ③ ④ ⑤	☐	☐
	① ② ③ ④ ⑤	☐	☐
	① ② ③ ④ ⑤	☐	☐
	① ② ③ ④ ⑤	☐	☐
	① ② ③ ④ ⑤	☐	☐
	① ② ③ ④ ⑤	☐	☐
	① ② ③ ④ ⑤	☐	☐

front ***back***

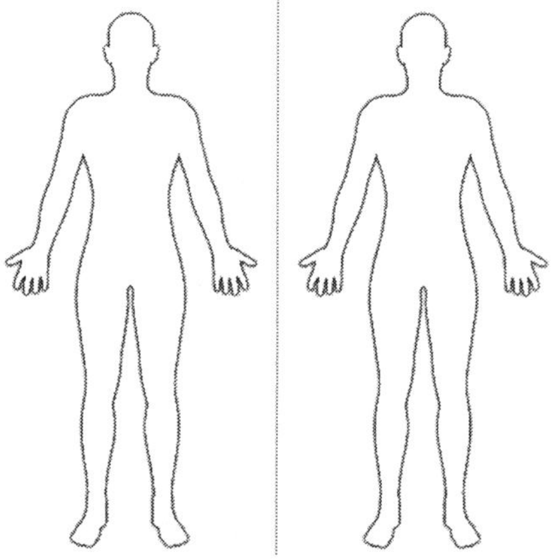

OTHER SYMPTOMS

general

Symptom	Severity	Time	
☐ Fatigue	① ② ③ ④ ⑤	☐ a.m.	☐ p.m.
☐ Lethargy	① ② ③ ④ ⑤	☐ a.m.	☐ p.m.
☐ Malaise	① ② ③ ④ ⑤	☐ a.m.	☐ p.m.
☐ Weakness	① ② ③ ④ ⑤	☐ a.m.	☐ p.m.
☐ Dizziness	① ② ③ ④ ⑤	☐ a.m.	☐ p.m.
☐ Trembling	① ② ③ ④ ⑤	☐ a.m.	☐ p.m.
☐ Twitching	① ② ③ ④ ⑤	☐ a.m.	☐ p.m.
☐ Insomnia	① ② ③ ④ ⑤	☐ a.m.	☐ p.m.

illness

Symptom	Severity	Time	
☐ Nausea	① ② ③ ④ ⑤	☐ a.m.	☐ p.m.
☐ Vomiting	① ② ③ ④ ⑤	☐ a.m.	☐ p.m.
☐ Constipation	① ② ③ ④ ⑤	☐ a.m.	☐ p.m.
☐ Diarrhea	① ② ③ ④ ⑤	☐ a.m.	☐ p.m.
☐ Sore throat	① ② ③ ④ ⑤	☐ a.m.	☐ p.m.
☐ Congestion	① ② ③ ④ ⑤	☐ a.m.	☐ p.m.
☐ Coughing	① ② ③ ④ ⑤	☐ a.m.	☐ p.m.
☐ Acid reflux	① ② ③ ④ ⑤	☐ a.m.	☐ p.m.

psychological

Symptom	Severity	Time	
☐ Anxiety	① ② ③ ④ ⑤	☐ a.m.	☐ p.m.
☐ Depression	① ② ③ ④ ⑤	☐ a.m.	☐ p.m.
☐ Memory loss	① ② ③ ④ ⑤	☐ a.m.	☐ p.m.
☐ Confusion	① ② ③ ④ ⑤	☐ a.m.	☐ p.m.
☐ Poor focus	① ② ③ ④ ⑤	☐ a.m.	☐ p.m.
☐ Mood swings	① ② ③ ④ ⑤	☐ a.m.	☐ p.m.
☐ Suicidal	① ② ③ ④ ⑤	☐ a.m.	☐ p.m.

other

Symptom	Severity	Time	
	① ② ③ ④ ⑤	☐ a.m.	☐ p.m.
	① ② ③ ④ ⑤	☐ a.m.	☐ p.m.
	① ② ③ ④ ⑤	☐ a.m.	☐ p.m.
	① ② ③ ④ ⑤	☐ a.m.	☐ p.m.
	① ② ③ ④ ⑤	☐ a.m.	☐ p.m.
	① ② ③ ④ ⑤	☐ a.m.	☐ p.m.
	① ② ③ ④ ⑤	☐ a.m.	☐ p.m.

SLEEP

hours ________ *quality* ① ② ③ ④ ⑤

STRESS LEVELS

None	Low	Medium	High	Max	@$#%!

WEATHER

☐ Cold ☐ Mild ☐ Hot
☐ Dry ☐ Humid ☐ Wet

Allergen Levels: ________

BM Pressure: ________

EXERCISE

☐ Heck yes, I worked out.
☐ I managed to exercise a bit.
☐ No, I haven't exercised at all.
☐ I did some stuff, and that counts.

DETAILS

FOOD / MEDICATION

Food / Drinks

Meds / Supplements	Time	Dose
☐ usual daily medication		

Water	*Caffeine*	*Alcohol*
	x ________	x ________

FOOD ANALYSIS

New food introduced?
☐ Yes ☐ No

Food reintroduction?
☐ Yes ☐ No

Details

MEDICATION ANALYSIS

New med/dose introduced?
☐ Yes ☐ No

Medication stopped?
☐ Yes ☐ No

Details

ACTIVITY ANALYSIS

Heightened exertion levels?
☐ Yes ☐ No

Lowered exertion levels?
☐ Yes ☐ No

Details

SLEEP ANALYSIS

When you woke up this morning, did you feel well-rested?	☐ Yes	☐ No	☐ A bit
Did you snore or stop breathing throughout the night?	☐ Yes	☐ No	☐ Not sure
Roughly how many times did you wake up throughout the night?			

Notes / Suspected Triggers

ENTRY #12 | M T W T F S S | DATE:

HOW ARE YOU *Feeling today?*

Amazing!	Meh
Great	Not good
Good	Terrible!

RATE YOUR PAIN LEVEL

① ② ③ ④ ⑤ ⑥ ⑦ ⑧ ⑨ ⑩

WHAT ABOUT YOUR...?

Mood	① ② ③ ④ ⑤ ⑥ ⑦ ⑧ ⑨ ⑩
Energy Levels	① ② ③ ④ ⑤ ⑥ ⑦ ⑧ ⑨ ⑩
Mental Clarity	① ② ③ ④ ⑤ ⑥ ⑦ ⑧ ⑨ ⑩

PAIN & PHYSICAL SYMPTOMS

Symptom	Severity	am	pm
	① ② ③ ④ ⑤	☐	☐
	① ② ③ ④ ⑤	☐	☐
	① ② ③ ④ ⑤	☐	☐
	① ② ③ ④ ⑤	☐	☐
	① ② ③ ④ ⑤	☐	☐
	① ② ③ ④ ⑤	☐	☐
	① ② ③ ④ ⑤	☐	☐
	① ② ③ ④ ⑤	☐	☐

front

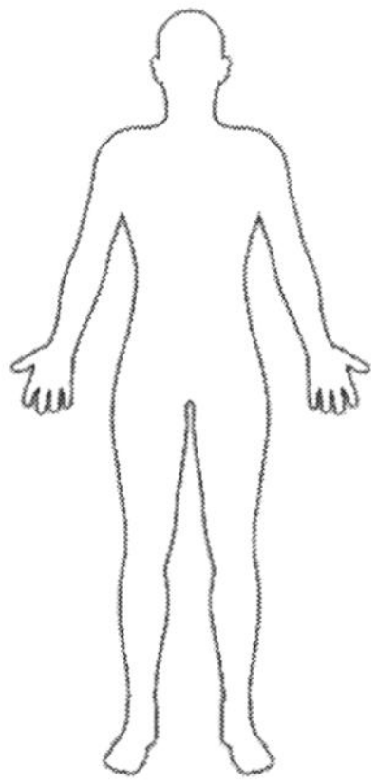

back

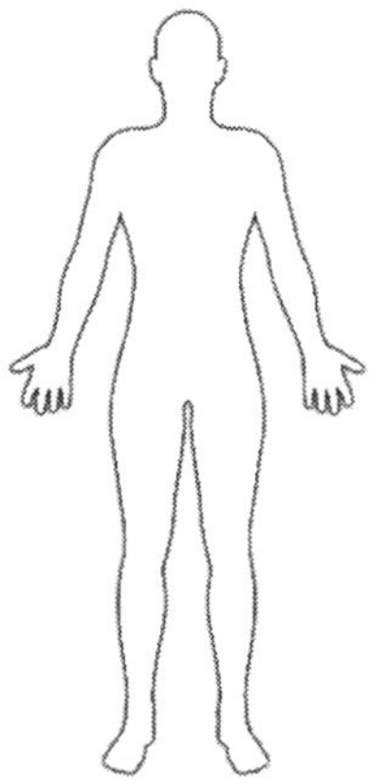

OTHER SYMPTOMS

general

Symptom	Severity	Time	
☐ Fatigue	① ② ③ ④ ⑤	☐ a.m.	☐ p.m.
☐ Lethargy	① ② ③ ④ ⑤	☐ a.m.	☐ p.m.
☐ Malaise	① ② ③ ④ ⑤	☐ a.m.	☐ p.m.
☐ Weakness	① ② ③ ④ ⑤	☐ a.m.	☐ p.m.
☐ Dizziness	① ② ③ ④ ⑤	☐ a.m.	☐ p.m.
☐ Trembling	① ② ③ ④ ⑤	☐ a.m.	☐ p.m.
☐ Twitching	① ② ③ ④ ⑤	☐ a.m.	☐ p.m.
☐ Insomnia	① ② ③ ④ ⑤	☐ a.m.	☐ p.m.

illness

Symptom	Severity	Time	
☐ Nausea	① ② ③ ④ ⑤	☐ a.m.	☐ p.m.
☐ Vomiting	① ② ③ ④ ⑤	☐ a.m.	☐ p.m.
☐ Constipation	① ② ③ ④ ⑤	☐ a.m.	☐ p.m.
☐ Diarrhea	① ② ③ ④ ⑤	☐ a.m.	☐ p.m.
☐ Sore throat	① ② ③ ④ ⑤	☐ a.m.	☐ p.m.
☐ Congestion	① ② ③ ④ ⑤	☐ a.m.	☐ p.m.
☐ Coughing	① ② ③ ④ ⑤	☐ a.m.	☐ p.m.
☐ Acid reflux	① ② ③ ④ ⑤	☐ a.m.	☐ p.m.

psychological

Symptom	Severity	Time	
☐ Anxiety	① ② ③ ④ ⑤	☐ a.m.	☐ p.m.
☐ Depression	① ② ③ ④ ⑤	☐ a.m.	☐ p.m.
☐ Memory loss	① ② ③ ④ ⑤	☐ a.m.	☐ p.m.
☐ Confusion	① ② ③ ④ ⑤	☐ a.m.	☐ p.m.
☐ Poor focus	① ② ③ ④ ⑤	☐ a.m.	☐ p.m.
☐ Mood swings	① ② ③ ④ ⑤	☐ a.m.	☐ p.m.
☐ Suicidal	① ② ③ ④ ⑤	☐ a.m.	☐ p.m.

other

Symptom	Severity	Time	
	① ② ③ ④ ⑤	☐ a.m.	☐ p.m.
	① ② ③ ④ ⑤	☐ a.m.	☐ p.m.
	① ② ③ ④ ⑤	☐ a.m.	☐ p.m.
	① ② ③ ④ ⑤	☐ a.m.	☐ p.m.
	① ② ③ ④ ⑤	☐ a.m.	☐ p.m.
	① ② ③ ④ ⑤	☐ a.m.	☐ p.m.
	① ② ③ ④ ⑤	☐ a.m.	☐ p.m.

SLEEP

hours ________ *quality* ① ② ③ ④ ⑤

STRESS LEVELS

None	Low	Medium	High	Max	@$#%!

WEATHER

☐ Cold ☐ Mild ☐ Hot
☐ Dry ☐ Humid ☐ Wet

Allergen Levels: ________
BM Pressure: ________

EXERCISE

☐ Heck yes, I worked out.
☐ I managed to exercise a bit.
☐ No, I haven't exercised at all.
☐ I did some stuff, and that counts.

DETAILS

FOOD / MEDICATION

Food / Drinks

Meds / Supplements	Time	Dose

☐ usual daily medication

Water *Caffeine* *Alcohol*

x ________ x ________

FOOD ANALYSIS

New food introduced?
☐ Yes ☐ No
Food reintroduction?
☐ Yes ☐ No

Details

MEDICATION ANALYSIS

New med/dose introduced?
☐ Yes ☐ No
Medication stopped?
☐ Yes ☐ No

Details

ACTIVITY ANALYSIS

Heightened exertion levels?
☐ Yes ☐ No
Lowered exertion levels?
☐ Yes ☐ No

Details

SLEEP ANALYSIS

When you woke up this morning, did you feel well-rested?	☐ Yes	☐ No	☐ A bit
Did you snore or stop breathing throughout the night?	☐ Yes	☐ No	☐ Not sure
Roughly how many times did you wake up throughout the night?			

Notes / Suspected Triggers

ENTRY #13 | M T W T F S S | DATE:

HOW ARE YOU *Feeling today?*

Amazing!	Meh
Great	Not good
Good	Terrible!

RATE YOUR PAIN LEVEL

① ② ③ ④ ⑤ ⑥ ⑦ ⑧ ⑨ ⑩

WHAT ABOUT YOUR...?

Mood	① ② ③ ④ ⑤ ⑥ ⑦ ⑧ ⑨ ⑩
Energy Levels	① ② ③ ④ ⑤ ⑥ ⑦ ⑧ ⑨ ⑩
Mental Clarity	① ② ③ ④ ⑤ ⑥ ⑦ ⑧ ⑨ ⑩

PAIN & PHYSICAL SYMPTOMS

Symptom	Severity	am	pm
	① ② ③ ④ ⑤	☐	☐
	① ② ③ ④ ⑤	☐	☐
	① ② ③ ④ ⑤	☐	☐
	① ② ③ ④ ⑤	☐	☐
	① ② ③ ④ ⑤	☐	☐
	① ② ③ ④ ⑤	☐	☐
	① ② ③ ④ ⑤	☐	☐
	① ② ③ ④ ⑤	☐	☐

front ***back***

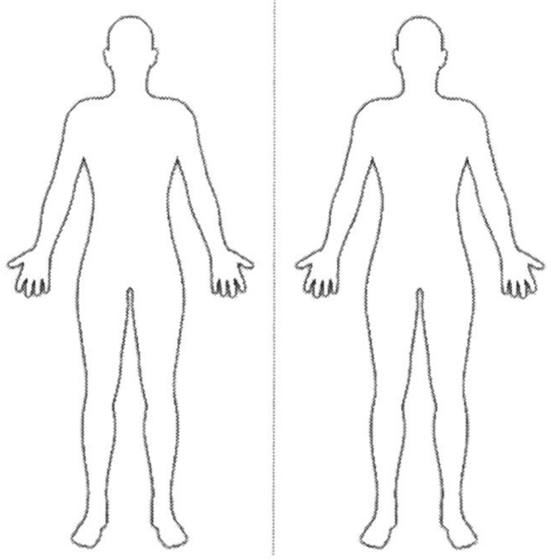

OTHER SYMPTOMS

general

Symptom	Severity	Time	
☐ Fatigue	① ② ③ ④ ⑤	☐ a.m.	☐ p.m.
☐ Lethargy	① ② ③ ④ ⑤	☐ a.m.	☐ p.m.
☐ Malaise	① ② ③ ④ ⑤	☐ a.m.	☐ p.m.
☐ Weakness	① ② ③ ④ ⑤	☐ a.m.	☐ p.m.
☐ Dizziness	① ② ③ ④ ⑤	☐ a.m.	☐ p.m.
☐ Trembling	① ② ③ ④ ⑤	☐ a.m.	☐ p.m.
☐ Twitching	① ② ③ ④ ⑤	☐ a.m.	☐ p.m.
☐ Insomnia	① ② ③ ④ ⑤	☐ a.m.	☐ p.m.

illness

Symptom	Severity	Time	
☐ Nausea	① ② ③ ④ ⑤	☐ a.m.	☐ p.m.
☐ Vomiting	① ② ③ ④ ⑤	☐ a.m.	☐ p.m.
☐ Constipation	① ② ③ ④ ⑤	☐ a.m.	☐ p.m.
☐ Diarrhea	① ② ③ ④ ⑤	☐ a.m.	☐ p.m.
☐ Sore throat	① ② ③ ④ ⑤	☐ a.m.	☐ p.m.
☐ Congestion	① ② ③ ④ ⑤	☐ a.m.	☐ p.m.
☐ Coughing	① ② ③ ④ ⑤	☐ a.m.	☐ p.m.
☐ Acid reflux	① ② ③ ④ ⑤	☐ a.m.	☐ p.m.

psychological

Symptom	Severity	Time	
☐ Anxiety	① ② ③ ④ ⑤	☐ a.m.	☐ p.m.
☐ Depression	① ② ③ ④ ⑤	☐ a.m.	☐ p.m.
☐ Memory loss	① ② ③ ④ ⑤	☐ a.m.	☐ p.m.
☐ Confusion	① ② ③ ④ ⑤	☐ a.m.	☐ p.m.
☐ Poor focus	① ② ③ ④ ⑤	☐ a.m.	☐ p.m.
☐ Mood swings	① ② ③ ④ ⑤	☐ a.m.	☐ p.m.
☐ Suicidal	① ② ③ ④ ⑤	☐ a.m.	☐ p.m.

other

Symptom	Severity	Time	
	① ② ③ ④ ⑤	☐ a.m.	☐ p.m.
	① ② ③ ④ ⑤	☐ a.m.	☐ p.m.
	① ② ③ ④ ⑤	☐ a.m.	☐ p.m.
	① ② ③ ④ ⑤	☐ a.m.	☐ p.m.
	① ② ③ ④ ⑤	☐ a.m.	☐ p.m.
	① ② ③ ④ ⑤	☐ a.m.	☐ p.m.
	① ② ③ ④ ⑤	☐ a.m.	☐ p.m.

SLEEP

hours ________ *quality* ① ② ③ ④ ⑤

STRESS LEVELS

None	Low	Medium	High	Max	@$#%!

WEATHER

☐ Cold ☐ Mild ☐ Hot
☐ Dry ☐ Humid ☐ Wet

Allergen Levels: ________

BM Pressure: ________

EXERCISE

☐ Heck yes, I worked out.
☐ I managed to exercise a bit.
☐ No, I haven't exercised at all.
☐ I did some stuff, and that counts.

DETAILS

FOOD / MEDICATION

Food / Drinks

Meds / Supplements	Time	Dose

☐ usual daily medication

Water *Caffeine* *Alcohol*

x ________ x ________

FOOD ANALYSIS

New food introduced?
☐ Yes ☐ No
Food reintroduction?
☐ Yes ☐ No

Details

MEDICATION ANALYSIS

New med/dose introduced?
☐ Yes ☐ No
Medication stopped?
☐ Yes ☐ No

Details

ACTIVITY ANALYSIS

Heightened exertion levels?
☐ Yes ☐ No
Lowered exertion levels?
☐ Yes ☐ No

Details

SLEEP ANALYSIS

When you woke up this morning, did you feel well-rested? ☐ Yes ☐ No ☐ A bit
Did you snore or stop breathing throughout the night? ☐ Yes ☐ No ☐ Not sure
Roughly how many times did you wake up throughout the night?

Notes / Suspected Triggers

ENTRY #14	M T W T F S S	DATE:

HOW ARE YOU *Feeling today?*

Amazing!	Meh
Great	Not good
Good	Terrible!

RATE YOUR PAIN LEVEL

① ② ③ ④ ⑤ ⑥ ⑦ ⑧ ⑨ ⑩

WHAT ABOUT YOUR...?

Mood	① ② ③ ④ ⑤ ⑥ ⑦ ⑧ ⑨ ⑩
Energy Levels	① ② ③ ④ ⑤ ⑥ ⑦ ⑧ ⑨ ⑩
Mental Clarity	① ② ③ ④ ⑤ ⑥ ⑦ ⑧ ⑨ ⑩

PAIN & PHYSICAL SYMPTOMS

Symptom	Severity	am	pm
	① ② ③ ④ ⑤	☐	☐
	① ② ③ ④ ⑤	☐	☐
	① ② ③ ④ ⑤	☐	☐
	① ② ③ ④ ⑤	☐	☐
	① ② ③ ④ ⑤	☐	☐
	① ② ③ ④ ⑤	☐	☐
	① ② ③ ④ ⑤	☐	☐
	① ② ③ ④ ⑤	☐	☐

front *back*

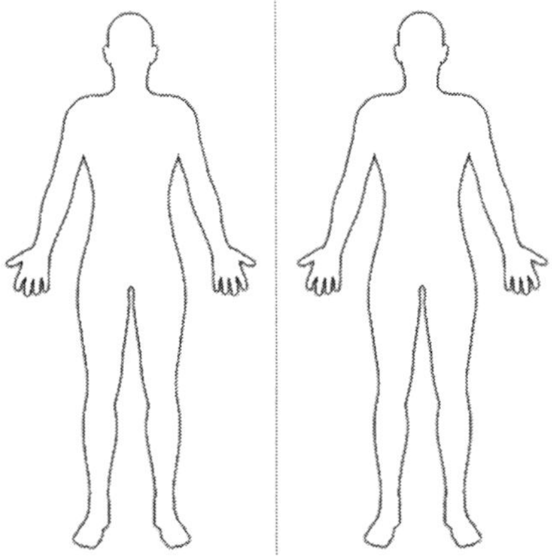

OTHER SYMPTOMS

general

Symptom	Severity	Time	
☐ Fatigue	① ② ③ ④ ⑤	☐ a.m.	☐ p.m.
☐ Lethargy	① ② ③ ④ ⑤	☐ a.m.	☐ p.m.
☐ Malaise	① ② ③ ④ ⑤	☐ a.m.	☐ p.m.
☐ Weakness	① ② ③ ④ ⑤	☐ a.m.	☐ p.m.
☐ Dizziness	① ② ③ ④ ⑤	☐ a.m.	☐ p.m.
☐ Trembling	① ② ③ ④ ⑤	☐ a.m.	☐ p.m.
☐ Twitching	① ② ③ ④ ⑤	☐ a.m.	☐ p.m.
☐ Insomnia	① ② ③ ④ ⑤	☐ a.m.	☐ p.m.

illness

Symptom	Severity	Time	
☐ Nausea	① ② ③ ④ ⑤	☐ a.m.	☐ p.m.
☐ Vomiting	① ② ③ ④ ⑤	☐ a.m.	☐ p.m.
☐ Constipation	① ② ③ ④ ⑤	☐ a.m.	☐ p.m.
☐ Diarrhea	① ② ③ ④ ⑤	☐ a.m.	☐ p.m.
☐ Sore throat	① ② ③ ④ ⑤	☐ a.m.	☐ p.m.
☐ Congestion	① ② ③ ④ ⑤	☐ a.m.	☐ p.m.
☐ Coughing	① ② ③ ④ ⑤	☐ a.m.	☐ p.m.
☐ Acid reflux	① ② ③ ④ ⑤	☐ a.m.	☐ p.m.

psychological

Symptom	Severity	Time	
☐ Anxiety	① ② ③ ④ ⑤	☐ a.m.	☐ p.m.
☐ Depression	① ② ③ ④ ⑤	☐ a.m.	☐ p.m.
☐ Memory loss	① ② ③ ④ ⑤	☐ a.m.	☐ p.m.
☐ Confusion	① ② ③ ④ ⑤	☐ a.m.	☐ p.m.
☐ Poor focus	① ② ③ ④ ⑤	☐ a.m.	☐ p.m.
☐ Mood swings	① ② ③ ④ ⑤	☐ a.m.	☐ p.m.
☐ Suicidal	① ② ③ ④ ⑤	☐ a.m.	☐ p.m.

other

Symptom	Severity	Time	
	① ② ③ ④ ⑤	☐ a.m.	☐ p.m.
	① ② ③ ④ ⑤	☐ a.m.	☐ p.m.
	① ② ③ ④ ⑤	☐ a.m.	☐ p.m.
	① ② ③ ④ ⑤	☐ a.m.	☐ p.m.
	① ② ③ ④ ⑤	☐ a.m.	☐ p.m.
	① ② ③ ④ ⑤	☐ a.m.	☐ p.m.
	① ② ③ ④ ⑤	☐ a.m.	☐ p.m.

SLEEP

hours ________

quality ① ② ③ ④ ⑤

STRESS LEVELS

None	Low	Medium	High	Max	@$#%!

WEATHER

☐ Cold ☐ Mild ☐ Hot
☐ Dry ☐ Humid ☐ Wet

Allergen Levels: ________

BM Pressure: ________

EXERCISE

☐ Heck yes, I worked out.
☐ I managed to exercise a bit.
☐ No, I haven't exercised at all.
☐ I did some stuff, and that counts.

DETAILS

FOOD / MEDICATION

Food / Drinks

Meds / Supplements	Time	Dose

☐ usual daily medication

Water *Caffeine* *Alcohol*

x ________ x ________

FOOD ANALYSIS

New food introduced?
☐ Yes ☐ No
Food reintroduction?
☐ Yes ☐ No
Details

MEDICATION ANALYSIS

New med/dose introduced?
☐ Yes ☐ No
Medication stopped?
☐ Yes ☐ No
Details

ACTIVITY ANALYSIS

Heightened exertion levels?
☐ Yes ☐ No
Lowered exertion levels?
☐ Yes ☐ No
Details

SLEEP ANALYSIS

When you woke up this morning, did you feel well-rested?	☐ Yes	☐ No	☐ A bit
Did you snore or stop breathing throughout the night?	☐ Yes	☐ No	☐ Not sure
Roughly how many times did you wake up throughout the night?			

Notes / Suspected Triggers

ENTRY #15 | M T W T F S S | DATE:

HOW ARE YOU *Feeling today?*

Amazing!	Meh
Great	Not good
Good	Terrible!

RATE YOUR PAIN LEVEL

① ② ③ ④ ⑤ ⑥ ⑦ ⑧ ⑨ ⑩

WHAT ABOUT YOUR...?

Mood	① ② ③ ④ ⑤ ⑥ ⑦ ⑧ ⑨ ⑩
Energy Levels	① ② ③ ④ ⑤ ⑥ ⑦ ⑧ ⑨ ⑩
Mental Clarity	① ② ③ ④ ⑤ ⑥ ⑦ ⑧ ⑨ ⑩

PAIN & PHYSICAL SYMPTOMS

Symptom	Severity	am	pm
	① ② ③ ④ ⑤	☐	☐
	① ② ③ ④ ⑤	☐	☐
	① ② ③ ④ ⑤	☐	☐
	① ② ③ ④ ⑤	☐	☐
	① ② ③ ④ ⑤	☐	☐
	① ② ③ ④ ⑤	☐	☐
	① ② ③ ④ ⑤	☐	☐
	① ② ③ ④ ⑤	☐	☐

front *back*

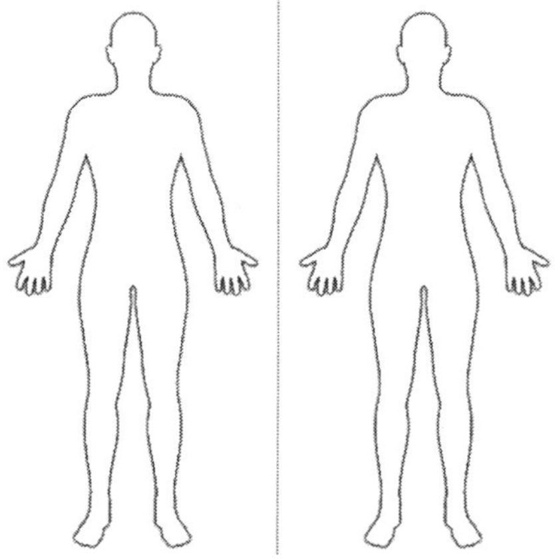

OTHER SYMPTOMS

general

Symptom	Severity	Time	
☐ Fatigue	① ② ③ ④ ⑤	☐ a.m.	☐ p.m.
☐ Lethargy	① ② ③ ④ ⑤	☐ a.m.	☐ p.m.
☐ Malaise	① ② ③ ④ ⑤	☐ a.m.	☐ p.m.
☐ Weakness	① ② ③ ④ ⑤	☐ a.m.	☐ p.m.
☐ Dizziness	① ② ③ ④ ⑤	☐ a.m.	☐ p.m.
☐ Trembling	① ② ③ ④ ⑤	☐ a.m.	☐ p.m.
☐ Twitching	① ② ③ ④ ⑤	☐ a.m.	☐ p.m.
☐ Insomnia	① ② ③ ④ ⑤	☐ a.m.	☐ p.m.

illness

Symptom	Severity	Time	
☐ Nausea	① ② ③ ④ ⑤	☐ a.m.	☐ p.m.
☐ Vomiting	① ② ③ ④ ⑤	☐ a.m.	☐ p.m.
☐ Constipation	① ② ③ ④ ⑤	☐ a.m.	☐ p.m.
☐ Diarrhea	① ② ③ ④ ⑤	☐ a.m.	☐ p.m.
☐ Sore throat	① ② ③ ④ ⑤	☐ a.m.	☐ p.m.
☐ Congestion	① ② ③ ④ ⑤	☐ a.m.	☐ p.m.
☐ Coughing	① ② ③ ④ ⑤	☐ a.m.	☐ p.m.
☐ Acid reflux	① ② ③ ④ ⑤	☐ a.m.	☐ p.m.

psychological

Symptom	Severity	Time	
☐ Anxiety	① ② ③ ④ ⑤	☐ a.m.	☐ p.m.
☐ Depression	① ② ③ ④ ⑤	☐ a.m.	☐ p.m.
☐ Memory loss	① ② ③ ④ ⑤	☐ a.m.	☐ p.m.
☐ Confusion	① ② ③ ④ ⑤	☐ a.m.	☐ p.m.
☐ Poor focus	① ② ③ ④ ⑤	☐ a.m.	☐ p.m.
☐ Mood swings	① ② ③ ④ ⑤	☐ a.m.	☐ p.m.
☐ Suicidal	① ② ③ ④ ⑤	☐ a.m.	☐ p.m.

other

Symptom	Severity	Time	
	① ② ③ ④ ⑤	☐ a.m.	☐ p.m.
	① ② ③ ④ ⑤	☐ a.m.	☐ p.m.
	① ② ③ ④ ⑤	☐ a.m.	☐ p.m.
	① ② ③ ④ ⑤	☐ a.m.	☐ p.m.
	① ② ③ ④ ⑤	☐ a.m.	☐ p.m.
	① ② ③ ④ ⑤	☐ a.m.	☐ p.m.
	① ② ③ ④ ⑤	☐ a.m.	☐ p.m.

SLEEP

hours ________

quality ① ② ③ ④ ⑤

STRESS LEVELS

None	Low	Medium	High	Max	@$#%!

WEATHER

☐ Cold ☐ Mild ☐ Hot
☐ Dry ☐ Humid ☐ Wet

Allergen Levels: ________

BM Pressure: ________

EXERCISE

☐ Heck yes, I worked out.
☐ I managed to exercise a bit.
☐ No, I haven't exercised at all.
☐ I did some stuff, and that counts.

DETAILS

FOOD / MEDICATION

Food / Drinks

Meds / Supplements	Time	Dose
☐ usual daily medication		

Water	Caffeine	Alcohol
	x ________	x ________

FOOD ANALYSIS

New food introduced?
☐ Yes ☐ No

Food reintroduction?
☐ Yes ☐ No

Details

MEDICATION ANALYSIS

New med/dose introduced?
☐ Yes ☐ No

Medication stopped?
☐ Yes ☐ No

Details

ACTIVITY ANALYSIS

Heightened exertion levels?
☐ Yes ☐ No

Lowered exertion levels?
☐ Yes ☐ No

Details

SLEEP ANALYSIS

When you woke up this morning, did you feel well-rested?	☐ Yes	☐ No	☐ A bit
Did you snore or stop breathing throughout the night?	☐ Yes	☐ No	☐ Not sure
Roughly how many times did you wake up throughout the night?			

Notes / Suspected Triggers

ENTRY #16 | M T W T F S S | DATE:

HOW ARE YOU *Feeling today?*

Amazing!	Meh
Great	Not good
Good	Terrible!

RATE YOUR PAIN LEVEL

① ② ③ ④ ⑤ ⑥ ⑦ ⑧ ⑨ ⑩

WHAT ABOUT YOUR...?

Mood	① ② ③ ④ ⑤ ⑥ ⑦ ⑧ ⑨ ⑩
Energy Levels	① ② ③ ④ ⑤ ⑥ ⑦ ⑧ ⑨ ⑩
Mental Clarity	① ② ③ ④ ⑤ ⑥ ⑦ ⑧ ⑨ ⑩

PAIN & PHYSICAL SYMPTOMS

Symptom	Severity	am	pm
	① ② ③ ④ ⑤	☐	☐
	① ② ③ ④ ⑤	☐	☐
	① ② ③ ④ ⑤	☐	☐
	① ② ③ ④ ⑤	☐	☐
	① ② ③ ④ ⑤	☐	☐
	① ② ③ ④ ⑤	☐	☐
	① ② ③ ④ ⑤	☐	☐
	① ② ③ ④ ⑤	☐	☐

front *back*

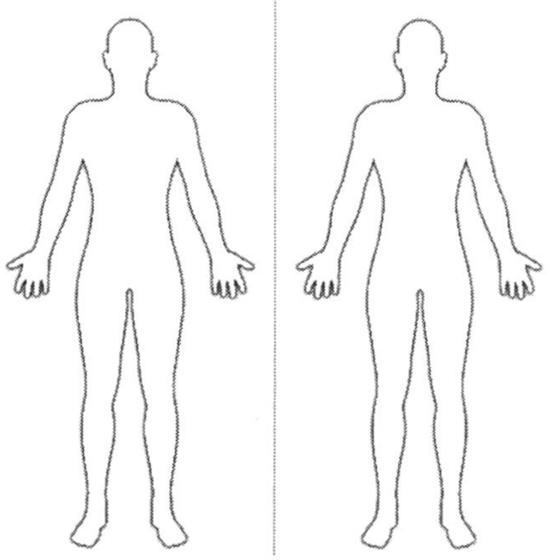

OTHER SYMPTOMS

general

Symptom	Severity	Time	
☐ Fatigue	① ② ③ ④ ⑤	☐ a.m.	☐ p.m.
☐ Lethargy	① ② ③ ④ ⑤	☐ a.m.	☐ p.m.
☐ Malaise	① ② ③ ④ ⑤	☐ a.m.	☐ p.m.
☐ Weakness	① ② ③ ④ ⑤	☐ a.m.	☐ p.m.
☐ Dizziness	① ② ③ ④ ⑤	☐ a.m.	☐ p.m.
☐ Trembling	① ② ③ ④ ⑤	☐ a.m.	☐ p.m.
☐ Twitching	① ② ③ ④ ⑤	☐ a.m.	☐ p.m.
☐ Insomnia	① ② ③ ④ ⑤	☐ a.m.	☐ p.m.

illness

Symptom	Severity	Time	
☐ Nausea	① ② ③ ④ ⑤	☐ a.m.	☐ p.m.
☐ Vomiting	① ② ③ ④ ⑤	☐ a.m.	☐ p.m.
☐ Constipation	① ② ③ ④ ⑤	☐ a.m.	☐ p.m.
☐ Diarrhea	① ② ③ ④ ⑤	☐ a.m.	☐ p.m.
☐ Sore throat	① ② ③ ④ ⑤	☐ a.m.	☐ p.m.
☐ Congestion	① ② ③ ④ ⑤	☐ a.m.	☐ p.m.
☐ Coughing	① ② ③ ④ ⑤	☐ a.m.	☐ p.m.
☐ Acid reflux	① ② ③ ④ ⑤	☐ a.m.	☐ p.m.

psychological

Symptom	Severity	Time	
☐ Anxiety	① ② ③ ④ ⑤	☐ a.m.	☐ p.m.
☐ Depression	① ② ③ ④ ⑤	☐ a.m.	☐ p.m.
☐ Memory loss	① ② ③ ④ ⑤	☐ a.m.	☐ p.m.
☐ Confusion	① ② ③ ④ ⑤	☐ a.m.	☐ p.m.
☐ Poor focus	① ② ③ ④ ⑤	☐ a.m.	☐ p.m.
☐ Mood swings	① ② ③ ④ ⑤	☐ a.m.	☐ p.m.
☐ Suicidal	① ② ③ ④ ⑤	☐ a.m.	☐ p.m.

other

Symptom	Severity	Time	
	① ② ③ ④ ⑤	☐ a.m.	☐ p.m.
	① ② ③ ④ ⑤	☐ a.m.	☐ p.m.
	① ② ③ ④ ⑤	☐ a.m.	☐ p.m.
	① ② ③ ④ ⑤	☐ a.m.	☐ p.m.
	① ② ③ ④ ⑤	☐ a.m.	☐ p.m.
	① ② ③ ④ ⑤	☐ a.m.	☐ p.m.
	① ② ③ ④ ⑤	☐ a.m.	☐ p.m.

SLEEP

hours ________ quality ① ② ③ ④ ⑤

STRESS LEVELS

None	Low	Medium	High	Max	@$#%!

WEATHER

☐ Cold ☐ Mild ☐ Hot
☐ Dry ☐ Humid ☐ Wet

Allergen Levels: ________

BM Pressure: ________

EXERCISE

☐ Heck yes, I worked out.
☐ I managed to exercise a bit.
☐ No, I haven't exercised at all.
☐ I did some stuff, and that counts.

DETAILS

FOOD / MEDICATION

Food / Drinks

Meds / Supplements	Time	Dose

☐ usual daily medication

Water	Caffeine	Alcohol
	x ________	x ________

FOOD ANALYSIS

New food introduced?
☐ Yes ☐ No

Food reintroduction?
☐ Yes ☐ No

Details

MEDICATION ANALYSIS

New med/dose introduced?
☐ Yes ☐ No

Medication stopped?
☐ Yes ☐ No

Details

ACTIVITY ANALYSIS

Heightened exertion levels?
☐ Yes ☐ No

Lowered exertion levels?
☐ Yes ☐ No

Details

SLEEP ANALYSIS

When you woke up this morning, did you feel well-rested?	☐ Yes	☐ No	☐ A bit
Did you snore or stop breathing throughout the night?	☐ Yes	☐ No	☐ Not sure
Roughly how many times did you wake up throughout the night?			

Notes / Suspected Triggers

ENTRY #17 | M T W T F S S | DATE:

HOW ARE YOU *Feeling today?*

Amazing!	Meh
Great	Not good
Good	Terrible!

RATE YOUR PAIN LEVEL

① ② ③ ④ ⑤ ⑥ ⑦ ⑧ ⑨ ⑩

WHAT ABOUT YOUR...?

Mood	① ② ③ ④ ⑤ ⑥ ⑦ ⑧ ⑨ ⑩
Energy Levels	① ② ③ ④ ⑤ ⑥ ⑦ ⑧ ⑨ ⑩
Mental Clarity	① ② ③ ④ ⑤ ⑥ ⑦ ⑧ ⑨ ⑩

PAIN & PHYSICAL SYMPTOMS

Symptom	Severity	am	pm
	① ② ③ ④ ⑤	☐	☐
	① ② ③ ④ ⑤	☐	☐
	① ② ③ ④ ⑤	☐	☐
	① ② ③ ④ ⑤	☐	☐
	① ② ③ ④ ⑤	☐	☐
	① ② ③ ④ ⑤	☐	☐
	① ② ③ ④ ⑤	☐	☐
	① ② ③ ④ ⑤	☐	☐

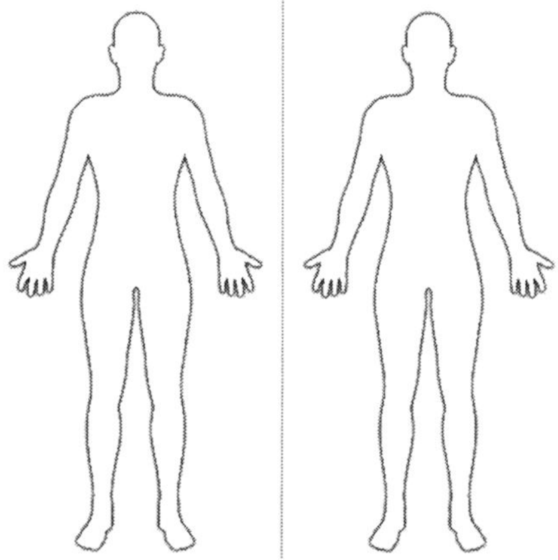

OTHER SYMPTOMS

general

Symptom	Severity	Time	
☐ Fatigue	① ② ③ ④ ⑤	☐ a.m.	☐ p.m.
☐ Lethargy	① ② ③ ④ ⑤	☐ a.m.	☐ p.m.
☐ Malaise	① ② ③ ④ ⑤	☐ a.m.	☐ p.m.
☐ Weakness	① ② ③ ④ ⑤	☐ a.m.	☐ p.m.
☐ Dizziness	① ② ③ ④ ⑤	☐ a.m.	☐ p.m.
☐ Trembling	① ② ③ ④ ⑤	☐ a.m.	☐ p.m.
☐ Twitching	① ② ③ ④ ⑤	☐ a.m.	☐ p.m.
☐ Insomnia	① ② ③ ④ ⑤	☐ a.m.	☐ p.m.

illness

Symptom	Severity	Time	
☐ Nausea	① ② ③ ④ ⑤	☐ a.m.	☐ p.m.
☐ Vomiting	① ② ③ ④ ⑤	☐ a.m.	☐ p.m.
☐ Constipation	① ② ③ ④ ⑤	☐ a.m.	☐ p.m.
☐ Diarrhea	① ② ③ ④ ⑤	☐ a.m.	☐ p.m.
☐ Sore throat	① ② ③ ④ ⑤	☐ a.m.	☐ p.m.
☐ Congestion	① ② ③ ④ ⑤	☐ a.m.	☐ p.m.
☐ Coughing	① ② ③ ④ ⑤	☐ a.m.	☐ p.m.
☐ Acid reflux	① ② ③ ④ ⑤	☐ a.m.	☐ p.m.

psychological

Symptom	Severity	Time	
☐ Anxiety	① ② ③ ④ ⑤	☐ a.m.	☐ p.m.
☐ Depression	① ② ③ ④ ⑤	☐ a.m.	☐ p.m.
☐ Memory loss	① ② ③ ④ ⑤	☐ a.m.	☐ p.m.
☐ Confusion	① ② ③ ④ ⑤	☐ a.m.	☐ p.m.
☐ Poor focus	① ② ③ ④ ⑤	☐ a.m.	☐ p.m.
☐ Mood swings	① ② ③ ④ ⑤	☐ a.m.	☐ p.m.
☐ Suicidal	① ② ③ ④ ⑤	☐ a.m.	☐ p.m.

other

Symptom	Severity	Time	
	① ② ③ ④ ⑤	☐ a.m.	☐ p.m.
	① ② ③ ④ ⑤	☐ a.m.	☐ p.m.
	① ② ③ ④ ⑤	☐ a.m.	☐ p.m.
	① ② ③ ④ ⑤	☐ a.m.	☐ p.m.
	① ② ③ ④ ⑤	☐ a.m.	☐ p.m.
	① ② ③ ④ ⑤	☐ a.m.	☐ p.m.
	① ② ③ ④ ⑤	☐ a.m.	☐ p.m.

SLEEP

hours ________

quality ① ② ③ ④ ⑤

STRESS LEVELS

None	Low	Medium	High	Max	@$#%!

WEATHER

☐ Cold ☐ Mild ☐ Hot
☐ Dry ☐ Humid ☐ Wet

Allergen Levels: ________

BM Pressure: ________

EXERCISE

☐ Heck yes, I worked out.
☐ I managed to exercise a bit.
☐ No, I haven't exercised at all.
☐ I did some stuff, and that counts.

DETAILS

FOOD / MEDICATION

Food / Drinks

Meds / Supplements	Time	Dose
☐ usual daily medication		

Water	Caffeine	Alcohol
	x ________	x ________

FOOD ANALYSIS		MEDICATION ANALYSIS		ACTIVITY ANALYSIS	
New food introduced?		New med/dose introduced?		Heightened exertion levels?	
☐ Yes	☐ No	☐ Yes	☐ No	☐ Yes	☐ No
Food reintroduction?		Medication stopped?		Lowered exertion levels?	
☐ Yes	☐ No	☐ Yes	☐ No	☐ Yes	☐ No
Details		Details		Details	

SLEEP ANALYSIS

When you woke up this morning, did you feel well-rested?	☐ Yes	☐ No	☐ A bit
Did you snore or stop breathing throughout the night?	☐ Yes	☐ No	☐ Not sure
Roughly how many times did you wake up throughout the night?			

Notes / Suspected Triggers

ENTRY #18 | M T W T F S S | DATE:

HOW ARE YOU *Feeling today?*

Amazing!	Meh
Great	Not good
Good	Terrible!

RATE YOUR PAIN LEVEL

① ② ③ ④ ⑤ ⑥ ⑦ ⑧ ⑨ ⑩

WHAT ABOUT YOUR...?

Mood	① ② ③ ④ ⑤ ⑥ ⑦ ⑧ ⑨ ⑩
Energy Levels	① ② ③ ④ ⑤ ⑥ ⑦ ⑧ ⑨ ⑩
Mental Clarity	① ② ③ ④ ⑤ ⑥ ⑦ ⑧ ⑨ ⑩

PAIN & PHYSICAL SYMPTOMS

Symptom	Severity	am	pm
	① ② ③ ④ ⑤	☐	☐
	① ② ③ ④ ⑤	☐	☐
	① ② ③ ④ ⑤	☐	☐
	① ② ③ ④ ⑤	☐	☐
	① ② ③ ④ ⑤	☐	☐
	① ② ③ ④ ⑤	☐	☐
	① ② ③ ④ ⑤	☐	☐
	① ② ③ ④ ⑤	☐	☐

front ***back***

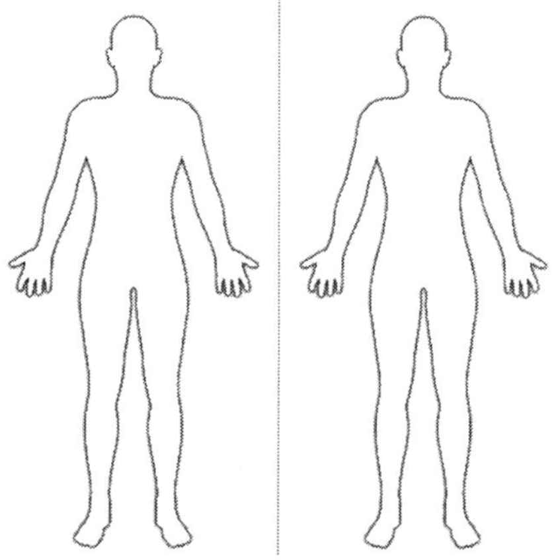

OTHER SYMPTOMS

general

Symptom	Severity	Time	
☐ Fatigue	① ② ③ ④ ⑤	☐ a.m.	☐ p.m.
☐ Lethargy	① ② ③ ④ ⑤	☐ a.m.	☐ p.m.
☐ Malaise	① ② ③ ④ ⑤	☐ a.m.	☐ p.m.
☐ Weakness	① ② ③ ④ ⑤	☐ a.m.	☐ p.m.
☐ Dizziness	① ② ③ ④ ⑤	☐ a.m.	☐ p.m.
☐ Trembling	① ② ③ ④ ⑤	☐ a.m.	☐ p.m.
☐ Twitching	① ② ③ ④ ⑤	☐ a.m.	☐ p.m.
☐ Insomnia	① ② ③ ④ ⑤	☐ a.m.	☐ p.m.

illness

Symptom	Severity	Time	
☐ Nausea	① ② ③ ④ ⑤	☐ a.m.	☐ p.m.
☐ Vomiting	① ② ③ ④ ⑤	☐ a.m.	☐ p.m.
☐ Constipation	① ② ③ ④ ⑤	☐ a.m.	☐ p.m.
☐ Diarrhea	① ② ③ ④ ⑤	☐ a.m.	☐ p.m.
☐ Sore throat	① ② ③ ④ ⑤	☐ a.m.	☐ p.m.
☐ Congestion	① ② ③ ④ ⑤	☐ a.m.	☐ p.m.
☐ Coughing	① ② ③ ④ ⑤	☐ a.m.	☐ p.m.
☐ Acid reflux	① ② ③ ④ ⑤	☐ a.m.	☐ p.m.

psychological

Symptom	Severity	Time	
☐ Anxiety	① ② ③ ④ ⑤	☐ a.m.	☐ p.m.
☐ Depression	① ② ③ ④ ⑤	☐ a.m.	☐ p.m.
☐ Memory loss	① ② ③ ④ ⑤	☐ a.m.	☐ p.m.
☐ Confusion	① ② ③ ④ ⑤	☐ a.m.	☐ p.m.
☐ Poor focus	① ② ③ ④ ⑤	☐ a.m.	☐ p.m.
☐ Mood swings	① ② ③ ④ ⑤	☐ a.m.	☐ p.m.
☐ Suicidal	① ② ③ ④ ⑤	☐ a.m.	☐ p.m.

other

Symptom	Severity	Time	
	① ② ③ ④ ⑤	☐ a.m.	☐ p.m.
	① ② ③ ④ ⑤	☐ a.m.	☐ p.m.
	① ② ③ ④ ⑤	☐ a.m.	☐ p.m.
	① ② ③ ④ ⑤	☐ a.m.	☐ p.m.
	① ② ③ ④ ⑤	☐ a.m.	☐ p.m.
	① ② ③ ④ ⑤	☐ a.m.	☐ p.m.
	① ② ③ ④ ⑤	☐ a.m.	☐ p.m.

SLEEP

hours ________ quality ① ② ③ ④ ⑤

STRESS LEVELS

None	Low	Medium	High	Max	@$#%!

WEATHER

- ☐ Cold ☐ Mild ☐ Hot
- ☐ Dry ☐ Humid ☐ Wet

Allergen Levels: ________

BM Pressure: ________

EXERCISE

- ☐ Heck yes, I worked out.
- ☐ I managed to exercise a bit.
- ☐ No, I haven't exercised at all.
- ☐ I did some stuff, and that counts.

DETAILS

FOOD / MEDICATION

Food / Drinks

Meds / Supplements	Time	Dose

☐ usual daily medication

Water Caffeine Alcohol

x ________ x ________

FOOD ANALYSIS

New food introduced?

☐ Yes ☐ No

Food reintroduction?

☐ Yes ☐ No

Details

MEDICATION ANALYSIS

New med/dose introduced?

☐ Yes ☐ No

Medication stopped?

☐ Yes ☐ No

Details

ACTIVITY ANALYSIS

Heightened exertion levels?

☐ Yes ☐ No

Lowered exertion levels?

☐ Yes ☐ No

Details

SLEEP ANALYSIS

When you woke up this morning, did you feel well-rested?	☐ Yes	☐ No	☐ A bit
Did you snore or stop breathing throughout the night?	☐ Yes	☐ No	☐ Not sure
Roughly how many times did you wake up throughout the night?			

Notes / Suspected Triggers

ENTRY #19 | M T W T F S S | DATE:

HOW ARE YOU *Feeling today?*

Amazing!	Meh
Great	Not good
Good	Terrible!

RATE YOUR PAIN LEVEL

① ② ③ ④ ⑤ ⑥ ⑦ ⑧ ⑨ ⑩

WHAT ABOUT YOUR...?

Mood	① ② ③ ④ ⑤ ⑥ ⑦ ⑧ ⑨ ⑩
Energy Levels	① ② ③ ④ ⑤ ⑥ ⑦ ⑧ ⑨ ⑩
Mental Clarity	① ② ③ ④ ⑤ ⑥ ⑦ ⑧ ⑨ ⑩

PAIN & PHYSICAL SYMPTOMS

Symptom	Severity	am	pm
	① ② ③ ④ ⑤	☐	☐
	① ② ③ ④ ⑤	☐	☐
	① ② ③ ④ ⑤	☐	☐
	① ② ③ ④ ⑤	☐	☐
	① ② ③ ④ ⑤	☐	☐
	① ② ③ ④ ⑤	☐	☐
	① ② ③ ④ ⑤	☐	☐
	① ② ③ ④ ⑤	☐	☐

front *back*

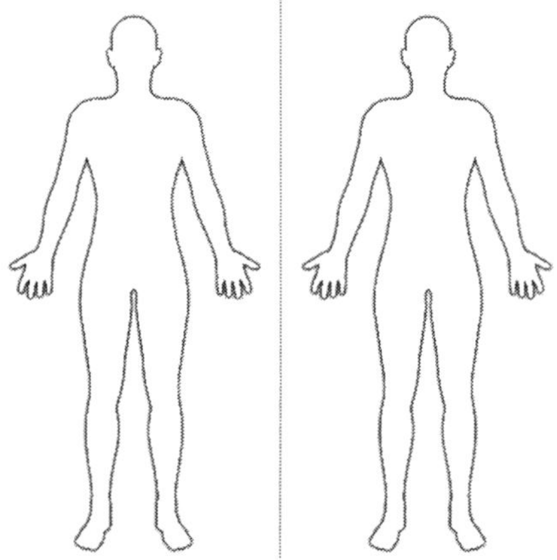

OTHER SYMPTOMS

general

Symptom	Severity	Time	
☐ Fatigue	① ② ③ ④ ⑤	☐ a.m.	☐ p.m.
☐ Lethargy	① ② ③ ④ ⑤	☐ a.m.	☐ p.m.
☐ Malaise	① ② ③ ④ ⑤	☐ a.m.	☐ p.m.
☐ Weakness	① ② ③ ④ ⑤	☐ a.m.	☐ p.m.
☐ Dizziness	① ② ③ ④ ⑤	☐ a.m.	☐ p.m.
☐ Trembling	① ② ③ ④ ⑤	☐ a.m.	☐ p.m.
☐ Twitching	① ② ③ ④ ⑤	☐ a.m.	☐ p.m.
☐ Insomnia	① ② ③ ④ ⑤	☐ a.m.	☐ p.m.

illness

Symptom	Severity	Time	
☐ Nausea	① ② ③ ④ ⑤	☐ a.m.	☐ p.m.
☐ Vomiting	① ② ③ ④ ⑤	☐ a.m.	☐ p.m.
☐ Constipation	① ② ③ ④ ⑤	☐ a.m.	☐ p.m.
☐ Diarrhea	① ② ③ ④ ⑤	☐ a.m.	☐ p.m.
☐ Sore throat	① ② ③ ④ ⑤	☐ a.m.	☐ p.m.
☐ Congestion	① ② ③ ④ ⑤	☐ a.m.	☐ p.m.
☐ Coughing	① ② ③ ④ ⑤	☐ a.m.	☐ p.m.
☐ Acid reflux	① ② ③ ④ ⑤	☐ a.m.	☐ p.m.

psychological

Symptom	Severity	Time	
☐ Anxiety	① ② ③ ④ ⑤	☐ a.m.	☐ p.m.
☐ Depression	① ② ③ ④ ⑤	☐ a.m.	☐ p.m.
☐ Memory loss	① ② ③ ④ ⑤	☐ a.m.	☐ p.m.
☐ Confusion	① ② ③ ④ ⑤	☐ a.m.	☐ p.m.
☐ Poor focus	① ② ③ ④ ⑤	☐ a.m.	☐ p.m.
☐ Mood swings	① ② ③ ④ ⑤	☐ a.m.	☐ p.m.
☐ Suicidal	① ② ③ ④ ⑤	☐ a.m.	☐ p.m.

other

Symptom	Severity	Time	
	① ② ③ ④ ⑤	☐ a.m.	☐ p.m.
	① ② ③ ④ ⑤	☐ a.m.	☐ p.m.
	① ② ③ ④ ⑤	☐ a.m.	☐ p.m.
	① ② ③ ④ ⑤	☐ a.m.	☐ p.m.
	① ② ③ ④ ⑤	☐ a.m.	☐ p.m.
	① ② ③ ④ ⑤	☐ a.m.	☐ p.m.
	① ② ③ ④ ⑤	☐ a.m.	☐ p.m.

SLEEP

hours ________ *quality* ① ② ③ ④ ⑤

STRESS LEVELS

None	Low	Medium	High	Max	@$#%!

WEATHER

☐ Cold ☐ Mild ☐ Hot
☐ Dry ☐ Humid ☐ Wet

Allergen Levels: ________
BM Pressure: ________

EXERCISE

☐ Heck yes, I worked out.
☐ I managed to exercise a bit.
☐ No, I haven't exercised at all.
☐ I did some stuff, and that counts.

DETAILS

FOOD / MEDICATION

Food / Drinks

Meds / Supplements	Time	Dose
☐ usual daily medication		

Water	*Caffeine*	*Alcohol*
☐☐☐☐☐☐☐☐☐☐	x ________	x ________

FOOD ANALYSIS

New food introduced?
☐ Yes ☐ No
Food reintroduction?
☐ Yes ☐ No

Details

MEDICATION ANALYSIS

New med/dose introduced?
☐ Yes ☐ No
Medication stopped?
☐ Yes ☐ No

Details

ACTIVITY ANALYSIS

Heightened exertion levels?
☐ Yes ☐ No
Lowered exertion levels?
☐ Yes ☐ No

Details

SLEEP ANALYSIS

When you woke up this morning, did you feel well-rested?	☐ Yes	☐ No	☐ A bit
Did you snore or stop breathing throughout the night?	☐ Yes	☐ No	☐ Not sure
Roughly how many times did you wake up throughout the night?			

Notes / Suspected Triggers

ENTRY #20 | M T W T F S S | DATE:

HOW ARE YOU *Feeling today?*

Amazing!	Meh
Great	Not good
Good	Terrible!

RATE YOUR PAIN LEVEL

① ② ③ ④ ⑤ ⑥ ⑦ ⑧ ⑨ ⑩

WHAT ABOUT YOUR...?

Mood	① ② ③ ④ ⑤ ⑥ ⑦ ⑧ ⑨ ⑩
Energy Levels	① ② ③ ④ ⑤ ⑥ ⑦ ⑧ ⑨ ⑩
Mental Clarity	① ② ③ ④ ⑤ ⑥ ⑦ ⑧ ⑨ ⑩

PAIN & PHYSICAL SYMPTOMS

Symptom	Severity	am	pm
	① ② ③ ④ ⑤	☐	☐
	① ② ③ ④ ⑤	☐	☐
	① ② ③ ④ ⑤	☐	☐
	① ② ③ ④ ⑤	☐	☐
	① ② ③ ④ ⑤	☐	☐
	① ② ③ ④ ⑤	☐	☐
	① ② ③ ④ ⑤	☐	☐
	① ② ③ ④ ⑤	☐	☐

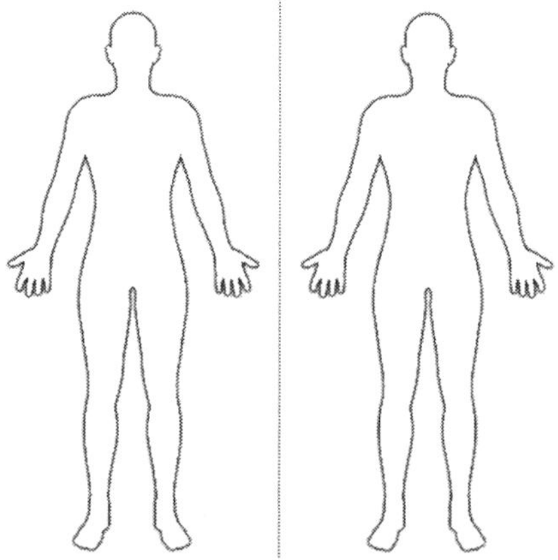

OTHER SYMPTOMS

general

Symptom	Severity	Time	
☐ Fatigue	① ② ③ ④ ⑤	☐ a.m.	☐ p.m.
☐ Lethargy	① ② ③ ④ ⑤	☐ a.m.	☐ p.m.
☐ Malaise	① ② ③ ④ ⑤	☐ a.m.	☐ p.m.
☐ Weakness	① ② ③ ④ ⑤	☐ a.m.	☐ p.m.
☐ Dizziness	① ② ③ ④ ⑤	☐ a.m.	☐ p.m.
☐ Trembling	① ② ③ ④ ⑤	☐ a.m.	☐ p.m.
☐ Twitching	① ② ③ ④ ⑤	☐ a.m.	☐ p.m.
☐ Insomnia	① ② ③ ④ ⑤	☐ a.m.	☐ p.m.

illness

Symptom	Severity	Time	
☐ Nausea	① ② ③ ④ ⑤	☐ a.m.	☐ p.m.
☐ Vomiting	① ② ③ ④ ⑤	☐ a.m.	☐ p.m.
☐ Constipation	① ② ③ ④ ⑤	☐ a.m.	☐ p.m.
☐ Diarrhea	① ② ③ ④ ⑤	☐ a.m.	☐ p.m.
☐ Sore throat	① ② ③ ④ ⑤	☐ a.m.	☐ p.m.
☐ Congestion	① ② ③ ④ ⑤	☐ a.m.	☐ p.m.
☐ Coughing	① ② ③ ④ ⑤	☐ a.m.	☐ p.m.
☐ Acid reflux	① ② ③ ④ ⑤	☐ a.m.	☐ p.m.

psychological

Symptom	Severity	Time	
☐ Anxiety	① ② ③ ④ ⑤	☐ a.m.	☐ p.m.
☐ Depression	① ② ③ ④ ⑤	☐ a.m.	☐ p.m.
☐ Memory loss	① ② ③ ④ ⑤	☐ a.m.	☐ p.m.
☐ Confusion	① ② ③ ④ ⑤	☐ a.m.	☐ p.m.
☐ Poor focus	① ② ③ ④ ⑤	☐ a.m.	☐ p.m.
☐ Mood swings	① ② ③ ④ ⑤	☐ a.m.	☐ p.m.
☐ Suicidal	① ② ③ ④ ⑤	☐ a.m.	☐ p.m.

other

Symptom	Severity	Time	
	① ② ③ ④ ⑤	☐ a.m.	☐ p.m.
	① ② ③ ④ ⑤	☐ a.m.	☐ p.m.
	① ② ③ ④ ⑤	☐ a.m.	☐ p.m.
	① ② ③ ④ ⑤	☐ a.m.	☐ p.m.
	① ② ③ ④ ⑤	☐ a.m.	☐ p.m.
	① ② ③ ④ ⑤	☐ a.m.	☐ p.m.
	① ② ③ ④ ⑤	☐ a.m.	☐ p.m.

SLEEP

hours ________ quality (1) (2) (3) (4) (5)

STRESS LEVELS

None	Low	Medium	High	Max	@$#%!

WEATHER

☐ Cold ☐ Mild ☐ Hot

☐ Dry ☐ Humid ☐ Wet

Allergen Levels: ________

BM Pressure: ________

EXERCISE

☐ Heck yes, I worked out.

☐ I managed to exercise a bit.

☐ No, I haven't exercised at all.

☐ I did some stuff, and that counts.

DETAILS

FOOD / MEDICATION

Food / Drinks

Meds / Supplements	Time	Dose

☐ usual daily medication

Water	Caffeine	Alcohol
	x ________	x ________

FOOD ANALYSIS

New food introduced?

☐ Yes ☐ No

Food reintroduction?

☐ Yes ☐ No

Details

MEDICATION ANALYSIS

New med/dose introduced?

☐ Yes ☐ No

Medication stopped?

☐ Yes ☐ No

Details

ACTIVITY ANALYSIS

Heightened exertion levels?

☐ Yes ☐ No

Lowered exertion levels?

☐ Yes ☐ No

Details

SLEEP ANALYSIS

When you woke up this morning, did you feel well-rested?	☐ Yes	☐ No	☐ A bit
Did you snore or stop breathing throughout the night?	☐ Yes	☐ No	☐ Not sure
Roughly how many times did you wake up throughout the night?			

Notes / Suspected Triggers

ENTRY #21 | M T W T F S S | DATE:

HOW ARE YOU *Feeling today?*

Amazing!	Meh
Great	Not good
Good	Terrible!

RATE YOUR PAIN LEVEL

① ② ③ ④ ⑤ ⑥ ⑦ ⑧ ⑨ ⑩

WHAT ABOUT YOUR...?

Mood	① ② ③ ④ ⑤ ⑥ ⑦ ⑧ ⑨ ⑩
Energy Levels	① ② ③ ④ ⑤ ⑥ ⑦ ⑧ ⑨ ⑩
Mental Clarity	① ② ③ ④ ⑤ ⑥ ⑦ ⑧ ⑨ ⑩

PAIN & PHYSICAL SYMPTOMS

Symptom	Severity	am	pm
	① ② ③ ④ ⑤	☐	☐
	① ② ③ ④ ⑤	☐	☐
	① ② ③ ④ ⑤	☐	☐
	① ② ③ ④ ⑤	☐	☐
	① ② ③ ④ ⑤	☐	☐
	① ② ③ ④ ⑤	☐	☐
	① ② ③ ④ ⑤	☐	☐
	① ② ③ ④ ⑤	☐	☐

front

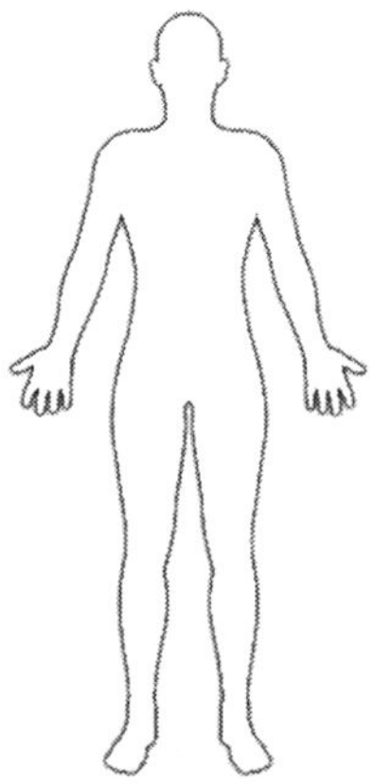

back

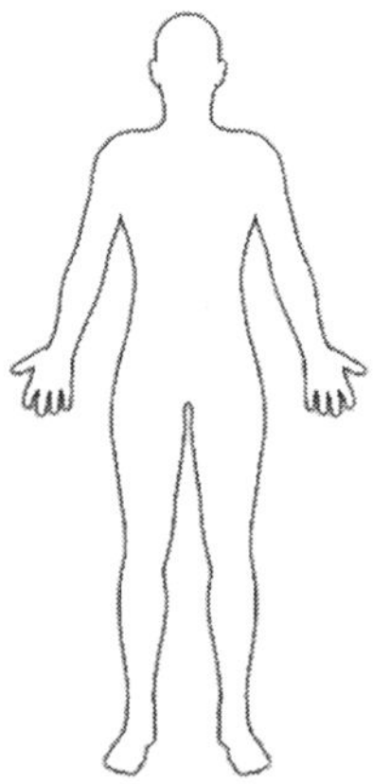

OTHER SYMPTOMS

general

Symptom	Severity	Time	
☐ Fatigue	① ② ③ ④ ⑤	☐ a.m.	☐ p.m.
☐ Lethargy	① ② ③ ④ ⑤	☐ a.m.	☐ p.m.
☐ Malaise	① ② ③ ④ ⑤	☐ a.m.	☐ p.m.
☐ Weakness	① ② ③ ④ ⑤	☐ a.m.	☐ p.m.
☐ Dizziness	① ② ③ ④ ⑤	☐ a.m.	☐ p.m.
☐ Trembling	① ② ③ ④ ⑤	☐ a.m.	☐ p.m.
☐ Twitching	① ② ③ ④ ⑤	☐ a.m.	☐ p.m.
☐ Insomnia	① ② ③ ④ ⑤	☐ a.m.	☐ p.m.

illness

Symptom	Severity	Time	
☐ Nausea	① ② ③ ④ ⑤	☐ a.m.	☐ p.m.
☐ Vomiting	① ② ③ ④ ⑤	☐ a.m.	☐ p.m.
☐ Constipation	① ② ③ ④ ⑤	☐ a.m.	☐ p.m.
☐ Diarrhea	① ② ③ ④ ⑤	☐ a.m.	☐ p.m.
☐ Sore throat	① ② ③ ④ ⑤	☐ a.m.	☐ p.m.
☐ Congestion	① ② ③ ④ ⑤	☐ a.m.	☐ p.m.
☐ Coughing	① ② ③ ④ ⑤	☐ a.m.	☐ p.m.
☐ Acid reflux	① ② ③ ④ ⑤	☐ a.m.	☐ p.m.

psychological

Symptom	Severity	Time	
☐ Anxiety	① ② ③ ④ ⑤	☐ a.m.	☐ p.m.
☐ Depression	① ② ③ ④ ⑤	☐ a.m.	☐ p.m.
☐ Memory loss	① ② ③ ④ ⑤	☐ a.m.	☐ p.m.
☐ Confusion	① ② ③ ④ ⑤	☐ a.m.	☐ p.m.
☐ Poor focus	① ② ③ ④ ⑤	☐ a.m.	☐ p.m.
☐ Mood swings	① ② ③ ④ ⑤	☐ a.m.	☐ p.m.
☐ Suicidal	① ② ③ ④ ⑤	☐ a.m.	☐ p.m.

other

Symptom	Severity	Time	
	① ② ③ ④ ⑤	☐ a.m.	☐ p.m.
	① ② ③ ④ ⑤	☐ a.m.	☐ p.m.
	① ② ③ ④ ⑤	☐ a.m.	☐ p.m.
	① ② ③ ④ ⑤	☐ a.m.	☐ p.m.
	① ② ③ ④ ⑤	☐ a.m.	☐ p.m.
	① ② ③ ④ ⑤	☐ a.m.	☐ p.m.
	① ② ③ ④ ⑤	☐ a.m.	☐ p.m.

SLEEP

hours ________ *quality* ① ② ③ ④ ⑤

STRESS LEVELS

None	Low	Medium	High	Max	@$#%!

WEATHER

☐ Cold ☐ Mild ☐ Hot
☐ Dry ☐ Humid ☐ Wet

Allergen Levels: ________
BM Pressure: ________

EXERCISE

☐ Heck yes, I worked out.
☐ I managed to exercise a bit.
☐ No, I haven't exercised at all.
☐ I did some stuff, and that counts.

DETAILS

FOOD / MEDICATION

Food / Drinks

Meds / Supplements	Time	Dose
☐ usual daily medication		

Water *Caffeine* *Alcohol*

x ________ x ________

FOOD ANALYSIS

New food introduced?
☐ Yes ☐ No
Food reintroduction?
☐ Yes ☐ No

Details

MEDICATION ANALYSIS

New med/dose introduced?
☐ Yes ☐ No
Medication stopped?
☐ Yes ☐ No

Details

ACTIVITY ANALYSIS

Heightened exertion levels?
☐ Yes ☐ No
Lowered exertion levels?
☐ Yes ☐ No

Details

SLEEP ANALYSIS

When you woke up this morning, did you feel well-rested?	☐ Yes	☐ No	☐ A bit
Did you snore or stop breathing throughout the night?	☐ Yes	☐ No	☐ Not sure
Roughly how many times did you wake up throughout the night?			

Notes / Suspected Triggers

ENTRY #22 | M T W T F S S | DATE:

HOW ARE YOU *Feeling today?*

Amazing!	Meh
Great	Not good
Good	Terrible!

RATE YOUR PAIN LEVEL

① ② ③ ④ ⑤ ⑥ ⑦ ⑧ ⑨ ⑩

WHAT ABOUT YOUR...?

Mood	① ② ③ ④ ⑤ ⑥ ⑦ ⑧ ⑨ ⑩
Energy Levels	① ② ③ ④ ⑤ ⑥ ⑦ ⑧ ⑨ ⑩
Mental Clarity	① ② ③ ④ ⑤ ⑥ ⑦ ⑧ ⑨ ⑩

PAIN & PHYSICAL SYMPTOMS

Symptom	Severity	am	pm
	① ② ③ ④ ⑤	☐	☐
	① ② ③ ④ ⑤	☐	☐
	① ② ③ ④ ⑤	☐	☐
	① ② ③ ④ ⑤	☐	☐
	① ② ③ ④ ⑤	☐	☐
	① ② ③ ④ ⑤	☐	☐
	① ② ③ ④ ⑤	☐	☐
	① ② ③ ④ ⑤	☐	☐

front

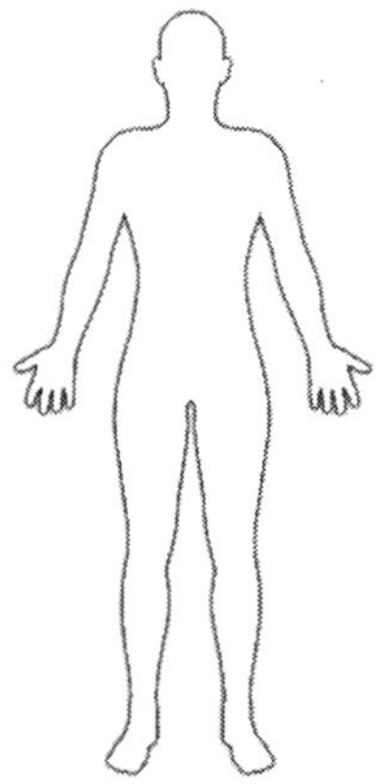

back

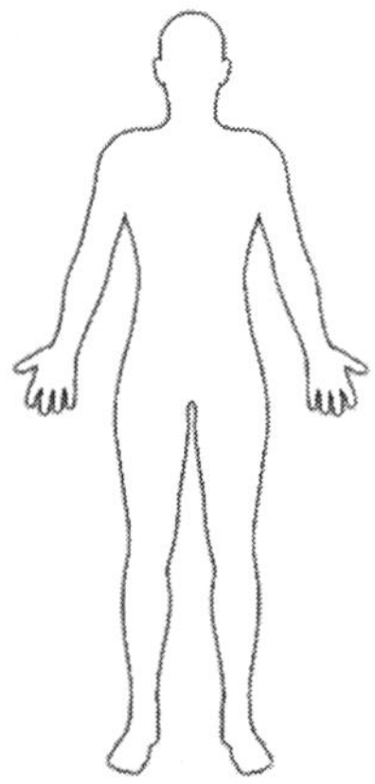

OTHER SYMPTOMS

general

Symptom	Severity	Time	
☐ Fatigue	① ② ③ ④ ⑤	☐ a.m.	☐ p.m.
☐ Lethargy	① ② ③ ④ ⑤	☐ a.m.	☐ p.m.
☐ Malaise	① ② ③ ④ ⑤	☐ a.m.	☐ p.m.
☐ Weakness	① ② ③ ④ ⑤	☐ a.m.	☐ p.m.
☐ Dizziness	① ② ③ ④ ⑤	☐ a.m.	☐ p.m.
☐ Trembling	① ② ③ ④ ⑤	☐ a.m.	☐ p.m.
☐ Twitching	① ② ③ ④ ⑤	☐ a.m.	☐ p.m.
☐ Insomnia	① ② ③ ④ ⑤	☐ a.m.	☐ p.m.

illness

Symptom	Severity	Time	
☐ Nausea	① ② ③ ④ ⑤	☐ a.m.	☐ p.m.
☐ Vomiting	① ② ③ ④ ⑤	☐ a.m.	☐ p.m.
☐ Constipation	① ② ③ ④ ⑤	☐ a.m.	☐ p.m.
☐ Diarrhea	① ② ③ ④ ⑤	☐ a.m.	☐ p.m.
☐ Sore throat	① ② ③ ④ ⑤	☐ a.m.	☐ p.m.
☐ Congestion	① ② ③ ④ ⑤	☐ a.m.	☐ p.m.
☐ Coughing	① ② ③ ④ ⑤	☐ a.m.	☐ p.m.
☐ Acid reflux	① ② ③ ④ ⑤	☐ a.m.	☐ p.m.

psychological

Symptom	Severity	Time	
☐ Anxiety	① ② ③ ④ ⑤	☐ a.m.	☐ p.m.
☐ Depression	① ② ③ ④ ⑤	☐ a.m.	☐ p.m.
☐ Memory loss	① ② ③ ④ ⑤	☐ a.m.	☐ p.m.
☐ Confusion	① ② ③ ④ ⑤	☐ a.m.	☐ p.m.
☐ Poor focus	① ② ③ ④ ⑤	☐ a.m.	☐ p.m.
☐ Mood swings	① ② ③ ④ ⑤	☐ a.m.	☐ p.m.
☐ Suicidal	① ② ③ ④ ⑤	☐ a.m.	☐ p.m.

other

Symptom	Severity	Time	
	① ② ③ ④ ⑤	☐ a.m.	☐ p.m.
	① ② ③ ④ ⑤	☐ a.m.	☐ p.m.
	① ② ③ ④ ⑤	☐ a.m.	☐ p.m.
	① ② ③ ④ ⑤	☐ a.m.	☐ p.m.
	① ② ③ ④ ⑤	☐ a.m.	☐ p.m.
	① ② ③ ④ ⑤	☐ a.m.	☐ p.m.
	① ② ③ ④ ⑤	☐ a.m.	☐ p.m.

SLEEP

hours ________

quality ① ② ③ ④ ⑤

STRESS LEVELS

None	Low	Medium	High	Max	@$#%!

WEATHER

☐ Cold ☐ Mild ☐ Hot
☐ Dry ☐ Humid ☐ Wet

Allergen Levels: ________

BM Pressure: ________

EXERCISE

☐ Heck yes, I worked out.
☐ I managed to exercise a bit.
☐ No, I haven't exercised at all.
☐ I did some stuff, and that counts.

DETAILS

FOOD / MEDICATION

Food / Drinks

Meds / Supplements	Time	Dose

☐ usual daily medication

Water	Caffeine	Alcohol
	x ________	x ________

FOOD ANALYSIS

New food introduced?
☐ Yes ☐ No
Food reintroduction?
☐ Yes ☐ No

Details

MEDICATION ANALYSIS

New med/dose introduced?
☐ Yes ☐ No
Medication stopped?
☐ Yes ☐ No

Details

ACTIVITY ANALYSIS

Heightened exertion levels?
☐ Yes ☐ No
Lowered exertion levels?
☐ Yes ☐ No

Details

SLEEP ANALYSIS

When you woke up this morning, did you feel well-rested?	☐ Yes	☐ No	☐ A bit
Did you snore or stop breathing throughout the night?	☐ Yes	☐ No	☐ Not sure
Roughly how many times did you wake up throughout the night?			

Notes / Suspected Triggers

ENTRY #23 | M T W T F S S | DATE:

HOW ARE YOU *Feeling today?*

Amazing!	Meh
Great	Not good
Good	Terrible!

RATE YOUR PAIN LEVEL

① ② ③ ④ ⑤ ⑥ ⑦ ⑧ ⑨ ⑩

WHAT ABOUT YOUR...?

Mood	① ② ③ ④ ⑤ ⑥ ⑦ ⑧ ⑨ ⑩
Energy Levels	① ② ③ ④ ⑤ ⑥ ⑦ ⑧ ⑨ ⑩
Mental Clarity	① ② ③ ④ ⑤ ⑥ ⑦ ⑧ ⑨ ⑩

PAIN & PHYSICAL SYMPTOMS

Symptom	Severity	am	pm
	① ② ③ ④ ⑤	☐	☐
	① ② ③ ④ ⑤	☐	☐
	① ② ③ ④ ⑤	☐	☐
	① ② ③ ④ ⑤	☐	☐
	① ② ③ ④ ⑤	☐	☐
	① ② ③ ④ ⑤	☐	☐
	① ② ③ ④ ⑤	☐	☐
	① ② ③ ④ ⑤	☐	☐

front *back*

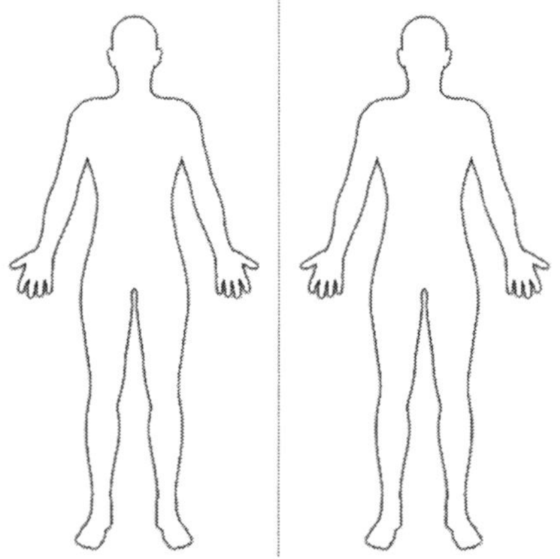

OTHER SYMPTOMS

general

Symptom	Severity	Time	
☐ Fatigue	① ② ③ ④ ⑤	☐ a.m.	☐ p.m.
☐ Lethargy	① ② ③ ④ ⑤	☐ a.m.	☐ p.m.
☐ Malaise	① ② ③ ④ ⑤	☐ a.m.	☐ p.m.
☐ Weakness	① ② ③ ④ ⑤	☐ a.m.	☐ p.m.
☐ Dizziness	① ② ③ ④ ⑤	☐ a.m.	☐ p.m.
☐ Trembling	① ② ③ ④ ⑤	☐ a.m.	☐ p.m.
☐ Twitching	① ② ③ ④ ⑤	☐ a.m.	☐ p.m.
☐ Insomnia	① ② ③ ④ ⑤	☐ a.m.	☐ p.m.

illness

Symptom	Severity	Time	
☐ Nausea	① ② ③ ④ ⑤	☐ a.m.	☐ p.m.
☐ Vomiting	① ② ③ ④ ⑤	☐ a.m.	☐ p.m.
☐ Constipation	① ② ③ ④ ⑤	☐ a.m.	☐ p.m.
☐ Diarrhea	① ② ③ ④ ⑤	☐ a.m.	☐ p.m.
☐ Sore throat	① ② ③ ④ ⑤	☐ a.m.	☐ p.m.
☐ Congestion	① ② ③ ④ ⑤	☐ a.m.	☐ p.m.
☐ Coughing	① ② ③ ④ ⑤	☐ a.m.	☐ p.m.
☐ Acid reflux	① ② ③ ④ ⑤	☐ a.m.	☐ p.m.

psychological

Symptom	Severity	Time	
☐ Anxiety	① ② ③ ④ ⑤	☐ a.m.	☐ p.m.
☐ Depression	① ② ③ ④ ⑤	☐ a.m.	☐ p.m.
☐ Memory loss	① ② ③ ④ ⑤	☐ a.m.	☐ p.m.
☐ Confusion	① ② ③ ④ ⑤	☐ a.m.	☐ p.m.
☐ Poor focus	① ② ③ ④ ⑤	☐ a.m.	☐ p.m.
☐ Mood swings	① ② ③ ④ ⑤	☐ a.m.	☐ p.m.
☐ Suicidal	① ② ③ ④ ⑤	☐ a.m.	☐ p.m.

other

Symptom	Severity	Time	
	① ② ③ ④ ⑤	☐ a.m.	☐ p.m.
	① ② ③ ④ ⑤	☐ a.m.	☐ p.m.
	① ② ③ ④ ⑤	☐ a.m.	☐ p.m.
	① ② ③ ④ ⑤	☐ a.m.	☐ p.m.
	① ② ③ ④ ⑤	☐ a.m.	☐ p.m.
	① ② ③ ④ ⑤	☐ a.m.	☐ p.m.
	① ② ③ ④ ⑤	☐ a.m.	☐ p.m.

SLEEP

hours ________ quality ① ② ③ ④ ⑤

STRESS LEVELS

None	Low	Medium	High	Max	@$#%!

WEATHER

☐ Cold ☐ Mild ☐ Hot
☐ Dry ☐ Humid ☐ Wet

Allergen Levels: ________
BM Pressure: ________

EXERCISE

☐ Heck yes, I worked out.
☐ I managed to exercise a bit.
☐ No, I haven't exercised at all.
☐ I did some stuff, and that counts.

DETAILS

FOOD / MEDICATION

Food / Drinks

Meds / Supplements	Time	Dose

☐ usual daily medication

Water	Caffeine	Alcohol
☐☐☐☐☐☐☐☐☐☐	x ________	x ________

FOOD ANALYSIS

New food introduced?
☐ Yes ☐ No

Food reintroduction?
☐ Yes ☐ No

Details

MEDICATION ANALYSIS

New med/dose introduced?
☐ Yes ☐ No

Medication stopped?
☐ Yes ☐ No

Details

ACTIVITY ANALYSIS

Heightened exertion levels?
☐ Yes ☐ No

Lowered exertion levels?
☐ Yes ☐ No

Details

SLEEP ANALYSIS

When you woke up this morning, did you feel well-rested?	☐ Yes	☐ No	☐ A bit
Did you snore or stop breathing throughout the night?	☐ Yes	☐ No	☐ Not sure
Roughly how many times did you wake up throughout the night?			

Notes / Suspected Triggers

ENTRY #24 | M T W T F S S | DATE:

HOW ARE YOU *Feeling today?*

Amazing!	Meh
Great	Not good
Good	Terrible!

RATE YOUR PAIN LEVEL

① ② ③ ④ ⑤ ⑥ ⑦ ⑧ ⑨ ⑩

WHAT ABOUT YOUR...?

Mood	① ② ③ ④ ⑤ ⑥ ⑦ ⑧ ⑨ ⑩
Energy Levels	① ② ③ ④ ⑤ ⑥ ⑦ ⑧ ⑨ ⑩
Mental Clarity	① ② ③ ④ ⑤ ⑥ ⑦ ⑧ ⑨ ⑩

PAIN & PHYSICAL SYMPTOMS

Symptom	Severity	am	pm
	① ② ③ ④ ⑤	☐	☐
	① ② ③ ④ ⑤	☐	☐
	① ② ③ ④ ⑤	☐	☐
	① ② ③ ④ ⑤	☐	☐
	① ② ③ ④ ⑤	☐	☐
	① ② ③ ④ ⑤	☐	☐
	① ② ③ ④ ⑤	☐	☐
	① ② ③ ④ ⑤	☐	☐

front *back*

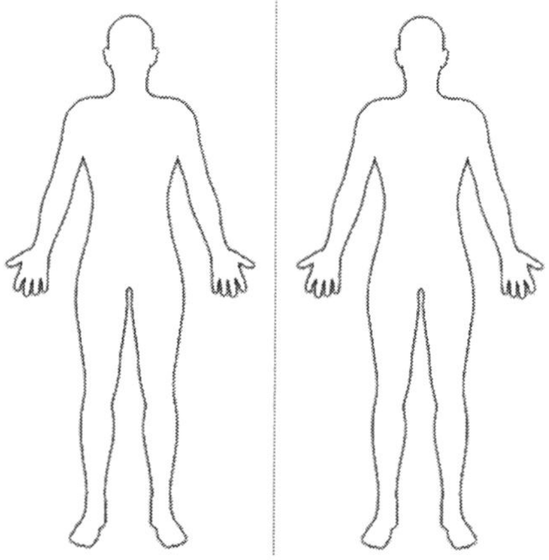

OTHER SYMPTOMS

general

Symptom	Severity	Time	
☐ Fatigue	① ② ③ ④ ⑤	☐ a.m.	☐ p.m.
☐ Lethargy	① ② ③ ④ ⑤	☐ a.m.	☐ p.m.
☐ Malaise	① ② ③ ④ ⑤	☐ a.m.	☐ p.m.
☐ Weakness	① ② ③ ④ ⑤	☐ a.m.	☐ p.m.
☐ Dizziness	① ② ③ ④ ⑤	☐ a.m.	☐ p.m.
☐ Trembling	① ② ③ ④ ⑤	☐ a.m.	☐ p.m.
☐ Twitching	① ② ③ ④ ⑤	☐ a.m.	☐ p.m.
☐ Insomnia	① ② ③ ④ ⑤	☐ a.m.	☐ p.m.

illness

Symptom	Severity	Time	
☐ Nausea	① ② ③ ④ ⑤	☐ a.m.	☐ p.m.
☐ Vomiting	① ② ③ ④ ⑤	☐ a.m.	☐ p.m.
☐ Constipation	① ② ③ ④ ⑤	☐ a.m.	☐ p.m.
☐ Diarrhea	① ② ③ ④ ⑤	☐ a.m.	☐ p.m.
☐ Sore throat	① ② ③ ④ ⑤	☐ a.m.	☐ p.m.
☐ Congestion	① ② ③ ④ ⑤	☐ a.m.	☐ p.m.
☐ Coughing	① ② ③ ④ ⑤	☐ a.m.	☐ p.m.
☐ Acid reflux	① ② ③ ④ ⑤	☐ a.m.	☐ p.m.

psychological

Symptom	Severity	Time	
☐ Anxiety	① ② ③ ④ ⑤	☐ a.m.	☐ p.m.
☐ Depression	① ② ③ ④ ⑤	☐ a.m.	☐ p.m.
☐ Memory loss	① ② ③ ④ ⑤	☐ a.m.	☐ p.m.
☐ Confusion	① ② ③ ④ ⑤	☐ a.m.	☐ p.m.
☐ Poor focus	① ② ③ ④ ⑤	☐ a.m.	☐ p.m.
☐ Mood swings	① ② ③ ④ ⑤	☐ a.m.	☐ p.m.
☐ Suicidal	① ② ③ ④ ⑤	☐ a.m.	☐ p.m.

other

Symptom	Severity	Time	
	① ② ③ ④ ⑤	☐ a.m.	☐ p.m.
	① ② ③ ④ ⑤	☐ a.m.	☐ p.m.
	① ② ③ ④ ⑤	☐ a.m.	☐ p.m.
	① ② ③ ④ ⑤	☐ a.m.	☐ p.m.
	① ② ③ ④ ⑤	☐ a.m.	☐ p.m.
	① ② ③ ④ ⑤	☐ a.m.	☐ p.m.
	① ② ③ ④ ⑤	☐ a.m.	☐ p.m.

SLEEP

hours ________ quality ① ② ③ ④ ⑤

STRESS LEVELS

None	Low	Medium	High	Max	@$#%!

WEATHER

☐ Cold ☐ Mild ☐ Hot
☐ Dry ☐ Humid ☐ Wet

Allergen Levels: ________

BM Pressure: ________

EXERCISE

☐ Heck yes, I worked out.
☐ I managed to exercise a bit.
☐ No, I haven't exercised at all.
☐ I did some stuff, and that counts.

DETAILS

FOOD / MEDICATION

Food / Drinks

Meds / Supplements	Time	Dose
☐ usual daily medication		

Water | Caffeine | Alcohol

☕ x ________ 🍷 x ________

FOOD ANALYSIS

New food introduced?
☐ Yes ☐ No

Food reintroduction?
☐ Yes ☐ No

Details

MEDICATION ANALYSIS

New med/dose introduced?
☐ Yes ☐ No

Medication stopped?
☐ Yes ☐ No

Details

ACTIVITY ANALYSIS

Heightened exertion levels?
☐ Yes ☐ No

Lowered exertion levels?
☐ Yes ☐ No

Details

SLEEP ANALYSIS

When you woke up this morning, did you feel well-rested? ☐ Yes ☐ No ☐ A bit

Did you snore or stop breathing throughout the night? ☐ Yes ☐ No ☐ Not sure

Roughly how many times did you wake up throughout the night?

Notes / Suspected Triggers

ENTRY #25 | M T W T F S S | DATE:

HOW ARE YOU *Feeling today?*

Amazing!	Meh
Great	Not good
Good	Terrible!

RATE YOUR PAIN LEVEL

① ② ③ ④ ⑤ ⑥ ⑦ ⑧ ⑨ ⑩

WHAT ABOUT YOUR...?

Mood	① ② ③ ④ ⑤ ⑥ ⑦ ⑧ ⑨ ⑩
Energy Levels	① ② ③ ④ ⑤ ⑥ ⑦ ⑧ ⑨ ⑩
Mental Clarity	① ② ③ ④ ⑤ ⑥ ⑦ ⑧ ⑨ ⑩

PAIN & PHYSICAL SYMPTOMS

Symptom	Severity	am	pm
	① ② ③ ④ ⑤	☐	☐
	① ② ③ ④ ⑤	☐	☐
	① ② ③ ④ ⑤	☐	☐
	① ② ③ ④ ⑤	☐	☐
	① ② ③ ④ ⑤	☐	☐
	① ② ③ ④ ⑤	☐	☐
	① ② ③ ④ ⑤	☐	☐
	① ② ③ ④ ⑤	☐	☐

front *back*

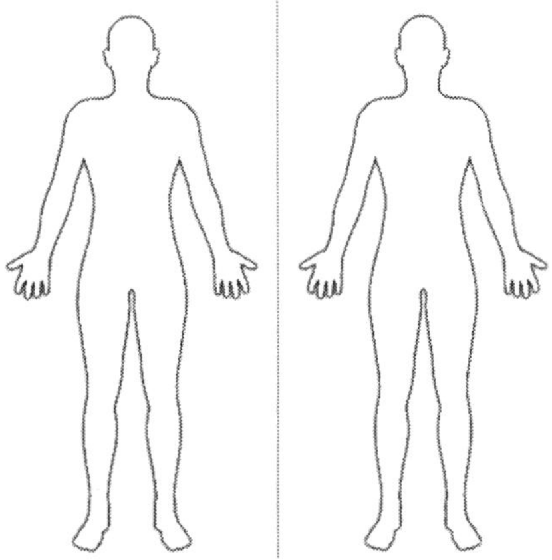

OTHER SYMPTOMS

general

Symptom	Severity	Time	
☐ Fatigue	① ② ③ ④ ⑤	☐ a.m.	☐ p.m.
☐ Lethargy	① ② ③ ④ ⑤	☐ a.m.	☐ p.m.
☐ Malaise	① ② ③ ④ ⑤	☐ a.m.	☐ p.m.
☐ Weakness	① ② ③ ④ ⑤	☐ a.m.	☐ p.m.
☐ Dizziness	① ② ③ ④ ⑤	☐ a.m.	☐ p.m.
☐ Trembling	① ② ③ ④ ⑤	☐ a.m.	☐ p.m.
☐ Twitching	① ② ③ ④ ⑤	☐ a.m.	☐ p.m.
☐ Insomnia	① ② ③ ④ ⑤	☐ a.m.	☐ p.m.

illness

Symptom	Severity	Time	
☐ Nausea	① ② ③ ④ ⑤	☐ a.m.	☐ p.m.
☐ Vomiting	① ② ③ ④ ⑤	☐ a.m.	☐ p.m.
☐ Constipation	① ② ③ ④ ⑤	☐ a.m.	☐ p.m.
☐ Diarrhea	① ② ③ ④ ⑤	☐ a.m.	☐ p.m.
☐ Sore throat	① ② ③ ④ ⑤	☐ a.m.	☐ p.m.
☐ Congestion	① ② ③ ④ ⑤	☐ a.m.	☐ p.m.
☐ Coughing	① ② ③ ④ ⑤	☐ a.m.	☐ p.m.
☐ Acid reflux	① ② ③ ④ ⑤	☐ a.m.	☐ p.m.

psychological

Symptom	Severity	Time	
☐ Anxiety	① ② ③ ④ ⑤	☐ a.m.	☐ p.m.
☐ Depression	① ② ③ ④ ⑤	☐ a.m.	☐ p.m.
☐ Memory loss	① ② ③ ④ ⑤	☐ a.m.	☐ p.m.
☐ Confusion	① ② ③ ④ ⑤	☐ a.m.	☐ p.m.
☐ Poor focus	① ② ③ ④ ⑤	☐ a.m.	☐ p.m.
☐ Mood swings	① ② ③ ④ ⑤	☐ a.m.	☐ p.m.
☐ Suicidal	① ② ③ ④ ⑤	☐ a.m.	☐ p.m.

other

Symptom	Severity	Time	
	① ② ③ ④ ⑤	☐ a.m.	☐ p.m.
	① ② ③ ④ ⑤	☐ a.m.	☐ p.m.
	① ② ③ ④ ⑤	☐ a.m.	☐ p.m.
	① ② ③ ④ ⑤	☐ a.m.	☐ p.m.
	① ② ③ ④ ⑤	☐ a.m.	☐ p.m.
	① ② ③ ④ ⑤	☐ a.m.	☐ p.m.
	① ② ③ ④ ⑤	☐ a.m.	☐ p.m.

SLEEP

hours ________ quality ① ② ③ ④ ⑤

STRESS LEVELS

None	Low	Medium	High	Max	@$#%!

WEATHER

☐ Cold ☐ Mild ☐ Hot
☐ Dry ☐ Humid ☐ Wet

Allergen Levels: ________
BM Pressure: ________

EXERCISE

☐ Heck yes, I worked out.
☐ I managed to exercise a bit.
☐ No, I haven't exercised at all.
☐ I did some stuff, and that counts.

DETAILS

FOOD / MEDICATION

Food / Drinks

Meds / Supplements	Time	Dose

☐ usual daily medication

Water | Caffeine | Alchohol

x ________ x ________

FOOD ANALYSIS

New food introduced?
☐ Yes ☐ No
Food reintroduction?
☐ Yes ☐ No
Details

MEDICATION ANALYSIS

New med/dose introduced?
☐ Yes ☐ No
Medication stopped?
☐ Yes ☐ No
Details

ACTIVITY ANALYSIS

Heightened exertion levels?
☐ Yes ☐ No
Lowered exertion levels?
☐ Yes ☐ No
Details

SLEEP ANALYSIS

When you woke up this morning, did you feel well-rested? ☐ Yes ☐ No ☐ A bit
Did you snore or stop breathing throughout the night? ☐ Yes ☐ No ☐ Not sure
Roughly how many times did you wake up throughout the night?

Notes / Suspected Triggers

ENTRY #26 | M T W T F S S | DATE:

HOW ARE YOU *Feeling today?*

Amazing!	Meh
Great	Not good
Good	Terrible!

RATE YOUR PAIN LEVEL

① ② ③ ④ ⑤ ⑥ ⑦ ⑧ ⑨ ⑩

WHAT ABOUT YOUR...?

Mood	① ② ③ ④ ⑤ ⑥ ⑦ ⑧ ⑨ ⑩
Energy Levels	① ② ③ ④ ⑤ ⑥ ⑦ ⑧ ⑨ ⑩
Mental Clarity	① ② ③ ④ ⑤ ⑥ ⑦ ⑧ ⑨ ⑩

PAIN & PHYSICAL SYMPTOMS

Symptom	Severity	am	pm
	① ② ③ ④ ⑤	☐	☐
	① ② ③ ④ ⑤	☐	☐
	① ② ③ ④ ⑤	☐	☐
	① ② ③ ④ ⑤	☐	☐
	① ② ③ ④ ⑤	☐	☐
	① ② ③ ④ ⑤	☐	☐
	① ② ③ ④ ⑤	☐	☐
	① ② ③ ④ ⑤	☐	☐

front *back*

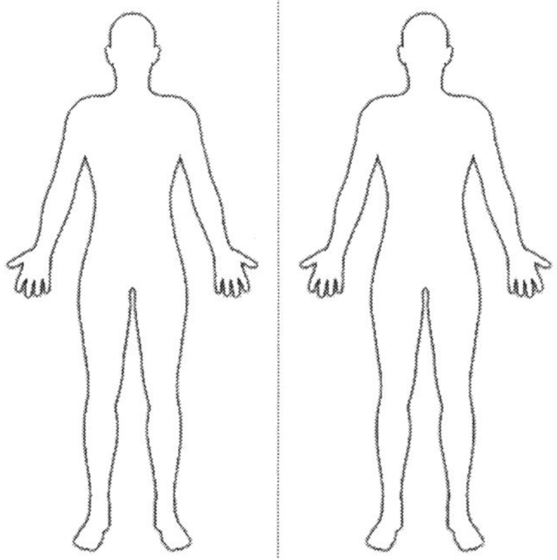

OTHER SYMPTOMS

general

Symptom	Severity	Time	
☐ Fatigue	① ② ③ ④ ⑤	☐ a.m.	☐ p.m.
☐ Lethargy	① ② ③ ④ ⑤	☐ a.m.	☐ p.m.
☐ Malaise	① ② ③ ④ ⑤	☐ a.m.	☐ p.m.
☐ Weakness	① ② ③ ④ ⑤	☐ a.m.	☐ p.m.
☐ Dizziness	① ② ③ ④ ⑤	☐ a.m.	☐ p.m.
☐ Trembling	① ② ③ ④ ⑤	☐ a.m.	☐ p.m.
☐ Twitching	① ② ③ ④ ⑤	☐ a.m.	☐ p.m.
☐ Insomnia	① ② ③ ④ ⑤	☐ a.m.	☐ p.m.

illness

Symptom	Severity	Time	
☐ Nausea	① ② ③ ④ ⑤	☐ a.m.	☐ p.m.
☐ Vomiting	① ② ③ ④ ⑤	☐ a.m.	☐ p.m.
☐ Constipation	① ② ③ ④ ⑤	☐ a.m.	☐ p.m.
☐ Diarrhea	① ② ③ ④ ⑤	☐ a.m.	☐ p.m.
☐ Sore throat	① ② ③ ④ ⑤	☐ a.m.	☐ p.m.
☐ Congestion	① ② ③ ④ ⑤	☐ a.m.	☐ p.m.
☐ Coughing	① ② ③ ④ ⑤	☐ a.m.	☐ p.m.
☐ Acid reflux	① ② ③ ④ ⑤	☐ a.m.	☐ p.m.

psychological

Symptom	Severity	Time	
☐ Anxiety	① ② ③ ④ ⑤	☐ a.m.	☐ p.m.
☐ Depression	① ② ③ ④ ⑤	☐ a.m.	☐ p.m.
☐ Memory loss	① ② ③ ④ ⑤	☐ a.m.	☐ p.m.
☐ Confusion	① ② ③ ④ ⑤	☐ a.m.	☐ p.m.
☐ Poor focus	① ② ③ ④ ⑤	☐ a.m.	☐ p.m.
☐ Mood swings	① ② ③ ④ ⑤	☐ a.m.	☐ p.m.
☐ Suicidal	① ② ③ ④ ⑤	☐ a.m.	☐ p.m.

other

Symptom	Severity	Time	
	① ② ③ ④ ⑤	☐ a.m.	☐ p.m.
	① ② ③ ④ ⑤	☐ a.m.	☐ p.m.
	① ② ③ ④ ⑤	☐ a.m.	☐ p.m.
	① ② ③ ④ ⑤	☐ a.m.	☐ p.m.
	① ② ③ ④ ⑤	☐ a.m.	☐ p.m.
	① ② ③ ④ ⑤	☐ a.m.	☐ p.m.
	① ② ③ ④ ⑤	☐ a.m.	☐ p.m.

SLEEP

hours ________ *quality* ① ② ③ ④ ⑤

STRESS LEVELS

None	Low	Medium	High	Max	@$#%!

WEATHER

☐ Cold ☐ Mild ☐ Hot
☐ Dry ☐ Humid ☐ Wet

Allergen Levels: ________
BM Pressure: ________

EXERCISE

☐ Heck yes, I worked out.
☐ I managed to exercise a bit.
☐ No, I haven't exercised at all.
☐ I did some stuff, and that counts.

DETAILS

FOOD / MEDICATION

Food / Drinks

Meds / Supplements	Time	Dose

☐ usual daily medication

Water	*Caffeine*	*Alcohol*
	x ________	x ________

FOOD ANALYSIS

New food introduced?
☐ Yes ☐ No
Food reintroduction?
☐ Yes ☐ No

Details

MEDICATION ANALYSIS

New med/dose introduced?
☐ Yes ☐ No
Medication stopped?
☐ Yes ☐ No

Details

ACTIVITY ANALYSIS

Heightened exertion levels?
☐ Yes ☐ No
Lowered exertion levels?
☐ Yes ☐ No

Details

SLEEP ANALYSIS

When you woke up this morning, did you feel well-rested?	☐ Yes	☐ No	☐ A bit
Did you snore or stop breathing throughout the night?	☐ Yes	☐ No	☐ Not sure
Roughly how many times did you wake up throughout the night?			

Notes / Suspected Triggers

ENTRY #27	M T W T F S S	DATE:

HOW ARE YOU *Feeling today?*

Amazing!	Meh
Great	Not good
Good	Terrible!

RATE YOUR PAIN LEVEL

① ② ③ ④ ⑤ ⑥ ⑦ ⑧ ⑨ ⑩

WHAT ABOUT YOUR...?

Mood	① ② ③ ④ ⑤ ⑥ ⑦ ⑧ ⑨ ⑩
Energy Levels	① ② ③ ④ ⑤ ⑥ ⑦ ⑧ ⑨ ⑩
Mental Clarity	① ② ③ ④ ⑤ ⑥ ⑦ ⑧ ⑨ ⑩

PAIN & PHYSICAL SYMPTOMS

Symptom	Severity	am	pm
	① ② ③ ④ ⑤	☐	☐
	① ② ③ ④ ⑤	☐	☐
	① ② ③ ④ ⑤	☐	☐
	① ② ③ ④ ⑤	☐	☐
	① ② ③ ④ ⑤	☐	☐
	① ② ③ ④ ⑤	☐	☐
	① ② ③ ④ ⑤	☐	☐
	① ② ③ ④ ⑤	☐	☐

front *back*

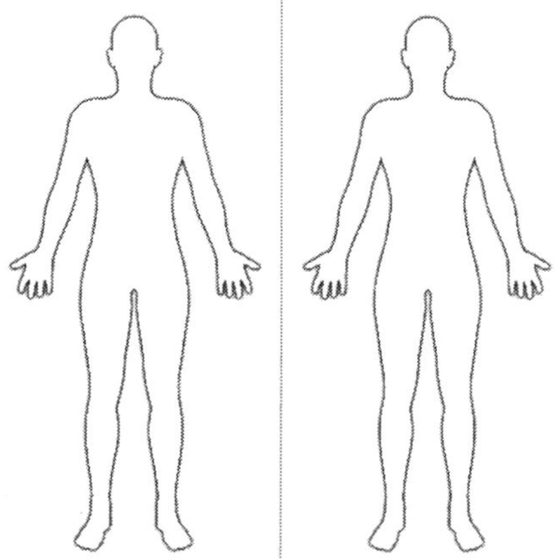

OTHER SYMPTOMS

general

Symptom	Severity	Time	
☐ Fatigue	① ② ③ ④ ⑤	☐ a.m.	☐ p.m.
☐ Lethargy	① ② ③ ④ ⑤	☐ a.m.	☐ p.m.
☐ Malaise	① ② ③ ④ ⑤	☐ a.m.	☐ p.m.
☐ Weakness	① ② ③ ④ ⑤	☐ a.m.	☐ p.m.
☐ Dizziness	① ② ③ ④ ⑤	☐ a.m.	☐ p.m.
☐ Trembling	① ② ③ ④ ⑤	☐ a.m.	☐ p.m.
☐ Twitching	① ② ③ ④ ⑤	☐ a.m.	☐ p.m.
☐ Insomnia	① ② ③ ④ ⑤	☐ a.m.	☐ p.m.

illness

Symptom	Severity	Time	
☐ Nausea	① ② ③ ④ ⑤	☐ a.m.	☐ p.m.
☐ Vomiting	① ② ③ ④ ⑤	☐ a.m.	☐ p.m.
☐ Constipation	① ② ③ ④ ⑤	☐ a.m.	☐ p.m.
☐ Diarrhea	① ② ③ ④ ⑤	☐ a.m.	☐ p.m.
☐ Sore throat	① ② ③ ④ ⑤	☐ a.m.	☐ p.m.
☐ Congestion	① ② ③ ④ ⑤	☐ a.m.	☐ p.m.
☐ Coughing	① ② ③ ④ ⑤	☐ a.m.	☐ p.m.
☐ Acid reflux	① ② ③ ④ ⑤	☐ a.m.	☐ p.m.

psychological

Symptom	Severity	Time	
☐ Anxiety	① ② ③ ④ ⑤	☐ a.m.	☐ p.m.
☐ Depression	① ② ③ ④ ⑤	☐ a.m.	☐ p.m.
☐ Memory loss	① ② ③ ④ ⑤	☐ a.m.	☐ p.m.
☐ Confusion	① ② ③ ④ ⑤	☐ a.m.	☐ p.m.
☐ Poor focus	① ② ③ ④ ⑤	☐ a.m.	☐ p.m.
☐ Mood swings	① ② ③ ④ ⑤	☐ a.m.	☐ p.m.
☐ Suicidal	① ② ③ ④ ⑤	☐ a.m.	☐ p.m.

other

Symptom	Severity	Time	
	① ② ③ ④ ⑤	☐ a.m.	☐ p.m.
	① ② ③ ④ ⑤	☐ a.m.	☐ p.m.
	① ② ③ ④ ⑤	☐ a.m.	☐ p.m.
	① ② ③ ④ ⑤	☐ a.m.	☐ p.m.
	① ② ③ ④ ⑤	☐ a.m.	☐ p.m.
	① ② ③ ④ ⑤	☐ a.m.	☐ p.m.
	① ② ③ ④ ⑤	☐ a.m.	☐ p.m.

SLEEP

hours ________ *quality* ① ② ③ ④ ⑤

STRESS LEVELS

None	Low	Medium	High	Max	@$#%!

WEATHER

☐ Cold ☐ Mild ☐ Hot
☐ Dry ☐ Humid ☐ Wet

Allergen Levels: ________
BM Pressure: ________

EXERCISE

☐ Heck yes, I worked out.
☐ I managed to exercise a bit.
☐ No, I haven't exercised at all.
☐ I did some stuff, and that counts.

DETAILS

FOOD / MEDICATION

Food / Drinks

Meds / Supplements	Time	Dose
☐ usual daily medication		

Water	*Caffeine*	*Alcohol*
	x ________	x ________

FOOD ANALYSIS

New food introduced?
☐ Yes ☐ No
Food reintroduction?
☐ Yes ☐ No
Details

MEDICATION ANALYSIS

New med/dose introduced?
☐ Yes ☐ No
Medication stopped?
☐ Yes ☐ No
Details

ACTIVITY ANALYSIS

Heightened exertion levels?
☐ Yes ☐ No
Lowered exertion levels?
☐ Yes ☐ No
Details

SLEEP ANALYSIS

When you woke up this morning, did you feel well-rested?	☐ Yes	☐ No	☐ A bit
Did you snore or stop breathing throughout the night?	☐ Yes	☐ No	☐ Not sure
Roughly how many times did you wake up throughout the night?			

Notes / Suspected Triggers

ENTRY #28	M T W T F S S	DATE:

HOW ARE YOU *Feeling today?*

Amazing!	Meh
Great	Not good
Good	Terrible!

RATE YOUR PAIN LEVEL

① ② ③ ④ ⑤ ⑥ ⑦ ⑧ ⑨ ⑩

WHAT ABOUT YOUR...?

Mood	① ② ③ ④ ⑤ ⑥ ⑦ ⑧ ⑨ ⑩
Energy Levels	① ② ③ ④ ⑤ ⑥ ⑦ ⑧ ⑨ ⑩
Mental Clarity	① ② ③ ④ ⑤ ⑥ ⑦ ⑧ ⑨ ⑩

PAIN & PHYSICAL SYMPTOMS

Symptom	Severity	am	pm
	① ② ③ ④ ⑤	☐	☐
	① ② ③ ④ ⑤	☐	☐
	① ② ③ ④ ⑤	☐	☐
	① ② ③ ④ ⑤	☐	☐
	① ② ③ ④ ⑤	☐	☐
	① ② ③ ④ ⑤	☐	☐
	① ② ③ ④ ⑤	☐	☐
	① ② ③ ④ ⑤	☐	☐

front ***back***

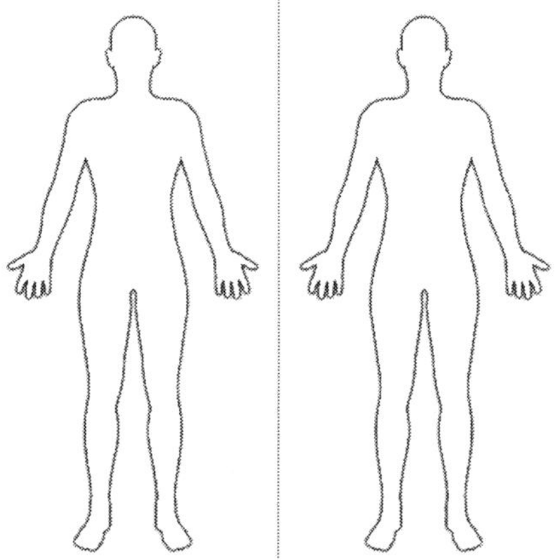

OTHER SYMPTOMS

general

Symptom	Severity	Time	
☐ Fatigue	① ② ③ ④ ⑤	☐ a.m.	☐ p.m.
☐ Lethargy	① ② ③ ④ ⑤	☐ a.m.	☐ p.m.
☐ Malaise	① ② ③ ④ ⑤	☐ a.m.	☐ p.m.
☐ Weakness	① ② ③ ④ ⑤	☐ a.m.	☐ p.m.
☐ Dizziness	① ② ③ ④ ⑤	☐ a.m.	☐ p.m.
☐ Trembling	① ② ③ ④ ⑤	☐ a.m.	☐ p.m.
☐ Twitching	① ② ③ ④ ⑤	☐ a.m.	☐ p.m.
☐ Insomnia	① ② ③ ④ ⑤	☐ a.m.	☐ p.m.

illness

Symptom	Severity	Time	
☐ Nausea	① ② ③ ④ ⑤	☐ a.m.	☐ p.m.
☐ Vomiting	① ② ③ ④ ⑤	☐ a.m.	☐ p.m.
☐ Constipation	① ② ③ ④ ⑤	☐ a.m.	☐ p.m.
☐ Diarrhea	① ② ③ ④ ⑤	☐ a.m.	☐ p.m.
☐ Sore throat	① ② ③ ④ ⑤	☐ a.m.	☐ p.m.
☐ Congestion	① ② ③ ④ ⑤	☐ a.m.	☐ p.m.
☐ Coughing	① ② ③ ④ ⑤	☐ a.m.	☐ p.m.
☐ Acid reflux	① ② ③ ④ ⑤	☐ a.m.	☐ p.m.

psychological

Symptom	Severity	Time	
☐ Anxiety	① ② ③ ④ ⑤	☐ a.m.	☐ p.m.
☐ Depression	① ② ③ ④ ⑤	☐ a.m.	☐ p.m.
☐ Memory loss	① ② ③ ④ ⑤	☐ a.m.	☐ p.m.
☐ Confusion	① ② ③ ④ ⑤	☐ a.m.	☐ p.m.
☐ Poor focus	① ② ③ ④ ⑤	☐ a.m.	☐ p.m.
☐ Mood swings	① ② ③ ④ ⑤	☐ a.m.	☐ p.m.
☐ Suicidal	① ② ③ ④ ⑤	☐ a.m.	☐ p.m.

other

Symptom	Severity	Time	
	① ② ③ ④ ⑤	☐ a.m.	☐ p.m.
	① ② ③ ④ ⑤	☐ a.m.	☐ p.m.
	① ② ③ ④ ⑤	☐ a.m.	☐ p.m.
	① ② ③ ④ ⑤	☐ a.m.	☐ p.m.
	① ② ③ ④ ⑤	☐ a.m.	☐ p.m.
	① ② ③ ④ ⑤	☐ a.m.	☐ p.m.
	① ② ③ ④ ⑤	☐ a.m.	☐ p.m.

SLEEP

hours ________ quality ① ② ③ ④ ⑤

STRESS LEVELS

None	Low	Medium	High	Max	@$#%!

WEATHER

☐ Cold ☐ Mild ☐ Hot
☐ Dry ☐ Humid ☐ Wet

Allergen Levels: ________
BM Pressure: ________

EXERCISE

☐ Heck yes, I worked out.
☐ I managed to exercise a bit.
☐ No, I haven't exercised at all.
☐ I did some stuff, and that counts.

DETAILS

FOOD / MEDICATION

Food / Drinks

Meds / Supplements	Time	Dose

☐ usual daily medication

Water *Caffeine* *Alcohol*

x ________ x ________

FOOD ANALYSIS

New food introduced?
☐ Yes ☐ No
Food reintroduction?
☐ Yes ☐ No

Details

MEDICATION ANALYSIS

New med/dose introduced?
☐ Yes ☐ No
Medication stopped?
☐ Yes ☐ No

Details

ACTIVITY ANALYSIS

Heightened exertion levels?
☐ Yes ☐ No
Lowered exertion levels?
☐ Yes ☐ No

Details

SLEEP ANALYSIS

When you woke up this morning, did you feel well-rested?	☐ Yes	☐ No	☐ A bit
Did you snore or stop breathing throughout the night?	☐ Yes	☐ No	☐ Not sure
Roughly how many times did you wake up throughout the night?			

Notes / Suspected Triggers

ENTRY #29 | M T W T F S S | DATE:

HOW ARE YOU *Feeling today?*

Amazing!	Meh
Great	Not good
Good	Terrible!

RATE YOUR PAIN LEVEL

① ② ③ ④ ⑤ ⑥ ⑦ ⑧ ⑨ ⑩

WHAT ABOUT YOUR...?

Mood	① ② ③ ④ ⑤ ⑥ ⑦ ⑧ ⑨ ⑩
Energy Levels	① ② ③ ④ ⑤ ⑥ ⑦ ⑧ ⑨ ⑩
Mental Clarity	① ② ③ ④ ⑤ ⑥ ⑦ ⑧ ⑨ ⑩

PAIN & PHYSICAL SYMPTOMS

Symptom	Severity	am	pm
	① ② ③ ④ ⑤	☐	☐
	① ② ③ ④ ⑤	☐	☐
	① ② ③ ④ ⑤	☐	☐
	① ② ③ ④ ⑤	☐	☐
	① ② ③ ④ ⑤	☐	☐
	① ② ③ ④ ⑤	☐	☐
	① ② ③ ④ ⑤	☐	☐
	① ② ③ ④ ⑤	☐	☐

front

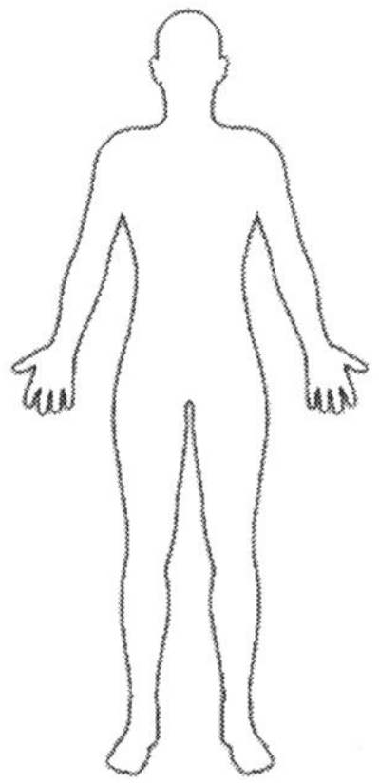

back

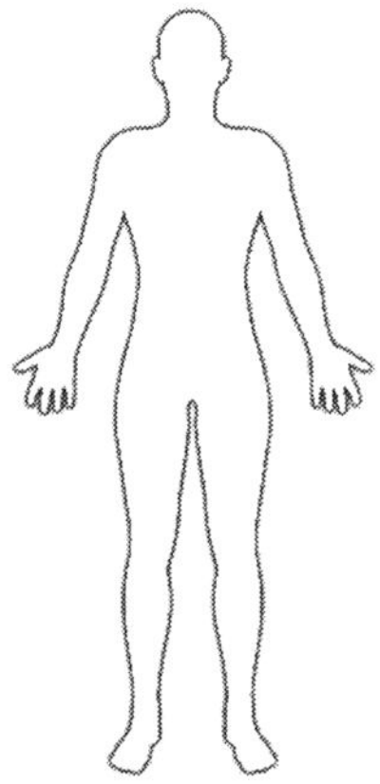

OTHER SYMPTOMS

general

Symptom	Severity	Time	
☐ Fatigue	① ② ③ ④ ⑤	☐ a.m.	☐ p.m.
☐ Lethargy	① ② ③ ④ ⑤	☐ a.m.	☐ p.m.
☐ Malaise	① ② ③ ④ ⑤	☐ a.m.	☐ p.m.
☐ Weakness	① ② ③ ④ ⑤	☐ a.m.	☐ p.m.
☐ Dizziness	① ② ③ ④ ⑤	☐ a.m.	☐ p.m.
☐ Trembling	① ② ③ ④ ⑤	☐ a.m.	☐ p.m.
☐ Twitching	① ② ③ ④ ⑤	☐ a.m.	☐ p.m.
☐ Insomnia	① ② ③ ④ ⑤	☐ a.m.	☐ p.m.

illness

Symptom	Severity	Time	
☐ Nausea	① ② ③ ④ ⑤	☐ a.m.	☐ p.m.
☐ Vomiting	① ② ③ ④ ⑤	☐ a.m.	☐ p.m.
☐ Constipation	① ② ③ ④ ⑤	☐ a.m.	☐ p.m.
☐ Diarrhea	① ② ③ ④ ⑤	☐ a.m.	☐ p.m.
☐ Sore throat	① ② ③ ④ ⑤	☐ a.m.	☐ p.m.
☐ Congestion	① ② ③ ④ ⑤	☐ a.m.	☐ p.m.
☐ Coughing	① ② ③ ④ ⑤	☐ a.m.	☐ p.m.
☐ Acid reflux	① ② ③ ④ ⑤	☐ a.m.	☐ p.m.

psychological

Symptom	Severity	Time	
☐ Anxiety	① ② ③ ④ ⑤	☐ a.m.	☐ p.m.
☐ Depression	① ② ③ ④ ⑤	☐ a.m.	☐ p.m.
☐ Memory loss	① ② ③ ④ ⑤	☐ a.m.	☐ p.m.
☐ Confusion	① ② ③ ④ ⑤	☐ a.m.	☐ p.m.
☐ Poor focus	① ② ③ ④ ⑤	☐ a.m.	☐ p.m.
☐ Mood swings	① ② ③ ④ ⑤	☐ a.m.	☐ p.m.
☐ Suicidal	① ② ③ ④ ⑤	☐ a.m.	☐ p.m.

other

Symptom	Severity	Time	
	① ② ③ ④ ⑤	☐ a.m.	☐ p.m.
	① ② ③ ④ ⑤	☐ a.m.	☐ p.m.
	① ② ③ ④ ⑤	☐ a.m.	☐ p.m.
	① ② ③ ④ ⑤	☐ a.m.	☐ p.m.
	① ② ③ ④ ⑤	☐ a.m.	☐ p.m.
	① ② ③ ④ ⑤	☐ a.m.	☐ p.m.
	① ② ③ ④ ⑤	☐ a.m.	☐ p.m.

SLEEP

hours ________

quality ① ② ③ ④ ⑤

STRESS LEVELS

None	Low	Medium	High	Max	@$#%!

WEATHER

☐ Cold ☐ Mild ☐ Hot

☐ Dry ☐ Humid ☐ Wet

Allergen Levels: ________

BM Pressure: ________

EXERCISE

☐ Heck yes, I worked out.

☐ I managed to exercise a bit.

☐ No, I haven't exercised at all.

☐ I did some stuff, and that counts.

DETAILS

FOOD / MEDICATION

Food / Drinks

Meds / Supplements	Time	Dose
☐ usual daily medication		

Water	Caffeine	Alcohol
☐☐☐☐☐☐☐☐☐☐	x ________	x ________

FOOD ANALYSIS

New food introduced?

☐ Yes ☐ No

Food reintroduction?

☐ Yes ☐ No

Details

MEDICATION ANALYSIS

New med/dose introduced?

☐ Yes ☐ No

Medication stopped?

☐ Yes ☐ No

Details

ACTIVITY ANALYSIS

Heightened exertion levels?

☐ Yes ☐ No

Lowered exertion levels?

☐ Yes ☐ No

Details

SLEEP ANALYSIS

When you woke up this morning, did you feel well-rested?	☐ Yes	☐ No	☐ A bit
Did you snore or stop breathing throughout the night?	☐ Yes	☐ No	☐ Not sure
Roughly how many times did you wake up throughout the night?			

Notes / Suspected Triggers

ENTRY #30 | M T W T F S S | DATE:

HOW ARE YOU *Feeling today?*

Amazing!	Meh
Great	Not good
Good	Terrible!

RATE YOUR PAIN LEVEL

① ② ③ ④ ⑤ ⑥ ⑦ ⑧ ⑨ ⑩

WHAT ABOUT YOUR...?

Mood	① ② ③ ④ ⑤ ⑥ ⑦ ⑧ ⑨ ⑩
Energy Levels	① ② ③ ④ ⑤ ⑥ ⑦ ⑧ ⑨ ⑩
Mental Clarity	① ② ③ ④ ⑤ ⑥ ⑦ ⑧ ⑨ ⑩

PAIN & PHYSICAL SYMPTOMS

Symptom	Severity	am	pm
	① ② ③ ④ ⑤	☐	☐
	① ② ③ ④ ⑤	☐	☐
	① ② ③ ④ ⑤	☐	☐
	① ② ③ ④ ⑤	☐	☐
	① ② ③ ④ ⑤	☐	☐
	① ② ③ ④ ⑤	☐	☐
	① ② ③ ④ ⑤	☐	☐
	① ② ③ ④ ⑤	☐	☐

front

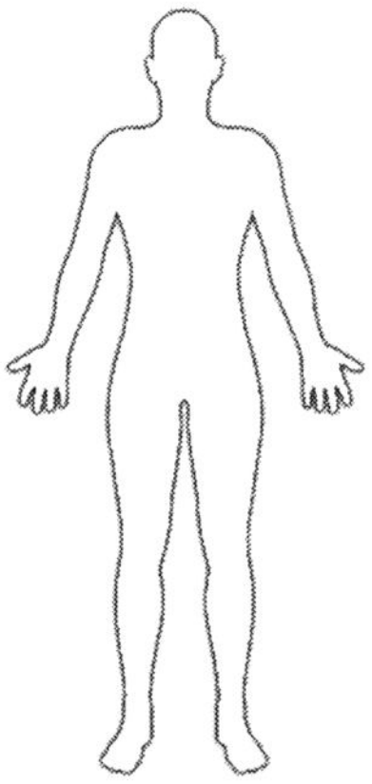

back

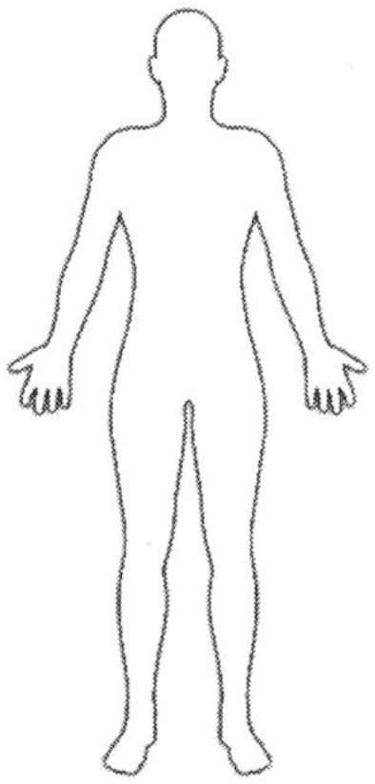

OTHER SYMPTOMS

general

Symptom	Severity	Time	
☐ Fatigue	① ② ③ ④ ⑤	☐ a.m.	☐ p.m.
☐ Lethargy	① ② ③ ④ ⑤	☐ a.m.	☐ p.m.
☐ Malaise	① ② ③ ④ ⑤	☐ a.m.	☐ p.m.
☐ Weakness	① ② ③ ④ ⑤	☐ a.m.	☐ p.m.
☐ Dizziness	① ② ③ ④ ⑤	☐ a.m.	☐ p.m.
☐ Trembling	① ② ③ ④ ⑤	☐ a.m.	☐ p.m.
☐ Twitching	① ② ③ ④ ⑤	☐ a.m.	☐ p.m.
☐ Insomnia	① ② ③ ④ ⑤	☐ a.m.	☐ p.m.

illness

Symptom	Severity	Time	
☐ Nausea	① ② ③ ④ ⑤	☐ a.m.	☐ p.m.
☐ Vomiting	① ② ③ ④ ⑤	☐ a.m.	☐ p.m.
☐ Constipation	① ② ③ ④ ⑤	☐ a.m.	☐ p.m.
☐ Diarrhea	① ② ③ ④ ⑤	☐ a.m.	☐ p.m.
☐ Sore throat	① ② ③ ④ ⑤	☐ a.m.	☐ p.m.
☐ Congestion	① ② ③ ④ ⑤	☐ a.m.	☐ p.m.
☐ Coughing	① ② ③ ④ ⑤	☐ a.m.	☐ p.m.
☐ Acid reflux	① ② ③ ④ ⑤	☐ a.m.	☐ p.m.

psychological

Symptom	Severity	Time	
☐ Anxiety	① ② ③ ④ ⑤	☐ a.m.	☐ p.m.
☐ Depression	① ② ③ ④ ⑤	☐ a.m.	☐ p.m.
☐ Memory loss	① ② ③ ④ ⑤	☐ a.m.	☐ p.m.
☐ Confusion	① ② ③ ④ ⑤	☐ a.m.	☐ p.m.
☐ Poor focus	① ② ③ ④ ⑤	☐ a.m.	☐ p.m.
☐ Mood swings	① ② ③ ④ ⑤	☐ a.m.	☐ p.m.
☐ Suicidal	① ② ③ ④ ⑤	☐ a.m.	☐ p.m.

other

Symptom	Severity	Time	
	① ② ③ ④ ⑤	☐ a.m.	☐ p.m.
	① ② ③ ④ ⑤	☐ a.m.	☐ p.m.
	① ② ③ ④ ⑤	☐ a.m.	☐ p.m.
	① ② ③ ④ ⑤	☐ a.m.	☐ p.m.
	① ② ③ ④ ⑤	☐ a.m.	☐ p.m.
	① ② ③ ④ ⑤	☐ a.m.	☐ p.m.
	① ② ③ ④ ⑤	☐ a.m.	☐ p.m.

SLEEP

hours ________ quality ① ② ③ ④ ⑤

STRESS LEVELS

None	Low	Medium	High	Max	@$#%!

WEATHER

☐ Cold ☐ Mild ☐ Hot
☐ Dry ☐ Humid ☐ Wet

Allergen Levels: ________

BM Pressure: ________

EXERCISE

☐ Heck yes, I worked out.
☐ I managed to exercise a bit.
☐ No, I haven't exercised at all.
☐ I did some stuff, and that counts.

DETAILS

FOOD / MEDICATION

Food / Drinks

Meds / Supplements	Time	Dose
☐ usual daily medication		

Water	Caffeine	Alcohol
	x ________	x ________

FOOD ANALYSIS

New food introduced?
☐ Yes ☐ No

Food reintroduction?
☐ Yes ☐ No

Details

MEDICATION ANALYSIS

New med/dose introduced?
☐ Yes ☐ No

Medication stopped?
☐ Yes ☐ No

Details

ACTIVITY ANALYSIS

Heightened exertion levels?
☐ Yes ☐ No

Lowered exertion levels?
☐ Yes ☐ No

Details

SLEEP ANALYSIS

When you woke up this morning, did you feel well-rested?	☐ Yes	☐ No	☐ A bit
Did you snore or stop breathing throughout the night?	☐ Yes	☐ No	☐ Not sure
Roughly how many times did you wake up throughout the night?			

Notes / Suspected Triggers

ENTRY #31 | M T W T F S S | DATE:

HOW ARE YOU *Feeling today?*

Amazing!	Meh
Great	Not good
Good	Terrible!

RATE YOUR PAIN LEVEL

① ② ③ ④ ⑤ ⑥ ⑦ ⑧ ⑨ ⑩

WHAT ABOUT YOUR...?

Mood	① ② ③ ④ ⑤ ⑥ ⑦ ⑧ ⑨ ⑩
Energy Levels	① ② ③ ④ ⑤ ⑥ ⑦ ⑧ ⑨ ⑩
Mental Clarity	① ② ③ ④ ⑤ ⑥ ⑦ ⑧ ⑨ ⑩

PAIN & PHYSICAL SYMPTOMS

Symptom	Severity	am	pm
	① ② ③ ④ ⑤	☐	☐
	① ② ③ ④ ⑤	☐	☐
	① ② ③ ④ ⑤	☐	☐
	① ② ③ ④ ⑤	☐	☐
	① ② ③ ④ ⑤	☐	☐
	① ② ③ ④ ⑤	☐	☐
	① ② ③ ④ ⑤	☐	☐
	① ② ③ ④ ⑤	☐	☐

front

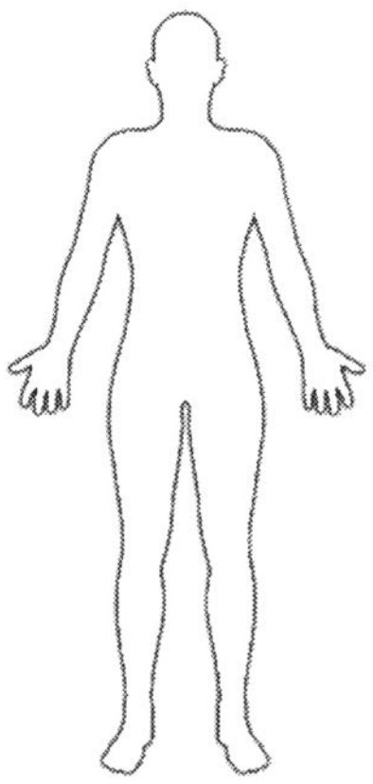

back

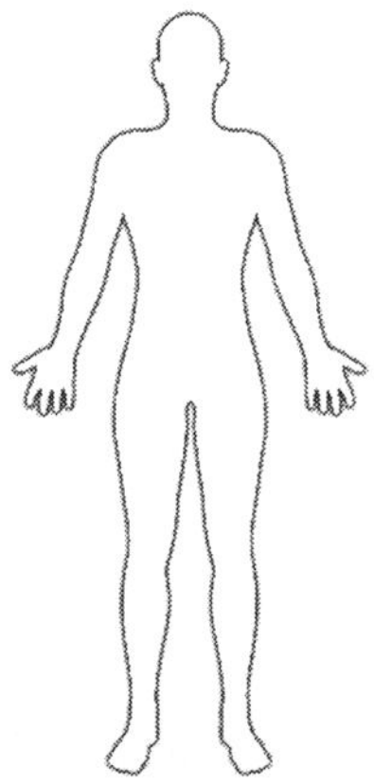

OTHER SYMPTOMS

general

Symptom	Severity	Time	
☐ Fatigue	① ② ③ ④ ⑤	☐ a.m.	☐ p.m.
☐ Lethargy	① ② ③ ④ ⑤	☐ a.m.	☐ p.m.
☐ Malaise	① ② ③ ④ ⑤	☐ a.m.	☐ p.m.
☐ Weakness	① ② ③ ④ ⑤	☐ a.m.	☐ p.m.
☐ Dizziness	① ② ③ ④ ⑤	☐ a.m.	☐ p.m.
☐ Trembling	① ② ③ ④ ⑤	☐ a.m.	☐ p.m.
☐ Twitching	① ② ③ ④ ⑤	☐ a.m.	☐ p.m.
☐ Insomnia	① ② ③ ④ ⑤	☐ a.m.	☐ p.m.

illness

Symptom	Severity	Time	
☐ Nausea	① ② ③ ④ ⑤	☐ a.m.	☐ p.m.
☐ Vomiting	① ② ③ ④ ⑤	☐ a.m.	☐ p.m.
☐ Constipation	① ② ③ ④ ⑤	☐ a.m.	☐ p.m.
☐ Diarrhea	① ② ③ ④ ⑤	☐ a.m.	☐ p.m.
☐ Sore throat	① ② ③ ④ ⑤	☐ a.m.	☐ p.m.
☐ Congestion	① ② ③ ④ ⑤	☐ a.m.	☐ p.m.
☐ Coughing	① ② ③ ④ ⑤	☐ a.m.	☐ p.m.
☐ Acid reflux	① ② ③ ④ ⑤	☐ a.m.	☐ p.m.

psychological

Symptom	Severity	Time	
☐ Anxiety	① ② ③ ④ ⑤	☐ a.m.	☐ p.m.
☐ Depression	① ② ③ ④ ⑤	☐ a.m.	☐ p.m.
☐ Memory loss	① ② ③ ④ ⑤	☐ a.m.	☐ p.m.
☐ Confusion	① ② ③ ④ ⑤	☐ a.m.	☐ p.m.
☐ Poor focus	① ② ③ ④ ⑤	☐ a.m.	☐ p.m.
☐ Mood swings	① ② ③ ④ ⑤	☐ a.m.	☐ p.m.
☐ Suicidal	① ② ③ ④ ⑤	☐ a.m.	☐ p.m.

other

Symptom	Severity	Time	
	① ② ③ ④ ⑤	☐ a.m.	☐ p.m.
	① ② ③ ④ ⑤	☐ a.m.	☐ p.m.
	① ② ③ ④ ⑤	☐ a.m.	☐ p.m.
	① ② ③ ④ ⑤	☐ a.m.	☐ p.m.
	① ② ③ ④ ⑤	☐ a.m.	☐ p.m.
	① ② ③ ④ ⑤	☐ a.m.	☐ p.m.
	① ② ③ ④ ⑤	☐ a.m.	☐ p.m.

SLEEP

hours ________ quality ① ② ③ ④ ⑤

STRESS LEVELS

None	Low	Medium	High	Max	@$#%!

WEATHER

☐ Cold ☐ Mild ☐ Hot
☐ Dry ☐ Humid ☐ Wet

Allergen Levels: ________

BM Pressure: ________

EXERCISE

☐ Heck yes, I worked out.
☐ I managed to exercise a bit.
☐ No, I haven't exercised at all.
☐ I did some stuff, and that counts.

DETAILS

FOOD / MEDICATION

Food / Drinks

Meds / Supplements	Time	Dose

☐ usual daily medication

Water	Caffeine	Alchohol
	x ________	x ________

FOOD ANALYSIS

New food introduced?
☐ Yes ☐ No

Food reintroduction?
☐ Yes ☐ No

Details

MEDICATION ANALYSIS

New med/dose introduced?
☐ Yes ☐ No

Medication stopped?
☐ Yes ☐ No

Details

ACTIVITY ANALYSIS

Heightened exertion levels?
☐ Yes ☐ No

Lowered exertion levels?
☐ Yes ☐ No

Details

SLEEP ANALYSIS

When you woke up this morning, did you feel well-rested?	☐ Yes	☐ No	☐ A bit
Did you snore or stop breathing throughout the night?	☐ Yes	☐ No	☐ Not sure
Roughly how many times did you wake up throughout the night?			

Notes / Suspected Triggers

ENTRY #32 | M T W T F S S | DATE:

HOW ARE YOU *Feeling today?*

Amazing!	Meh
Great	Not good
Good	Terrible!

RATE YOUR PAIN LEVEL

① ② ③ ④ ⑤ ⑥ ⑦ ⑧ ⑨ ⑩

WHAT ABOUT YOUR...?

Mood	① ② ③ ④ ⑤ ⑥ ⑦ ⑧ ⑨ ⑩
Energy Levels	① ② ③ ④ ⑤ ⑥ ⑦ ⑧ ⑨ ⑩
Mental Clarity	① ② ③ ④ ⑤ ⑥ ⑦ ⑧ ⑨ ⑩

PAIN & PHYSICAL SYMPTOMS

Symptom	Severity	am	pm
	① ② ③ ④ ⑤	☐	☐
	① ② ③ ④ ⑤	☐	☐
	① ② ③ ④ ⑤	☐	☐
	① ② ③ ④ ⑤	☐	☐
	① ② ③ ④ ⑤	☐	☐
	① ② ③ ④ ⑤	☐	☐
	① ② ③ ④ ⑤	☐	☐
	① ② ③ ④ ⑤	☐	☐

front

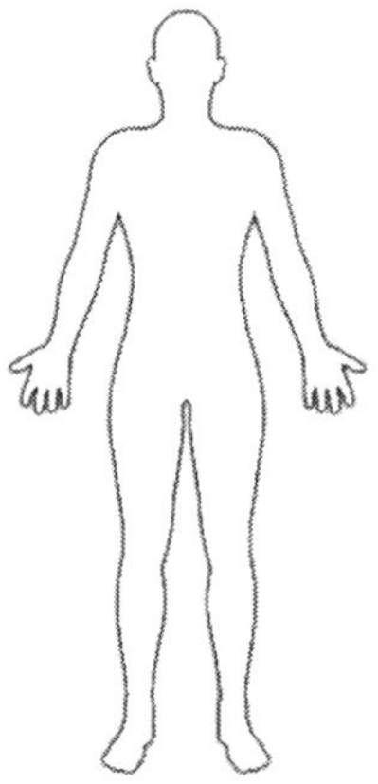

back

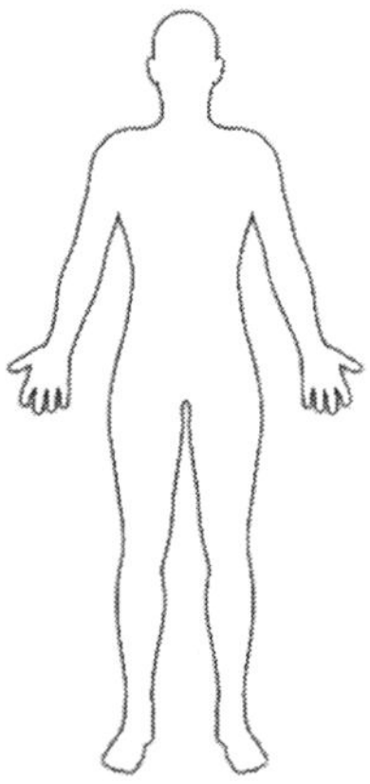

OTHER SYMPTOMS

general

Symptom	Severity	Time	
☐ Fatigue	① ② ③ ④ ⑤	☐ a.m.	☐ p.m.
☐ Lethargy	① ② ③ ④ ⑤	☐ a.m.	☐ p.m.
☐ Malaise	① ② ③ ④ ⑤	☐ a.m.	☐ p.m.
☐ Weakness	① ② ③ ④ ⑤	☐ a.m.	☐ p.m.
☐ Dizziness	① ② ③ ④ ⑤	☐ a.m.	☐ p.m.
☐ Trembling	① ② ③ ④ ⑤	☐ a.m.	☐ p.m.
☐ Twitching	① ② ③ ④ ⑤	☐ a.m.	☐ p.m.
☐ Insomnia	① ② ③ ④ ⑤	☐ a.m.	☐ p.m.

illness

Symptom	Severity	Time	
☐ Nausea	① ② ③ ④ ⑤	☐ a.m.	☐ p.m.
☐ Vomiting	① ② ③ ④ ⑤	☐ a.m.	☐ p.m.
☐ Constipation	① ② ③ ④ ⑤	☐ a.m.	☐ p.m.
☐ Diarrhea	① ② ③ ④ ⑤	☐ a.m.	☐ p.m.
☐ Sore throat	① ② ③ ④ ⑤	☐ a.m.	☐ p.m.
☐ Congestion	① ② ③ ④ ⑤	☐ a.m.	☐ p.m.
☐ Coughing	① ② ③ ④ ⑤	☐ a.m.	☐ p.m.
☐ Acid reflux	① ② ③ ④ ⑤	☐ a.m.	☐ p.m.

psychological

Symptom	Severity	Time	
☐ Anxiety	① ② ③ ④ ⑤	☐ a.m.	☐ p.m.
☐ Depression	① ② ③ ④ ⑤	☐ a.m.	☐ p.m.
☐ Memory loss	① ② ③ ④ ⑤	☐ a.m.	☐ p.m.
☐ Confusion	① ② ③ ④ ⑤	☐ a.m.	☐ p.m.
☐ Poor focus	① ② ③ ④ ⑤	☐ a.m.	☐ p.m.
☐ Mood swings	① ② ③ ④ ⑤	☐ a.m.	☐ p.m.
☐ Suicidal	① ② ③ ④ ⑤	☐ a.m.	☐ p.m.

other

Symptom	Severity	Time	
	① ② ③ ④ ⑤	☐ a.m.	☐ p.m.
	① ② ③ ④ ⑤	☐ a.m.	☐ p.m.
	① ② ③ ④ ⑤	☐ a.m.	☐ p.m.
	① ② ③ ④ ⑤	☐ a.m.	☐ p.m.
	① ② ③ ④ ⑤	☐ a.m.	☐ p.m.
	① ② ③ ④ ⑤	☐ a.m.	☐ p.m.
	① ② ③ ④ ⑤	☐ a.m.	☐ p.m.

SLEEP

hours ________

quality ① ② ③ ④ ⑤

STRESS LEVELS

None	Low	Medium	High	Max	@$#%!

WEATHER

☐ Cold ☐ Mild ☐ Hot
☐ Dry ☐ Humid ☐ Wet

Allergen Levels: ________

BM Pressure: ________

EXERCISE

☐ Heck yes, I worked out.
☐ I managed to exercise a bit.
☐ No, I haven't exercised at all.
☐ I did some stuff, and that counts.

DETAILS

FOOD / MEDICATION

Food / Drinks

Meds / Supplements	Time	Dose

☐ usual daily medication

Water *Caffeine* *Alcohol*

x ________ x ________

FOOD ANALYSIS

New food introduced?
☐ Yes ☐ No

Food reintroduction?
☐ Yes ☐ No

Details

MEDICATION ANALYSIS

New med/dose introduced?
☐ Yes ☐ No

Medication stopped?
☐ Yes ☐ No

Details

ACTIVITY ANALYSIS

Heightened exertion levels?
☐ Yes ☐ No

Lowered exertion levels?
☐ Yes ☐ No

Details

SLEEP ANALYSIS

When you woke up this morning, did you feel well-rested?	☐ Yes	☐ No	☐ A bit
Did you snore or stop breathing throughout the night?	☐ Yes	☐ No	☐ Not sure

Roughly how many times did you wake up throughout the night?

Notes / Suspected Triggers

ENTRY #33 | M T W T F S S | DATE:

HOW ARE YOU *Feeling today?*

Amazing!	Meh
Great	Not good
Good	Terrible!

RATE YOUR PAIN LEVEL

① ② ③ ④ ⑤ ⑥ ⑦ ⑧ ⑨ ⑩

WHAT ABOUT YOUR...?

Mood	① ② ③ ④ ⑤ ⑥ ⑦ ⑧ ⑨ ⑩
Energy Levels	① ② ③ ④ ⑤ ⑥ ⑦ ⑧ ⑨ ⑩
Mental Clarity	① ② ③ ④ ⑤ ⑥ ⑦ ⑧ ⑨ ⑩

PAIN & PHYSICAL SYMPTOMS

Symptom	Severity	am	pm
	① ② ③ ④ ⑤	☐	☐
	① ② ③ ④ ⑤	☐	☐
	① ② ③ ④ ⑤	☐	☐
	① ② ③ ④ ⑤	☐	☐
	① ② ③ ④ ⑤	☐	☐
	① ② ③ ④ ⑤	☐	☐
	① ② ③ ④ ⑤	☐	☐
	① ② ③ ④ ⑤	☐	☐

front ***back***

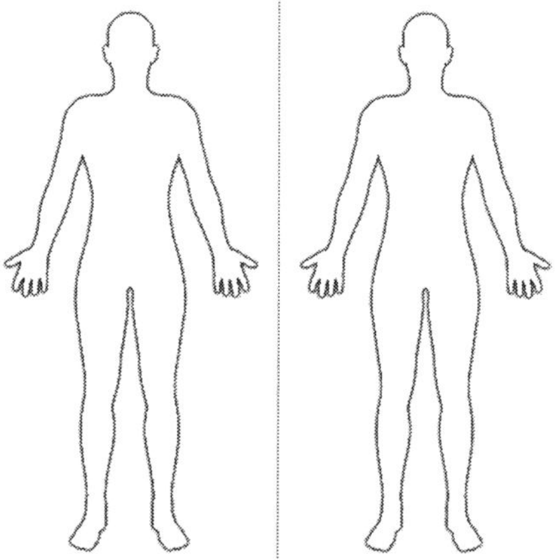

OTHER SYMPTOMS

general

Symptom	Severity	Time	
☐ Fatigue	① ② ③ ④ ⑤	☐ a.m.	☐ p.m.
☐ Lethargy	① ② ③ ④ ⑤	☐ a.m.	☐ p.m.
☐ Malaise	① ② ③ ④ ⑤	☐ a.m.	☐ p.m.
☐ Weakness	① ② ③ ④ ⑤	☐ a.m.	☐ p.m.
☐ Dizziness	① ② ③ ④ ⑤	☐ a.m.	☐ p.m.
☐ Trembling	① ② ③ ④ ⑤	☐ a.m.	☐ p.m.
☐ Twitching	① ② ③ ④ ⑤	☐ a.m.	☐ p.m.
☐ Insomnia	① ② ③ ④ ⑤	☐ a.m.	☐ p.m.

illness

Symptom	Severity	Time	
☐ Nausea	① ② ③ ④ ⑤	☐ a.m.	☐ p.m.
☐ Vomiting	① ② ③ ④ ⑤	☐ a.m.	☐ p.m.
☐ Constipation	① ② ③ ④ ⑤	☐ a.m.	☐ p.m.
☐ Diarrhea	① ② ③ ④ ⑤	☐ a.m.	☐ p.m.
☐ Sore throat	① ② ③ ④ ⑤	☐ a.m.	☐ p.m.
☐ Congestion	① ② ③ ④ ⑤	☐ a.m.	☐ p.m.
☐ Coughing	① ② ③ ④ ⑤	☐ a.m.	☐ p.m.
☐ Acid reflux	① ② ③ ④ ⑤	☐ a.m.	☐ p.m.

psychological

Symptom	Severity	Time	
☐ Anxiety	① ② ③ ④ ⑤	☐ a.m.	☐ p.m.
☐ Depression	① ② ③ ④ ⑤	☐ a.m.	☐ p.m.
☐ Memory loss	① ② ③ ④ ⑤	☐ a.m.	☐ p.m.
☐ Confusion	① ② ③ ④ ⑤	☐ a.m.	☐ p.m.
☐ Poor focus	① ② ③ ④ ⑤	☐ a.m.	☐ p.m.
☐ Mood swings	① ② ③ ④ ⑤	☐ a.m.	☐ p.m.
☐ Suicidal	① ② ③ ④ ⑤	☐ a.m.	☐ p.m.

other

Symptom	Severity	Time	
	① ② ③ ④ ⑤	☐ a.m.	☐ p.m.
	① ② ③ ④ ⑤	☐ a.m.	☐ p.m.
	① ② ③ ④ ⑤	☐ a.m.	☐ p.m.
	① ② ③ ④ ⑤	☐ a.m.	☐ p.m.
	① ② ③ ④ ⑤	☐ a.m.	☐ p.m.
	① ② ③ ④ ⑤	☐ a.m.	☐ p.m.
	① ② ③ ④ ⑤	☐ a.m.	☐ p.m.

SLEEP

hours ________ *quality* ① ② ③ ④ ⑤

STRESS LEVELS

None	Low	Medium	High	Max	@$#%!

WEATHER

☐ Cold ☐ Mild ☐ Hot
☐ Dry ☐ Humid ☐ Wet

Allergen Levels: ________
BM Pressure: ________

EXERCISE

☐ Heck yes, I worked out.
☐ I managed to exercise a bit.
☐ No, I haven't exercised at all.
☐ I did some stuff, and that counts.

DETAILS

FOOD / MEDICATION

Food / Drinks

Meds / Supplements	Time	Dose

☐ usual daily medication

Water	*Caffeine*	*Alcohol*
	x ________	x ________

FOOD ANALYSIS

New food introduced?
☐ Yes ☐ No
Food reintroduction?
☐ Yes ☐ No

Details

MEDICATION ANALYSIS

New med/dose introduced?
☐ Yes ☐ No
Medication stopped?
☐ Yes ☐ No

Details

ACTIVITY ANALYSIS

Heightened exertion levels?
☐ Yes ☐ No
Lowered exertion levels?
☐ Yes ☐ No

Details

SLEEP ANALYSIS

When you woke up this morning, did you feel well-rested?	☐ Yes	☐ No	☐ A bit
Did you snore or stop breathing throughout the night?	☐ Yes	☐ No	☐ Not sure
Roughly how many times did you wake up throughout the night?			

Notes / Suspected Triggers

ENTRY #34 | M T W T F S S | DATE:

HOW ARE YOU *Feeling today?*

RATE YOUR PAIN LEVEL

① ② ③ ④ ⑤ ⑥ ⑦ ⑧ ⑨ ⑩

WHAT ABOUT YOUR...?

Mood	① ② ③ ④ ⑤ ⑥ ⑦ ⑧ ⑨ ⑩
Energy Levels	① ② ③ ④ ⑤ ⑥ ⑦ ⑧ ⑨ ⑩
Mental Clarity	① ② ③ ④ ⑤ ⑥ ⑦ ⑧ ⑨ ⑩

PAIN & PHYSICAL SYMPTOMS

Symptom	Severity	am	pm
	① ② ③ ④ ⑤	☐	☐
	① ② ③ ④ ⑤	☐	☐
	① ② ③ ④ ⑤	☐	☐
	① ② ③ ④ ⑤	☐	☐
	① ② ③ ④ ⑤	☐	☐
	① ② ③ ④ ⑤	☐	☐
	① ② ③ ④ ⑤	☐	☐
	① ② ③ ④ ⑤	☐	☐

front

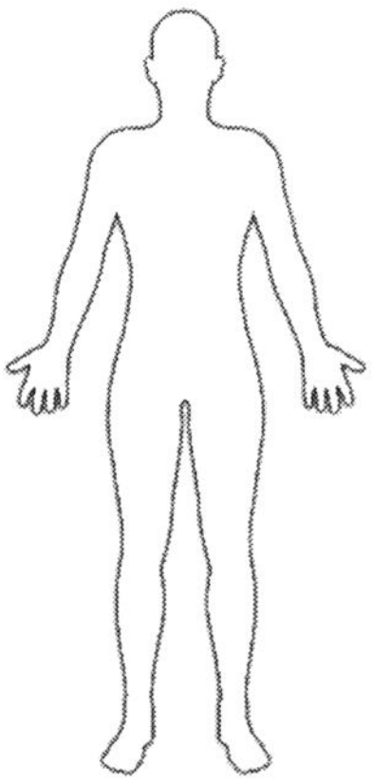

back

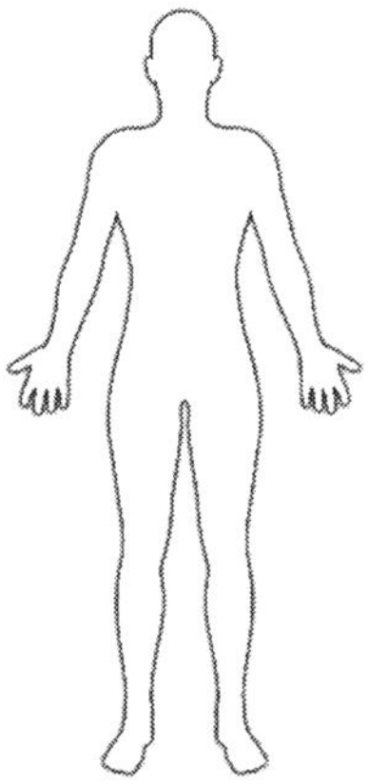

OTHER SYMPTOMS

general

Symptom	Severity	Time	
☐ Fatigue	① ② ③ ④ ⑤	☐ a.m.	☐ p.m.
☐ Lethargy	① ② ③ ④ ⑤	☐ a.m.	☐ p.m.
☐ Malaise	① ② ③ ④ ⑤	☐ a.m.	☐ p.m.
☐ Weakness	① ② ③ ④ ⑤	☐ a.m.	☐ p.m.
☐ Dizziness	① ② ③ ④ ⑤	☐ a.m.	☐ p.m.
☐ Trembling	① ② ③ ④ ⑤	☐ a.m.	☐ p.m.
☐ Twitching	① ② ③ ④ ⑤	☐ a.m.	☐ p.m.
☐ Insomnia	① ② ③ ④ ⑤	☐ a.m.	☐ p.m.

illness

Symptom	Severity	Time	
☐ Nausea	① ② ③ ④ ⑤	☐ a.m.	☐ p.m.
☐ Vomiting	① ② ③ ④ ⑤	☐ a.m.	☐ p.m.
☐ Constipation	① ② ③ ④ ⑤	☐ a.m.	☐ p.m.
☐ Diarrhea	① ② ③ ④ ⑤	☐ a.m.	☐ p.m.
☐ Sore throat	① ② ③ ④ ⑤	☐ a.m.	☐ p.m.
☐ Congestion	① ② ③ ④ ⑤	☐ a.m.	☐ p.m.
☐ Coughing	① ② ③ ④ ⑤	☐ a.m.	☐ p.m.
☐ Acid reflux	① ② ③ ④ ⑤	☐ a.m.	☐ p.m.

psychological

Symptom	Severity	Time	
☐ Anxiety	① ② ③ ④ ⑤	☐ a.m.	☐ p.m.
☐ Depression	① ② ③ ④ ⑤	☐ a.m.	☐ p.m.
☐ Memory loss	① ② ③ ④ ⑤	☐ a.m.	☐ p.m.
☐ Confusion	① ② ③ ④ ⑤	☐ a.m.	☐ p.m.
☐ Poor focus	① ② ③ ④ ⑤	☐ a.m.	☐ p.m.
☐ Mood swings	① ② ③ ④ ⑤	☐ a.m.	☐ p.m.
☐ Suicidal	① ② ③ ④ ⑤	☐ a.m.	☐ p.m.

other

Symptom	Severity	Time	
	① ② ③ ④ ⑤	☐ a.m.	☐ p.m.
	① ② ③ ④ ⑤	☐ a.m.	☐ p.m.
	① ② ③ ④ ⑤	☐ a.m.	☐ p.m.
	① ② ③ ④ ⑤	☐ a.m.	☐ p.m.
	① ② ③ ④ ⑤	☐ a.m.	☐ p.m.
	① ② ③ ④ ⑤	☐ a.m.	☐ p.m.
	① ② ③ ④ ⑤	☐ a.m.	☐ p.m.

SLEEP

hours ________ quality ① ② ③ ④ ⑤

STRESS LEVELS

None	Low	Medium	High	Max	@$#%!

WEATHER

☐ Cold ☐ Mild ☐ Hot
☐ Dry ☐ Humid ☐ Wet

Allergen Levels: ________

BM Pressure: ________

EXERCISE

☐ Heck yes, I worked out.
☐ I managed to exercise a bit.
☐ No, I haven't exercised at all.
☐ I did some stuff, and that counts.

DETAILS

FOOD / MEDICATION

Food / Drinks

Meds / Supplements	Time	Dose

☐ usual daily medication

Water | Caffeine | Alchohol

x ________ x ________

FOOD ANALYSIS

New food introduced?
☐ Yes ☐ No

Food reintroduction?
☐ Yes ☐ No

Details

MEDICATION ANALYSIS

New med/dose introduced?
☐ Yes ☐ No

Medication stopped?
☐ Yes ☐ No

Details

ACTIVITY ANALYSIS

Heightened exertion levels?
☐ Yes ☐ No

Lowered exertion levels?
☐ Yes ☐ No

Details

SLEEP ANALYSIS

When you woke up this morning, did you feel well-rested?	☐ Yes	☐ No	☐ A bit
Did you snore or stop breathing throughout the night?	☐ Yes	☐ No	☐ Not sure
Roughly how many times did you wake up throughout the night?			

Notes / Suspected Triggers

ENTRY #35 | M T W T F S S | DATE:

HOW ARE YOU *Feeling today?*

Amazing!	Meh
Great	Not good
Good	Terrible!

RATE YOUR PAIN LEVEL

① ② ③ ④ ⑤ ⑥ ⑦ ⑧ ⑨ ⑩

WHAT ABOUT YOUR...?

Mood	① ② ③ ④ ⑤ ⑥ ⑦ ⑧ ⑨ ⑩
Energy Levels	① ② ③ ④ ⑤ ⑥ ⑦ ⑧ ⑨ ⑩
Mental Clarity	① ② ③ ④ ⑤ ⑥ ⑦ ⑧ ⑨ ⑩

PAIN & PHYSICAL SYMPTOMS

Symptom	Severity	am	pm
	① ② ③ ④ ⑤	☐	☐
	① ② ③ ④ ⑤	☐	☐
	① ② ③ ④ ⑤	☐	☐
	① ② ③ ④ ⑤	☐	☐
	① ② ③ ④ ⑤	☐	☐
	① ② ③ ④ ⑤	☐	☐
	① ② ③ ④ ⑤	☐	☐
	① ② ③ ④ ⑤	☐	☐

front ***back***

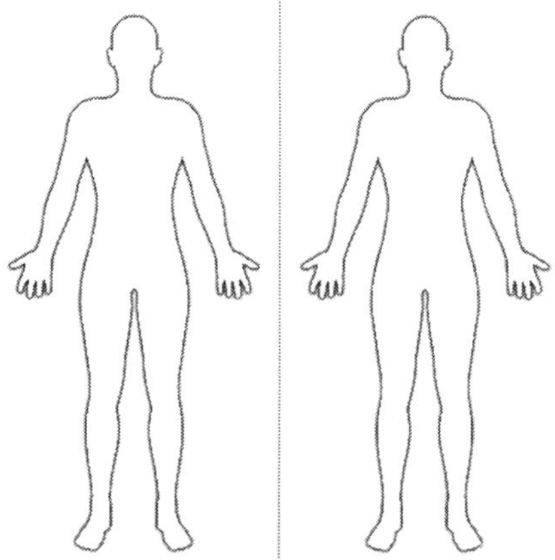

OTHER SYMPTOMS

general

Symptom	Severity	Time	
☐ Fatigue	① ② ③ ④ ⑤	☐ a.m.	☐ p.m.
☐ Lethargy	① ② ③ ④ ⑤	☐ a.m.	☐ p.m.
☐ Malaise	① ② ③ ④ ⑤	☐ a.m.	☐ p.m.
☐ Weakness	① ② ③ ④ ⑤	☐ a.m.	☐ p.m.
☐ Dizziness	① ② ③ ④ ⑤	☐ a.m.	☐ p.m.
☐ Trembling	① ② ③ ④ ⑤	☐ a.m.	☐ p.m.
☐ Twitching	① ② ③ ④ ⑤	☐ a.m.	☐ p.m.
☐ Insomnia	① ② ③ ④ ⑤	☐ a.m.	☐ p.m.

illness

Symptom	Severity	Time	
☐ Nausea	① ② ③ ④ ⑤	☐ a.m.	☐ p.m.
☐ Vomiting	① ② ③ ④ ⑤	☐ a.m.	☐ p.m.
☐ Constipation	① ② ③ ④ ⑤	☐ a.m.	☐ p.m.
☐ Diarrhea	① ② ③ ④ ⑤	☐ a.m.	☐ p.m.
☐ Sore throat	① ② ③ ④ ⑤	☐ a.m.	☐ p.m.
☐ Congestion	① ② ③ ④ ⑤	☐ a.m.	☐ p.m.
☐ Coughing	① ② ③ ④ ⑤	☐ a.m.	☐ p.m.
☐ Acid reflux	① ② ③ ④ ⑤	☐ a.m.	☐ p.m.

psychological

Symptom	Severity	Time	
☐ Anxiety	① ② ③ ④ ⑤	☐ a.m.	☐ p.m.
☐ Depression	① ② ③ ④ ⑤	☐ a.m.	☐ p.m.
☐ Memory loss	① ② ③ ④ ⑤	☐ a.m.	☐ p.m.
☐ Confusion	① ② ③ ④ ⑤	☐ a.m.	☐ p.m.
☐ Poor focus	① ② ③ ④ ⑤	☐ a.m.	☐ p.m.
☐ Mood swings	① ② ③ ④ ⑤	☐ a.m.	☐ p.m.
☐ Suicidal	① ② ③ ④ ⑤	☐ a.m.	☐ p.m.

other

Symptom	Severity	Time	
	① ② ③ ④ ⑤	☐ a.m.	☐ p.m.
	① ② ③ ④ ⑤	☐ a.m.	☐ p.m.
	① ② ③ ④ ⑤	☐ a.m.	☐ p.m.
	① ② ③ ④ ⑤	☐ a.m.	☐ p.m.
	① ② ③ ④ ⑤	☐ a.m.	☐ p.m.
	① ② ③ ④ ⑤	☐ a.m.	☐ p.m.
	① ② ③ ④ ⑤	☐ a.m.	☐ p.m.

SLEEP

hours ________

quality ① ② ③ ④ ⑤

STRESS LEVELS

None	Low	Medium	High	Max	@$#%!

WEATHER

☐ Cold ☐ Mild ☐ Hot

☐ Dry ☐ Humid ☐ Wet

Allergen Levels: ________

BM Pressure: ________

EXERCISE

☐ Heck yes, I worked out.

☐ I managed to exercise a bit.

☐ No, I haven't exercised at all.

☐ I did some stuff, and that counts.

DETAILS

FOOD / MEDICATION

Food / Drinks

Meds / Supplements	Time	Dose
☐ usual daily medication		

Water	Caffeine	Alohol
	x ________	x ________

FOOD ANALYSIS

New food introduced?

☐ Yes ☐ No

Food reintroduction?

☐ Yes ☐ No

Details

MEDICATION ANALYSIS

New med/dose introduced?

☐ Yes ☐ No

Medication stopped?

☐ Yes ☐ No

Details

ACTIVITY ANALYSIS

Heightened exertion levels?

☐ Yes ☐ No

Lowered exertion levels?

☐ Yes ☐ No

Details

SLEEP ANALYSIS

When you woke up this morning, did you feel well-rested?	☐ Yes	☐ No	☐ A bit
Did you snore or stop breathing throughout the night?	☐ Yes	☐ No	☐ Not sure
Roughly how many times did you wake up throughout the night?			

Notes / Suspected Triggers

ENTRY #36	M T W T F S S	DATE:

HOW ARE YOU *Feeling today?*

Amazing!	Meh
Great	Not good
Good	Terrible!

RATE YOUR PAIN LEVEL

① ② ③ ④ ⑤ ⑥ ⑦ ⑧ ⑨ ⑩

WHAT ABOUT YOUR...?

Mood	① ② ③ ④ ⑤ ⑥ ⑦ ⑧ ⑨ ⑩
Energy Levels	① ② ③ ④ ⑤ ⑥ ⑦ ⑧ ⑨ ⑩
Mental Clarity	① ② ③ ④ ⑤ ⑥ ⑦ ⑧ ⑨ ⑩

PAIN & PHYSICAL SYMPTOMS

Symptom	Severity	am	pm
	① ② ③ ④ ⑤	☐	☐
	① ② ③ ④ ⑤	☐	☐
	① ② ③ ④ ⑤	☐	☐
	① ② ③ ④ ⑤	☐	☐
	① ② ③ ④ ⑤	☐	☐
	① ② ③ ④ ⑤	☐	☐
	① ② ③ ④ ⑤	☐	☐
	① ② ③ ④ ⑤	☐	☐

front ***back***

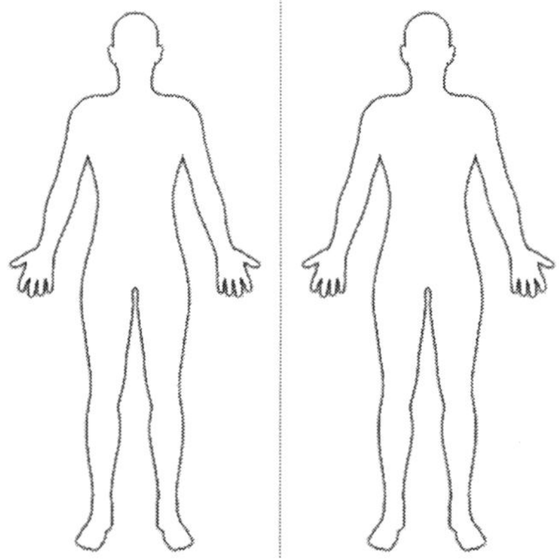

OTHER SYMPTOMS

general

Symptom	Severity	Time	
☐ Fatigue	① ② ③ ④ ⑤	☐ a.m.	☐ p.m.
☐ Lethargy	① ② ③ ④ ⑤	☐ a.m.	☐ p.m.
☐ Malaise	① ② ③ ④ ⑤	☐ a.m.	☐ p.m.
☐ Weakness	① ② ③ ④ ⑤	☐ a.m.	☐ p.m.
☐ Dizziness	① ② ③ ④ ⑤	☐ a.m.	☐ p.m.
☐ Trembling	① ② ③ ④ ⑤	☐ a.m.	☐ p.m.
☐ Twitching	① ② ③ ④ ⑤	☐ a.m.	☐ p.m.
☐ Insomnia	① ② ③ ④ ⑤	☐ a.m.	☐ p.m.

illness

Symptom	Severity	Time	
☐ Nausea	① ② ③ ④ ⑤	☐ a.m.	☐ p.m.
☐ Vomiting	① ② ③ ④ ⑤	☐ a.m.	☐ p.m.
☐ Constipation	① ② ③ ④ ⑤	☐ a.m.	☐ p.m.
☐ Diarrhea	① ② ③ ④ ⑤	☐ a.m.	☐ p.m.
☐ Sore throat	① ② ③ ④ ⑤	☐ a.m.	☐ p.m.
☐ Congestion	① ② ③ ④ ⑤	☐ a.m.	☐ p.m.
☐ Coughing	① ② ③ ④ ⑤	☐ a.m.	☐ p.m.
☐ Acid reflux	① ② ③ ④ ⑤	☐ a.m.	☐ p.m.

psychological

Symptom	Severity	Time	
☐ Anxiety	① ② ③ ④ ⑤	☐ a.m.	☐ p.m.
☐ Depression	① ② ③ ④ ⑤	☐ a.m.	☐ p.m.
☐ Memory loss	① ② ③ ④ ⑤	☐ a.m.	☐ p.m.
☐ Confusion	① ② ③ ④ ⑤	☐ a.m.	☐ p.m.
☐ Poor focus	① ② ③ ④ ⑤	☐ a.m.	☐ p.m.
☐ Mood swings	① ② ③ ④ ⑤	☐ a.m.	☐ p.m.
☐ Suicidal	① ② ③ ④ ⑤	☐ a.m.	☐ p.m.

other

Symptom	Severity	Time	
	① ② ③ ④ ⑤	☐ a.m.	☐ p.m.
	① ② ③ ④ ⑤	☐ a.m.	☐ p.m.
	① ② ③ ④ ⑤	☐ a.m.	☐ p.m.
	① ② ③ ④ ⑤	☐ a.m.	☐ p.m.
	① ② ③ ④ ⑤	☐ a.m.	☐ p.m.
	① ② ③ ④ ⑤	☐ a.m.	☐ p.m.
	① ② ③ ④ ⑤	☐ a.m.	☐ p.m.

SLEEP

hours ________ quality ① ② ③ ④ ⑤

STRESS LEVELS

None	Low	Medium	High	Max	@$#%!

WEATHER

☐ Cold ☐ Mild ☐ Hot
☐ Dry ☐ Humid ☐ Wet

Allergen Levels: ________
BM Pressure: ________

EXERCISE

☐ Heck yes, I worked out.
☐ I managed to exercise a bit.
☐ No, I haven't exercised at all.
☐ I did some stuff, and that counts.

DETAILS

FOOD / MEDICATION

Food / Drinks

Meds / Supplements	Time	Dose

☐ usual daily medication

Water	Caffeine	Alcohol
☐☐☐☐☐☐☐☐☐☐	x ________	x ________

FOOD ANALYSIS

New food introduced?
☐ Yes ☐ No
Food reintroduction?
☐ Yes ☐ No

Details

MEDICATION ANALYSIS

New med/dose introduced?
☐ Yes ☐ No
Medication stopped?
☐ Yes ☐ No

Details

ACTIVITY ANALYSIS

Heightened exertion levels?
☐ Yes ☐ No
Lowered exertion levels?
☐ Yes ☐ No

Details

SLEEP ANALYSIS

When you woke up this morning, did you feel well-rested?	☐ Yes	☐ No	☐ A bit
Did you snore or stop breathing throughout the night?	☐ Yes	☐ No	☐ Not sure
Roughly how many times did you wake up throughout the night?			

Notes / Suspected Triggers

ENTRY #37 | M T W T F S S | DATE:

HOW ARE YOU *Feeling today?*

Amazing!	Meh
Great	Not good
Good	Terrible!

RATE YOUR PAIN LEVEL

① ② ③ ④ ⑤ ⑥ ⑦ ⑧ ⑨ ⑩

WHAT ABOUT YOUR...?

Mood	① ② ③ ④ ⑤ ⑥ ⑦ ⑧ ⑨ ⑩
Energy Levels	① ② ③ ④ ⑤ ⑥ ⑦ ⑧ ⑨ ⑩
Mental Clarity	① ② ③ ④ ⑤ ⑥ ⑦ ⑧ ⑨ ⑩

PAIN & PHYSICAL SYMPTOMS

Symptom	Severity	am	pm
	① ② ③ ④ ⑤	☐	☐
	① ② ③ ④ ⑤	☐	☐
	① ② ③ ④ ⑤	☐	☐
	① ② ③ ④ ⑤	☐	☐
	① ② ③ ④ ⑤	☐	☐
	① ② ③ ④ ⑤	☐	☐
	① ② ③ ④ ⑤	☐	☐
	① ② ③ ④ ⑤	☐	☐

front ***back***

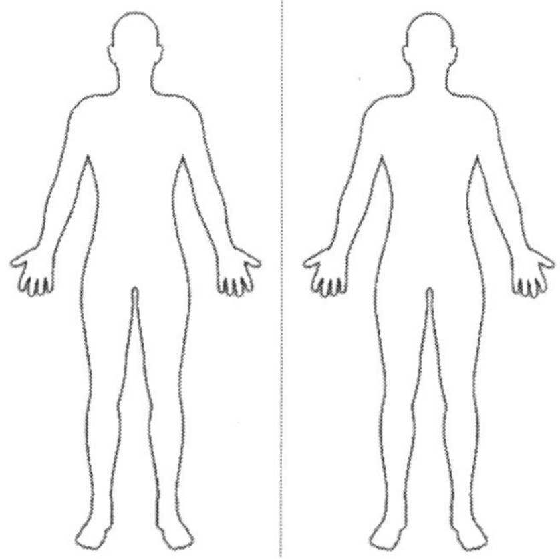

OTHER SYMPTOMS

general

Symptom	Severity	Time	
☐ Fatigue	① ② ③ ④ ⑤	☐ a.m.	☐ p.m.
☐ Lethargy	① ② ③ ④ ⑤	☐ a.m.	☐ p.m.
☐ Malaise	① ② ③ ④ ⑤	☐ a.m.	☐ p.m.
☐ Weakness	① ② ③ ④ ⑤	☐ a.m.	☐ p.m.
☐ Dizziness	① ② ③ ④ ⑤	☐ a.m.	☐ p.m.
☐ Trembling	① ② ③ ④ ⑤	☐ a.m.	☐ p.m.
☐ Twitching	① ② ③ ④ ⑤	☐ a.m.	☐ p.m.
☐ Insomnia	① ② ③ ④ ⑤	☐ a.m.	☐ p.m.

illness

Symptom	Severity	Time	
☐ Nausea	① ② ③ ④ ⑤	☐ a.m.	☐ p.m.
☐ Vomiting	① ② ③ ④ ⑤	☐ a.m.	☐ p.m.
☐ Constipation	① ② ③ ④ ⑤	☐ a.m.	☐ p.m.
☐ Diarrhea	① ② ③ ④ ⑤	☐ a.m.	☐ p.m.
☐ Sore throat	① ② ③ ④ ⑤	☐ a.m.	☐ p.m.
☐ Congestion	① ② ③ ④ ⑤	☐ a.m.	☐ p.m.
☐ Coughing	① ② ③ ④ ⑤	☐ a.m.	☐ p.m.
☐ Acid reflux	① ② ③ ④ ⑤	☐ a.m.	☐ p.m.

psychological

Symptom	Severity	Time	
☐ Anxiety	① ② ③ ④ ⑤	☐ a.m.	☐ p.m.
☐ Depression	① ② ③ ④ ⑤	☐ a.m.	☐ p.m.
☐ Memory loss	① ② ③ ④ ⑤	☐ a.m.	☐ p.m.
☐ Confusion	① ② ③ ④ ⑤	☐ a.m.	☐ p.m.
☐ Poor focus	① ② ③ ④ ⑤	☐ a.m.	☐ p.m.
☐ Mood swings	① ② ③ ④ ⑤	☐ a.m.	☐ p.m.
☐ Suicidal	① ② ③ ④ ⑤	☐ a.m.	☐ p.m.

other

Symptom	Severity	Time	
	① ② ③ ④ ⑤	☐ a.m.	☐ p.m.
	① ② ③ ④ ⑤	☐ a.m.	☐ p.m.
	① ② ③ ④ ⑤	☐ a.m.	☐ p.m.
	① ② ③ ④ ⑤	☐ a.m.	☐ p.m.
	① ② ③ ④ ⑤	☐ a.m.	☐ p.m.
	① ② ③ ④ ⑤	☐ a.m.	☐ p.m.
	① ② ③ ④ ⑤	☐ a.m.	☐ p.m.

SLEEP

hours ________

quality ① ② ③ ④ ⑤

STRESS LEVELS

None	Low	Medium	High	Max	@$#%!

WEATHER

☐ Cold ☐ Mild ☐ Hot
☐ Dry ☐ Humid ☐ Wet

Allergen Levels: ________

BM Pressure: ________

EXERCISE

☐ Heck yes, I worked out.
☐ I managed to exercise a bit.
☐ No, I haven't exercised at all.
☐ I did some stuff, and that counts.

DETAILS

FOOD / MEDICATION

Food / Drinks

Meds / Supplements	Time	Dose
☐ usual daily medication		

Water	*Caffeine*	*Alcohol*
	x ________	x ________

FOOD ANALYSIS

New food introduced?

☐ Yes ☐ No

Food reintroduction?

☐ Yes ☐ No

Details

MEDICATION ANALYSIS

New med/dose introduced?

☐ Yes ☐ No

Medication stopped?

☐ Yes ☐ No

Details

ACTIVITY ANALYSIS

Heightened exertion levels?

☐ Yes ☐ No

Lowered exertion levels?

☐ Yes ☐ No

Details

SLEEP ANALYSIS

When you woke up this morning, did you feel well-rested?	☐ Yes	☐ No	☐ A bit
Did you snore or stop breathing throughout the night?	☐ Yes	☐ No	☐ Not sure
Roughly how many times did you wake up throughout the night?			

Notes / Suspected Triggers

ENTRY #38 | M T W T F S S | DATE:

HOW ARE YOU *Feeling today?*

Amazing!	Meh
Great	Not good
Good	Terrible!

RATE YOUR PAIN LEVEL

① ② ③ ④ ⑤ ⑥ ⑦ ⑧ ⑨ ⑩

WHAT ABOUT YOUR...?

Mood	① ② ③ ④ ⑤ ⑥ ⑦ ⑧ ⑨ ⑩
Energy Levels	① ② ③ ④ ⑤ ⑥ ⑦ ⑧ ⑨ ⑩
Mental Clarity	① ② ③ ④ ⑤ ⑥ ⑦ ⑧ ⑨ ⑩

PAIN & PHYSICAL SYMPTOMS

Symptom	Severity	am	pm
	① ② ③ ④ ⑤	☐	☐
	① ② ③ ④ ⑤	☐	☐
	① ② ③ ④ ⑤	☐	☐
	① ② ③ ④ ⑤	☐	☐
	① ② ③ ④ ⑤	☐	☐
	① ② ③ ④ ⑤	☐	☐
	① ② ③ ④ ⑤	☐	☐
	① ② ③ ④ ⑤	☐	☐

front ***back***

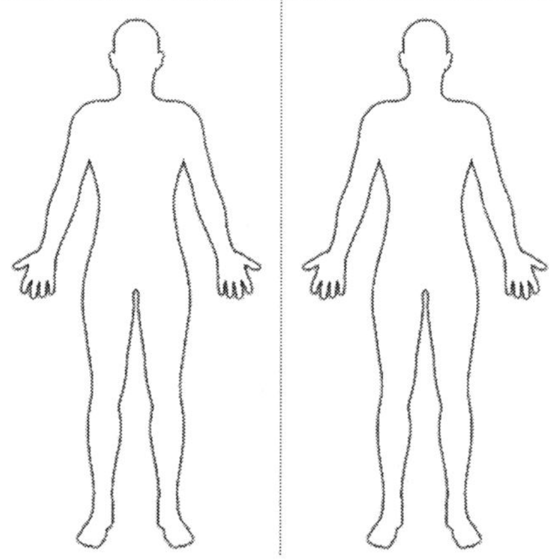

OTHER SYMPTOMS

general

Symptom	Severity	Time	
☐ Fatigue	① ② ③ ④ ⑤	☐ a.m.	☐ p.m.
☐ Lethargy	① ② ③ ④ ⑤	☐ a.m.	☐ p.m.
☐ Malaise	① ② ③ ④ ⑤	☐ a.m.	☐ p.m.
☐ Weakness	① ② ③ ④ ⑤	☐ a.m.	☐ p.m.
☐ Dizziness	① ② ③ ④ ⑤	☐ a.m.	☐ p.m.
☐ Trembling	① ② ③ ④ ⑤	☐ a.m.	☐ p.m.
☐ Twitching	① ② ③ ④ ⑤	☐ a.m.	☐ p.m.
☐ Insomnia	① ② ③ ④ ⑤	☐ a.m.	☐ p.m.

illness

Symptom	Severity	Time	
☐ Nausea	① ② ③ ④ ⑤	☐ a.m.	☐ p.m.
☐ Vomiting	① ② ③ ④ ⑤	☐ a.m.	☐ p.m.
☐ Constipation	① ② ③ ④ ⑤	☐ a.m.	☐ p.m.
☐ Diarrhea	① ② ③ ④ ⑤	☐ a.m.	☐ p.m.
☐ Sore throat	① ② ③ ④ ⑤	☐ a.m.	☐ p.m.
☐ Congestion	① ② ③ ④ ⑤	☐ a.m.	☐ p.m.
☐ Coughing	① ② ③ ④ ⑤	☐ a.m.	☐ p.m.
☐ Acid reflux	① ② ③ ④ ⑤	☐ a.m.	☐ p.m.

psychological

Symptom	Severity	Time	
☐ Anxiety	① ② ③ ④ ⑤	☐ a.m.	☐ p.m.
☐ Depression	① ② ③ ④ ⑤	☐ a.m.	☐ p.m.
☐ Memory loss	① ② ③ ④ ⑤	☐ a.m.	☐ p.m.
☐ Confusion	① ② ③ ④ ⑤	☐ a.m.	☐ p.m.
☐ Poor focus	① ② ③ ④ ⑤	☐ a.m.	☐ p.m.
☐ Mood swings	① ② ③ ④ ⑤	☐ a.m.	☐ p.m.
☐ Suicidal	① ② ③ ④ ⑤	☐ a.m.	☐ p.m.

other

Symptom	Severity	Time	
	① ② ③ ④ ⑤	☐ a.m.	☐ p.m.
	① ② ③ ④ ⑤	☐ a.m.	☐ p.m.
	① ② ③ ④ ⑤	☐ a.m.	☐ p.m.
	① ② ③ ④ ⑤	☐ a.m.	☐ p.m.
	① ② ③ ④ ⑤	☐ a.m.	☐ p.m.
	① ② ③ ④ ⑤	☐ a.m.	☐ p.m.
	① ② ③ ④ ⑤	☐ a.m.	☐ p.m.

SLEEP

hours ________ *quality* ① ② ③ ④ ⑤

STRESS LEVELS

None	Low	Medium	High	Max	@$#%!

WEATHER

☐ Cold ☐ Mild ☐ Hot
☐ Dry ☐ Humid ☐ Wet

Allergen Levels: ________

BM Pressure: ________

EXERCISE

☐ Heck yes, I worked out.
☐ I managed to exercise a bit.
☐ No, I haven't exercised at all.
☐ I did some stuff, and that counts.

DETAILS

FOOD / MEDICATION

Food / Drinks

Meds / Supplements	Time	Dose

☐ usual daily medication

Water *Caffeine* *Alcohol*

x ________ x ________

FOOD ANALYSIS

New food introduced?
☐ Yes ☐ No

Food reintroduction?
☐ Yes ☐ No

Details

MEDICATION ANALYSIS

New med/dose introduced?
☐ Yes ☐ No

Medication stopped?
☐ Yes ☐ No

Details

ACTIVITY ANALYSIS

Heightened exertion levels?
☐ Yes ☐ No

Lowered exertion levels?
☐ Yes ☐ No

Details

SLEEP ANALYSIS

When you woke up this morning, did you feel well-rested?	☐ Yes	☐ No	☐ A bit
Did you snore or stop breathing throughout the night?	☐ Yes	☐ No	☐ Not sure
Roughly how many times did you wake up throughout the night?			

Notes / Suspected Triggers

ENTRY #39 | M T W T F S S | DATE:

HOW ARE YOU *Feeling today?*

Amazing!	Meh
Great	Not good
Good	Terrible!

RATE YOUR PAIN LEVEL

① ② ③ ④ ⑤ ⑥ ⑦ ⑧ ⑨ ⑩

WHAT ABOUT YOUR...?

Mood	① ② ③ ④ ⑤ ⑥ ⑦ ⑧ ⑨ ⑩
Energy Levels	① ② ③ ④ ⑤ ⑥ ⑦ ⑧ ⑨ ⑩
Mental Clarity	① ② ③ ④ ⑤ ⑥ ⑦ ⑧ ⑨ ⑩

PAIN & PHYSICAL SYMPTOMS

Symptom	Severity	am	pm
	① ② ③ ④ ⑤	☐	☐
	① ② ③ ④ ⑤	☐	☐
	① ② ③ ④ ⑤	☐	☐
	① ② ③ ④ ⑤	☐	☐
	① ② ③ ④ ⑤	☐	☐
	① ② ③ ④ ⑤	☐	☐
	① ② ③ ④ ⑤	☐	☐
	① ② ③ ④ ⑤	☐	☐

front ***back***

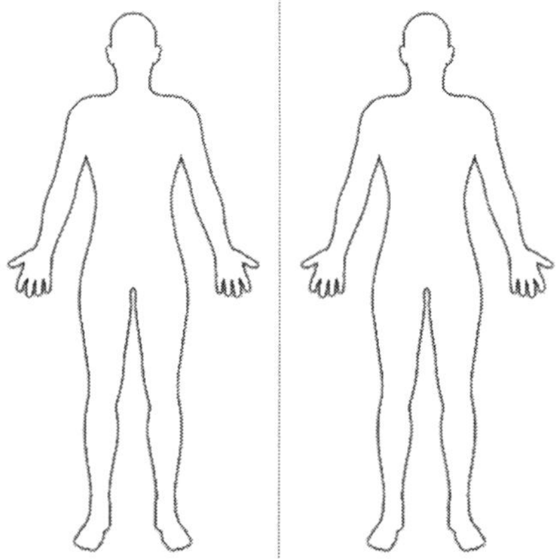

OTHER SYMPTOMS

general

Symptom	Severity	Time	
☐ Fatigue	① ② ③ ④ ⑤	☐ a.m.	☐ p.m.
☐ Lethargy	① ② ③ ④ ⑤	☐ a.m.	☐ p.m.
☐ Malaise	① ② ③ ④ ⑤	☐ a.m.	☐ p.m.
☐ Weakness	① ② ③ ④ ⑤	☐ a.m.	☐ p.m.
☐ Dizziness	① ② ③ ④ ⑤	☐ a.m.	☐ p.m.
☐ Trembling	① ② ③ ④ ⑤	☐ a.m.	☐ p.m.
☐ Twitching	① ② ③ ④ ⑤	☐ a.m.	☐ p.m.
☐ Insomnia	① ② ③ ④ ⑤	☐ a.m.	☐ p.m.

illness

Symptom	Severity	Time	
☐ Nausea	① ② ③ ④ ⑤	☐ a.m.	☐ p.m.
☐ Vomiting	① ② ③ ④ ⑤	☐ a.m.	☐ p.m.
☐ Constipation	① ② ③ ④ ⑤	☐ a.m.	☐ p.m.
☐ Diarrhea	① ② ③ ④ ⑤	☐ a.m.	☐ p.m.
☐ Sore throat	① ② ③ ④ ⑤	☐ a.m.	☐ p.m.
☐ Congestion	① ② ③ ④ ⑤	☐ a.m.	☐ p.m.
☐ Coughing	① ② ③ ④ ⑤	☐ a.m.	☐ p.m.
☐ Acid reflux	① ② ③ ④ ⑤	☐ a.m.	☐ p.m.

psychological

Symptom	Severity	Time	
☐ Anxiety	① ② ③ ④ ⑤	☐ a.m.	☐ p.m.
☐ Depression	① ② ③ ④ ⑤	☐ a.m.	☐ p.m.
☐ Memory loss	① ② ③ ④ ⑤	☐ a.m.	☐ p.m.
☐ Confusion	① ② ③ ④ ⑤	☐ a.m.	☐ p.m.
☐ Poor focus	① ② ③ ④ ⑤	☐ a.m.	☐ p.m.
☐ Mood swings	① ② ③ ④ ⑤	☐ a.m.	☐ p.m.
☐ Suicidal	① ② ③ ④ ⑤	☐ a.m.	☐ p.m.

other

Symptom	Severity	Time	
	① ② ③ ④ ⑤	☐ a.m.	☐ p.m.
	① ② ③ ④ ⑤	☐ a.m.	☐ p.m.
	① ② ③ ④ ⑤	☐ a.m.	☐ p.m.
	① ② ③ ④ ⑤	☐ a.m.	☐ p.m.
	① ② ③ ④ ⑤	☐ a.m.	☐ p.m.
	① ② ③ ④ ⑤	☐ a.m.	☐ p.m.
	① ② ③ ④ ⑤	☐ a.m.	☐ p.m.

SLEEP

hours ______ quality ① ② ③ ④ ⑤

STRESS LEVELS

None	Low	Medium	High	Max	@$#%!

WEATHER

☐ Cold ☐ Mild ☐ Hot
☐ Dry ☐ Humid ☐ Wet

Allergen Levels: ______

BM Pressure: ______

EXERCISE

☐ Heck yes, I worked out.
☐ I managed to exercise a bit.
☐ No, I haven't exercised at all.
☐ I did some stuff, and that counts.

DETAILS

FOOD / MEDICATION

Food / Drinks

Meds / Supplements	Time	Dose

☐ usual daily medication

Water	Caffeine	Alcohol
	x ______	x ______

FOOD ANALYSIS

New food introduced?
☐ Yes ☐ No

Food reintroduction?
☐ Yes ☐ No

Details

MEDICATION ANALYSIS

New med/dose introduced?
☐ Yes ☐ No

Medication stopped?
☐ Yes ☐ No

Details

ACTIVITY ANALYSIS

Heightened exertion levels?
☐ Yes ☐ No

Lowered exertion levels?
☐ Yes ☐ No

Details

SLEEP ANALYSIS

When you woke up this morning, did you feel well-rested?	☐ Yes	☐ No	☐ A bit
Did you snore or stop breathing throughout the night?	☐ Yes	☐ No	☐ Not sure
Roughly how many times did you wake up throughout the night?			

Notes / Suspected Triggers

ENTRY #40 | M T W T F S S | DATE:

HOW ARE YOU *Feeling today?*

Amazing!	Meh
Great	Not good
Good	Terrible!

RATE YOUR PAIN LEVEL

① ② ③ ④ ⑤ ⑥ ⑦ ⑧ ⑨ ⑩

WHAT ABOUT YOUR...?

Mood	① ② ③ ④ ⑤ ⑥ ⑦ ⑧ ⑨ ⑩
Energy Levels	① ② ③ ④ ⑤ ⑥ ⑦ ⑧ ⑨ ⑩
Mental Clarity	① ② ③ ④ ⑤ ⑥ ⑦ ⑧ ⑨ ⑩

PAIN & PHYSICAL SYMPTOMS

Symptom	Severity	am	pm
	① ② ③ ④ ⑤	☐	☐
	① ② ③ ④ ⑤	☐	☐
	① ② ③ ④ ⑤	☐	☐
	① ② ③ ④ ⑤	☐	☐
	① ② ③ ④ ⑤	☐	☐
	① ② ③ ④ ⑤	☐	☐
	① ② ③ ④ ⑤	☐	☐
	① ② ③ ④ ⑤	☐	☐

front

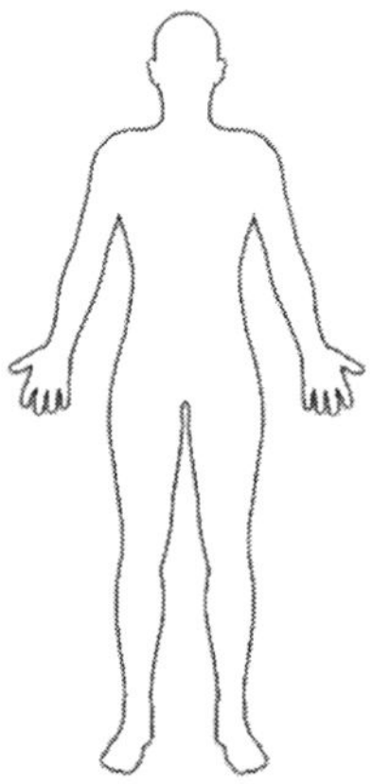

back

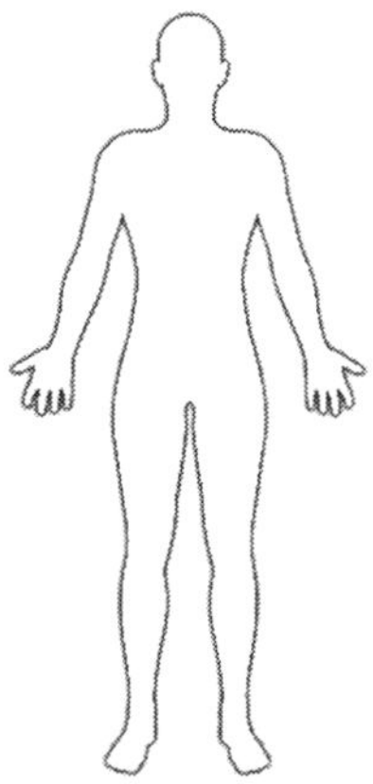

OTHER SYMPTOMS

general

Symptom	Severity	Time	
☐ Fatigue	① ② ③ ④ ⑤	☐ a.m.	☐ p.m.
☐ Lethargy	① ② ③ ④ ⑤	☐ a.m.	☐ p.m.
☐ Malaise	① ② ③ ④ ⑤	☐ a.m.	☐ p.m.
☐ Weakness	① ② ③ ④ ⑤	☐ a.m.	☐ p.m.
☐ Dizziness	① ② ③ ④ ⑤	☐ a.m.	☐ p.m.
☐ Trembling	① ② ③ ④ ⑤	☐ a.m.	☐ p.m.
☐ Twitching	① ② ③ ④ ⑤	☐ a.m.	☐ p.m.
☐ Insomnia	① ② ③ ④ ⑤	☐ a.m.	☐ p.m.

illness

Symptom	Severity	Time	
☐ Nausea	① ② ③ ④ ⑤	☐ a.m.	☐ p.m.
☐ Vomiting	① ② ③ ④ ⑤	☐ a.m.	☐ p.m.
☐ Constipation	① ② ③ ④ ⑤	☐ a.m.	☐ p.m.
☐ Diarrhea	① ② ③ ④ ⑤	☐ a.m.	☐ p.m.
☐ Sore throat	① ② ③ ④ ⑤	☐ a.m.	☐ p.m.
☐ Congestion	① ② ③ ④ ⑤	☐ a.m.	☐ p.m.
☐ Coughing	① ② ③ ④ ⑤	☐ a.m.	☐ p.m.
☐ Acid reflux	① ② ③ ④ ⑤	☐ a.m.	☐ p.m.

psychological

Symptom	Severity	Time	
☐ Anxiety	① ② ③ ④ ⑤	☐ a.m.	☐ p.m.
☐ Depression	① ② ③ ④ ⑤	☐ a.m.	☐ p.m.
☐ Memory loss	① ② ③ ④ ⑤	☐ a.m.	☐ p.m.
☐ Confusion	① ② ③ ④ ⑤	☐ a.m.	☐ p.m.
☐ Poor focus	① ② ③ ④ ⑤	☐ a.m.	☐ p.m.
☐ Mood swings	① ② ③ ④ ⑤	☐ a.m.	☐ p.m.
☐ Suicidal	① ② ③ ④ ⑤	☐ a.m.	☐ p.m.

other

Symptom	Severity	Time	
	① ② ③ ④ ⑤	☐ a.m.	☐ p.m.
	① ② ③ ④ ⑤	☐ a.m.	☐ p.m.
	① ② ③ ④ ⑤	☐ a.m.	☐ p.m.
	① ② ③ ④ ⑤	☐ a.m.	☐ p.m.
	① ② ③ ④ ⑤	☐ a.m.	☐ p.m.
	① ② ③ ④ ⑤	☐ a.m.	☐ p.m.
	① ② ③ ④ ⑤	☐ a.m.	☐ p.m.

SLEEP

hours ________ quality ① ② ③ ④ ⑤

STRESS LEVELS

None	Low	Medium	High	Max	@$#%!

WEATHER

☐ Cold ☐ Mild ☐ Hot
☐ Dry ☐ Humid ☐ Wet

Allergen Levels: ________
BM Pressure: ________

EXERCISE

☐ Heck yes, I worked out.
☐ I managed to exercise a bit.
☐ No, I haven't exercised at all.
☐ I did some stuff, and that counts.

DETAILS

FOOD / MEDICATION

Food / Drinks

Meds / Supplements	Time	Dose

☐ usual daily medication

Water *Caffeine* *Alcohol*

x ________ x ________

FOOD ANALYSIS

New food introduced?
☐ Yes ☐ No
Food reintroduction?
☐ Yes ☐ No

Details

MEDICATION ANALYSIS

New med/dose introduced?
☐ Yes ☐ No
Medication stopped?
☐ Yes ☐ No

Details

ACTIVITY ANALYSIS

Heightened exertion levels?
☐ Yes ☐ No
Lowered exertion levels?
☐ Yes ☐ No

Details

SLEEP ANALYSIS

When you woke up this morning, did you feel well-rested?	☐ Yes	☐ No	☐ A bit
Did you snore or stop breathing throughout the night?	☐ Yes	☐ No	☐ Not sure
Roughly how many times did you wake up throughout the night?			

Notes / Suspected Triggers

ENTRY #41 | M T W T F S S | DATE:

HOW ARE YOU *Feeling today?*

Amazing!	Meh
Great	Not good
Good	Terrible!

RATE YOUR PAIN LEVEL

① ② ③ ④ ⑤ ⑥ ⑦ ⑧ ⑨ ⑩

WHAT ABOUT YOUR...?

Mood	① ② ③ ④ ⑤ ⑥ ⑦ ⑧ ⑨ ⑩
Energy Levels	① ② ③ ④ ⑤ ⑥ ⑦ ⑧ ⑨ ⑩
Mental Clarity	① ② ③ ④ ⑤ ⑥ ⑦ ⑧ ⑨ ⑩

PAIN & PHYSICAL SYMPTOMS

Symptom	Severity	am	pm
	① ② ③ ④ ⑤	☐	☐
	① ② ③ ④ ⑤	☐	☐
	① ② ③ ④ ⑤	☐	☐
	① ② ③ ④ ⑤	☐	☐
	① ② ③ ④ ⑤	☐	☐
	① ② ③ ④ ⑤	☐	☐
	① ② ③ ④ ⑤	☐	☐
	① ② ③ ④ ⑤	☐	☐

front

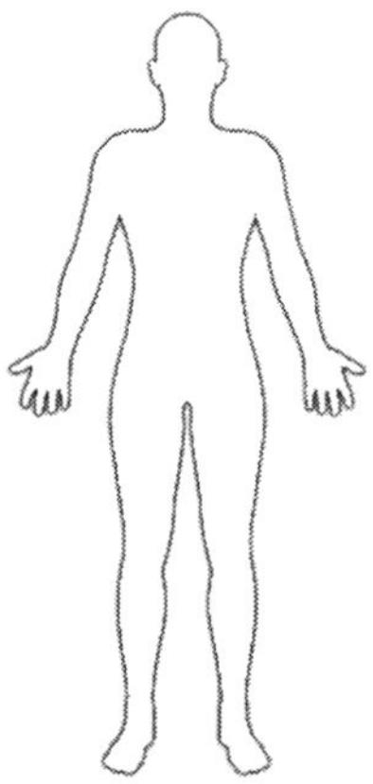

back

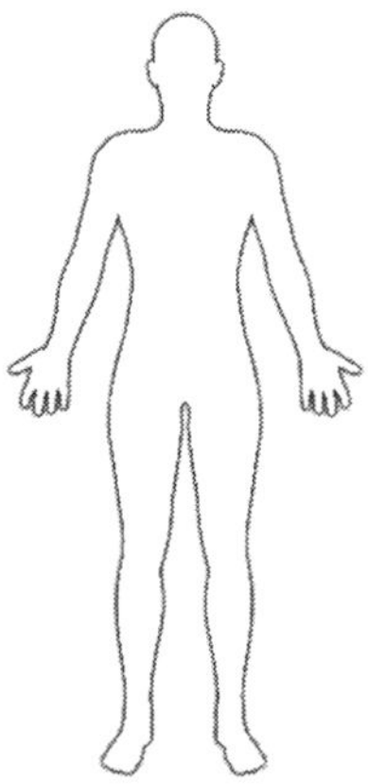

OTHER SYMPTOMS

general

Symptom	Severity	Time	
☐ Fatigue	① ② ③ ④ ⑤	☐ a.m.	☐ p.m.
☐ Lethargy	① ② ③ ④ ⑤	☐ a.m.	☐ p.m.
☐ Malaise	① ② ③ ④ ⑤	☐ a.m.	☐ p.m.
☐ Weakness	① ② ③ ④ ⑤	☐ a.m.	☐ p.m.
☐ Dizziness	① ② ③ ④ ⑤	☐ a.m.	☐ p.m.
☐ Trembling	① ② ③ ④ ⑤	☐ a.m.	☐ p.m.
☐ Twitching	① ② ③ ④ ⑤	☐ a.m.	☐ p.m.
☐ Insomnia	① ② ③ ④ ⑤	☐ a.m.	☐ p.m.

illness

Symptom	Severity	Time	
☐ Nausea	① ② ③ ④ ⑤	☐ a.m.	☐ p.m.
☐ Vomiting	① ② ③ ④ ⑤	☐ a.m.	☐ p.m.
☐ Constipation	① ② ③ ④ ⑤	☐ a.m.	☐ p.m.
☐ Diarrhea	① ② ③ ④ ⑤	☐ a.m.	☐ p.m.
☐ Sore throat	① ② ③ ④ ⑤	☐ a.m.	☐ p.m.
☐ Congestion	① ② ③ ④ ⑤	☐ a.m.	☐ p.m.
☐ Coughing	① ② ③ ④ ⑤	☐ a.m.	☐ p.m.
☐ Acid reflux	① ② ③ ④ ⑤	☐ a.m.	☐ p.m.

psychological

Symptom	Severity	Time	
☐ Anxiety	① ② ③ ④ ⑤	☐ a.m.	☐ p.m.
☐ Depression	① ② ③ ④ ⑤	☐ a.m.	☐ p.m.
☐ Memory loss	① ② ③ ④ ⑤	☐ a.m.	☐ p.m.
☐ Confusion	① ② ③ ④ ⑤	☐ a.m.	☐ p.m.
☐ Poor focus	① ② ③ ④ ⑤	☐ a.m.	☐ p.m.
☐ Mood swings	① ② ③ ④ ⑤	☐ a.m.	☐ p.m.
☐ Suicidal	① ② ③ ④ ⑤	☐ a.m.	☐ p.m.

other

Symptom	Severity	Time	
	① ② ③ ④ ⑤	☐ a.m.	☐ p.m.
	① ② ③ ④ ⑤	☐ a.m.	☐ p.m.
	① ② ③ ④ ⑤	☐ a.m.	☐ p.m.
	① ② ③ ④ ⑤	☐ a.m.	☐ p.m.
	① ② ③ ④ ⑤	☐ a.m.	☐ p.m.
	① ② ③ ④ ⑤	☐ a.m.	☐ p.m.
	① ② ③ ④ ⑤	☐ a.m.	☐ p.m.

SLEEP

hours ________ *quality* ① ② ③ ④ ⑤

STRESS LEVELS

None	Low	Medium	High	Max	@$#%!

WEATHER

☐ Cold ☐ Mild ☐ Hot
☐ Dry ☐ Humid ☐ Wet

Allergen Levels: ________
BM Pressure: ________

EXERCISE

☐ Heck yes, I worked out.
☐ I managed to exercise a bit.
☐ No, I haven't exercised at all.
☐ I did some stuff, and that counts.

DETAILS

FOOD / MEDICATION

Food / Drinks

Meds / Supplements	Time	Dose

☐ usual daily medication

Water *Caffeine* *Alcohol*

x ________ x ________

FOOD ANALYSIS

New food introduced?
☐ Yes ☐ No
Food reintroduction?
☐ Yes ☐ No

Details

MEDICATION ANALYSIS

New med/dose introduced?
☐ Yes ☐ No
Medication stopped?
☐ Yes ☐ No

Details

ACTIVITY ANALYSIS

Heightened exertion levels?
☐ Yes ☐ No
Lowered exertion levels?
☐ Yes ☐ No

Details

SLEEP ANALYSIS

When you woke up this morning, did you feel well-rested?	☐ Yes	☐ No	☐ A bit
Did you snore or stop breathing throughout the night?	☐ Yes	☐ No	☐ Not sure
Roughly how many times did you wake up throughout the night?			

Notes / Suspected Triggers

ENTRY #42 | M T W T F S S | DATE:

HOW ARE YOU *Feeling today?*

Amazing!	Meh
Great	Not good
Good	Terrible!

RATE YOUR PAIN LEVEL

① ② ③ ④ ⑤ ⑥ ⑦ ⑧ ⑨ ⑩

WHAT ABOUT YOUR...?

Mood	① ② ③ ④ ⑤ ⑥ ⑦ ⑧ ⑨ ⑩
Energy Levels	① ② ③ ④ ⑤ ⑥ ⑦ ⑧ ⑨ ⑩
Mental Clarity	① ② ③ ④ ⑤ ⑥ ⑦ ⑧ ⑨ ⑩

PAIN & PHYSICAL SYMPTOMS

Symptom	Severity	am	pm
	① ② ③ ④ ⑤	☐	☐
	① ② ③ ④ ⑤	☐	☐
	① ② ③ ④ ⑤	☐	☐
	① ② ③ ④ ⑤	☐	☐
	① ② ③ ④ ⑤	☐	☐
	① ② ③ ④ ⑤	☐	☐
	① ② ③ ④ ⑤	☐	☐
	① ② ③ ④ ⑤	☐	☐

front

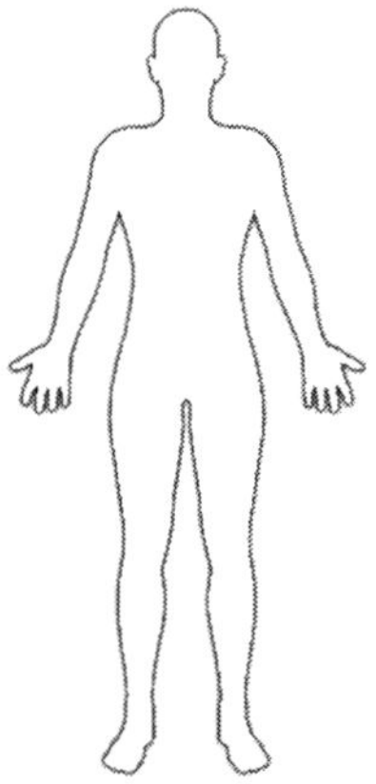

back

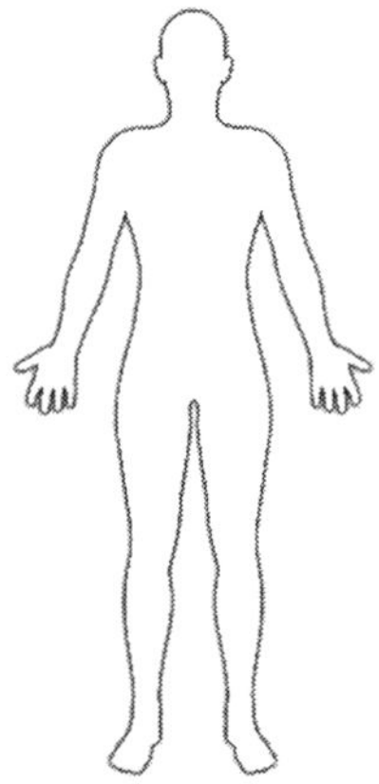

OTHER SYMPTOMS

general

Symptom	Severity	Time	
☐ Fatigue	① ② ③ ④ ⑤	☐ a.m.	☐ p.m.
☐ Lethargy	① ② ③ ④ ⑤	☐ a.m.	☐ p.m.
☐ Malaise	① ② ③ ④ ⑤	☐ a.m.	☐ p.m.
☐ Weakness	① ② ③ ④ ⑤	☐ a.m.	☐ p.m.
☐ Dizziness	① ② ③ ④ ⑤	☐ a.m.	☐ p.m.
☐ Trembling	① ② ③ ④ ⑤	☐ a.m.	☐ p.m.
☐ Twitching	① ② ③ ④ ⑤	☐ a.m.	☐ p.m.
☐ Insomnia	① ② ③ ④ ⑤	☐ a.m.	☐ p.m.

illness

Symptom	Severity	Time	
☐ Nausea	① ② ③ ④ ⑤	☐ a.m.	☐ p.m.
☐ Vomiting	① ② ③ ④ ⑤	☐ a.m.	☐ p.m.
☐ Constipation	① ② ③ ④ ⑤	☐ a.m.	☐ p.m.
☐ Diarrhea	① ② ③ ④ ⑤	☐ a.m.	☐ p.m.
☐ Sore throat	① ② ③ ④ ⑤	☐ a.m.	☐ p.m.
☐ Congestion	① ② ③ ④ ⑤	☐ a.m.	☐ p.m.
☐ Coughing	① ② ③ ④ ⑤	☐ a.m.	☐ p.m.
☐ Acid reflux	① ② ③ ④ ⑤	☐ a.m.	☐ p.m.

psychological

Symptom	Severity	Time	
☐ Anxiety	① ② ③ ④ ⑤	☐ a.m.	☐ p.m.
☐ Depression	① ② ③ ④ ⑤	☐ a.m.	☐ p.m.
☐ Memory loss	① ② ③ ④ ⑤	☐ a.m.	☐ p.m.
☐ Confusion	① ② ③ ④ ⑤	☐ a.m.	☐ p.m.
☐ Poor focus	① ② ③ ④ ⑤	☐ a.m.	☐ p.m.
☐ Mood swings	① ② ③ ④ ⑤	☐ a.m.	☐ p.m.
☐ Suicidal	① ② ③ ④ ⑤	☐ a.m.	☐ p.m.

other

Symptom	Severity	Time	
	① ② ③ ④ ⑤	☐ a.m.	☐ p.m.
	① ② ③ ④ ⑤	☐ a.m.	☐ p.m.
	① ② ③ ④ ⑤	☐ a.m.	☐ p.m.
	① ② ③ ④ ⑤	☐ a.m.	☐ p.m.
	① ② ③ ④ ⑤	☐ a.m.	☐ p.m.
	① ② ③ ④ ⑤	☐ a.m.	☐ p.m.
	① ② ③ ④ ⑤	☐ a.m.	☐ p.m.

SLEEP

hours ________ *quality* ① ② ③ ④ ⑤

STRESS LEVELS

None	Low	Medium	High	Max	@$#%!

WEATHER

☐ Cold ☐ Mild ☐ Hot
☐ Dry ☐ Humid ☐ Wet

Allergen Levels: ________

BM Pressure: ________

EXERCISE

☐ Heck yes, I worked out.
☐ I managed to exercise a bit.
☐ No, I haven't exercised at all.
☐ I did some stuff, and that counts.

DETAILS

FOOD / MEDICATION

Food / Drinks

Meds / Supplements	Time	Dose
☐ usual daily medication		

Water	*Caffeine*	*Alcohol*
	x ________	x ________

FOOD ANALYSIS

New food introduced?
☐ Yes ☐ No

Food reintroduction?
☐ Yes ☐ No

Details

MEDICATION ANALYSIS

New med/dose introduced?
☐ Yes ☐ No

Medication stopped?
☐ Yes ☐ No

Details

ACTIVITY ANALYSIS

Heightened exertion levels?
☐ Yes ☐ No

Lowered exertion levels?
☐ Yes ☐ No

Details

SLEEP ANALYSIS

When you woke up this morning, did you feel well-rested?	☐ Yes	☐ No	☐ A bit
Did you snore or stop breathing throughout the night?	☐ Yes	☐ No	☐ Not sure
Roughly how many times did you wake up throughout the night?			

Notes / Suspected Triggers

ENTRY #43 | M T W T F S S | DATE:

HOW ARE YOU *Feeling today?*

RATE YOUR PAIN LEVEL

① ② ③ ④ ⑤ ⑥ ⑦ ⑧ ⑨ ⑩

WHAT ABOUT YOUR...?

Mood	① ② ③ ④ ⑤ ⑥ ⑦ ⑧ ⑨ ⑩
Energy Levels	① ② ③ ④ ⑤ ⑥ ⑦ ⑧ ⑨ ⑩
Mental Clarity	① ② ③ ④ ⑤ ⑥ ⑦ ⑧ ⑨ ⑩

PAIN & PHYSICAL SYMPTOMS

Symptom	Severity	am	pm
	① ② ③ ④ ⑤	☐	☐
	① ② ③ ④ ⑤	☐	☐
	① ② ③ ④ ⑤	☐	☐
	① ② ③ ④ ⑤	☐	☐
	① ② ③ ④ ⑤	☐	☐
	① ② ③ ④ ⑤	☐	☐
	① ② ③ ④ ⑤	☐	☐
	① ② ③ ④ ⑤	☐	☐

front ***back***

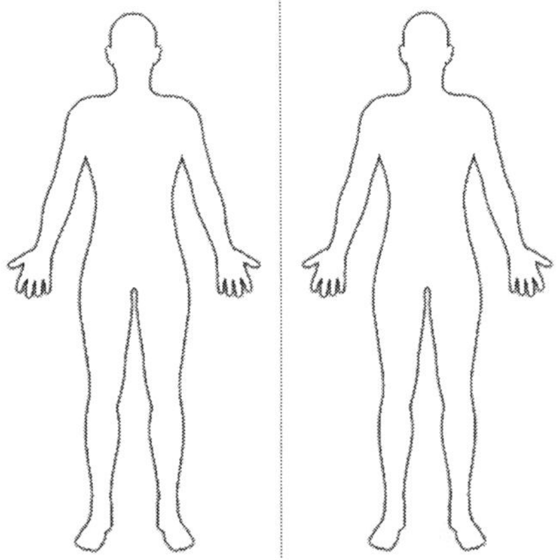

OTHER SYMPTOMS

general

Symptom	Severity	Time	
☐ Fatigue	① ② ③ ④ ⑤	☐ a.m.	☐ p.m.
☐ Lethargy	① ② ③ ④ ⑤	☐ a.m.	☐ p.m.
☐ Malaise	① ② ③ ④ ⑤	☐ a.m.	☐ p.m.
☐ Weakness	① ② ③ ④ ⑤	☐ a.m.	☐ p.m.
☐ Dizziness	① ② ③ ④ ⑤	☐ a.m.	☐ p.m.
☐ Trembling	① ② ③ ④ ⑤	☐ a.m.	☐ p.m.
☐ Twitching	① ② ③ ④ ⑤	☐ a.m.	☐ p.m.
☐ Insomnia	① ② ③ ④ ⑤	☐ a.m.	☐ p.m.

illness

Symptom	Severity	Time	
☐ Nausea	① ② ③ ④ ⑤	☐ a.m.	☐ p.m.
☐ Vomiting	① ② ③ ④ ⑤	☐ a.m.	☐ p.m.
☐ Constipation	① ② ③ ④ ⑤	☐ a.m.	☐ p.m.
☐ Diarrhea	① ② ③ ④ ⑤	☐ a.m.	☐ p.m.
☐ Sore throat	① ② ③ ④ ⑤	☐ a.m.	☐ p.m.
☐ Congestion	① ② ③ ④ ⑤	☐ a.m.	☐ p.m.
☐ Coughing	① ② ③ ④ ⑤	☐ a.m.	☐ p.m.
☐ Acid reflux	① ② ③ ④ ⑤	☐ a.m.	☐ p.m.

psychological

Symptom	Severity	Time	
☐ Anxiety	① ② ③ ④ ⑤	☐ a.m.	☐ p.m.
☐ Depression	① ② ③ ④ ⑤	☐ a.m.	☐ p.m.
☐ Memory loss	① ② ③ ④ ⑤	☐ a.m.	☐ p.m.
☐ Confusion	① ② ③ ④ ⑤	☐ a.m.	☐ p.m.
☐ Poor focus	① ② ③ ④ ⑤	☐ a.m.	☐ p.m.
☐ Mood swings	① ② ③ ④ ⑤	☐ a.m.	☐ p.m.
☐ Suicidal	① ② ③ ④ ⑤	☐ a.m.	☐ p.m.

other

Symptom	Severity	Time	
	① ② ③ ④ ⑤	☐ a.m.	☐ p.m.
	① ② ③ ④ ⑤	☐ a.m.	☐ p.m.
	① ② ③ ④ ⑤	☐ a.m.	☐ p.m.
	① ② ③ ④ ⑤	☐ a.m.	☐ p.m.
	① ② ③ ④ ⑤	☐ a.m.	☐ p.m.
	① ② ③ ④ ⑤	☐ a.m.	☐ p.m.
	① ② ③ ④ ⑤	☐ a.m.	☐ p.m.

SLEEP

hours ________

quality ① ② ③ ④ ⑤

STRESS LEVELS

None	Low	Medium	High	Max	@$#%!

WEATHER

☐ Cold ☐ Mild ☐ Hot
☐ Dry ☐ Humid ☐ Wet

Allergen Levels: ________

BM Pressure: ________

EXERCISE

☐ Heck yes, I worked out.
☐ I managed to exercise a bit.
☐ No, I haven't exercised at all.
☐ I did some stuff, and that counts.

DETAILS

FOOD / MEDICATION

Food / Drinks

Meds / Supplements	Time	Dose

☐ usual daily medication

Water	Caffeine	Alcohol
	x ________	x ________

FOOD ANALYSIS

New food introduced?
☐ Yes ☐ No

Food reintroduction?
☐ Yes ☐ No

Details

MEDICATION ANALYSIS

New med/dose introduced?
☐ Yes ☐ No

Medication stopped?
☐ Yes ☐ No

Details

ACTIVITY ANALYSIS

Heightened exertion levels?
☐ Yes ☐ No

Lowered exertion levels?
☐ Yes ☐ No

Details

SLEEP ANALYSIS

When you woke up this morning, did you feel well-rested?	☐ Yes	☐ No	☐ A bit
Did you snore or stop breathing throughout the night?	☐ Yes	☐ No	☐ Not sure
Roughly how many times did you wake up throughout the night?			

Notes / Suspected Triggers

ENTRY #44 | M T W T F S S | DATE:

HOW ARE YOU *Feeling today?*

Amazing!	Meh
Great	Not good
Good	Terrible!

RATE YOUR PAIN LEVEL

① ② ③ ④ ⑤ ⑥ ⑦ ⑧ ⑨ ⑩

WHAT ABOUT YOUR...?

Mood	① ② ③ ④ ⑤ ⑥ ⑦ ⑧ ⑨ ⑩
Energy Levels	① ② ③ ④ ⑤ ⑥ ⑦ ⑧ ⑨ ⑩
Mental Clarity	① ② ③ ④ ⑤ ⑥ ⑦ ⑧ ⑨ ⑩

PAIN & PHYSICAL SYMPTOMS

Symptom	Severity	am	pm
	① ② ③ ④ ⑤	☐	☐
	① ② ③ ④ ⑤	☐	☐
	① ② ③ ④ ⑤	☐	☐
	① ② ③ ④ ⑤	☐	☐
	① ② ③ ④ ⑤	☐	☐
	① ② ③ ④ ⑤	☐	☐
	① ② ③ ④ ⑤	☐	☐
	① ② ③ ④ ⑤	☐	☐

front ***back***

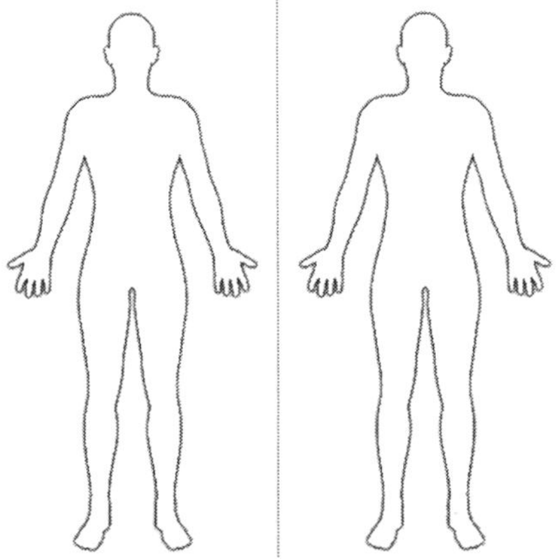

OTHER SYMPTOMS

general

Symptom	Severity	Time	
☐ Fatigue	① ② ③ ④ ⑤	☐ a.m.	☐ p.m.
☐ Lethargy	① ② ③ ④ ⑤	☐ a.m.	☐ p.m.
☐ Malaise	① ② ③ ④ ⑤	☐ a.m.	☐ p.m.
☐ Weakness	① ② ③ ④ ⑤	☐ a.m.	☐ p.m.
☐ Dizziness	① ② ③ ④ ⑤	☐ a.m.	☐ p.m.
☐ Trembling	① ② ③ ④ ⑤	☐ a.m.	☐ p.m.
☐ Twitching	① ② ③ ④ ⑤	☐ a.m.	☐ p.m.
☐ Insomnia	① ② ③ ④ ⑤	☐ a.m.	☐ p.m.

illness

Symptom	Severity	Time	
☐ Nausea	① ② ③ ④ ⑤	☐ a.m.	☐ p.m.
☐ Vomiting	① ② ③ ④ ⑤	☐ a.m.	☐ p.m.
☐ Constipation	① ② ③ ④ ⑤	☐ a.m.	☐ p.m.
☐ Diarrhea	① ② ③ ④ ⑤	☐ a.m.	☐ p.m.
☐ Sore throat	① ② ③ ④ ⑤	☐ a.m.	☐ p.m.
☐ Congestion	① ② ③ ④ ⑤	☐ a.m.	☐ p.m.
☐ Coughing	① ② ③ ④ ⑤	☐ a.m.	☐ p.m.
☐ Acid reflux	① ② ③ ④ ⑤	☐ a.m.	☐ p.m.

psychological

Symptom	Severity	Time	
☐ Anxiety	① ② ③ ④ ⑤	☐ a.m.	☐ p.m.
☐ Depression	① ② ③ ④ ⑤	☐ a.m.	☐ p.m.
☐ Memory loss	① ② ③ ④ ⑤	☐ a.m.	☐ p.m.
☐ Confusion	① ② ③ ④ ⑤	☐ a.m.	☐ p.m.
☐ Poor focus	① ② ③ ④ ⑤	☐ a.m.	☐ p.m.
☐ Mood swings	① ② ③ ④ ⑤	☐ a.m.	☐ p.m.
☐ Suicidal	① ② ③ ④ ⑤	☐ a.m.	☐ p.m.

other

Symptom	Severity	Time	
	① ② ③ ④ ⑤	☐ a.m.	☐ p.m.
	① ② ③ ④ ⑤	☐ a.m.	☐ p.m.
	① ② ③ ④ ⑤	☐ a.m.	☐ p.m.
	① ② ③ ④ ⑤	☐ a.m.	☐ p.m.
	① ② ③ ④ ⑤	☐ a.m.	☐ p.m.
	① ② ③ ④ ⑤	☐ a.m.	☐ p.m.
	① ② ③ ④ ⑤	☐ a.m.	☐ p.m.

SLEEP

hours ________

quality ① ② ③ ④ ⑤

STRESS LEVELS

None	Low	Medium	High	Max	@$#%!

WEATHER

☐ Cold ☐ Mild ☐ Hot
☐ Dry ☐ Humid ☐ Wet

Allergen Levels: ________

BM Pressure: ________

EXERCISE

☐ Heck yes, I worked out.
☐ I managed to exercise a bit.
☐ No, I haven't exercised at all.
☐ I did some stuff, and that counts.

DETAILS

FOOD / MEDICATION

Food / Drinks

Meds / Supplements	Time	Dose

☐ usual daily medication

Water | Caffeine | Alcohol

Caffeine x ________ Alcohol x ________

FOOD ANALYSIS

New food introduced?
☐ Yes ☐ No

Food reintroduction?
☐ Yes ☐ No

Details

MEDICATION ANALYSIS

New med/dose introduced?
☐ Yes ☐ No

Medication stopped?
☐ Yes ☐ No

Details

ACTIVITY ANALYSIS

Heightened exertion levels?
☐ Yes ☐ No

Lowered exertion levels?
☐ Yes ☐ No

Details

SLEEP ANALYSIS

When you woke up this morning, did you feel well-rested?	☐ Yes	☐ No	☐ A bit
Did you snore or stop breathing throughout the night?	☐ Yes	☐ No	☐ Not sure
Roughly how many times did you wake up throughout the night?			

Notes / Suspected Triggers

ENTRY #45 | M T W T F S S | DATE:

HOW ARE YOU *Feeling today?*

Amazing!	Meh
Great	Not good
Good	Terrible!

RATE YOUR PAIN LEVEL

① ② ③ ④ ⑤ ⑥ ⑦ ⑧ ⑨ ⑩

WHAT ABOUT YOUR...?

Mood	① ② ③ ④ ⑤ ⑥ ⑦ ⑧ ⑨ ⑩
Energy Levels	① ② ③ ④ ⑤ ⑥ ⑦ ⑧ ⑨ ⑩
Mental Clarity	① ② ③ ④ ⑤ ⑥ ⑦ ⑧ ⑨ ⑩

PAIN & PHYSICAL SYMPTOMS

Symptom	Severity	am	pm
	① ② ③ ④ ⑤	☐	☐
	① ② ③ ④ ⑤	☐	☐
	① ② ③ ④ ⑤	☐	☐
	① ② ③ ④ ⑤	☐	☐
	① ② ③ ④ ⑤	☐	☐
	① ② ③ ④ ⑤	☐	☐
	① ② ③ ④ ⑤	☐	☐
	① ② ③ ④ ⑤	☐	☐

front

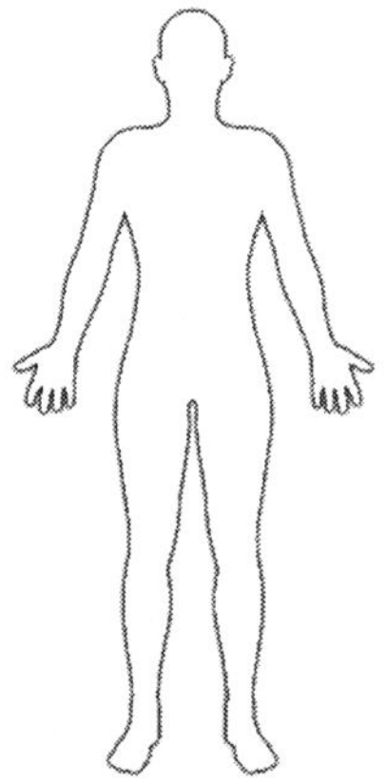

back

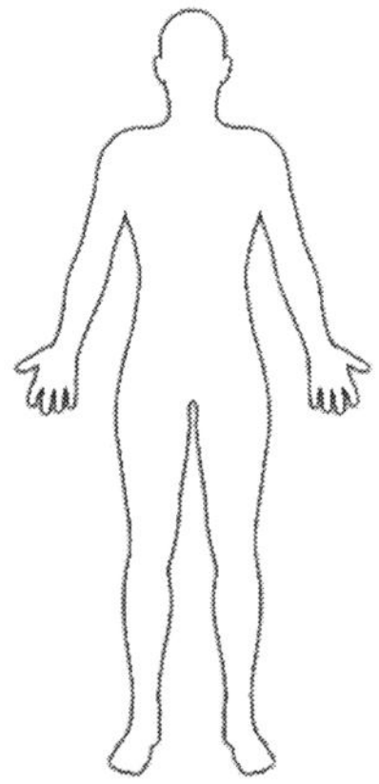

OTHER SYMPTOMS

general

Symptom	Severity	Time	
☐ Fatigue	① ② ③ ④ ⑤	☐ a.m.	☐ p.m.
☐ Lethargy	① ② ③ ④ ⑤	☐ a.m.	☐ p.m.
☐ Malaise	① ② ③ ④ ⑤	☐ a.m.	☐ p.m.
☐ Weakness	① ② ③ ④ ⑤	☐ a.m.	☐ p.m.
☐ Dizziness	① ② ③ ④ ⑤	☐ a.m.	☐ p.m.
☐ Trembling	① ② ③ ④ ⑤	☐ a.m.	☐ p.m.
☐ Twitching	① ② ③ ④ ⑤	☐ a.m.	☐ p.m.
☐ Insomnia	① ② ③ ④ ⑤	☐ a.m.	☐ p.m.

illness

Symptom	Severity	Time	
☐ Nausea	① ② ③ ④ ⑤	☐ a.m.	☐ p.m.
☐ Vomiting	① ② ③ ④ ⑤	☐ a.m.	☐ p.m.
☐ Constipation	① ② ③ ④ ⑤	☐ a.m.	☐ p.m.
☐ Diarrhea	① ② ③ ④ ⑤	☐ a.m.	☐ p.m.
☐ Sore throat	① ② ③ ④ ⑤	☐ a.m.	☐ p.m.
☐ Congestion	① ② ③ ④ ⑤	☐ a.m.	☐ p.m.
☐ Coughing	① ② ③ ④ ⑤	☐ a.m.	☐ p.m.
☐ Acid reflux	① ② ③ ④ ⑤	☐ a.m.	☐ p.m.

psychological

Symptom	Severity	Time	
☐ Anxiety	① ② ③ ④ ⑤	☐ a.m.	☐ p.m.
☐ Depression	① ② ③ ④ ⑤	☐ a.m.	☐ p.m.
☐ Memory loss	① ② ③ ④ ⑤	☐ a.m.	☐ p.m.
☐ Confusion	① ② ③ ④ ⑤	☐ a.m.	☐ p.m.
☐ Poor focus	① ② ③ ④ ⑤	☐ a.m.	☐ p.m.
☐ Mood swings	① ② ③ ④ ⑤	☐ a.m.	☐ p.m.
☐ Suicidal	① ② ③ ④ ⑤	☐ a.m.	☐ p.m.

other

Symptom	Severity	Time	
	① ② ③ ④ ⑤	☐ a.m.	☐ p.m.
	① ② ③ ④ ⑤	☐ a.m.	☐ p.m.
	① ② ③ ④ ⑤	☐ a.m.	☐ p.m.
	① ② ③ ④ ⑤	☐ a.m.	☐ p.m.
	① ② ③ ④ ⑤	☐ a.m.	☐ p.m.
	① ② ③ ④ ⑤	☐ a.m.	☐ p.m.
	① ② ③ ④ ⑤	☐ a.m.	☐ p.m.

SLEEP

hours ________ *quality* ① ② ③ ④ ⑤

STRESS LEVELS

None	Low	Medium	High	Max	@$#%!

WEATHER

☐ Cold ☐ Mild ☐ Hot
☐ Dry ☐ Humid ☐ Wet

Allergen Levels: ________
BM Pressure: ________

EXERCISE

☐ Heck yes, I worked out.
☐ I managed to exercise a bit.
☐ No, I haven't exercised at all.
☐ I did some stuff, and that counts.

DETAILS

FOOD / MEDICATION

Food / Drinks

Meds / Supplements	Time	Dose
☐ usual daily medication		

Water *Caffeine* *Alcohol*

x ________ x ________

FOOD ANALYSIS

New food introduced?
☐ Yes ☐ No
Food reintroduction?
☐ Yes ☐ No
Details

MEDICATION ANALYSIS

New med/dose introduced?
☐ Yes ☐ No
Medication stopped?
☐ Yes ☐ No
Details

ACTIVITY ANALYSIS

Heightened exertion levels?
☐ Yes ☐ No
Lowered exertion levels?
☐ Yes ☐ No
Details

SLEEP ANALYSIS

When you woke up this morning, did you feel well-rested?	☐ Yes	☐ No	☐ A bit
Did you snore or stop breathing throughout the night?	☐ Yes	☐ No	☐ Not sure

Roughly how many times did you wake up throughout the night?

Notes / Suspected Triggers

ENTRY #46 | M T W T F S S | DATE:

HOW ARE YOU *Feeling today?*

Amazing!	Meh
Great	Not good
Good	Terrible!

RATE YOUR PAIN LEVEL

① ② ③ ④ ⑤ ⑥ ⑦ ⑧ ⑨ ⑩

WHAT ABOUT YOUR...?

Mood	① ② ③ ④ ⑤ ⑥ ⑦ ⑧ ⑨ ⑩
Energy Levels	① ② ③ ④ ⑤ ⑥ ⑦ ⑧ ⑨ ⑩
Mental Clarity	① ② ③ ④ ⑤ ⑥ ⑦ ⑧ ⑨ ⑩

PAIN & PHYSICAL SYMPTOMS

Symptom	Severity	am	pm
	① ② ③ ④ ⑤	☐	☐
	① ② ③ ④ ⑤	☐	☐
	① ② ③ ④ ⑤	☐	☐
	① ② ③ ④ ⑤	☐	☐
	① ② ③ ④ ⑤	☐	☐
	① ② ③ ④ ⑤	☐	☐
	① ② ③ ④ ⑤	☐	☐
	① ② ③ ④ ⑤	☐	☐

front ***back***

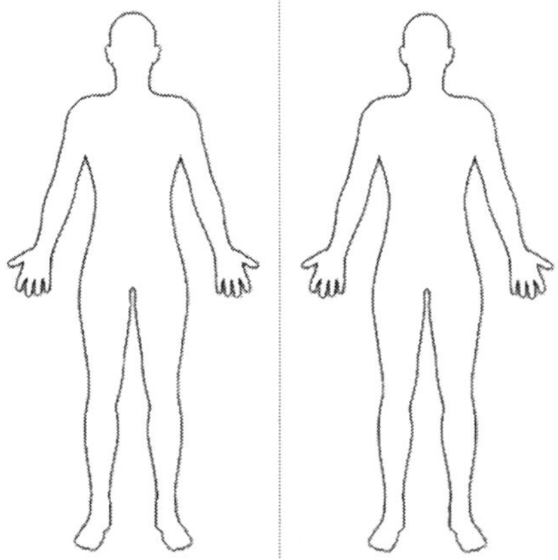

OTHER SYMPTOMS

general

Symptom	Severity	Time	
☐ Fatigue	① ② ③ ④ ⑤	☐ a.m.	☐ p.m.
☐ Lethargy	① ② ③ ④ ⑤	☐ a.m.	☐ p.m.
☐ Malaise	① ② ③ ④ ⑤	☐ a.m.	☐ p.m.
☐ Weakness	① ② ③ ④ ⑤	☐ a.m.	☐ p.m.
☐ Dizziness	① ② ③ ④ ⑤	☐ a.m.	☐ p.m.
☐ Trembling	① ② ③ ④ ⑤	☐ a.m.	☐ p.m.
☐ Twitching	① ② ③ ④ ⑤	☐ a.m.	☐ p.m.
☐ Insomnia	① ② ③ ④ ⑤	☐ a.m.	☐ p.m.

illness

Symptom	Severity	Time	
☐ Nausea	① ② ③ ④ ⑤	☐ a.m.	☐ p.m.
☐ Vomiting	① ② ③ ④ ⑤	☐ a.m.	☐ p.m.
☐ Constipation	① ② ③ ④ ⑤	☐ a.m.	☐ p.m.
☐ Diarrhea	① ② ③ ④ ⑤	☐ a.m.	☐ p.m.
☐ Sore throat	① ② ③ ④ ⑤	☐ a.m.	☐ p.m.
☐ Congestion	① ② ③ ④ ⑤	☐ a.m.	☐ p.m.
☐ Coughing	① ② ③ ④ ⑤	☐ a.m.	☐ p.m.
☐ Acid reflux	① ② ③ ④ ⑤	☐ a.m.	☐ p.m.

psychological

Symptom	Severity	Time	
☐ Anxiety	① ② ③ ④ ⑤	☐ a.m.	☐ p.m.
☐ Depression	① ② ③ ④ ⑤	☐ a.m.	☐ p.m.
☐ Memory loss	① ② ③ ④ ⑤	☐ a.m.	☐ p.m.
☐ Confusion	① ② ③ ④ ⑤	☐ a.m.	☐ p.m.
☐ Poor focus	① ② ③ ④ ⑤	☐ a.m.	☐ p.m.
☐ Mood swings	① ② ③ ④ ⑤	☐ a.m.	☐ p.m.
☐ Suicidal	① ② ③ ④ ⑤	☐ a.m.	☐ p.m.

other

Symptom	Severity	Time	
	① ② ③ ④ ⑤	☐ a.m.	☐ p.m.
	① ② ③ ④ ⑤	☐ a.m.	☐ p.m.
	① ② ③ ④ ⑤	☐ a.m.	☐ p.m.
	① ② ③ ④ ⑤	☐ a.m.	☐ p.m.
	① ② ③ ④ ⑤	☐ a.m.	☐ p.m.
	① ② ③ ④ ⑤	☐ a.m.	☐ p.m.
	① ② ③ ④ ⑤	☐ a.m.	☐ p.m.

SLEEP

hours ________ *quality* ① ② ③ ④ ⑤

STRESS LEVELS

None	Low	Medium	High	Max	@$#%!

WEATHER

☐ Cold ☐ Mild ☐ Hot
☐ Dry ☐ Humid ☐ Wet

Allergen Levels: ________

BM Pressure: ________

EXERCISE

☐ Heck yes, I worked out.
☐ I managed to exercise a bit.
☐ No, I haven't exercised at all.
☐ I did some stuff, and that counts.

DETAILS

FOOD / MEDICATION

Food / Drinks

Meds / Supplements	Time	Dose
☐ usual daily medication		

Water	*Caffeine*	*Alcohol*
☐☐☐☐☐☐☐☐☐☐	x ________	x ________

FOOD ANALYSIS

New food introduced?
☐ Yes ☐ No

Food reintroduction?
☐ Yes ☐ No

Details

MEDICATION ANALYSIS

New med/dose introduced?
☐ Yes ☐ No

Medication stopped?
☐ Yes ☐ No

Details

ACTIVITY ANALYSIS

Heightened exertion levels?
☐ Yes ☐ No

Lowered exertion levels?
☐ Yes ☐ No

Details

SLEEP ANALYSIS

When you woke up this morning, did you feel well-rested?	☐ Yes	☐ No	☐ A bit
Did you snore or stop breathing throughout the night?	☐ Yes	☐ No	☐ Not sure
Roughly how many times did you wake up throughout the night?			

Notes / Suspected Triggers

ENTRY #47 | M T W T F S S | DATE:

HOW ARE YOU *Feeling today?*

Amazing!	Meh
Great	Not good
Good	Terrible!

RATE YOUR PAIN LEVEL

① ② ③ ④ ⑤ ⑥ ⑦ ⑧ ⑨ ⑩

WHAT ABOUT YOUR...?

Mood	① ② ③ ④ ⑤ ⑥ ⑦ ⑧ ⑨ ⑩
Energy Levels	① ② ③ ④ ⑤ ⑥ ⑦ ⑧ ⑨ ⑩
Mental Clarity	① ② ③ ④ ⑤ ⑥ ⑦ ⑧ ⑨ ⑩

PAIN & PHYSICAL SYMPTOMS

Symptom	Severity	am	pm
	① ② ③ ④ ⑤	☐	☐
	① ② ③ ④ ⑤	☐	☐
	① ② ③ ④ ⑤	☐	☐
	① ② ③ ④ ⑤	☐	☐
	① ② ③ ④ ⑤	☐	☐
	① ② ③ ④ ⑤	☐	☐
	① ② ③ ④ ⑤	☐	☐
	① ② ③ ④ ⑤	☐	☐

front *back*

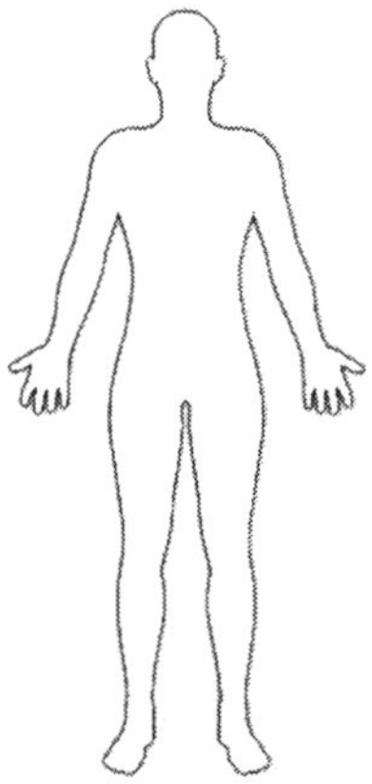

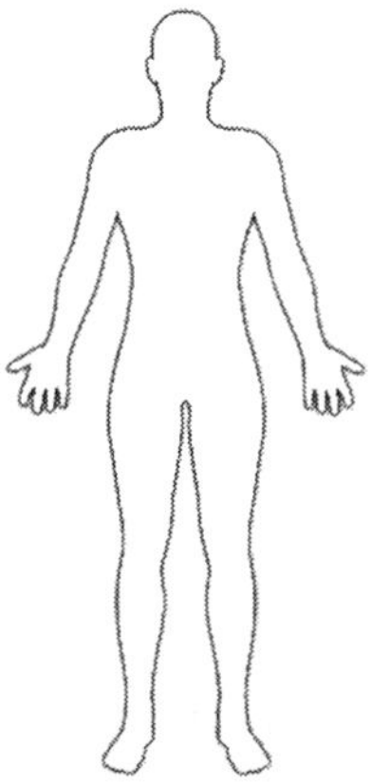

OTHER SYMPTOMS

general

Symptom	Severity	Time	
☐ Fatigue	① ② ③ ④ ⑤	☐ a.m.	☐ p.m.
☐ Lethargy	① ② ③ ④ ⑤	☐ a.m.	☐ p.m.
☐ Malaise	① ② ③ ④ ⑤	☐ a.m.	☐ p.m.
☐ Weakness	① ② ③ ④ ⑤	☐ a.m.	☐ p.m.
☐ Dizziness	① ② ③ ④ ⑤	☐ a.m.	☐ p.m.
☐ Trembling	① ② ③ ④ ⑤	☐ a.m.	☐ p.m.
☐ Twitching	① ② ③ ④ ⑤	☐ a.m.	☐ p.m.
☐ Insomnia	① ② ③ ④ ⑤	☐ a.m.	☐ p.m.

illness

Symptom	Severity	Time	
☐ Nausea	① ② ③ ④ ⑤	☐ a.m.	☐ p.m.
☐ Vomiting	① ② ③ ④ ⑤	☐ a.m.	☐ p.m.
☐ Constipation	① ② ③ ④ ⑤	☐ a.m.	☐ p.m.
☐ Diarrhea	① ② ③ ④ ⑤	☐ a.m.	☐ p.m.
☐ Sore throat	① ② ③ ④ ⑤	☐ a.m.	☐ p.m.
☐ Congestion	① ② ③ ④ ⑤	☐ a.m.	☐ p.m.
☐ Coughing	① ② ③ ④ ⑤	☐ a.m.	☐ p.m.
☐ Acid reflux	① ② ③ ④ ⑤	☐ a.m.	☐ p.m.

psychological

Symptom	Severity	Time	
☐ Anxiety	① ② ③ ④ ⑤	☐ a.m.	☐ p.m.
☐ Depression	① ② ③ ④ ⑤	☐ a.m.	☐ p.m.
☐ Memory loss	① ② ③ ④ ⑤	☐ a.m.	☐ p.m.
☐ Confusion	① ② ③ ④ ⑤	☐ a.m.	☐ p.m.
☐ Poor focus	① ② ③ ④ ⑤	☐ a.m.	☐ p.m.
☐ Mood swings	① ② ③ ④ ⑤	☐ a.m.	☐ p.m.
☐ Suicidal	① ② ③ ④ ⑤	☐ a.m.	☐ p.m.

other

Symptom	Severity	Time	
	① ② ③ ④ ⑤	☐ a.m.	☐ p.m.
	① ② ③ ④ ⑤	☐ a.m.	☐ p.m.
	① ② ③ ④ ⑤	☐ a.m.	☐ p.m.
	① ② ③ ④ ⑤	☐ a.m.	☐ p.m.
	① ② ③ ④ ⑤	☐ a.m.	☐ p.m.
	① ② ③ ④ ⑤	☐ a.m.	☐ p.m.
	① ② ③ ④ ⑤	☐ a.m.	☐ p.m.

SLEEP

hours ________ *quality* (1) (2) (3) (4) (5)

STRESS LEVELS

None	Low	Medium	High	Max	@$#%!

WEATHER

☐ Cold ☐ Mild ☐ Hot
☐ Dry ☐ Humid ☐ Wet

Allergen Levels: ________

BM Pressure: ________

EXERCISE

☐ Heck yes, I worked out.
☐ I managed to exercise a bit.
☐ No, I haven't exercised at all.
☐ I did some stuff, and that counts.

DETAILS

FOOD / MEDICATION

Food / Drinks

Meds / Supplements	Time	Dose
☐ usual daily medication		

Water	*Caffeine*	*Alcohol*
☐☐☐☐☐☐☐☐☐☐	x ________	x ________

FOOD ANALYSIS

New food introduced?

☐ Yes ☐ No

Food reintroduction?

☐ Yes ☐ No

Details

MEDICATION ANALYSIS

New med/dose introduced?

☐ Yes ☐ No

Medication stopped?

☐ Yes ☐ No

Details

ACTIVITY ANALYSIS

Heightened exertion levels?

☐ Yes ☐ No

Lowered exertion levels?

☐ Yes ☐ No

Details

SLEEP ANALYSIS

When you woke up this morning, did you feel well-rested?	☐ Yes	☐ No	☐ A bit
Did you snore or stop breathing throughout the night?	☐ Yes	☐ No	☐ Not sure
Roughly how many times did you wake up throughout the night?			

Notes / Suspected Triggers

ENTRY #48 | M T W T F S S | DATE:

HOW ARE YOU *Feeling today?*

Amazing!	Meh
Great	Not good
Good	Terrible!

RATE YOUR PAIN LEVEL

① ② ③ ④ ⑤ ⑥ ⑦ ⑧ ⑨ ⑩

WHAT ABOUT YOUR...?

Mood	① ② ③ ④ ⑤ ⑥ ⑦ ⑧ ⑨ ⑩
Energy Levels	① ② ③ ④ ⑤ ⑥ ⑦ ⑧ ⑨ ⑩
Mental Clarity	① ② ③ ④ ⑤ ⑥ ⑦ ⑧ ⑨ ⑩

PAIN & PHYSICAL SYMPTOMS

Symptom	Severity	am	pm
	① ② ③ ④ ⑤	☐	☐
	① ② ③ ④ ⑤	☐	☐
	① ② ③ ④ ⑤	☐	☐
	① ② ③ ④ ⑤	☐	☐
	① ② ③ ④ ⑤	☐	☐
	① ② ③ ④ ⑤	☐	☐
	① ② ③ ④ ⑤	☐	☐
	① ② ③ ④ ⑤	☐	☐

front

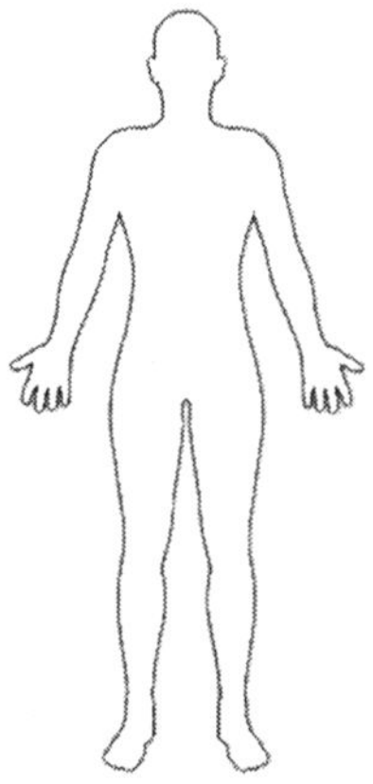

back

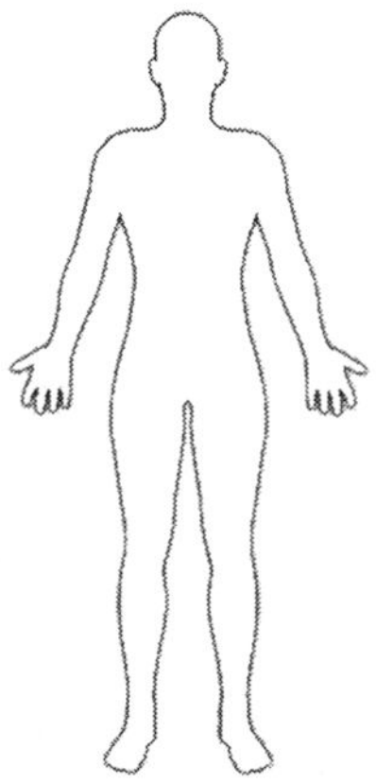

OTHER SYMPTOMS

general

Symptom	Severity	Time	
☐ Fatigue	① ② ③ ④ ⑤	☐ a.m.	☐ p.m.
☐ Lethargy	① ② ③ ④ ⑤	☐ a.m.	☐ p.m.
☐ Malaise	① ② ③ ④ ⑤	☐ a.m.	☐ p.m.
☐ Weakness	① ② ③ ④ ⑤	☐ a.m.	☐ p.m.
☐ Dizziness	① ② ③ ④ ⑤	☐ a.m.	☐ p.m.
☐ Trembling	① ② ③ ④ ⑤	☐ a.m.	☐ p.m.
☐ Twitching	① ② ③ ④ ⑤	☐ a.m.	☐ p.m.
☐ Insomnia	① ② ③ ④ ⑤	☐ a.m.	☐ p.m.

illness

Symptom	Severity	Time	
☐ Nausea	① ② ③ ④ ⑤	☐ a.m.	☐ p.m.
☐ Vomiting	① ② ③ ④ ⑤	☐ a.m.	☐ p.m.
☐ Constipation	① ② ③ ④ ⑤	☐ a.m.	☐ p.m.
☐ Diarrhea	① ② ③ ④ ⑤	☐ a.m.	☐ p.m.
☐ Sore throat	① ② ③ ④ ⑤	☐ a.m.	☐ p.m.
☐ Congestion	① ② ③ ④ ⑤	☐ a.m.	☐ p.m.
☐ Coughing	① ② ③ ④ ⑤	☐ a.m.	☐ p.m.
☐ Acid reflux	① ② ③ ④ ⑤	☐ a.m.	☐ p.m.

psychological

Symptom	Severity	Time	
☐ Anxiety	① ② ③ ④ ⑤	☐ a.m.	☐ p.m.
☐ Depression	① ② ③ ④ ⑤	☐ a.m.	☐ p.m.
☐ Memory loss	① ② ③ ④ ⑤	☐ a.m.	☐ p.m.
☐ Confusion	① ② ③ ④ ⑤	☐ a.m.	☐ p.m.
☐ Poor focus	① ② ③ ④ ⑤	☐ a.m.	☐ p.m.
☐ Mood swings	① ② ③ ④ ⑤	☐ a.m.	☐ p.m.
☐ Suicidal	① ② ③ ④ ⑤	☐ a.m.	☐ p.m.

other

Symptom	Severity	Time	
	① ② ③ ④ ⑤	☐ a.m.	☐ p.m.
	① ② ③ ④ ⑤	☐ a.m.	☐ p.m.
	① ② ③ ④ ⑤	☐ a.m.	☐ p.m.
	① ② ③ ④ ⑤	☐ a.m.	☐ p.m.
	① ② ③ ④ ⑤	☐ a.m.	☐ p.m.
	① ② ③ ④ ⑤	☐ a.m.	☐ p.m.
	① ② ③ ④ ⑤	☐ a.m.	☐ p.m.

SLEEP

hours ________

quality ① ② ③ ④ ⑤

STRESS LEVELS

None	Low	Medium	High	Max	@$#%!

WEATHER

☐ Cold ☐ Mild ☐ Hot

☐ Dry ☐ Humid ☐ Wet

Allergen Levels: ________

BM Pressure: ________

EXERCISE

☐ Heck yes, I worked out.

☐ I managed to exercise a bit.

☐ No, I haven't exercised at all.

☐ I did some stuff, and that counts.

DETAILS

FOOD / MEDICATION

Food / Drinks

Meds / Supplements	Time	Dose
☐ usual daily medication		

Water *Caffeine* *Alcohol*

x ________ x ________

FOOD ANALYSIS

New food introduced?

☐ Yes ☐ No

Food reintroduction?

☐ Yes ☐ No

Details

MEDICATION ANALYSIS

New med/dose introduced?

☐ Yes ☐ No

Medication stopped?

☐ Yes ☐ No

Details

ACTIVITY ANALYSIS

Heightened exertion levels?

☐ Yes ☐ No

Lowered exertion levels?

☐ Yes ☐ No

Details

SLEEP ANALYSIS

When you woke up this morning, did you feel well-rested? ☐ Yes ☐ No ☐ A bit

Did you snore or stop breathing throughout the night? ☐ Yes ☐ No ☐ Not sure

Roughly how many times did you wake up throughout the night?

Notes / Suspected Triggers

ENTRY #49 | M T W T F S S | DATE:

HOW ARE YOU *Feeling today?*

Amazing!	Meh
Great	Not good
Good	Terrible!

RATE YOUR PAIN LEVEL

① ② ③ ④ ⑤ ⑥ ⑦ ⑧ ⑨ ⑩

WHAT ABOUT YOUR...?

Mood	① ② ③ ④ ⑤ ⑥ ⑦ ⑧ ⑨ ⑩
Energy Levels	① ② ③ ④ ⑤ ⑥ ⑦ ⑧ ⑨ ⑩
Mental Clarity	① ② ③ ④ ⑤ ⑥ ⑦ ⑧ ⑨ ⑩

PAIN & PHYSICAL SYMPTOMS

Symptom	Severity	am	pm
	① ② ③ ④ ⑤	☐	☐
	① ② ③ ④ ⑤	☐	☐
	① ② ③ ④ ⑤	☐	☐
	① ② ③ ④ ⑤	☐	☐
	① ② ③ ④ ⑤	☐	☐
	① ② ③ ④ ⑤	☐	☐
	① ② ③ ④ ⑤	☐	☐
	① ② ③ ④ ⑤	☐	☐

front *back*

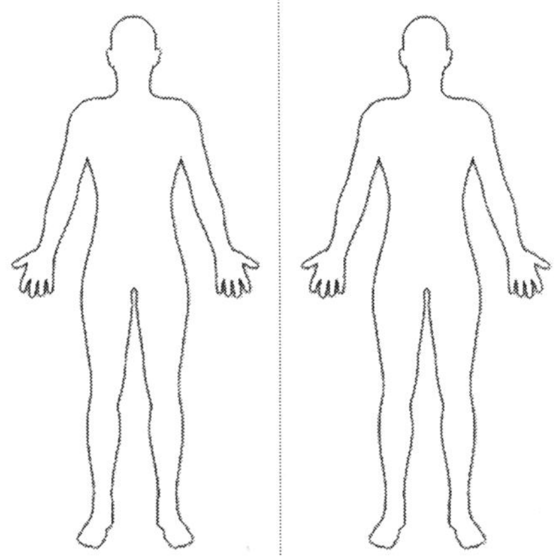

OTHER SYMPTOMS

general

Symptom	Severity	Time	
☐ Fatigue	① ② ③ ④ ⑤	☐ a.m.	☐ p.m.
☐ Lethargy	① ② ③ ④ ⑤	☐ a.m.	☐ p.m.
☐ Malaise	① ② ③ ④ ⑤	☐ a.m.	☐ p.m.
☐ Weakness	① ② ③ ④ ⑤	☐ a.m.	☐ p.m.
☐ Dizziness	① ② ③ ④ ⑤	☐ a.m.	☐ p.m.
☐ Trembling	① ② ③ ④ ⑤	☐ a.m.	☐ p.m.
☐ Twitching	① ② ③ ④ ⑤	☐ a.m.	☐ p.m.
☐ Insomnia	① ② ③ ④ ⑤	☐ a.m.	☐ p.m.

illness

Symptom	Severity	Time	
☐ Nausea	① ② ③ ④ ⑤	☐ a.m.	☐ p.m.
☐ Vomiting	① ② ③ ④ ⑤	☐ a.m.	☐ p.m.
☐ Constipation	① ② ③ ④ ⑤	☐ a.m.	☐ p.m.
☐ Diarrhea	① ② ③ ④ ⑤	☐ a.m.	☐ p.m.
☐ Sore throat	① ② ③ ④ ⑤	☐ a.m.	☐ p.m.
☐ Congestion	① ② ③ ④ ⑤	☐ a.m.	☐ p.m.
☐ Coughing	① ② ③ ④ ⑤	☐ a.m.	☐ p.m.
☐ Acid reflux	① ② ③ ④ ⑤	☐ a.m.	☐ p.m.

psychological

Symptom	Severity	Time	
☐ Anxiety	① ② ③ ④ ⑤	☐ a.m.	☐ p.m.
☐ Depression	① ② ③ ④ ⑤	☐ a.m.	☐ p.m.
☐ Memory loss	① ② ③ ④ ⑤	☐ a.m.	☐ p.m.
☐ Confusion	① ② ③ ④ ⑤	☐ a.m.	☐ p.m.
☐ Poor focus	① ② ③ ④ ⑤	☐ a.m.	☐ p.m.
☐ Mood swings	① ② ③ ④ ⑤	☐ a.m.	☐ p.m.
☐ Suicidal	① ② ③ ④ ⑤	☐ a.m.	☐ p.m.

other

Symptom	Severity	Time	
	① ② ③ ④ ⑤	☐ a.m.	☐ p.m.
	① ② ③ ④ ⑤	☐ a.m.	☐ p.m.
	① ② ③ ④ ⑤	☐ a.m.	☐ p.m.
	① ② ③ ④ ⑤	☐ a.m.	☐ p.m.
	① ② ③ ④ ⑤	☐ a.m.	☐ p.m.
	① ② ③ ④ ⑤	☐ a.m.	☐ p.m.
	① ② ③ ④ ⑤	☐ a.m.	☐ p.m.

SLEEP

hours ________ *quality* ① ② ③ ④ ⑤

STRESS LEVELS

None	Low	Medium	High	Max	@$#%!

WEATHER

☐ Cold ☐ Mild ☐ Hot
☐ Dry ☐ Humid ☐ Wet

Allergen Levels: ________

BM Pressure: ________

EXERCISE

☐ Heck yes, I worked out.
☐ I managed to exercise a bit.
☐ No, I haven't exercised at all.
☐ I did some stuff, and that counts.

DETAILS

FOOD / MEDICATION

Food / Drinks

Meds / Supplements	Time	Dose
☐ usual daily medication		

Water *Caffeine* *Alcohol*

x ________ x ________

FOOD ANALYSIS	
New food introduced?	
☐ Yes	☐ No
Food reintroduction?	
☐ Yes	☐ No
Details	

MEDICATION ANALYSIS	
New med/dose introduced?	
☐ Yes	☐ No
Medication stopped?	
☐ Yes	☐ No
Details	

ACTIVITY ANALYSIS	
Heightened exertion levels?	
☐ Yes	☐ No
Lowered exertion levels?	
☐ Yes	☐ No
Details	

SLEEP ANALYSIS

When you woke up this morning, did you feel well-rested?	☐ Yes	☐ No	☐ A bit
Did you snore or stop breathing throughout the night?	☐ Yes	☐ No	☐ Not sure
Roughly how many times did you wake up throughout the night?			

Notes / Suspected Triggers

ENTRY #50 | M T W T F S S | DATE:

HOW ARE YOU *Feeling today?*

Amazing!	Meh
Great	Not good
Good	Terrible!

RATE YOUR PAIN LEVEL

① ② ③ ④ ⑤ ⑥ ⑦ ⑧ ⑨ ⑩

WHAT ABOUT YOUR...?

Mood	① ② ③ ④ ⑤ ⑥ ⑦ ⑧ ⑨ ⑩
Energy Levels	① ② ③ ④ ⑤ ⑥ ⑦ ⑧ ⑨ ⑩
Mental Clarity	① ② ③ ④ ⑤ ⑥ ⑦ ⑧ ⑨ ⑩

PAIN & PHYSICAL SYMPTOMS

Symptom	Severity	am	pm
	① ② ③ ④ ⑤	☐	☐
	① ② ③ ④ ⑤	☐	☐
	① ② ③ ④ ⑤	☐	☐
	① ② ③ ④ ⑤	☐	☐
	① ② ③ ④ ⑤	☐	☐
	① ② ③ ④ ⑤	☐	☐
	① ② ③ ④ ⑤	☐	☐
	① ② ③ ④ ⑤	☐	☐

front *back*

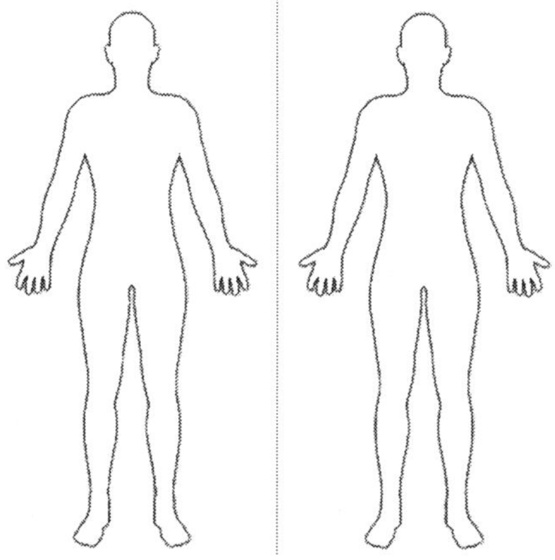

OTHER SYMPTOMS

general

Symptom	Severity	Time	
☐ Fatigue	① ② ③ ④ ⑤	☐ a.m.	☐ p.m.
☐ Lethargy	① ② ③ ④ ⑤	☐ a.m.	☐ p.m.
☐ Malaise	① ② ③ ④ ⑤	☐ a.m.	☐ p.m.
☐ Weakness	① ② ③ ④ ⑤	☐ a.m.	☐ p.m.
☐ Dizziness	① ② ③ ④ ⑤	☐ a.m.	☐ p.m.
☐ Trembling	① ② ③ ④ ⑤	☐ a.m.	☐ p.m.
☐ Twitching	① ② ③ ④ ⑤	☐ a.m.	☐ p.m.
☐ Insomnia	① ② ③ ④ ⑤	☐ a.m.	☐ p.m.

illness

Symptom	Severity	Time	
☐ Nausea	① ② ③ ④ ⑤	☐ a.m.	☐ p.m.
☐ Vomiting	① ② ③ ④ ⑤	☐ a.m.	☐ p.m.
☐ Constipation	① ② ③ ④ ⑤	☐ a.m.	☐ p.m.
☐ Diarrhea	① ② ③ ④ ⑤	☐ a.m.	☐ p.m.
☐ Sore throat	① ② ③ ④ ⑤	☐ a.m.	☐ p.m.
☐ Congestion	① ② ③ ④ ⑤	☐ a.m.	☐ p.m.
☐ Coughing	① ② ③ ④ ⑤	☐ a.m.	☐ p.m.
☐ Acid reflux	① ② ③ ④ ⑤	☐ a.m.	☐ p.m.

psychological

Symptom	Severity	Time	
☐ Anxiety	① ② ③ ④ ⑤	☐ a.m.	☐ p.m.
☐ Depression	① ② ③ ④ ⑤	☐ a.m.	☐ p.m.
☐ Memory loss	① ② ③ ④ ⑤	☐ a.m.	☐ p.m.
☐ Confusion	① ② ③ ④ ⑤	☐ a.m.	☐ p.m.
☐ Poor focus	① ② ③ ④ ⑤	☐ a.m.	☐ p.m.
☐ Mood swings	① ② ③ ④ ⑤	☐ a.m.	☐ p.m.
☐ Suicidal	① ② ③ ④ ⑤	☐ a.m.	☐ p.m.

other

Symptom	Severity	Time	
	① ② ③ ④ ⑤	☐ a.m.	☐ p.m.
	① ② ③ ④ ⑤	☐ a.m.	☐ p.m.
	① ② ③ ④ ⑤	☐ a.m.	☐ p.m.
	① ② ③ ④ ⑤	☐ a.m.	☐ p.m.
	① ② ③ ④ ⑤	☐ a.m.	☐ p.m.
	① ② ③ ④ ⑤	☐ a.m.	☐ p.m.
	① ② ③ ④ ⑤	☐ a.m.	☐ p.m.

SLEEP

hours ________ *quality* ① ② ③ ④ ⑤

STRESS LEVELS

None	Low	Medium	High	Max	@$#%!

WEATHER

☐ Cold ☐ Mild ☐ Hot
☐ Dry ☐ Humid ☐ Wet

Allergen Levels: ________
BM Pressure: ________

EXERCISE

☐ Heck yes, I worked out.
☐ I managed to exercise a bit.
☐ No, I haven't exercised at all.
☐ I did some stuff, and that counts.

DETAILS

FOOD / MEDICATION

Food / Drinks

Meds / Supplements	Time	Dose
☐ usual daily medication		

Water	*Caffeine*	*Alcohol*
	x ________	x ________

FOOD ANALYSIS		MEDICATION ANALYSIS		ACTIVITY ANALYSIS	
New food introduced?		New med/dose introduced?		Heightened exertion levels?	
☐ Yes	☐ No	☐ Yes	☐ No	☐ Yes	☐ No
Food reintroduction?		Medication stopped?		Lowered exertion levels?	
☐ Yes	☐ No	☐ Yes	☐ No	☐ Yes	☐ No
Details		*Details*		*Details*	

SLEEP ANALYSIS

When you woke up this morning, did you feel well-rested?	☐ Yes	☐ No	☐ A bit
Did you snore or stop breathing throughout the night?	☐ Yes	☐ No	☐ Not sure
Roughly how many times did you wake up throughout the night?			

Notes / Suspected Triggers

ENTRY #51 | M T W T F S S | DATE:

HOW ARE YOU *Feeling today?*

Amazing!	Meh
Great	Not good
Good	Terrible!

RATE YOUR PAIN LEVEL

① ② ③ ④ ⑤ ⑥ ⑦ ⑧ ⑨ ⑩

WHAT ABOUT YOUR...?

Mood	① ② ③ ④ ⑤ ⑥ ⑦ ⑧ ⑨ ⑩
Energy Levels	① ② ③ ④ ⑤ ⑥ ⑦ ⑧ ⑨ ⑩
Mental Clarity	① ② ③ ④ ⑤ ⑥ ⑦ ⑧ ⑨ ⑩

PAIN & PHYSICAL SYMPTOMS

Symptom	Severity	am	pm
	① ② ③ ④ ⑤	☐	☐
	① ② ③ ④ ⑤	☐	☐
	① ② ③ ④ ⑤	☐	☐
	① ② ③ ④ ⑤	☐	☐
	① ② ③ ④ ⑤	☐	☐
	① ② ③ ④ ⑤	☐	☐
	① ② ③ ④ ⑤	☐	☐
	① ② ③ ④ ⑤	☐	☐

front ***back***

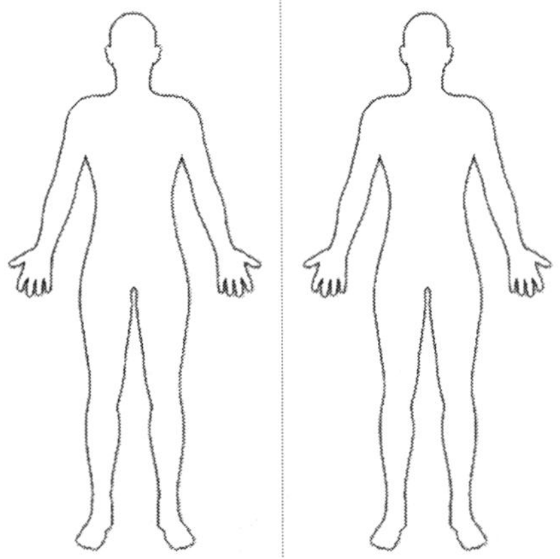

OTHER SYMPTOMS

general

Symptom	Severity	Time	
☐ Fatigue	① ② ③ ④ ⑤	☐ a.m.	☐ p.m.
☐ Lethargy	① ② ③ ④ ⑤	☐ a.m.	☐ p.m.
☐ Malaise	① ② ③ ④ ⑤	☐ a.m.	☐ p.m.
☐ Weakness	① ② ③ ④ ⑤	☐ a.m.	☐ p.m.
☐ Dizziness	① ② ③ ④ ⑤	☐ a.m.	☐ p.m.
☐ Trembling	① ② ③ ④ ⑤	☐ a.m.	☐ p.m.
☐ Twitching	① ② ③ ④ ⑤	☐ a.m.	☐ p.m.
☐ Insomnia	① ② ③ ④ ⑤	☐ a.m.	☐ p.m.

illness

Symptom	Severity	Time	
☐ Nausea	① ② ③ ④ ⑤	☐ a.m.	☐ p.m.
☐ Vomiting	① ② ③ ④ ⑤	☐ a.m.	☐ p.m.
☐ Constipation	① ② ③ ④ ⑤	☐ a.m.	☐ p.m.
☐ Diarrhea	① ② ③ ④ ⑤	☐ a.m.	☐ p.m.
☐ Sore throat	① ② ③ ④ ⑤	☐ a.m.	☐ p.m.
☐ Congestion	① ② ③ ④ ⑤	☐ a.m.	☐ p.m.
☐ Coughing	① ② ③ ④ ⑤	☐ a.m.	☐ p.m.
☐ Acid reflux	① ② ③ ④ ⑤	☐ a.m.	☐ p.m.

psychological

Symptom	Severity	Time	
☐ Anxiety	① ② ③ ④ ⑤	☐ a.m.	☐ p.m.
☐ Depression	① ② ③ ④ ⑤	☐ a.m.	☐ p.m.
☐ Memory loss	① ② ③ ④ ⑤	☐ a.m.	☐ p.m.
☐ Confusion	① ② ③ ④ ⑤	☐ a.m.	☐ p.m.
☐ Poor focus	① ② ③ ④ ⑤	☐ a.m.	☐ p.m.
☐ Mood swings	① ② ③ ④ ⑤	☐ a.m.	☐ p.m.
☐ Suicidal	① ② ③ ④ ⑤	☐ a.m.	☐ p.m.

other

Symptom	Severity	Time	
	① ② ③ ④ ⑤	☐ a.m.	☐ p.m.
	① ② ③ ④ ⑤	☐ a.m.	☐ p.m.
	① ② ③ ④ ⑤	☐ a.m.	☐ p.m.
	① ② ③ ④ ⑤	☐ a.m.	☐ p.m.
	① ② ③ ④ ⑤	☐ a.m.	☐ p.m.
	① ② ③ ④ ⑤	☐ a.m.	☐ p.m.
	① ② ③ ④ ⑤	☐ a.m.	☐ p.m.

SLEEP

hours ________

quality ① ② ③ ④ ⑤

STRESS LEVELS

None	Low	Medium	High	Max	@$#%!

WEATHER

☐ Cold ☐ Mild ☐ Hot
☐ Dry ☐ Humid ☐ Wet

Allergen Levels: ________

BM Pressure: ________

EXERCISE

☐ Heck yes, I worked out.
☐ I managed to exercise a bit.
☐ No, I haven't exercised at all.
☐ I did some stuff, and that counts.

DETAILS

FOOD / MEDICATION

Food / Drinks

Meds / Supplements	Time	Dose

☐ usual daily medication

Water *Caffeine* *Alcohol*

x ________ x ________

FOOD ANALYSIS

New food introduced?
☐ Yes ☐ No

Food reintroduction?
☐ Yes ☐ No

Details

MEDICATION ANALYSIS

New med/dose introduced?
☐ Yes ☐ No

Medication stopped?
☐ Yes ☐ No

Details

ACTIVITY ANALYSIS

Heightened exertion levels?
☐ Yes ☐ No

Lowered exertion levels?
☐ Yes ☐ No

Details

SLEEP ANALYSIS

When you woke up this morning, did you feel well-rested? ☐ Yes ☐ No ☐ A bit

Did you snore or stop breathing throughout the night? ☐ Yes ☐ No ☐ Not sure

Roughly how many times did you wake up throughout the night?

Notes / Suspected Triggers

ENTRY #52 | M T W T F S S | DATE:

HOW ARE YOU *Feeling today?*

RATE YOUR PAIN LEVEL

① ② ③ ④ ⑤ ⑥ ⑦ ⑧ ⑨ ⑩

WHAT ABOUT YOUR...?

Mood	① ② ③ ④ ⑤ ⑥ ⑦ ⑧ ⑨ ⑩
Energy Levels	① ② ③ ④ ⑤ ⑥ ⑦ ⑧ ⑨ ⑩
Mental Clarity	① ② ③ ④ ⑤ ⑥ ⑦ ⑧ ⑨ ⑩

PAIN & PHYSICAL SYMPTOMS

Symptom	Severity	am	pm
	① ② ③ ④ ⑤	☐	☐
	① ② ③ ④ ⑤	☐	☐
	① ② ③ ④ ⑤	☐	☐
	① ② ③ ④ ⑤	☐	☐
	① ② ③ ④ ⑤	☐	☐
	① ② ③ ④ ⑤	☐	☐
	① ② ③ ④ ⑤	☐	☐
	① ② ③ ④ ⑤	☐	☐

front *back*

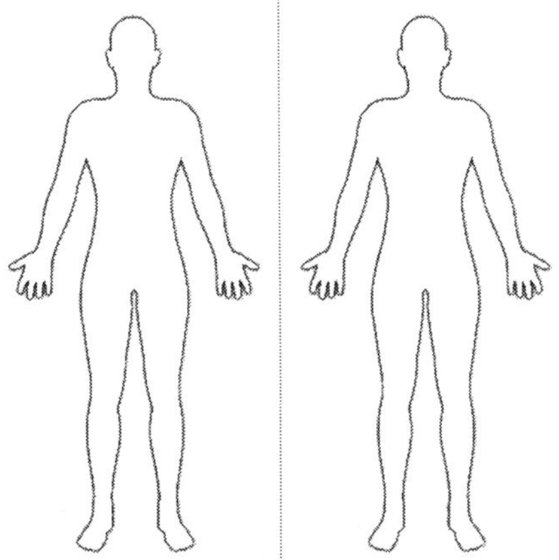

OTHER SYMPTOMS

general

Symptom	Severity	Time	
☐ Fatigue	① ② ③ ④ ⑤	☐ a.m.	☐ p.m.
☐ Lethargy	① ② ③ ④ ⑤	☐ a.m.	☐ p.m.
☐ Malaise	① ② ③ ④ ⑤	☐ a.m.	☐ p.m.
☐ Weakness	① ② ③ ④ ⑤	☐ a.m.	☐ p.m.
☐ Dizziness	① ② ③ ④ ⑤	☐ a.m.	☐ p.m.
☐ Trembling	① ② ③ ④ ⑤	☐ a.m.	☐ p.m.
☐ Twitching	① ② ③ ④ ⑤	☐ a.m.	☐ p.m.
☐ Insomnia	① ② ③ ④ ⑤	☐ a.m.	☐ p.m.

illness

Symptom	Severity	Time	
☐ Nausea	① ② ③ ④ ⑤	☐ a.m.	☐ p.m.
☐ Vomiting	① ② ③ ④ ⑤	☐ a.m.	☐ p.m.
☐ Constipation	① ② ③ ④ ⑤	☐ a.m.	☐ p.m.
☐ Diarrhea	① ② ③ ④ ⑤	☐ a.m.	☐ p.m.
☐ Sore throat	① ② ③ ④ ⑤	☐ a.m.	☐ p.m.
☐ Congestion	① ② ③ ④ ⑤	☐ a.m.	☐ p.m.
☐ Coughing	① ② ③ ④ ⑤	☐ a.m.	☐ p.m.
☐ Acid reflux	① ② ③ ④ ⑤	☐ a.m.	☐ p.m.

psychological

Symptom	Severity	Time	
☐ Anxiety	① ② ③ ④ ⑤	☐ a.m.	☐ p.m.
☐ Depression	① ② ③ ④ ⑤	☐ a.m.	☐ p.m.
☐ Memory loss	① ② ③ ④ ⑤	☐ a.m.	☐ p.m.
☐ Confusion	① ② ③ ④ ⑤	☐ a.m.	☐ p.m.
☐ Poor focus	① ② ③ ④ ⑤	☐ a.m.	☐ p.m.
☐ Mood swings	① ② ③ ④ ⑤	☐ a.m.	☐ p.m.
☐ Suicidal	① ② ③ ④ ⑤	☐ a.m.	☐ p.m.

other

Symptom	Severity	Time	
	① ② ③ ④ ⑤	☐ a.m.	☐ p.m.
	① ② ③ ④ ⑤	☐ a.m.	☐ p.m.
	① ② ③ ④ ⑤	☐ a.m.	☐ p.m.
	① ② ③ ④ ⑤	☐ a.m.	☐ p.m.
	① ② ③ ④ ⑤	☐ a.m.	☐ p.m.
	① ② ③ ④ ⑤	☐ a.m.	☐ p.m.
	① ② ③ ④ ⑤	☐ a.m.	☐ p.m.

SLEEP

hours ________ *quality* ① ② ③ ④ ⑤

STRESS LEVELS

None	Low	Medium	High	Max	@$#%!

WEATHER

☐ Cold ☐ Mild ☐ Hot

☐ Dry ☐ Humid ☐ Wet

Allergen Levels: ________

BM Pressure: ________

EXERCISE

☐ Heck yes, I worked out.

☐ I managed to exercise a bit.

☐ No, I haven't exercised at all.

☐ I did some stuff, and that counts.

DETAILS

FOOD / MEDICATION

Food / Drinks

Meds / Supplements	**Time**	**Dose**

☐ usual daily medication

Water *Caffeine* *Alcohol*

x ________ x ________

FOOD ANALYSIS

New food introduced?

☐ Yes ☐ No

Food reintroduction?

☐ Yes ☐ No

Details

MEDICATION ANALYSIS

New med/dose introduced?

☐ Yes ☐ No

Medication stopped?

☐ Yes ☐ No

Details

ACTIVITY ANALYSIS

Heightened exertion levels?

☐ Yes ☐ No

Lowered exertion levels?

☐ Yes ☐ No

Details

SLEEP ANALYSIS

When you woke up this morning, did you feel well-rested?	☐ Yes	☐ No	☐ A bit
Did you snore or stop breathing throughout the night?	☐ Yes	☐ No	☐ Not sure
Roughly how many times did you wake up throughout the night?			

Notes / Suspected Triggers

ENTRY #53 | M T W T F S S | DATE:

HOW ARE YOU *Feeling today?*

Amazing!	Meh
Great	Not good
Good	Terrible!

RATE YOUR PAIN LEVEL

① ② ③ ④ ⑤ ⑥ ⑦ ⑧ ⑨ ⑩

WHAT ABOUT YOUR...?

Mood	① ② ③ ④ ⑤ ⑥ ⑦ ⑧ ⑨ ⑩
Energy Levels	① ② ③ ④ ⑤ ⑥ ⑦ ⑧ ⑨ ⑩
Mental Clarity	① ② ③ ④ ⑤ ⑥ ⑦ ⑧ ⑨ ⑩

PAIN & PHYSICAL SYMPTOMS

Symptom	Severity	am	pm
	① ② ③ ④ ⑤	☐	☐
	① ② ③ ④ ⑤	☐	☐
	① ② ③ ④ ⑤	☐	☐
	① ② ③ ④ ⑤	☐	☐
	① ② ③ ④ ⑤	☐	☐
	① ② ③ ④ ⑤	☐	☐
	① ② ③ ④ ⑤	☐	☐
	① ② ③ ④ ⑤	☐	☐

front *back*

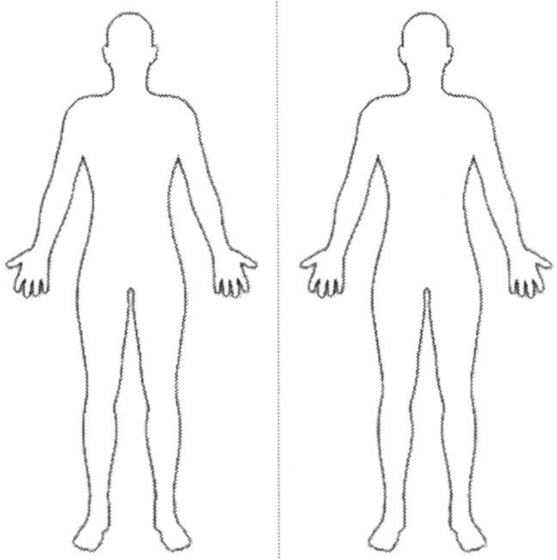

OTHER SYMPTOMS

general

Symptom	Severity	Time	
☐ Fatigue	① ② ③ ④ ⑤	☐ a.m.	☐ p.m.
☐ Lethargy	① ② ③ ④ ⑤	☐ a.m.	☐ p.m.
☐ Malaise	① ② ③ ④ ⑤	☐ a.m.	☐ p.m.
☐ Weakness	① ② ③ ④ ⑤	☐ a.m.	☐ p.m.
☐ Dizziness	① ② ③ ④ ⑤	☐ a.m.	☐ p.m.
☐ Trembling	① ② ③ ④ ⑤	☐ a.m.	☐ p.m.
☐ Twitching	① ② ③ ④ ⑤	☐ a.m.	☐ p.m.
☐ Insomnia	① ② ③ ④ ⑤	☐ a.m.	☐ p.m.

illness

Symptom	Severity	Time	
☐ Nausea	① ② ③ ④ ⑤	☐ a.m.	☐ p.m.
☐ Vomiting	① ② ③ ④ ⑤	☐ a.m.	☐ p.m.
☐ Constipation	① ② ③ ④ ⑤	☐ a.m.	☐ p.m.
☐ Diarrhea	① ② ③ ④ ⑤	☐ a.m.	☐ p.m.
☐ Sore throat	① ② ③ ④ ⑤	☐ a.m.	☐ p.m.
☐ Congestion	① ② ③ ④ ⑤	☐ a.m.	☐ p.m.
☐ Coughing	① ② ③ ④ ⑤	☐ a.m.	☐ p.m.
☐ Acid reflux	① ② ③ ④ ⑤	☐ a.m.	☐ p.m.

psychological

Symptom	Severity	Time	
☐ Anxiety	① ② ③ ④ ⑤	☐ a.m.	☐ p.m.
☐ Depression	① ② ③ ④ ⑤	☐ a.m.	☐ p.m.
☐ Memory loss	① ② ③ ④ ⑤	☐ a.m.	☐ p.m.
☐ Confusion	① ② ③ ④ ⑤	☐ a.m.	☐ p.m.
☐ Poor focus	① ② ③ ④ ⑤	☐ a.m.	☐ p.m.
☐ Mood swings	① ② ③ ④ ⑤	☐ a.m.	☐ p.m.
☐ Suicidal	① ② ③ ④ ⑤	☐ a.m.	☐ p.m.

other

Symptom	Severity	Time	
	① ② ③ ④ ⑤	☐ a.m.	☐ p.m.
	① ② ③ ④ ⑤	☐ a.m.	☐ p.m.
	① ② ③ ④ ⑤	☐ a.m.	☐ p.m.
	① ② ③ ④ ⑤	☐ a.m.	☐ p.m.
	① ② ③ ④ ⑤	☐ a.m.	☐ p.m.
	① ② ③ ④ ⑤	☐ a.m.	☐ p.m.
	① ② ③ ④ ⑤	☐ a.m.	☐ p.m.

SLEEP

hours ________ quality ① ② ③ ④ ⑤

STRESS LEVELS

None	Low	Medium	High	Max	@$#%!

WEATHER

☐ Cold ☐ Mild ☐ Hot
☐ Dry ☐ Humid ☐ Wet
Allergen Levels: ________
BM Pressure: ________

EXERCISE

☐ Heck yes, I worked out.
☐ I managed to exercise a bit.
☐ No, I haven't exercised at all.
☐ I did some stuff, and that counts.

DETAILS

FOOD / MEDICATION

Food / Drinks

Meds / Supplements	Time	Dose

☐ usual daily medication

Water | Caffeine | Alcohol

x ________ x ________

FOOD ANALYSIS

New food introduced?
☐ Yes ☐ No
Food reintroduction?
☐ Yes ☐ No
Details

MEDICATION ANALYSIS

New med/dose introduced?
☐ Yes ☐ No
Medication stopped?
☐ Yes ☐ No
Details

ACTIVITY ANALYSIS

Heightened exertion levels?
☐ Yes ☐ No
Lowered exertion levels?
☐ Yes ☐ No
Details

SLEEP ANALYSIS

When you woke up this morning, did you feel well-rested? ☐ Yes ☐ No ☐ A bit
Did you snore or stop breathing throughout the night? ☐ Yes ☐ No ☐ Not sure
Roughly how many times did you wake up throughout the night?

Notes / Suspected Triggers

ENTRY #54 | M T W T F S S | DATE:

HOW ARE YOU *Feeling today?*

Amazing!	Meh
Great	Not good
Good	Terrible!

RATE YOUR PAIN LEVEL

① ② ③ ④ ⑤ ⑥ ⑦ ⑧ ⑨ ⑩

WHAT ABOUT YOUR...?

Mood	① ② ③ ④ ⑤ ⑥ ⑦ ⑧ ⑨ ⑩
Energy Levels	① ② ③ ④ ⑤ ⑥ ⑦ ⑧ ⑨ ⑩
Mental Clarity	① ② ③ ④ ⑤ ⑥ ⑦ ⑧ ⑨ ⑩

PAIN & PHYSICAL SYMPTOMS

Symptom	Severity	am	pm
	① ② ③ ④ ⑤	☐	☐
	① ② ③ ④ ⑤	☐	☐
	① ② ③ ④ ⑤	☐	☐
	① ② ③ ④ ⑤	☐	☐
	① ② ③ ④ ⑤	☐	☐
	① ② ③ ④ ⑤	☐	☐
	① ② ③ ④ ⑤	☐	☐
	① ② ③ ④ ⑤	☐	☐

front ***back***

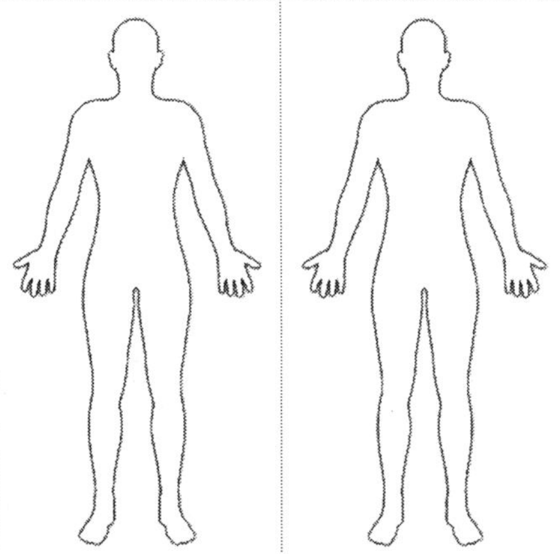

OTHER SYMPTOMS

general

Symptom	Severity	Time	
☐ Fatigue	① ② ③ ④ ⑤	☐ a.m.	☐ p.m.
☐ Lethargy	① ② ③ ④ ⑤	☐ a.m.	☐ p.m.
☐ Malaise	① ② ③ ④ ⑤	☐ a.m.	☐ p.m.
☐ Weakness	① ② ③ ④ ⑤	☐ a.m.	☐ p.m.
☐ Dizziness	① ② ③ ④ ⑤	☐ a.m.	☐ p.m.
☐ Trembling	① ② ③ ④ ⑤	☐ a.m.	☐ p.m.
☐ Twitching	① ② ③ ④ ⑤	☐ a.m.	☐ p.m.
☐ Insomnia	① ② ③ ④ ⑤	☐ a.m.	☐ p.m.

illness

Symptom	Severity	Time	
☐ Nausea	① ② ③ ④ ⑤	☐ a.m.	☐ p.m.
☐ Vomiting	① ② ③ ④ ⑤	☐ a.m.	☐ p.m.
☐ Constipation	① ② ③ ④ ⑤	☐ a.m.	☐ p.m.
☐ Diarrhea	① ② ③ ④ ⑤	☐ a.m.	☐ p.m.
☐ Sore throat	① ② ③ ④ ⑤	☐ a.m.	☐ p.m.
☐ Congestion	① ② ③ ④ ⑤	☐ a.m.	☐ p.m.
☐ Coughing	① ② ③ ④ ⑤	☐ a.m.	☐ p.m.
☐ Acid reflux	① ② ③ ④ ⑤	☐ a.m.	☐ p.m.

psychological

Symptom	Severity	Time	
☐ Anxiety	① ② ③ ④ ⑤	☐ a.m.	☐ p.m.
☐ Depression	① ② ③ ④ ⑤	☐ a.m.	☐ p.m.
☐ Memory loss	① ② ③ ④ ⑤	☐ a.m.	☐ p.m.
☐ Confusion	① ② ③ ④ ⑤	☐ a.m.	☐ p.m.
☐ Poor focus	① ② ③ ④ ⑤	☐ a.m.	☐ p.m.
☐ Mood swings	① ② ③ ④ ⑤	☐ a.m.	☐ p.m.
☐ Suicidal	① ② ③ ④ ⑤	☐ a.m.	☐ p.m.

other

Symptom	Severity	Time	
	① ② ③ ④ ⑤	☐ a.m.	☐ p.m.
	① ② ③ ④ ⑤	☐ a.m.	☐ p.m.
	① ② ③ ④ ⑤	☐ a.m.	☐ p.m.
	① ② ③ ④ ⑤	☐ a.m.	☐ p.m.
	① ② ③ ④ ⑤	☐ a.m.	☐ p.m.
	① ② ③ ④ ⑤	☐ a.m.	☐ p.m.
	① ② ③ ④ ⑤	☐ a.m.	☐ p.m.

SLEEP

hours ________ *quality* ① ② ③ ④ ⑤

STRESS LEVELS

None	Low	Medium	High	Max	@$#%!

WEATHER

☐ Cold ☐ Mild ☐ Hot
☐ Dry ☐ Humid ☐ Wet

Allergen Levels: ________
BM Pressure: ________

EXERCISE

☐ Heck yes, I worked out.
☐ I managed to exercise a bit.
☐ No, I haven't exercised at all.
☐ I did some stuff, and that counts.

DETAILS

FOOD / MEDICATION

Food / Drinks

Meds / Supplements	Time	Dose

☐ usual daily medication

Water	*Caffeine*	*Alcohol*
	x ________	x ________

FOOD ANALYSIS

New food introduced?
☐ Yes ☐ No

Food reintroduction?
☐ Yes ☐ No

Details

MEDICATION ANALYSIS

New med/dose introduced?
☐ Yes ☐ No

Medication stopped?
☐ Yes ☐ No

Details

ACTIVITY ANALYSIS

Heightened exertion levels?
☐ Yes ☐ No

Lowered exertion levels?
☐ Yes ☐ No

Details

SLEEP ANALYSIS

When you woke up this morning, did you feel well-rested?	☐ Yes	☐ No	☐ A bit
Did you snore or stop breathing throughout the night?	☐ Yes	☐ No	☐ Not sure
Roughly how many times did you wake up throughout the night?			

Notes / Suspected Triggers

ENTRY #55 | M T W T F S S | DATE:

HOW ARE YOU *Feeling today?*

Amazing!	Meh
Great	Not good
Good	Terrible!

RATE YOUR PAIN LEVEL

① ② ③ ④ ⑤ ⑥ ⑦ ⑧ ⑨ ⑩

WHAT ABOUT YOUR...?

Mood	① ② ③ ④ ⑤ ⑥ ⑦ ⑧ ⑨ ⑩
Energy Levels	① ② ③ ④ ⑤ ⑥ ⑦ ⑧ ⑨ ⑩
Mental Clarity	① ② ③ ④ ⑤ ⑥ ⑦ ⑧ ⑨ ⑩

PAIN & PHYSICAL SYMPTOMS

Symptom	Severity	am	pm
	① ② ③ ④ ⑤	☐	☐
	① ② ③ ④ ⑤	☐	☐
	① ② ③ ④ ⑤	☐	☐
	① ② ③ ④ ⑤	☐	☐
	① ② ③ ④ ⑤	☐	☐
	① ② ③ ④ ⑤	☐	☐
	① ② ③ ④ ⑤	☐	☐
	① ② ③ ④ ⑤	☐	☐

front ***back***

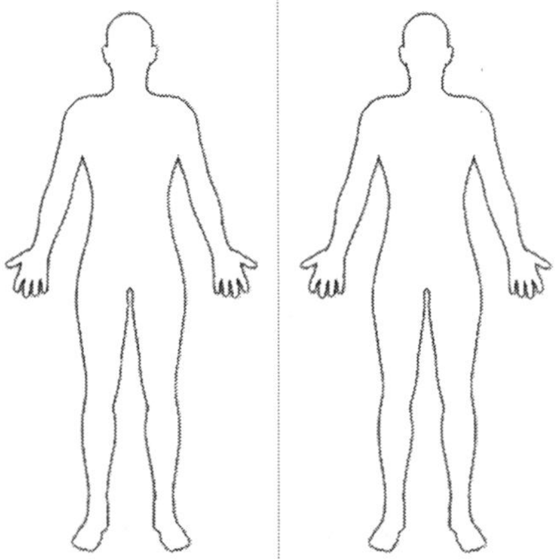

OTHER SYMPTOMS

general

Symptom	Severity	Time	
☐ Fatigue	① ② ③ ④ ⑤	☐ a.m.	☐ p.m.
☐ Lethargy	① ② ③ ④ ⑤	☐ a.m.	☐ p.m.
☐ Malaise	① ② ③ ④ ⑤	☐ a.m.	☐ p.m.
☐ Weakness	① ② ③ ④ ⑤	☐ a.m.	☐ p.m.
☐ Dizziness	① ② ③ ④ ⑤	☐ a.m.	☐ p.m.
☐ Trembling	① ② ③ ④ ⑤	☐ a.m.	☐ p.m.
☐ Twitching	① ② ③ ④ ⑤	☐ a.m.	☐ p.m.
☐ Insomnia	① ② ③ ④ ⑤	☐ a.m.	☐ p.m.

illness

Symptom	Severity	Time	
☐ Nausea	① ② ③ ④ ⑤	☐ a.m.	☐ p.m.
☐ Vomiting	① ② ③ ④ ⑤	☐ a.m.	☐ p.m.
☐ Constipation	① ② ③ ④ ⑤	☐ a.m.	☐ p.m.
☐ Diarrhea	① ② ③ ④ ⑤	☐ a.m.	☐ p.m.
☐ Sore throat	① ② ③ ④ ⑤	☐ a.m.	☐ p.m.
☐ Congestion	① ② ③ ④ ⑤	☐ a.m.	☐ p.m.
☐ Coughing	① ② ③ ④ ⑤	☐ a.m.	☐ p.m.
☐ Acid reflux	① ② ③ ④ ⑤	☐ a.m.	☐ p.m.

psychological

Symptom	Severity	Time	
☐ Anxiety	① ② ③ ④ ⑤	☐ a.m.	☐ p.m.
☐ Depression	① ② ③ ④ ⑤	☐ a.m.	☐ p.m.
☐ Memory loss	① ② ③ ④ ⑤	☐ a.m.	☐ p.m.
☐ Confusion	① ② ③ ④ ⑤	☐ a.m.	☐ p.m.
☐ Poor focus	① ② ③ ④ ⑤	☐ a.m.	☐ p.m.
☐ Mood swings	① ② ③ ④ ⑤	☐ a.m.	☐ p.m.
☐ Suicidal	① ② ③ ④ ⑤	☐ a.m.	☐ p.m.

other

Symptom	Severity	Time	
	① ② ③ ④ ⑤	☐ a.m.	☐ p.m.
	① ② ③ ④ ⑤	☐ a.m.	☐ p.m.
	① ② ③ ④ ⑤	☐ a.m.	☐ p.m.
	① ② ③ ④ ⑤	☐ a.m.	☐ p.m.
	① ② ③ ④ ⑤	☐ a.m.	☐ p.m.
	① ② ③ ④ ⑤	☐ a.m.	☐ p.m.
	① ② ③ ④ ⑤	☐ a.m.	☐ p.m.

SLEEP

hours ________ *quality* ① ② ③ ④ ⑤

STRESS LEVELS

None	Low	Medium	High	Max	@$#%!

WEATHER

☐ Cold ☐ Mild ☐ Hot
☐ Dry ☐ Humid ☐ Wet

Allergen Levels: ________
BM Pressure: ________

EXERCISE

☐ Heck yes, I worked out.
☐ I managed to exercise a bit.
☐ No, I haven't exercised at all.
☐ I did some stuff, and that counts.

DETAILS

FOOD / MEDICATION

Food / Drinks

Meds / Supplements	Time	Dose

☐ usual daily medication

Water *Caffeine* *Alcohol*

x ________ x ________

FOOD ANALYSIS

New food introduced?
☐ Yes ☐ No
Food reintroduction?
☐ Yes ☐ No
Details

MEDICATION ANALYSIS

New med/dose introduced?
☐ Yes ☐ No
Medication stopped?
☐ Yes ☐ No
Details

ACTIVITY ANALYSIS

Heightened exertion levels?
☐ Yes ☐ No
Lowered exertion levels?
☐ Yes ☐ No
Details

SLEEP ANALYSIS

When you woke up this morning, did you feel well-rested? ☐ Yes ☐ No ☐ A bit
Did you snore or stop breathing throughout the night? ☐ Yes ☐ No ☐ Not sure
Roughly how many times did you wake up throughout the night?

Notes / Suspected Triggers

ENTRY #56 | M T W T F S S | DATE:

HOW ARE YOU *Feeling today?*

Amazing!	Meh
Great	Not good
Good	Terrible!

RATE YOUR PAIN LEVEL

① ② ③ ④ ⑤ ⑥ ⑦ ⑧ ⑨ ⑩

WHAT ABOUT YOUR...?

Mood	① ② ③ ④ ⑤ ⑥ ⑦ ⑧ ⑨ ⑩
Energy Levels	① ② ③ ④ ⑤ ⑥ ⑦ ⑧ ⑨ ⑩
Mental Clarity	① ② ③ ④ ⑤ ⑥ ⑦ ⑧ ⑨ ⑩

PAIN & PHYSICAL SYMPTOMS

Symptom	Severity	am	pm
	① ② ③ ④ ⑤	☐	☐
	① ② ③ ④ ⑤	☐	☐
	① ② ③ ④ ⑤	☐	☐
	① ② ③ ④ ⑤	☐	☐
	① ② ③ ④ ⑤	☐	☐
	① ② ③ ④ ⑤	☐	☐
	① ② ③ ④ ⑤	☐	☐
	① ② ③ ④ ⑤	☐	☐

front *back*

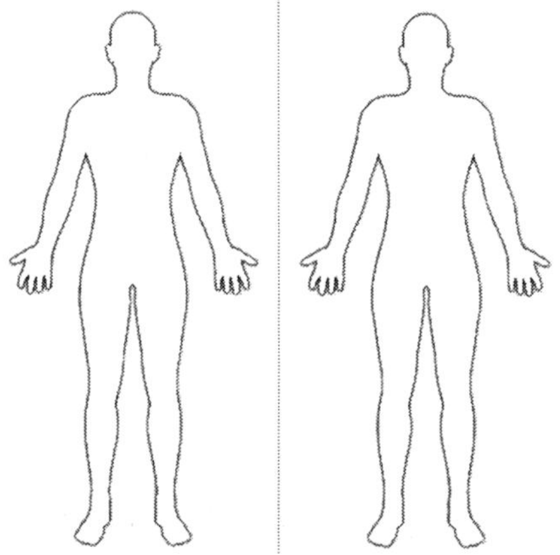

OTHER SYMPTOMS

general

Symptom	Severity	Time	
☐ Fatigue	① ② ③ ④ ⑤	☐ a.m.	☐ p.m.
☐ Lethargy	① ② ③ ④ ⑤	☐ a.m.	☐ p.m.
☐ Malaise	① ② ③ ④ ⑤	☐ a.m.	☐ p.m.
☐ Weakness	① ② ③ ④ ⑤	☐ a.m.	☐ p.m.
☐ Dizziness	① ② ③ ④ ⑤	☐ a.m.	☐ p.m.
☐ Trembling	① ② ③ ④ ⑤	☐ a.m.	☐ p.m.
☐ Twitching	① ② ③ ④ ⑤	☐ a.m.	☐ p.m.
☐ Insomnia	① ② ③ ④ ⑤	☐ a.m.	☐ p.m.

illness

Symptom	Severity	Time	
☐ Nausea	① ② ③ ④ ⑤	☐ a.m.	☐ p.m.
☐ Vomiting	① ② ③ ④ ⑤	☐ a.m.	☐ p.m.
☐ Constipation	① ② ③ ④ ⑤	☐ a.m.	☐ p.m.
☐ Diarrhea	① ② ③ ④ ⑤	☐ a.m.	☐ p.m.
☐ Sore throat	① ② ③ ④ ⑤	☐ a.m.	☐ p.m.
☐ Congestion	① ② ③ ④ ⑤	☐ a.m.	☐ p.m.
☐ Coughing	① ② ③ ④ ⑤	☐ a.m.	☐ p.m.
☐ Acid reflux	① ② ③ ④ ⑤	☐ a.m.	☐ p.m.

psychological

Symptom	Severity	Time	
☐ Anxiety	① ② ③ ④ ⑤	☐ a.m.	☐ p.m.
☐ Depression	① ② ③ ④ ⑤	☐ a.m.	☐ p.m.
☐ Memory loss	① ② ③ ④ ⑤	☐ a.m.	☐ p.m.
☐ Confusion	① ② ③ ④ ⑤	☐ a.m.	☐ p.m.
☐ Poor focus	① ② ③ ④ ⑤	☐ a.m.	☐ p.m.
☐ Mood swings	① ② ③ ④ ⑤	☐ a.m.	☐ p.m.
☐ Suicidal	① ② ③ ④ ⑤	☐ a.m.	☐ p.m.

other

Symptom	Severity	Time	
	① ② ③ ④ ⑤	☐ a.m.	☐ p.m.
	① ② ③ ④ ⑤	☐ a.m.	☐ p.m.
	① ② ③ ④ ⑤	☐ a.m.	☐ p.m.
	① ② ③ ④ ⑤	☐ a.m.	☐ p.m.
	① ② ③ ④ ⑤	☐ a.m.	☐ p.m.
	① ② ③ ④ ⑤	☐ a.m.	☐ p.m.
	① ② ③ ④ ⑤	☐ a.m.	☐ p.m.

SLEEP

hours ________ *quality* ① ② ③ ④ ⑤

STRESS LEVELS

None	Low	Medium	High	Max	@$#%!

WEATHER

☐ Cold ☐ Mild ☐ Hot
☐ Dry ☐ Humid ☐ Wet

Allergen Levels: ________

BM Pressure: ________

EXERCISE

☐ Heck yes, I worked out.
☐ I managed to exercise a bit.
☐ No, I haven't exercised at all.
☐ I did some stuff, and that counts.

DETAILS

FOOD / MEDICATION

Food / Drinks

Meds / Supplements	Time	Dose
☐ usual daily medication		

Water	*Caffeine*	*Alcohol*
☐☐☐☐☐☐☐☐☐☐	x ________	x ________

FOOD ANALYSIS

New food introduced?

☐ Yes ☐ No

Food reintroduction?

☐ Yes ☐ No

Details

MEDICATION ANALYSIS

New med/dose introduced?

☐ Yes ☐ No

Medication stopped?

☐ Yes ☐ No

Details

ACTIVITY ANALYSIS

Heightened exertion levels?

☐ Yes ☐ No

Lowered exertion levels?

☐ Yes ☐ No

Details

SLEEP ANALYSIS

When you woke up this morning, did you feel well-rested?	☐ Yes	☐ No	☐ A bit
Did you snore or stop breathing throughout the night?	☐ Yes	☐ No	☐ Not sure
Roughly how many times did you wake up throughout the night?			

Notes / Suspected Triggers

ENTRY #57 | M T W T F S S | DATE:

HOW ARE YOU *Feeling today?*

Amazing!	Meh
Great	Not good
Good	Terrible!

RATE YOUR PAIN LEVEL

① ② ③ ④ ⑤ ⑥ ⑦ ⑧ ⑨ ⑩

WHAT ABOUT YOUR...?

Mood	① ② ③ ④ ⑤ ⑥ ⑦ ⑧ ⑨ ⑩
Energy Levels	① ② ③ ④ ⑤ ⑥ ⑦ ⑧ ⑨ ⑩
Mental Clarity	① ② ③ ④ ⑤ ⑥ ⑦ ⑧ ⑨ ⑩

PAIN & PHYSICAL SYMPTOMS

Symptom	Severity	am	pm
	① ② ③ ④ ⑤	☐	☐
	① ② ③ ④ ⑤	☐	☐
	① ② ③ ④ ⑤	☐	☐
	① ② ③ ④ ⑤	☐	☐
	① ② ③ ④ ⑤	☐	☐
	① ② ③ ④ ⑤	☐	☐
	① ② ③ ④ ⑤	☐	☐
	① ② ③ ④ ⑤	☐	☐

front ***back***

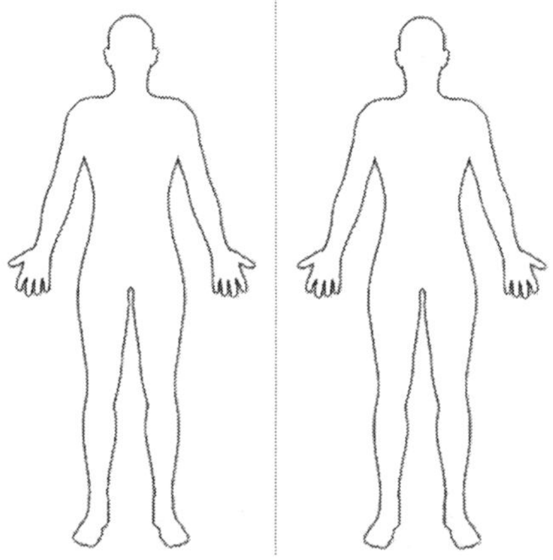

OTHER SYMPTOMS

general

Symptom	Severity	Time	
☐ Fatigue	① ② ③ ④ ⑤	☐ a.m.	☐ p.m.
☐ Lethargy	① ② ③ ④ ⑤	☐ a.m.	☐ p.m.
☐ Malaise	① ② ③ ④ ⑤	☐ a.m.	☐ p.m.
☐ Weakness	① ② ③ ④ ⑤	☐ a.m.	☐ p.m.
☐ Dizziness	① ② ③ ④ ⑤	☐ a.m.	☐ p.m.
☐ Trembling	① ② ③ ④ ⑤	☐ a.m.	☐ p.m.
☐ Twitching	① ② ③ ④ ⑤	☐ a.m.	☐ p.m.
☐ Insomnia	① ② ③ ④ ⑤	☐ a.m.	☐ p.m.

illness

Symptom	Severity	Time	
☐ Nausea	① ② ③ ④ ⑤	☐ a.m.	☐ p.m.
☐ Vomiting	① ② ③ ④ ⑤	☐ a.m.	☐ p.m.
☐ Constipation	① ② ③ ④ ⑤	☐ a.m.	☐ p.m.
☐ Diarrhea	① ② ③ ④ ⑤	☐ a.m.	☐ p.m.
☐ Sore throat	① ② ③ ④ ⑤	☐ a.m.	☐ p.m.
☐ Congestion	① ② ③ ④ ⑤	☐ a.m.	☐ p.m.
☐ Coughing	① ② ③ ④ ⑤	☐ a.m.	☐ p.m.
☐ Acid reflux	① ② ③ ④ ⑤	☐ a.m.	☐ p.m.

psychological

Symptom	Severity	Time	
☐ Anxiety	① ② ③ ④ ⑤	☐ a.m.	☐ p.m.
☐ Depression	① ② ③ ④ ⑤	☐ a.m.	☐ p.m.
☐ Memory loss	① ② ③ ④ ⑤	☐ a.m.	☐ p.m.
☐ Confusion	① ② ③ ④ ⑤	☐ a.m.	☐ p.m.
☐ Poor focus	① ② ③ ④ ⑤	☐ a.m.	☐ p.m.
☐ Mood swings	① ② ③ ④ ⑤	☐ a.m.	☐ p.m.
☐ Suicidal	① ② ③ ④ ⑤	☐ a.m.	☐ p.m.

other

Symptom	Severity	Time	
	① ② ③ ④ ⑤	☐ a.m.	☐ p.m.
	① ② ③ ④ ⑤	☐ a.m.	☐ p.m.
	① ② ③ ④ ⑤	☐ a.m.	☐ p.m.
	① ② ③ ④ ⑤	☐ a.m.	☐ p.m.
	① ② ③ ④ ⑤	☐ a.m.	☐ p.m.
	① ② ③ ④ ⑤	☐ a.m.	☐ p.m.
	① ② ③ ④ ⑤	☐ a.m.	☐ p.m.

SLEEP

hours ________ *quality* ① ② ③ ④ ⑤

STRESS LEVELS

None	Low	Medium	High	Max	@$#%!

WEATHER

☐ Cold ☐ Mild ☐ Hot
☐ Dry ☐ Humid ☐ Wet

Allergen Levels: ________

BM Pressure: ________

EXERCISE

☐ Heck yes, I worked out.
☐ I managed to exercise a bit.
☐ No, I haven't exercised at all.
☐ I did some stuff, and that counts.

DETAILS

FOOD / MEDICATION

Food / Drinks

Meds / Supplements	Time	Dose

☐ usual daily medication

Water	*Caffeine*	*Alcohol*
	x ________	x ________

FOOD ANALYSIS

New food introduced?

☐ Yes ☐ No

Food reintroduction?

☐ Yes ☐ No

Details

MEDICATION ANALYSIS

New med/dose introduced?

☐ Yes ☐ No

Medication stopped?

☐ Yes ☐ No

Details

ACTIVITY ANALYSIS

Heightened exertion levels?

☐ Yes ☐ No

Lowered exertion levels?

☐ Yes ☐ No

Details

SLEEP ANALYSIS

When you woke up this morning, did you feel well-rested?	☐ Yes	☐ No	☐ A bit
Did you snore or stop breathing throughout the night?	☐ Yes	☐ No	☐ Not sure
Roughly how many times did you wake up throughout the night?			

Notes / Suspected Triggers

ENTRY #58	M T W T F S S	DATE:

HOW ARE YOU *Feeling today?*

Amazing!	Meh
Great	Not good
Good	Terrible!

RATE YOUR PAIN LEVEL

① ② ③ ④ ⑤ ⑥ ⑦ ⑧ ⑨ ⑩

WHAT ABOUT YOUR...?

Mood	① ② ③ ④ ⑤ ⑥ ⑦ ⑧ ⑨ ⑩
Energy Levels	① ② ③ ④ ⑤ ⑥ ⑦ ⑧ ⑨ ⑩
Mental Clarity	① ② ③ ④ ⑤ ⑥ ⑦ ⑧ ⑨ ⑩

PAIN & PHYSICAL SYMPTOMS

Symptom	Severity	am	pm
	① ② ③ ④ ⑤	☐	☐
	① ② ③ ④ ⑤	☐	☐
	① ② ③ ④ ⑤	☐	☐
	① ② ③ ④ ⑤	☐	☐
	① ② ③ ④ ⑤	☐	☐
	① ② ③ ④ ⑤	☐	☐
	① ② ③ ④ ⑤	☐	☐
	① ② ③ ④ ⑤	☐	☐

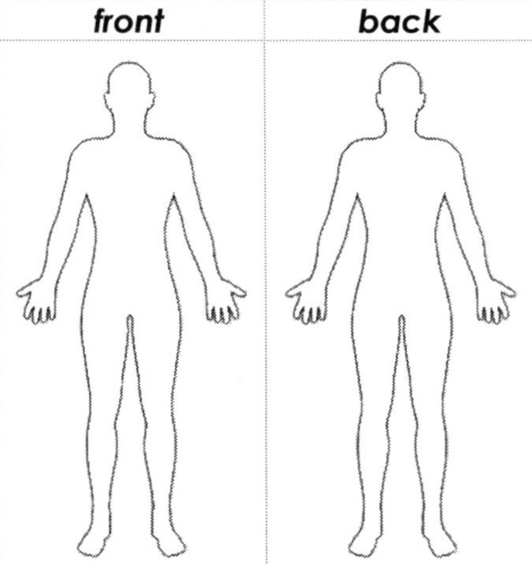

OTHER SYMPTOMS

general

Symptom	Severity	Time	
☐ Fatigue	① ② ③ ④ ⑤	☐ a.m.	☐ p.m.
☐ Lethargy	① ② ③ ④ ⑤	☐ a.m.	☐ p.m.
☐ Malaise	① ② ③ ④ ⑤	☐ a.m.	☐ p.m.
☐ Weakness	① ② ③ ④ ⑤	☐ a.m.	☐ p.m.
☐ Dizziness	① ② ③ ④ ⑤	☐ a.m.	☐ p.m.
☐ Trembling	① ② ③ ④ ⑤	☐ a.m.	☐ p.m.
☐ Twitching	① ② ③ ④ ⑤	☐ a.m.	☐ p.m.
☐ Insomnia	① ② ③ ④ ⑤	☐ a.m.	☐ p.m.

illness

Symptom	Severity	Time	
☐ Nausea	① ② ③ ④ ⑤	☐ a.m.	☐ p.m.
☐ Vomiting	① ② ③ ④ ⑤	☐ a.m.	☐ p.m.
☐ Constipation	① ② ③ ④ ⑤	☐ a.m.	☐ p.m.
☐ Diarrhea	① ② ③ ④ ⑤	☐ a.m.	☐ p.m.
☐ Sore throat	① ② ③ ④ ⑤	☐ a.m.	☐ p.m.
☐ Congestion	① ② ③ ④ ⑤	☐ a.m.	☐ p.m.
☐ Coughing	① ② ③ ④ ⑤	☐ a.m.	☐ p.m.
☐ Acid reflux	① ② ③ ④ ⑤	☐ a.m.	☐ p.m.

psychological

Symptom	Severity	Time	
☐ Anxiety	① ② ③ ④ ⑤	☐ a.m.	☐ p.m.
☐ Depression	① ② ③ ④ ⑤	☐ a.m.	☐ p.m.
☐ Memory loss	① ② ③ ④ ⑤	☐ a.m.	☐ p.m.
☐ Confusion	① ② ③ ④ ⑤	☐ a.m.	☐ p.m.
☐ Poor focus	① ② ③ ④ ⑤	☐ a.m.	☐ p.m.
☐ Mood swings	① ② ③ ④ ⑤	☐ a.m.	☐ p.m.
☐ Suicidal	① ② ③ ④ ⑤	☐ a.m.	☐ p.m.

other

Symptom	Severity	Time	
	① ② ③ ④ ⑤	☐ a.m.	☐ p.m.
	① ② ③ ④ ⑤	☐ a.m.	☐ p.m.
	① ② ③ ④ ⑤	☐ a.m.	☐ p.m.
	① ② ③ ④ ⑤	☐ a.m.	☐ p.m.
	① ② ③ ④ ⑤	☐ a.m.	☐ p.m.
	① ② ③ ④ ⑤	☐ a.m.	☐ p.m.
	① ② ③ ④ ⑤	☐ a.m.	☐ p.m.

SLEEP

hours ________ quality ① ② ③ ④ ⑤

STRESS LEVELS

None	Low	Medium	High	Max	@$#%!

WEATHER

☐ Cold ☐ Mild ☐ Hot
☐ Dry ☐ Humid ☐ Wet

Allergen Levels: ________

BM Pressure: ________

EXERCISE

☐ Heck yes, I worked out.
☐ I managed to exercise a bit.
☐ No, I haven't exercised at all.
☐ I did some stuff, and that counts.

DETAILS

FOOD / MEDICATION

Food / Drinks

Meds / Supplements	Time	Dose

☐ usual daily medication

Water	Caffeine	Alcohol
	x ________	x ________

FOOD ANALYSIS

New food introduced?
☐ Yes ☐ No

Food reintroduction?
☐ Yes ☐ No

Details

MEDICATION ANALYSIS

New med/dose introduced?
☐ Yes ☐ No

Medication stopped?
☐ Yes ☐ No

Details

ACTIVITY ANALYSIS

Heightened exertion levels?
☐ Yes ☐ No

Lowered exertion levels?
☐ Yes ☐ No

Details

SLEEP ANALYSIS

When you woke up this morning, did you feel well-rested?	☐ Yes	☐ No	☐ A bit
Did you snore or stop breathing throughout the night?	☐ Yes	☐ No	☐ Not sure
Roughly how many times did you wake up throughout the night?			

Notes / Suspected Triggers

ENTRY #59 | M T W T F S S | DATE:

HOW ARE YOU *Feeling today?*

Amazing!	Meh
Great	Not good
Good	Terrible!

RATE YOUR PAIN LEVEL

① ② ③ ④ ⑤ ⑥ ⑦ ⑧ ⑨ ⑩

WHAT ABOUT YOUR...?

Mood	① ② ③ ④ ⑤ ⑥ ⑦ ⑧ ⑨ ⑩
Energy Levels	① ② ③ ④ ⑤ ⑥ ⑦ ⑧ ⑨ ⑩
Mental Clarity	① ② ③ ④ ⑤ ⑥ ⑦ ⑧ ⑨ ⑩

PAIN & PHYSICAL SYMPTOMS

Symptom	Severity	am	pm
	① ② ③ ④ ⑤	☐	☐
	① ② ③ ④ ⑤	☐	☐
	① ② ③ ④ ⑤	☐	☐
	① ② ③ ④ ⑤	☐	☐
	① ② ③ ④ ⑤	☐	☐
	① ② ③ ④ ⑤	☐	☐
	① ② ③ ④ ⑤	☐	☐
	① ② ③ ④ ⑤	☐	☐

front

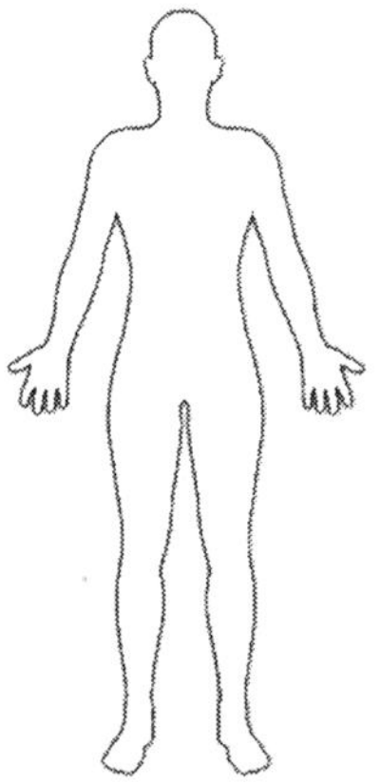

back

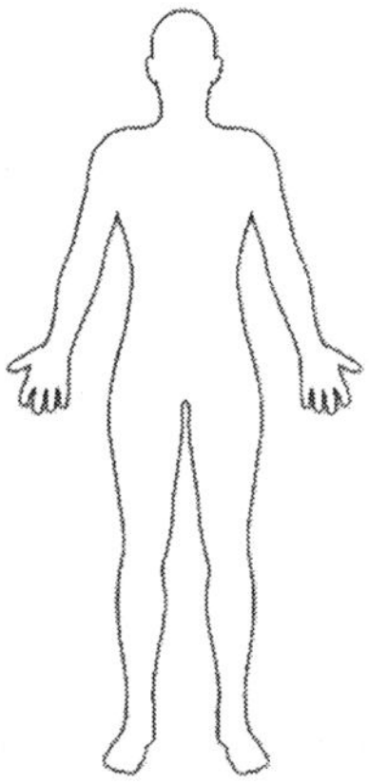

OTHER SYMPTOMS

general

Symptom	Severity	Time	
☐ Fatigue	① ② ③ ④ ⑤	☐ a.m.	☐ p.m.
☐ Lethargy	① ② ③ ④ ⑤	☐ a.m.	☐ p.m.
☐ Malaise	① ② ③ ④ ⑤	☐ a.m.	☐ p.m.
☐ Weakness	① ② ③ ④ ⑤	☐ a.m.	☐ p.m.
☐ Dizziness	① ② ③ ④ ⑤	☐ a.m.	☐ p.m.
☐ Trembling	① ② ③ ④ ⑤	☐ a.m.	☐ p.m.
☐ Twitching	① ② ③ ④ ⑤	☐ a.m.	☐ p.m.
☐ Insomnia	① ② ③ ④ ⑤	☐ a.m.	☐ p.m.

illness

Symptom	Severity	Time	
☐ Nausea	① ② ③ ④ ⑤	☐ a.m.	☐ p.m.
☐ Vomiting	① ② ③ ④ ⑤	☐ a.m.	☐ p.m.
☐ Constipation	① ② ③ ④ ⑤	☐ a.m.	☐ p.m.
☐ Diarrhea	① ② ③ ④ ⑤	☐ a.m.	☐ p.m.
☐ Sore throat	① ② ③ ④ ⑤	☐ a.m.	☐ p.m.
☐ Congestion	① ② ③ ④ ⑤	☐ a.m.	☐ p.m.
☐ Coughing	① ② ③ ④ ⑤	☐ a.m.	☐ p.m.
☐ Acid reflux	① ② ③ ④ ⑤	☐ a.m.	☐ p.m.

psychological

Symptom	Severity	Time	
☐ Anxiety	① ② ③ ④ ⑤	☐ a.m.	☐ p.m.
☐ Depression	① ② ③ ④ ⑤	☐ a.m.	☐ p.m.
☐ Memory loss	① ② ③ ④ ⑤	☐ a.m.	☐ p.m.
☐ Confusion	① ② ③ ④ ⑤	☐ a.m.	☐ p.m.
☐ Poor focus	① ② ③ ④ ⑤	☐ a.m.	☐ p.m.
☐ Mood swings	① ② ③ ④ ⑤	☐ a.m.	☐ p.m.
☐ Suicidal	① ② ③ ④ ⑤	☐ a.m.	☐ p.m.

other

Symptom	Severity	Time	
	① ② ③ ④ ⑤	☐ a.m.	☐ p.m.
	① ② ③ ④ ⑤	☐ a.m.	☐ p.m.
	① ② ③ ④ ⑤	☐ a.m.	☐ p.m.
	① ② ③ ④ ⑤	☐ a.m.	☐ p.m.
	① ② ③ ④ ⑤	☐ a.m.	☐ p.m.
	① ② ③ ④ ⑤	☐ a.m.	☐ p.m.
	① ② ③ ④ ⑤	☐ a.m.	☐ p.m.

SLEEP

hours ________ *quality* ① ② ③ ④ ⑤

STRESS LEVELS

None	Low	Medium	High	Max	@$#%!

WEATHER

☐ Cold ☐ Mild ☐ Hot

☐ Dry ☐ Humid ☐ Wet

Allergen Levels: ________

BM Pressure: ________

EXERCISE

☐ Heck yes, I worked out.

☐ I managed to exercise a bit.

☐ No, I haven't exercised at all.

☐ I did some stuff, and that counts.

DETAILS

FOOD / MEDICATION

Food / Drinks

Meds / Supplements	Time	Dose

☐ usual daily medication

Water *Caffeine* *Alcohol*

x ________ x ________

FOOD ANALYSIS

New food introduced?

☐ Yes ☐ No

Food reintroduction?

☐ Yes ☐ No

Details

MEDICATION ANALYSIS

New med/dose introduced?

☐ Yes ☐ No

Medication stopped?

☐ Yes ☐ No

Details

ACTIVITY ANALYSIS

Heightened exertion levels?

☐ Yes ☐ No

Lowered exertion levels?

☐ Yes ☐ No

Details

SLEEP ANALYSIS

When you woke up this morning, did you feel well-rested?	☐ Yes	☐ No	☐ A bit
Did you snore or stop breathing throughout the night?	☐ Yes	☐ No	☐ Not sure
Roughly how many times did you wake up throughout the night?			

Notes / Suspected Triggers

ENTRY #60 | M T W T F S S | DATE:

HOW ARE YOU *Feeling today?*

Amazing!	Meh
Great	Not good
Good	Terrible!

RATE YOUR PAIN LEVEL

① ② ③ ④ ⑤ ⑥ ⑦ ⑧ ⑨ ⑩

WHAT ABOUT YOUR...?

Mood	① ② ③ ④ ⑤ ⑥ ⑦ ⑧ ⑨ ⑩
Energy Levels	① ② ③ ④ ⑤ ⑥ ⑦ ⑧ ⑨ ⑩
Mental Clarity	① ② ③ ④ ⑤ ⑥ ⑦ ⑧ ⑨ ⑩

PAIN & PHYSICAL SYMPTOMS

Symptom	Severity	am	pm
	① ② ③ ④ ⑤	☐	☐
	① ② ③ ④ ⑤	☐	☐
	① ② ③ ④ ⑤	☐	☐
	① ② ③ ④ ⑤	☐	☐
	① ② ③ ④ ⑤	☐	☐
	① ② ③ ④ ⑤	☐	☐
	① ② ③ ④ ⑤	☐	☐
	① ② ③ ④ ⑤	☐	☐

front *back*

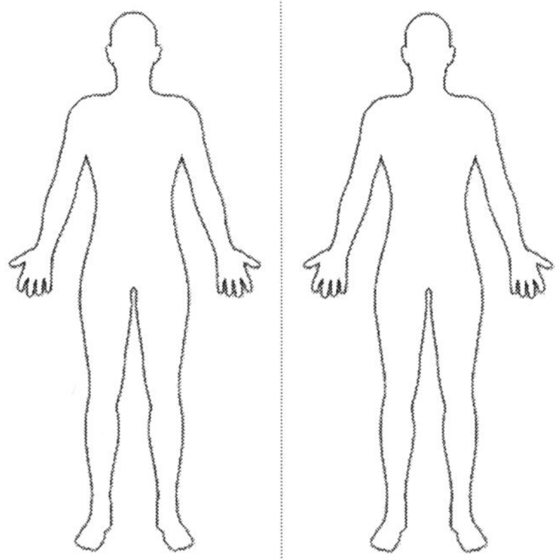

OTHER SYMPTOMS

general

Symptom	Severity	Time	
☐ Fatigue	① ② ③ ④ ⑤	☐ a.m.	☐ p.m.
☐ Lethargy	① ② ③ ④ ⑤	☐ a.m.	☐ p.m.
☐ Malaise	① ② ③ ④ ⑤	☐ a.m.	☐ p.m.
☐ Weakness	① ② ③ ④ ⑤	☐ a.m.	☐ p.m.
☐ Dizziness	① ② ③ ④ ⑤	☐ a.m.	☐ p.m.
☐ Trembling	① ② ③ ④ ⑤	☐ a.m.	☐ p.m.
☐ Twitching	① ② ③ ④ ⑤	☐ a.m.	☐ p.m.
☐ Insomnia	① ② ③ ④ ⑤	☐ a.m.	☐ p.m.

illness

Symptom	Severity	Time	
☐ Nausea	① ② ③ ④ ⑤	☐ a.m.	☐ p.m.
☐ Vomiting	① ② ③ ④ ⑤	☐ a.m.	☐ p.m.
☐ Constipation	① ② ③ ④ ⑤	☐ a.m.	☐ p.m.
☐ Diarrhea	① ② ③ ④ ⑤	☐ a.m.	☐ p.m.
☐ Sore throat	① ② ③ ④ ⑤	☐ a.m.	☐ p.m.
☐ Congestion	① ② ③ ④ ⑤	☐ a.m.	☐ p.m.
☐ Coughing	① ② ③ ④ ⑤	☐ a.m.	☐ p.m.
☐ Acid reflux	① ② ③ ④ ⑤	☐ a.m.	☐ p.m.

psychological

Symptom	Severity	Time	
☐ Anxiety	① ② ③ ④ ⑤	☐ a.m.	☐ p.m.
☐ Depression	① ② ③ ④ ⑤	☐ a.m.	☐ p.m.
☐ Memory loss	① ② ③ ④ ⑤	☐ a.m.	☐ p.m.
☐ Confusion	① ② ③ ④ ⑤	☐ a.m.	☐ p.m.
☐ Poor focus	① ② ③ ④ ⑤	☐ a.m.	☐ p.m.
☐ Mood swings	① ② ③ ④ ⑤	☐ a.m.	☐ p.m.
☐ Suicidal	① ② ③ ④ ⑤	☐ a.m.	☐ p.m.

other

Symptom	Severity	Time	
	① ② ③ ④ ⑤	☐ a.m.	☐ p.m.
	① ② ③ ④ ⑤	☐ a.m.	☐ p.m.
	① ② ③ ④ ⑤	☐ a.m.	☐ p.m.
	① ② ③ ④ ⑤	☐ a.m.	☐ p.m.
	① ② ③ ④ ⑤	☐ a.m.	☐ p.m.
	① ② ③ ④ ⑤	☐ a.m.	☐ p.m.
	① ② ③ ④ ⑤	☐ a.m.	☐ p.m.

SLEEP

hours ________ *quality* ① ② ③ ④ ⑤

STRESS LEVELS

None	Low	Medium	High	Max	@$#%!

WEATHER

☐ Cold ☐ Mild ☐ Hot
☐ Dry ☐ Humid ☐ Wet

Allergen Levels: ________
BM Pressure: ________

EXERCISE

☐ Heck yes, I worked out.
☐ I managed to exercise a bit.
☐ No, I haven't exercised at all.
☐ I did some stuff, and that counts.

DETAILS

FOOD / MEDICATION

Food / Drinks

Meds / Supplements	Time	Dose
☐ usual daily medication		

Water *Caffeine* x ________ *Alcohol* x ________

FOOD ANALYSIS		MEDICATION ANALYSIS		ACTIVITY ANALYSIS	
New food introduced?		New med/dose introduced?		Heightened exertion levels?	
☐ Yes	☐ No	☐ Yes	☐ No	☐ Yes	☐ No
Food reintroduction?		Medication stopped?		Lowered exertion levels?	
☐ Yes	☐ No	☐ Yes	☐ No	☐ Yes	☐ No
Details		*Details*		*Details*	

SLEEP ANALYSIS

When you woke up this morning, did you feel well-rested?	☐ Yes	☐ No	☐ A bit
Did you snore or stop breathing throughout the night?	☐ Yes	☐ No	☐ Not sure
Roughly how many times did you wake up throughout the night?			

Notes / Suspected Triggers

ENTRY #61 | M T W T F S S | DATE:

HOW ARE YOU *Feeling today?*

Amazing!	Meh
Great	Not good
Good	Terrible!

RATE YOUR PAIN LEVEL

① ② ③ ④ ⑤ ⑥ ⑦ ⑧ ⑨ ⑩

WHAT ABOUT YOUR...?

Mood	① ② ③ ④ ⑤ ⑥ ⑦ ⑧ ⑨ ⑩
Energy Levels	① ② ③ ④ ⑤ ⑥ ⑦ ⑧ ⑨ ⑩
Mental Clarity	① ② ③ ④ ⑤ ⑥ ⑦ ⑧ ⑨ ⑩

PAIN & PHYSICAL SYMPTOMS

Symptom	Severity	am	pm
	① ② ③ ④ ⑤	☐	☐
	① ② ③ ④ ⑤	☐	☐
	① ② ③ ④ ⑤	☐	☐
	① ② ③ ④ ⑤	☐	☐
	① ② ③ ④ ⑤	☐	☐
	① ② ③ ④ ⑤	☐	☐
	① ② ③ ④ ⑤	☐	☐
	① ② ③ ④ ⑤	☐	☐

front ***back***

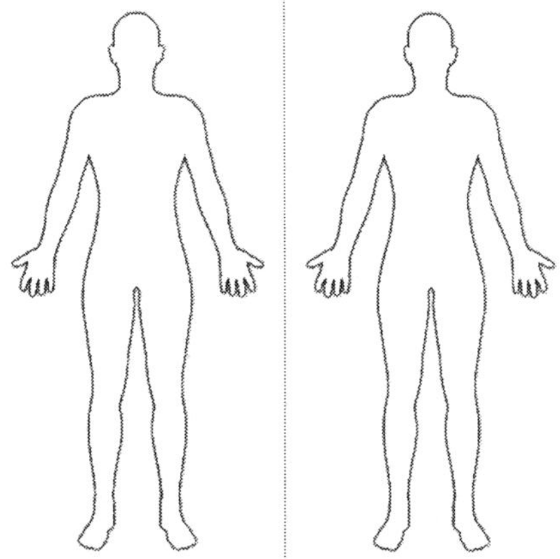

OTHER SYMPTOMS

general

Symptom	Severity	Time	
☐ Fatigue	① ② ③ ④ ⑤	☐ a.m.	☐ p.m.
☐ Lethargy	① ② ③ ④ ⑤	☐ a.m.	☐ p.m.
☐ Malaise	① ② ③ ④ ⑤	☐ a.m.	☐ p.m.
☐ Weakness	① ② ③ ④ ⑤	☐ a.m.	☐ p.m.
☐ Dizziness	① ② ③ ④ ⑤	☐ a.m.	☐ p.m.
☐ Trembling	① ② ③ ④ ⑤	☐ a.m.	☐ p.m.
☐ Twitching	① ② ③ ④ ⑤	☐ a.m.	☐ p.m.
☐ Insomnia	① ② ③ ④ ⑤	☐ a.m.	☐ p.m.

illness

Symptom	Severity	Time	
☐ Nausea	① ② ③ ④ ⑤	☐ a.m.	☐ p.m.
☐ Vomiting	① ② ③ ④ ⑤	☐ a.m.	☐ p.m.
☐ Constipation	① ② ③ ④ ⑤	☐ a.m.	☐ p.m.
☐ Diarrhea	① ② ③ ④ ⑤	☐ a.m.	☐ p.m.
☐ Sore throat	① ② ③ ④ ⑤	☐ a.m.	☐ p.m.
☐ Congestion	① ② ③ ④ ⑤	☐ a.m.	☐ p.m.
☐ Coughing	① ② ③ ④ ⑤	☐ a.m.	☐ p.m.
☐ Acid reflux	① ② ③ ④ ⑤	☐ a.m.	☐ p.m.

psychological

Symptom	Severity	Time	
☐ Anxiety	① ② ③ ④ ⑤	☐ a.m.	☐ p.m.
☐ Depression	① ② ③ ④ ⑤	☐ a.m.	☐ p.m.
☐ Memory loss	① ② ③ ④ ⑤	☐ a.m.	☐ p.m.
☐ Confusion	① ② ③ ④ ⑤	☐ a.m.	☐ p.m.
☐ Poor focus	① ② ③ ④ ⑤	☐ a.m.	☐ p.m.
☐ Mood swings	① ② ③ ④ ⑤	☐ a.m.	☐ p.m.
☐ Suicidal	① ② ③ ④ ⑤	☐ a.m.	☐ p.m.

other

Symptom	Severity	Time	
	① ② ③ ④ ⑤	☐ a.m.	☐ p.m.
	① ② ③ ④ ⑤	☐ a.m.	☐ p.m.
	① ② ③ ④ ⑤	☐ a.m.	☐ p.m.
	① ② ③ ④ ⑤	☐ a.m.	☐ p.m.
	① ② ③ ④ ⑤	☐ a.m.	☐ p.m.
	① ② ③ ④ ⑤	☐ a.m.	☐ p.m.
	① ② ③ ④ ⑤	☐ a.m.	☐ p.m.

SLEEP

hours ________ *quality* ① ② ③ ④ ⑤

STRESS LEVELS

None	Low	Medium	High	Max	@$#%!

WEATHER

☐ Cold ☐ Mild ☐ Hot

☐ Dry ☐ Humid ☐ Wet

Allergen Levels: ________

BM Pressure: ________

EXERCISE

☐ Heck yes, I worked out.

☐ I managed to exercise a bit.

☐ No, I haven't exercised at all.

☐ I did some stuff, and that counts.

DETAILS

FOOD / MEDICATION

Food / Drinks

Meds / Supplements	Time	Dose

☐ usual daily medication

Water *Caffeine* *Alcohol*

x ________ x ________

FOOD ANALYSIS

New food introduced?

☐ Yes ☐ No

Food reintroduction?

☐ Yes ☐ No

Details

MEDICATION ANALYSIS

New med/dose introduced?

☐ Yes ☐ No

Medication stopped?

☐ Yes ☐ No

Details

ACTIVITY ANALYSIS

Heightened exertion levels?

☐ Yes ☐ No

Lowered exertion levels?

☐ Yes ☐ No

Details

SLEEP ANALYSIS

When you woke up this morning, did you feel well-rested?	☐ Yes	☐ No	☐ A bit
Did you snore or stop breathing throughout the night?	☐ Yes	☐ No	☐ Not sure
Roughly how many times did you wake up throughout the night?			

Notes / Suspected Triggers

ENTRY #62 | M T W T F S S | DATE:

HOW ARE YOU *Feeling today?*

Amazing!	Meh
Great	Not good
Good	Terrible!

RATE YOUR PAIN LEVEL

① ② ③ ④ ⑤ ⑥ ⑦ ⑧ ⑨ ⑩

WHAT ABOUT YOUR...?

Mood	① ② ③ ④ ⑤ ⑥ ⑦ ⑧ ⑨ ⑩
Energy Levels	① ② ③ ④ ⑤ ⑥ ⑦ ⑧ ⑨ ⑩
Mental Clarity	① ② ③ ④ ⑤ ⑥ ⑦ ⑧ ⑨ ⑩

PAIN & PHYSICAL SYMPTOMS

Symptom	Severity	am	pm
	① ② ③ ④ ⑤	☐	☐
	① ② ③ ④ ⑤	☐	☐
	① ② ③ ④ ⑤	☐	☐
	① ② ③ ④ ⑤	☐	☐
	① ② ③ ④ ⑤	☐	☐
	① ② ③ ④ ⑤	☐	☐
	① ② ③ ④ ⑤	☐	☐
	① ② ③ ④ ⑤	☐	☐

front *back*

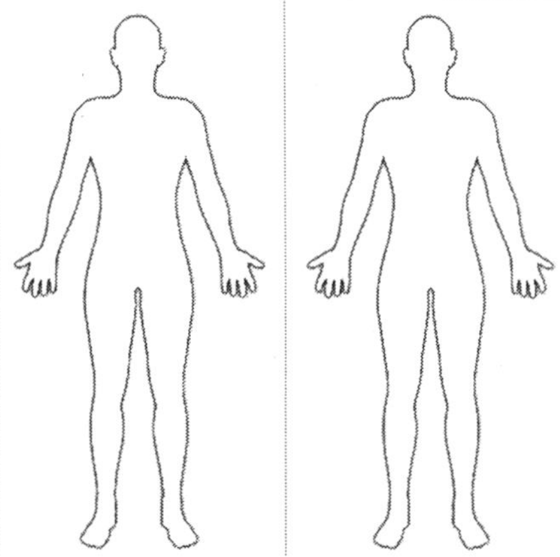

OTHER SYMPTOMS

general

Symptom	Severity	Time	
☐ Fatigue	① ② ③ ④ ⑤	☐ a.m.	☐ p.m.
☐ Lethargy	① ② ③ ④ ⑤	☐ a.m.	☐ p.m.
☐ Malaise	① ② ③ ④ ⑤	☐ a.m.	☐ p.m.
☐ Weakness	① ② ③ ④ ⑤	☐ a.m.	☐ p.m.
☐ Dizziness	① ② ③ ④ ⑤	☐ a.m.	☐ p.m.
☐ Trembling	① ② ③ ④ ⑤	☐ a.m.	☐ p.m.
☐ Twitching	① ② ③ ④ ⑤	☐ a.m.	☐ p.m.
☐ Insomnia	① ② ③ ④ ⑤	☐ a.m.	☐ p.m.

illness

Symptom	Severity	Time	
☐ Nausea	① ② ③ ④ ⑤	☐ a.m.	☐ p.m.
☐ Vomiting	① ② ③ ④ ⑤	☐ a.m.	☐ p.m.
☐ Constipation	① ② ③ ④ ⑤	☐ a.m.	☐ p.m.
☐ Diarrhea	① ② ③ ④ ⑤	☐ a.m.	☐ p.m.
☐ Sore throat	① ② ③ ④ ⑤	☐ a.m.	☐ p.m.
☐ Congestion	① ② ③ ④ ⑤	☐ a.m.	☐ p.m.
☐ Coughing	① ② ③ ④ ⑤	☐ a.m.	☐ p.m.
☐ Acid reflux	① ② ③ ④ ⑤	☐ a.m.	☐ p.m.

psychological

Symptom	Severity	Time	
☐ Anxiety	① ② ③ ④ ⑤	☐ a.m.	☐ p.m.
☐ Depression	① ② ③ ④ ⑤	☐ a.m.	☐ p.m.
☐ Memory loss	① ② ③ ④ ⑤	☐ a.m.	☐ p.m.
☐ Confusion	① ② ③ ④ ⑤	☐ a.m.	☐ p.m.
☐ Poor focus	① ② ③ ④ ⑤	☐ a.m.	☐ p.m.
☐ Mood swings	① ② ③ ④ ⑤	☐ a.m.	☐ p.m.
☐ Suicidal	① ② ③ ④ ⑤	☐ a.m.	☐ p.m.

other

Symptom	Severity	Time	
	① ② ③ ④ ⑤	☐ a.m.	☐ p.m.
	① ② ③ ④ ⑤	☐ a.m.	☐ p.m.
	① ② ③ ④ ⑤	☐ a.m.	☐ p.m.
	① ② ③ ④ ⑤	☐ a.m.	☐ p.m.
	① ② ③ ④ ⑤	☐ a.m.	☐ p.m.
	① ② ③ ④ ⑤	☐ a.m.	☐ p.m.
	① ② ③ ④ ⑤	☐ a.m.	☐ p.m.

SLEEP

hours ________ quality ① ② ③ ④ ⑤

STRESS LEVELS

None	Low	Medium	High	Max	@$#%!

WEATHER

☐ Cold ☐ Mild ☐ Hot
☐ Dry ☐ Humid ☐ Wet

Allergen Levels: ________

BM Pressure: ________

EXERCISE

☐ Heck yes, I worked out.
☐ I managed to exercise a bit.
☐ No, I haven't exercised at all.
☐ I did some stuff, and that counts.

DETAILS

FOOD / MEDICATION

Food / Drinks

Meds / Supplements	Time	Dose

☐ usual daily medication

Water *Caffeine* *Alcohol*

x ________ x ________

FOOD ANALYSIS

New food introduced?

☐ Yes ☐ No

Food reintroduction?

☐ Yes ☐ No

Details

MEDICATION ANALYSIS

New med/dose introduced?

☐ Yes ☐ No

Medication stopped?

☐ Yes ☐ No

Details

ACTIVITY ANALYSIS

Heightened exertion levels?

☐ Yes ☐ No

Lowered exertion levels?

☐ Yes ☐ No

Details

SLEEP ANALYSIS

When you woke up this morning, did you feel well-rested?	☐ Yes	☐ No	☐ A bit
Did you snore or stop breathing throughout the night?	☐ Yes	☐ No	☐ Not sure
Roughly how many times did you wake up throughout the night?			

Notes / Suspected Triggers

ENTRY #63	M T W T F S S	DATE:

HOW ARE YOU *Feeling today?*

Amazing!	Meh
Great	Not good
Good	Terrible!

RATE YOUR PAIN LEVEL

① ② ③ ④ ⑤ ⑥ ⑦ ⑧ ⑨ ⑩

WHAT ABOUT YOUR...?

Mood	① ② ③ ④ ⑤ ⑥ ⑦ ⑧ ⑨ ⑩
Energy Levels	① ② ③ ④ ⑤ ⑥ ⑦ ⑧ ⑨ ⑩
Mental Clarity	① ② ③ ④ ⑤ ⑥ ⑦ ⑧ ⑨ ⑩

PAIN & PHYSICAL SYMPTOMS

Symptom	Severity	am	pm
	① ② ③ ④ ⑤	☐	☐
	① ② ③ ④ ⑤	☐	☐
	① ② ③ ④ ⑤	☐	☐
	① ② ③ ④ ⑤	☐	☐
	① ② ③ ④ ⑤	☐	☐
	① ② ③ ④ ⑤	☐	☐
	① ② ③ ④ ⑤	☐	☐
	① ② ③ ④ ⑤	☐	☐

front ***back***

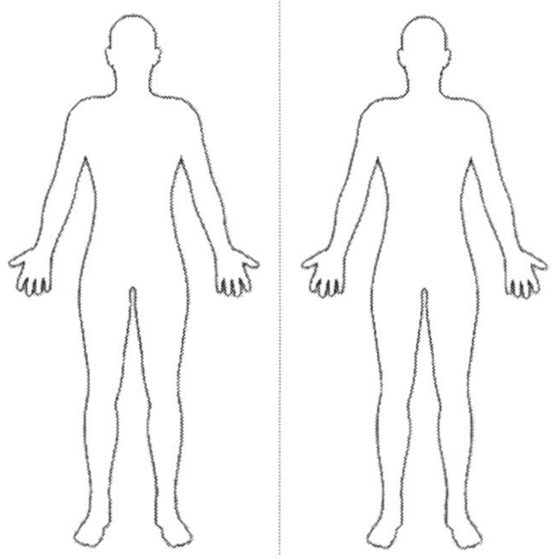

OTHER SYMPTOMS

general

Symptom	Severity	Time	
☐ Fatigue	① ② ③ ④ ⑤	☐ a.m.	☐ p.m.
☐ Lethargy	① ② ③ ④ ⑤	☐ a.m.	☐ p.m.
☐ Malaise	① ② ③ ④ ⑤	☐ a.m.	☐ p.m.
☐ Weakness	① ② ③ ④ ⑤	☐ a.m.	☐ p.m.
☐ Dizziness	① ② ③ ④ ⑤	☐ a.m.	☐ p.m.
☐ Trembling	① ② ③ ④ ⑤	☐ a.m.	☐ p.m.
☐ Twitching	① ② ③ ④ ⑤	☐ a.m.	☐ p.m.
☐ Insomnia	① ② ③ ④ ⑤	☐ a.m.	☐ p.m.

illness

Symptom	Severity	Time	
☐ Nausea	① ② ③ ④ ⑤	☐ a.m.	☐ p.m.
☐ Vomiting	① ② ③ ④ ⑤	☐ a.m.	☐ p.m.
☐ Constipation	① ② ③ ④ ⑤	☐ a.m.	☐ p.m.
☐ Diarrhea	① ② ③ ④ ⑤	☐ a.m.	☐ p.m.
☐ Sore throat	① ② ③ ④ ⑤	☐ a.m.	☐ p.m.
☐ Congestion	① ② ③ ④ ⑤	☐ a.m.	☐ p.m.
☐ Coughing	① ② ③ ④ ⑤	☐ a.m.	☐ p.m.
☐ Acid reflux	① ② ③ ④ ⑤	☐ a.m.	☐ p.m.

psychological

Symptom	Severity	Time	
☐ Anxiety	① ② ③ ④ ⑤	☐ a.m.	☐ p.m.
☐ Depression	① ② ③ ④ ⑤	☐ a.m.	☐ p.m.
☐ Memory loss	① ② ③ ④ ⑤	☐ a.m.	☐ p.m.
☐ Confusion	① ② ③ ④ ⑤	☐ a.m.	☐ p.m.
☐ Poor focus	① ② ③ ④ ⑤	☐ a.m.	☐ p.m.
☐ Mood swings	① ② ③ ④ ⑤	☐ a.m.	☐ p.m.
☐ Suicidal	① ② ③ ④ ⑤	☐ a.m.	☐ p.m.

other

Symptom	Severity	Time	
	① ② ③ ④ ⑤	☐ a.m.	☐ p.m.
	① ② ③ ④ ⑤	☐ a.m.	☐ p.m.
	① ② ③ ④ ⑤	☐ a.m.	☐ p.m.
	① ② ③ ④ ⑤	☐ a.m.	☐ p.m.
	① ② ③ ④ ⑤	☐ a.m.	☐ p.m.
	① ② ③ ④ ⑤	☐ a.m.	☐ p.m.
	① ② ③ ④ ⑤	☐ a.m.	☐ p.m.

SLEEP

hours ________

quality ① ② ③ ④ ⑤

STRESS LEVELS

None	Low	Medium	High	Max	@$#%!

WEATHER

☐ Cold ☐ Mild ☐ Hot
☐ Dry ☐ Humid ☐ Wet

Allergen Levels: ________

BM Pressure: ________

EXERCISE

☐ Heck yes, I worked out.
☐ I managed to exercise a bit.
☐ No, I haven't exercised at all.
☐ I did some stuff, and that counts.

DETAILS

FOOD / MEDICATION

Food / Drinks

Meds / Supplements	Time	Dose

☐ usual daily medication

Water *Caffeine* *Alcohol*

x ________ x ________

FOOD ANALYSIS

New food introduced?

☐ Yes ☐ No

Food reintroduction?

☐ Yes ☐ No

Details

MEDICATION ANALYSIS

New med/dose introduced?

☐ Yes ☐ No

Medication stopped?

☐ Yes ☐ No

Details

ACTIVITY ANALYSIS

Heightened exertion levels?

☐ Yes ☐ No

Lowered exertion levels?

☐ Yes ☐ No

Details

SLEEP ANALYSIS

When you woke up this morning, did you feel well-rested?	☐ Yes	☐ No	☐ A bit
Did you snore or stop breathing throughout the night?	☐ Yes	☐ No	☐ Not sure

Roughly how many times did you wake up throughout the night?

Notes / Suspected Triggers

ENTRY #64 | M T W T F S S | DATE:

HOW ARE YOU *Feeling today?*

Amazing!	Meh
Great	Not good
Good	Terrible!

RATE YOUR PAIN LEVEL

① ② ③ ④ ⑤ ⑥ ⑦ ⑧ ⑨ ⑩

WHAT ABOUT YOUR...?

Mood	① ② ③ ④ ⑤ ⑥ ⑦ ⑧ ⑨ ⑩
Energy Levels	① ② ③ ④ ⑤ ⑥ ⑦ ⑧ ⑨ ⑩
Mental Clarity	① ② ③ ④ ⑤ ⑥ ⑦ ⑧ ⑨ ⑩

PAIN & PHYSICAL SYMPTOMS

Symptom	Severity	am	pm
	① ② ③ ④ ⑤	☐	☐
	① ② ③ ④ ⑤	☐	☐
	① ② ③ ④ ⑤	☐	☐
	① ② ③ ④ ⑤	☐	☐
	① ② ③ ④ ⑤	☐	☐
	① ② ③ ④ ⑤	☐	☐
	① ② ③ ④ ⑤	☐	☐
	① ② ③ ④ ⑤	☐	☐

front ***back***

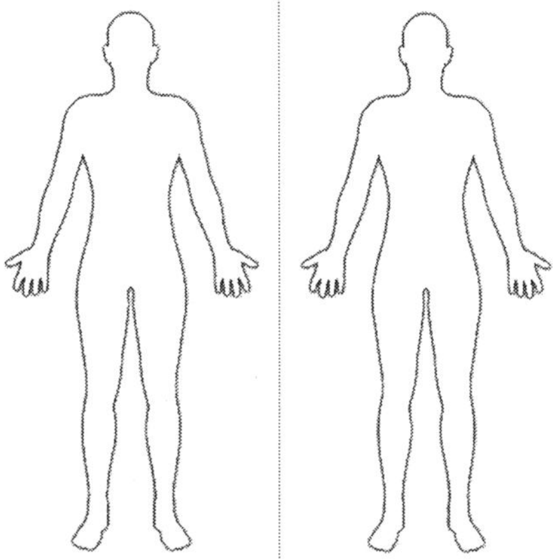

OTHER SYMPTOMS

general

Symptom	Severity	Time	
☐ Fatigue	① ② ③ ④ ⑤	☐ a.m.	☐ p.m.
☐ Lethargy	① ② ③ ④ ⑤	☐ a.m.	☐ p.m.
☐ Malaise	① ② ③ ④ ⑤	☐ a.m.	☐ p.m.
☐ Weakness	① ② ③ ④ ⑤	☐ a.m.	☐ p.m.
☐ Dizziness	① ② ③ ④ ⑤	☐ a.m.	☐ p.m.
☐ Trembling	① ② ③ ④ ⑤	☐ a.m.	☐ p.m.
☐ Twitching	① ② ③ ④ ⑤	☐ a.m.	☐ p.m.
☐ Insomnia	① ② ③ ④ ⑤	☐ a.m.	☐ p.m.

illness

Symptom	Severity	Time	
☐ Nausea	① ② ③ ④ ⑤	☐ a.m.	☐ p.m.
☐ Vomiting	① ② ③ ④ ⑤	☐ a.m.	☐ p.m.
☐ Constipation	① ② ③ ④ ⑤	☐ a.m.	☐ p.m.
☐ Diarrhea	① ② ③ ④ ⑤	☐ a.m.	☐ p.m.
☐ Sore throat	① ② ③ ④ ⑤	☐ a.m.	☐ p.m.
☐ Congestion	① ② ③ ④ ⑤	☐ a.m.	☐ p.m.
☐ Coughing	① ② ③ ④ ⑤	☐ a.m.	☐ p.m.
☐ Acid reflux	① ② ③ ④ ⑤	☐ a.m.	☐ p.m.

psychological

Symptom	Severity	Time	
☐ Anxiety	① ② ③ ④ ⑤	☐ a.m.	☐ p.m.
☐ Depression	① ② ③ ④ ⑤	☐ a.m.	☐ p.m.
☐ Memory loss	① ② ③ ④ ⑤	☐ a.m.	☐ p.m.
☐ Confusion	① ② ③ ④ ⑤	☐ a.m.	☐ p.m.
☐ Poor focus	① ② ③ ④ ⑤	☐ a.m.	☐ p.m.
☐ Mood swings	① ② ③ ④ ⑤	☐ a.m.	☐ p.m.
☐ Suicidal	① ② ③ ④ ⑤	☐ a.m.	☐ p.m.

other

Symptom	Severity	Time	
	① ② ③ ④ ⑤	☐ a.m.	☐ p.m.
	① ② ③ ④ ⑤	☐ a.m.	☐ p.m.
	① ② ③ ④ ⑤	☐ a.m.	☐ p.m.
	① ② ③ ④ ⑤	☐ a.m.	☐ p.m.
	① ② ③ ④ ⑤	☐ a.m.	☐ p.m.
	① ② ③ ④ ⑤	☐ a.m.	☐ p.m.
	① ② ③ ④ ⑤	☐ a.m.	☐ p.m.

SLEEP

hours ________ *quality* ① ② ③ ④ ⑤

STRESS LEVELS

None	Low	Medium	High	Max	@$#%!

WEATHER

☐ Cold ☐ Mild ☐ Hot
☐ Dry ☐ Humid ☐ Wet

Allergen Levels: ________

BM Pressure: ________

EXERCISE

☐ Heck yes, I worked out.
☐ I managed to exercise a bit.
☐ No, I haven't exercised at all.
☐ I did some stuff, and that counts.

DETAILS

FOOD / MEDICATION

Food / Drinks

Meds / Supplements	Time	Dose
☐ usual daily medication		

Water	*Caffeine*	*Alcohol*
	x ________	x ________

FOOD ANALYSIS

New food introduced?

☐ Yes ☐ No

Food reintroduction?

☐ Yes ☐ No

Details

MEDICATION ANALYSIS

New med/dose introduced?

☐ Yes ☐ No

Medication stopped?

☐ Yes ☐ No

Details

ACTIVITY ANALYSIS

Heightened exertion levels?

☐ Yes ☐ No

Lowered exertion levels?

☐ Yes ☐ No

Details

SLEEP ANALYSIS

When you woke up this morning, did you feel well-rested?	☐ Yes	☐ No	☐ A bit
Did you snore or stop breathing throughout the night?	☐ Yes	☐ No	☐ Not sure
Roughly how many times did you wake up throughout the night?			

Notes / Suspected Triggers

ENTRY #65 | M T W T F S S | DATE:

HOW ARE YOU *Feeling today?*

Amazing!	Meh
Great	Not good
Good	Terrible!

RATE YOUR PAIN LEVEL

① ② ③ ④ ⑤ ⑥ ⑦ ⑧ ⑨ ⑩

WHAT ABOUT YOUR...?

Mood	① ② ③ ④ ⑤ ⑥ ⑦ ⑧ ⑨ ⑩
Energy Levels	① ② ③ ④ ⑤ ⑥ ⑦ ⑧ ⑨ ⑩
Mental Clarity	① ② ③ ④ ⑤ ⑥ ⑦ ⑧ ⑨ ⑩

PAIN & PHYSICAL SYMPTOMS

Symptom	Severity	am	pm
	① ② ③ ④ ⑤	☐	☐
	① ② ③ ④ ⑤	☐	☐
	① ② ③ ④ ⑤	☐	☐
	① ② ③ ④ ⑤	☐	☐
	① ② ③ ④ ⑤	☐	☐
	① ② ③ ④ ⑤	☐	☐
	① ② ③ ④ ⑤	☐	☐
	① ② ③ ④ ⑤	☐	☐

front

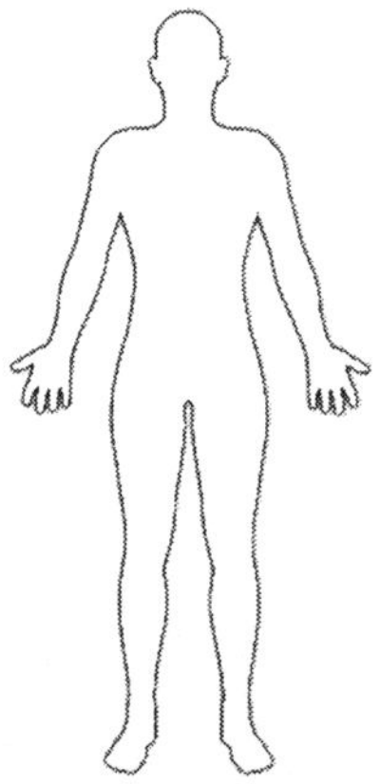

back

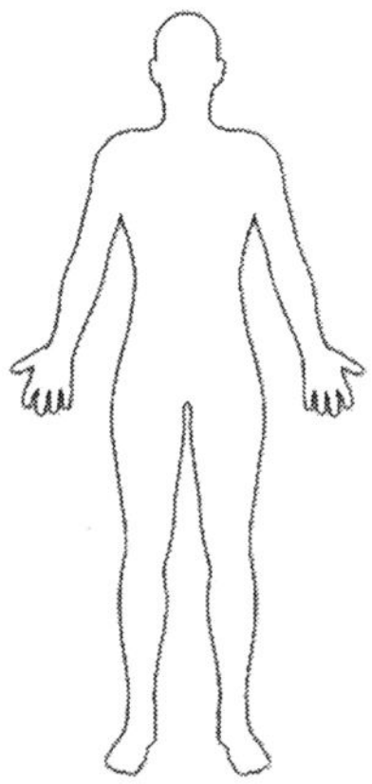

OTHER SYMPTOMS

general

Symptom	Severity	Time	
☐ Fatigue	① ② ③ ④ ⑤	☐ a.m.	☐ p.m.
☐ Lethargy	① ② ③ ④ ⑤	☐ a.m.	☐ p.m.
☐ Malaise	① ② ③ ④ ⑤	☐ a.m.	☐ p.m.
☐ Weakness	① ② ③ ④ ⑤	☐ a.m.	☐ p.m.
☐ Dizziness	① ② ③ ④ ⑤	☐ a.m.	☐ p.m.
☐ Trembling	① ② ③ ④ ⑤	☐ a.m.	☐ p.m.
☐ Twitching	① ② ③ ④ ⑤	☐ a.m.	☐ p.m.
☐ Insomnia	① ② ③ ④ ⑤	☐ a.m.	☐ p.m.

illness

Symptom	Severity	Time	
☐ Nausea	① ② ③ ④ ⑤	☐ a.m.	☐ p.m.
☐ Vomiting	① ② ③ ④ ⑤	☐ a.m.	☐ p.m.
☐ Constipation	① ② ③ ④ ⑤	☐ a.m.	☐ p.m.
☐ Diarrhea	① ② ③ ④ ⑤	☐ a.m.	☐ p.m.
☐ Sore throat	① ② ③ ④ ⑤	☐ a.m.	☐ p.m.
☐ Congestion	① ② ③ ④ ⑤	☐ a.m.	☐ p.m.
☐ Coughing	① ② ③ ④ ⑤	☐ a.m.	☐ p.m.
☐ Acid reflux	① ② ③ ④ ⑤	☐ a.m.	☐ p.m.

psychological

Symptom	Severity	Time	
☐ Anxiety	① ② ③ ④ ⑤	☐ a.m.	☐ p.m.
☐ Depression	① ② ③ ④ ⑤	☐ a.m.	☐ p.m.
☐ Memory loss	① ② ③ ④ ⑤	☐ a.m.	☐ p.m.
☐ Confusion	① ② ③ ④ ⑤	☐ a.m.	☐ p.m.
☐ Poor focus	① ② ③ ④ ⑤	☐ a.m.	☐ p.m.
☐ Mood swings	① ② ③ ④ ⑤	☐ a.m.	☐ p.m.
☐ Suicidal	① ② ③ ④ ⑤	☐ a.m.	☐ p.m.

other

Symptom	Severity	Time	
	① ② ③ ④ ⑤	☐ a.m.	☐ p.m.
	① ② ③ ④ ⑤	☐ a.m.	☐ p.m.
	① ② ③ ④ ⑤	☐ a.m.	☐ p.m.
	① ② ③ ④ ⑤	☐ a.m.	☐ p.m.
	① ② ③ ④ ⑤	☐ a.m.	☐ p.m.
	① ② ③ ④ ⑤	☐ a.m.	☐ p.m.
	① ② ③ ④ ⑤	☐ a.m.	☐ p.m.

SLEEP

hours ________ *quality* ① ② ③ ④ ⑤

STRESS LEVELS

None	Low	Medium	High	Max	@$#%!

WEATHER

☐ Cold ☐ Mild ☐ Hot
☐ Dry ☐ Humid ☐ Wet

Allergen Levels: ________

BM Pressure: ________

EXERCISE

☐ Heck yes, I worked out.
☐ I managed to exercise a bit.
☐ No, I haven't exercised at all.
☐ I did some stuff, and that counts.

DETAILS

FOOD / MEDICATION

Food / Drinks

Meds / Supplements	Time	Dose
☐ usual daily medication		

Water	*Caffeine*	*Alcohol*
	x ________	x ________

FOOD ANALYSIS		MEDICATION ANALYSIS		ACTIVITY ANALYSIS	
New food introduced?		New med/dose introduced?		Heightened exertion levels?	
☐ Yes	☐ No	☐ Yes	☐ No	☐ Yes	☐ No
Food reintroduction?		Medication stopped?		Lowered exertion levels?	
☐ Yes	☐ No	☐ Yes	☐ No	☐ Yes	☐ No
Details		*Details*		*Details*	

SLEEP ANALYSIS

When you woke up this morning, did you feel well-rested?	☐ Yes	☐ No	☐ A bit
Did you snore or stop breathing throughout the night?	☐ Yes	☐ No	☐ Not sure
Roughly how many times did you wake up throughout the night?			

Notes / Suspected Triggers

ENTRY #66 | M T W T F S S | DATE:

HOW ARE YOU *Feeling today?*

Amazing!	Meh
Great	Not good
Good	Terrible!

RATE YOUR PAIN LEVEL

① ② ③ ④ ⑤ ⑥ ⑦ ⑧ ⑨ ⑩

WHAT ABOUT YOUR...?

Mood	① ② ③ ④ ⑤ ⑥ ⑦ ⑧ ⑨ ⑩
Energy Levels	① ② ③ ④ ⑤ ⑥ ⑦ ⑧ ⑨ ⑩
Mental Clarity	① ② ③ ④ ⑤ ⑥ ⑦ ⑧ ⑨ ⑩

PAIN & PHYSICAL SYMPTOMS

Symptom	Severity	am	pm
	① ② ③ ④ ⑤	☐	☐
	① ② ③ ④ ⑤	☐	☐
	① ② ③ ④ ⑤	☐	☐
	① ② ③ ④ ⑤	☐	☐
	① ② ③ ④ ⑤	☐	☐
	① ② ③ ④ ⑤	☐	☐
	① ② ③ ④ ⑤	☐	☐
	① ② ③ ④ ⑤	☐	☐

front *back*

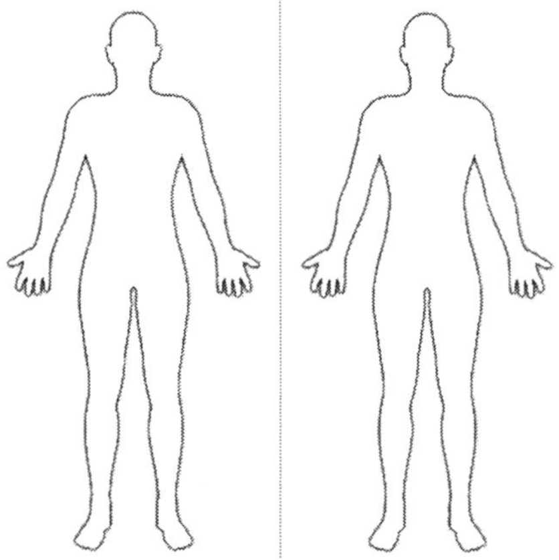

OTHER SYMPTOMS

general

Symptom	Severity	Time	
☐ Fatigue	① ② ③ ④ ⑤	☐ a.m.	☐ p.m.
☐ Lethargy	① ② ③ ④ ⑤	☐ a.m.	☐ p.m.
☐ Malaise	① ② ③ ④ ⑤	☐ a.m.	☐ p.m.
☐ Weakness	① ② ③ ④ ⑤	☐ a.m.	☐ p.m.
☐ Dizziness	① ② ③ ④ ⑤	☐ a.m.	☐ p.m.
☐ Trembling	① ② ③ ④ ⑤	☐ a.m.	☐ p.m.
☐ Twitching	① ② ③ ④ ⑤	☐ a.m.	☐ p.m.
☐ Insomnia	① ② ③ ④ ⑤	☐ a.m.	☐ p.m.

illness

Symptom	Severity	Time	
☐ Nausea	① ② ③ ④ ⑤	☐ a.m.	☐ p.m.
☐ Vomiting	① ② ③ ④ ⑤	☐ a.m.	☐ p.m.
☐ Constipation	① ② ③ ④ ⑤	☐ a.m.	☐ p.m.
☐ Diarrhea	① ② ③ ④ ⑤	☐ a.m.	☐ p.m.
☐ Sore throat	① ② ③ ④ ⑤	☐ a.m.	☐ p.m.
☐ Congestion	① ② ③ ④ ⑤	☐ a.m.	☐ p.m.
☐ Coughing	① ② ③ ④ ⑤	☐ a.m.	☐ p.m.
☐ Acid reflux	① ② ③ ④ ⑤	☐ a.m.	☐ p.m.

psychological

Symptom	Severity	Time	
☐ Anxiety	① ② ③ ④ ⑤	☐ a.m.	☐ p.m.
☐ Depression	① ② ③ ④ ⑤	☐ a.m.	☐ p.m.
☐ Memory loss	① ② ③ ④ ⑤	☐ a.m.	☐ p.m.
☐ Confusion	① ② ③ ④ ⑤	☐ a.m.	☐ p.m.
☐ Poor focus	① ② ③ ④ ⑤	☐ a.m.	☐ p.m.
☐ Mood swings	① ② ③ ④ ⑤	☐ a.m.	☐ p.m.
☐ Suicidal	① ② ③ ④ ⑤	☐ a.m.	☐ p.m.

other

Symptom	Severity	Time	
	① ② ③ ④ ⑤	☐ a.m.	☐ p.m.
	① ② ③ ④ ⑤	☐ a.m.	☐ p.m.
	① ② ③ ④ ⑤	☐ a.m.	☐ p.m.
	① ② ③ ④ ⑤	☐ a.m.	☐ p.m.
	① ② ③ ④ ⑤	☐ a.m.	☐ p.m.
	① ② ③ ④ ⑤	☐ a.m.	☐ p.m.
	① ② ③ ④ ⑤	☐ a.m.	☐ p.m.

SLEEP

hours ________ *quality* ① ② ③ ④ ⑤

STRESS LEVELS

None	Low	Medium	High	Max	@$#%!

WEATHER

☐ Cold ☐ Mild ☐ Hot
☐ Dry ☐ Humid ☐ Wet

Allergen Levels: ________
BM Pressure: ________

EXERCISE

☐ Heck yes, I worked out.
☐ I managed to exercise a bit.
☐ No, I haven't exercised at all.
☐ I did some stuff, and that counts.

DETAILS

FOOD / MEDICATION

Food / Drinks

Meds / Supplements	Time	Dose

☐ usual daily medication

Water *Caffeine* *Alcohol*

x ________ x ________

FOOD ANALYSIS

New food introduced?
☐ Yes ☐ No
Food reintroduction?
☐ Yes ☐ No
Details

MEDICATION ANALYSIS

New med/dose introduced?
☐ Yes ☐ No
Medication stopped?
☐ Yes ☐ No
Details

ACTIVITY ANALYSIS

Heightened exertion levels?
☐ Yes ☐ No
Lowered exertion levels?
☐ Yes ☐ No
Details

SLEEP ANALYSIS

When you woke up this morning, did you feel well-rested?	☐ Yes	☐ No	☐ A bit
Did you snore or stop breathing throughout the night?	☐ Yes	☐ No	☐ Not sure
Roughly how many times did you wake up throughout the night?			

Notes / Suspected Triggers

ENTRY #67 | M T W T F S S | DATE:

HOW ARE YOU *Feeling today?*

Amazing!	Meh
Great	Not good
Good	Terrible!

RATE YOUR PAIN LEVEL

1 2 3 4 5 6 7 8 9 10

WHAT ABOUT YOUR...?

Mood	1 2 3 4 5 6 7 8 9 10
Energy Levels	1 2 3 4 5 6 7 8 9 10
Mental Clarity	1 2 3 4 5 6 7 8 9 10

PAIN & PHYSICAL SYMPTOMS

Symptom	Severity	am	pm
	1 2 3 4 5	☐	☐
	1 2 3 4 5	☐	☐
	1 2 3 4 5	☐	☐
	1 2 3 4 5	☐	☐
	1 2 3 4 5	☐	☐
	1 2 3 4 5	☐	☐
	1 2 3 4 5	☐	☐
	1 2 3 4 5	☐	☐

front *back*

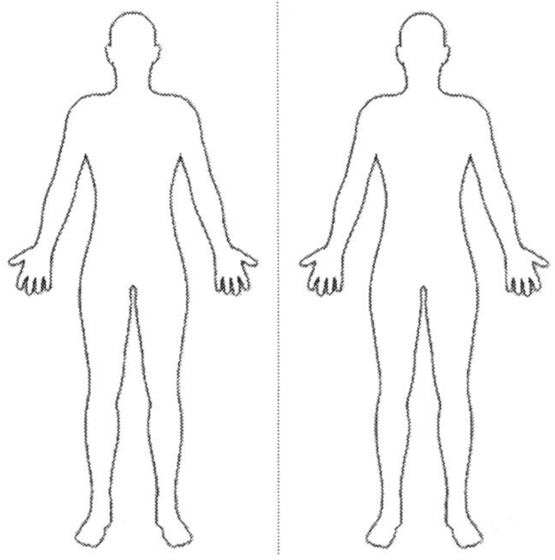

OTHER SYMPTOMS

general

Symptom	Severity	Time	
☐ Fatigue	1 2 3 4 5	☐ a.m.	☐ p.m.
☐ Lethargy	1 2 3 4 5	☐ a.m.	☐ p.m.
☐ Malaise	1 2 3 4 5	☐ a.m.	☐ p.m.
☐ Weakness	1 2 3 4 5	☐ a.m.	☐ p.m.
☐ Dizziness	1 2 3 4 5	☐ a.m.	☐ p.m.
☐ Trembling	1 2 3 4 5	☐ a.m.	☐ p.m.
☐ Twitching	1 2 3 4 5	☐ a.m.	☐ p.m.
☐ Insomnia	1 2 3 4 5	☐ a.m.	☐ p.m.

illness

Symptom	Severity	Time	
☐ Nausea	1 2 3 4 5	☐ a.m.	☐ p.m.
☐ Vomiting	1 2 3 4 5	☐ a.m.	☐ p.m.
☐ Constipation	1 2 3 4 5	☐ a.m.	☐ p.m.
☐ Diarrhea	1 2 3 4 5	☐ a.m.	☐ p.m.
☐ Sore throat	1 2 3 4 5	☐ a.m.	☐ p.m.
☐ Congestion	1 2 3 4 5	☐ a.m.	☐ p.m.
☐ Coughing	1 2 3 4 5	☐ a.m.	☐ p.m.
☐ Acid reflux	1 2 3 4 5	☐ a.m.	☐ p.m.

psychological

Symptom	Severity	Time	
☐ Anxiety	1 2 3 4 5	☐ a.m.	☐ p.m.
☐ Depression	1 2 3 4 5	☐ a.m.	☐ p.m.
☐ Memory loss	1 2 3 4 5	☐ a.m.	☐ p.m.
☐ Confusion	1 2 3 4 5	☐ a.m.	☐ p.m.
☐ Poor focus	1 2 3 4 5	☐ a.m.	☐ p.m.
☐ Mood swings	1 2 3 4 5	☐ a.m.	☐ p.m.
☐ Suicidal	1 2 3 4 5	☐ a.m.	☐ p.m.

other

Symptom	Severity	Time	
	1 2 3 4 5	☐ a.m.	☐ p.m.
	1 2 3 4 5	☐ a.m.	☐ p.m.
	1 2 3 4 5	☐ a.m.	☐ p.m.
	1 2 3 4 5	☐ a.m.	☐ p.m.
	1 2 3 4 5	☐ a.m.	☐ p.m.
	1 2 3 4 5	☐ a.m.	☐ p.m.
	1 2 3 4 5	☐ a.m.	☐ p.m.

SLEEP

hours ________ quality ① ② ③ ④ ⑤

STRESS LEVELS

None	Low	Medium	High	Max	@$#%!

WEATHER

☐ Cold ☐ Mild ☐ Hot
☐ Dry ☐ Humid ☐ Wet

Allergen Levels: ________

BM Pressure: ________

EXERCISE

☐ Heck yes, I worked out.
☐ I managed to exercise a bit.
☐ No, I haven't exercised at all.
☐ I did some stuff, and that counts.

DETAILS

FOOD / MEDICATION

Food / Drinks

Meds / Supplements	Time	Dose

☐ usual daily medication

Water Caffeine Alcohol

x ________ x ________

FOOD ANALYSIS

New food introduced?

☐ Yes ☐ No

Food reintroduction?

☐ Yes ☐ No

Details

MEDICATION ANALYSIS

New med/dose introduced?

☐ Yes ☐ No

Medication stopped?

☐ Yes ☐ No

Details

ACTIVITY ANALYSIS

Heightened exertion levels?

☐ Yes ☐ No

Lowered exertion levels?

☐ Yes ☐ No

Details

SLEEP ANALYSIS

When you woke up this morning, did you feel well-rested?	☐ Yes	☐ No	☐ A bit
Did you snore or stop breathing throughout the night?	☐ Yes	☐ No	☐ Not sure
Roughly how many times did you wake up throughout the night?			

Notes / Suspected Triggers

ENTRY #68 | M T W T F S S | DATE:

HOW ARE YOU *Feeling today?*

Amazing!	Meh
Great	Not good
Good	Terrible!

RATE YOUR PAIN LEVEL

(1) (2) (3) (4) (5) (6) (7) (8) (9) (10)

WHAT ABOUT YOUR...?

Mood	(1) (2) (3) (4) (5) (6) (7) (8) (9) (10)
Energy Levels	(1) (2) (3) (4) (5) (6) (7) (8) (9) (10)
Mental Clarity	(1) (2) (3) (4) (5) (6) (7) (8) (9) (10)

PAIN & PHYSICAL SYMPTOMS

Symptom	Severity	am	pm
	(1) (2) (3) (4) (5)	☐	☐
	(1) (2) (3) (4) (5)	☐	☐
	(1) (2) (3) (4) (5)	☐	☐
	(1) (2) (3) (4) (5)	☐	☐
	(1) (2) (3) (4) (5)	☐	☐
	(1) (2) (3) (4) (5)	☐	☐
	(1) (2) (3) (4) (5)	☐	☐
	(1) (2) (3) (4) (5)	☐	☐

front

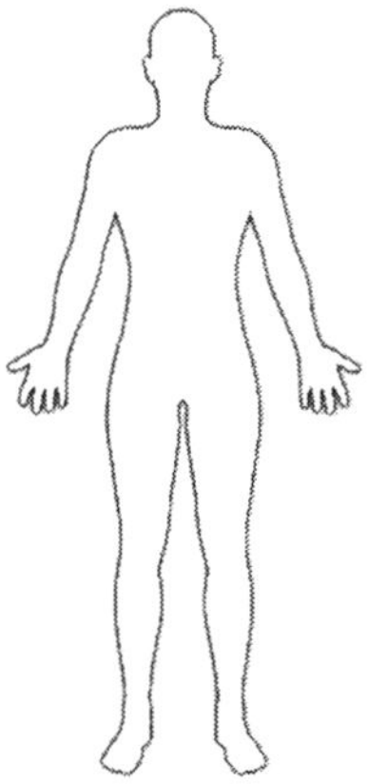

back

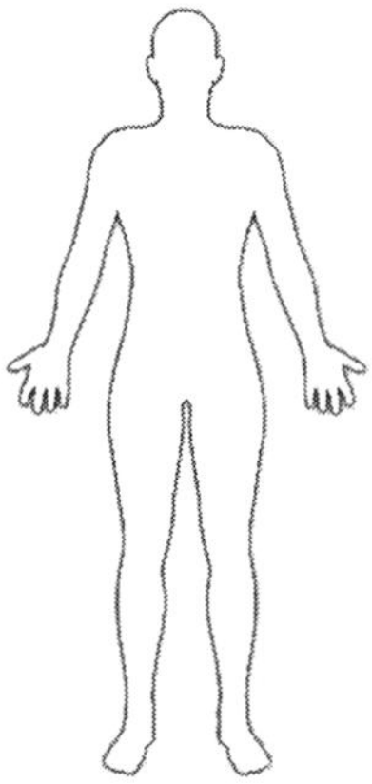

OTHER SYMPTOMS

general

Symptom	Severity	Time	
☐ Fatigue	(1) (2) (3) (4) (5)	☐ a.m.	☐ p.m.
☐ Lethargy	(1) (2) (3) (4) (5)	☐ a.m.	☐ p.m.
☐ Malaise	(1) (2) (3) (4) (5)	☐ a.m.	☐ p.m.
☐ Weakness	(1) (2) (3) (4) (5)	☐ a.m.	☐ p.m.
☐ Dizziness	(1) (2) (3) (4) (5)	☐ a.m.	☐ p.m.
☐ Trembling	(1) (2) (3) (4) (5)	☐ a.m.	☐ p.m.
☐ Twitching	(1) (2) (3) (4) (5)	☐ a.m.	☐ p.m.
☐ Insomnia	(1) (2) (3) (4) (5)	☐ a.m.	☐ p.m.

illness

Symptom	Severity	Time	
☐ Nausea	(1) (2) (3) (4) (5)	☐ a.m.	☐ p.m.
☐ Vomiting	(1) (2) (3) (4) (5)	☐ a.m.	☐ p.m.
☐ Constipation	(1) (2) (3) (4) (5)	☐ a.m.	☐ p.m.
☐ Diarrhea	(1) (2) (3) (4) (5)	☐ a.m.	☐ p.m.
☐ Sore throat	(1) (2) (3) (4) (5)	☐ a.m.	☐ p.m.
☐ Congestion	(1) (2) (3) (4) (5)	☐ a.m.	☐ p.m.
☐ Coughing	(1) (2) (3) (4) (5)	☐ a.m.	☐ p.m.
☐ Acid reflux	(1) (2) (3) (4) (5)	☐ a.m.	☐ p.m.

psychological

Symptom	Severity	Time	
☐ Anxiety	(1) (2) (3) (4) (5)	☐ a.m.	☐ p.m.
☐ Depression	(1) (2) (3) (4) (5)	☐ a.m.	☐ p.m.
☐ Memory loss	(1) (2) (3) (4) (5)	☐ a.m.	☐ p.m.
☐ Confusion	(1) (2) (3) (4) (5)	☐ a.m.	☐ p.m.
☐ Poor focus	(1) (2) (3) (4) (5)	☐ a.m.	☐ p.m.
☐ Mood swings	(1) (2) (3) (4) (5)	☐ a.m.	☐ p.m.
☐ Suicidal	(1) (2) (3) (4) (5)	☐ a.m.	☐ p.m.

other

Symptom	Severity	Time	
	(1) (2) (3) (4) (5)	☐ a.m.	☐ p.m.
	(1) (2) (3) (4) (5)	☐ a.m.	☐ p.m.
	(1) (2) (3) (4) (5)	☐ a.m.	☐ p.m.
	(1) (2) (3) (4) (5)	☐ a.m.	☐ p.m.
	(1) (2) (3) (4) (5)	☐ a.m.	☐ p.m.
	(1) (2) (3) (4) (5)	☐ a.m.	☐ p.m.
	(1) (2) (3) (4) (5)	☐ a.m.	☐ p.m.

SLEEP

hours ________ *quality* ① ② ③ ④ ⑤

STRESS LEVELS

None	Low	Medium	High	Max	@$#%!

WEATHER

☐ Cold ☐ Mild ☐ Hot
☐ Dry ☐ Humid ☐ Wet

Allergen Levels: ________
BM Pressure: ________

EXERCISE

☐ Heck yes, I worked out.
☐ I managed to exercise a bit.
☐ No, I haven't exercised at all.
☐ I did some stuff, and that counts.

DETAILS

FOOD / MEDICATION

Food / Drinks

Meds / Supplements	Time	Dose

☐ usual daily medication

Water *Caffeine* *Alcohol*

x ________ x ________

FOOD ANALYSIS

New food introduced?
☐ Yes ☐ No

Food reintroduction?
☐ Yes ☐ No

Details

MEDICATION ANALYSIS

New med/dose introduced?
☐ Yes ☐ No

Medication stopped?
☐ Yes ☐ No

Details

ACTIVITY ANALYSIS

Heightened exertion levels?
☐ Yes ☐ No

Lowered exertion levels?
☐ Yes ☐ No

Details

SLEEP ANALYSIS

When you woke up this morning, did you feel well-rested?	☐ Yes	☐ No	☐ A bit
Did you snore or stop breathing throughout the night?	☐ Yes	☐ No	☐ Not sure
Roughly how many times did you wake up throughout the night?			

Notes / Suspected Triggers

ENTRY #69 | M T W T F S S | DATE:

HOW ARE YOU *Feeling today?*

Amazing!	Meh
Great	Not good
Good	Terrible!

RATE YOUR PAIN LEVEL

① ② ③ ④ ⑤ ⑥ ⑦ ⑧ ⑨ ⑩

WHAT ABOUT YOUR...?

Mood	① ② ③ ④ ⑤ ⑥ ⑦ ⑧ ⑨ ⑩
Energy Levels	① ② ③ ④ ⑤ ⑥ ⑦ ⑧ ⑨ ⑩
Mental Clarity	① ② ③ ④ ⑤ ⑥ ⑦ ⑧ ⑨ ⑩

PAIN & PHYSICAL SYMPTOMS

Symptom	Severity	am	pm
	① ② ③ ④ ⑤	☐	☐
	① ② ③ ④ ⑤	☐	☐
	① ② ③ ④ ⑤	☐	☐
	① ② ③ ④ ⑤	☐	☐
	① ② ③ ④ ⑤	☐	☐
	① ② ③ ④ ⑤	☐	☐
	① ② ③ ④ ⑤	☐	☐
	① ② ③ ④ ⑤	☐	☐

front *back*

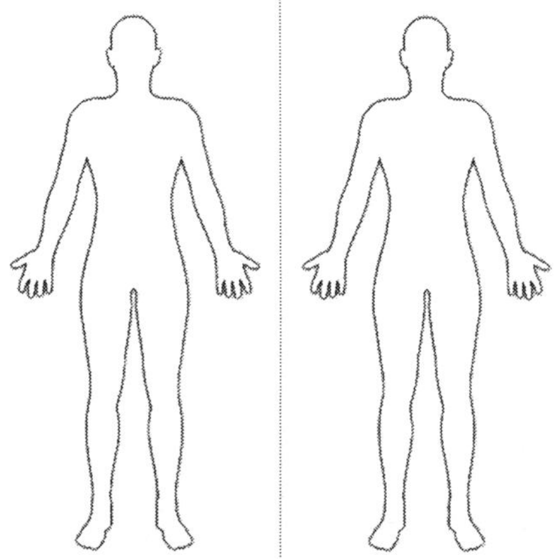

OTHER SYMPTOMS

general

Symptom	Severity	Time	
☐ Fatigue	① ② ③ ④ ⑤	☐ a.m.	☐ p.m.
☐ Lethargy	① ② ③ ④ ⑤	☐ a.m.	☐ p.m.
☐ Malaise	① ② ③ ④ ⑤	☐ a.m.	☐ p.m.
☐ Weakness	① ② ③ ④ ⑤	☐ a.m.	☐ p.m.
☐ Dizziness	① ② ③ ④ ⑤	☐ a.m.	☐ p.m.
☐ Trembling	① ② ③ ④ ⑤	☐ a.m.	☐ p.m.
☐ Twitching	① ② ③ ④ ⑤	☐ a.m.	☐ p.m.
☐ Insomnia	① ② ③ ④ ⑤	☐ a.m.	☐ p.m.

illness

Symptom	Severity	Time	
☐ Nausea	① ② ③ ④ ⑤	☐ a.m.	☐ p.m.
☐ Vomiting	① ② ③ ④ ⑤	☐ a.m.	☐ p.m.
☐ Constipation	① ② ③ ④ ⑤	☐ a.m.	☐ p.m.
☐ Diarrhea	① ② ③ ④ ⑤	☐ a.m.	☐ p.m.
☐ Sore throat	① ② ③ ④ ⑤	☐ a.m.	☐ p.m.
☐ Congestion	① ② ③ ④ ⑤	☐ a.m.	☐ p.m.
☐ Coughing	① ② ③ ④ ⑤	☐ a.m.	☐ p.m.
☐ Acid reflux	① ② ③ ④ ⑤	☐ a.m.	☐ p.m.

psychological

Symptom	Severity	Time	
☐ Anxiety	① ② ③ ④ ⑤	☐ a.m.	☐ p.m.
☐ Depression	① ② ③ ④ ⑤	☐ a.m.	☐ p.m.
☐ Memory loss	① ② ③ ④ ⑤	☐ a.m.	☐ p.m.
☐ Confusion	① ② ③ ④ ⑤	☐ a.m.	☐ p.m.
☐ Poor focus	① ② ③ ④ ⑤	☐ a.m.	☐ p.m.
☐ Mood swings	① ② ③ ④ ⑤	☐ a.m.	☐ p.m.
☐ Suicidal	① ② ③ ④ ⑤	☐ a.m.	☐ p.m.

other

Symptom	Severity	Time	
	① ② ③ ④ ⑤	☐ a.m.	☐ p.m.
	① ② ③ ④ ⑤	☐ a.m.	☐ p.m.
	① ② ③ ④ ⑤	☐ a.m.	☐ p.m.
	① ② ③ ④ ⑤	☐ a.m.	☐ p.m.
	① ② ③ ④ ⑤	☐ a.m.	☐ p.m.
	① ② ③ ④ ⑤	☐ a.m.	☐ p.m.
	① ② ③ ④ ⑤	☐ a.m.	☐ p.m.

SLEEP

hours ________ quality ① ② ③ ④ ⑤

STRESS LEVELS

None	Low	Medium	High	Max	@$#%!

WEATHER

☐ Cold ☐ Mild ☐ Hot
☐ Dry ☐ Humid ☐ Wet

Allergen Levels: ________
BM Pressure: ________

EXERCISE

☐ Heck yes, I worked out.
☐ I managed to exercise a bit.
☐ No, I haven't exercised at all.
☐ I did some stuff, and that counts.

DETAILS

FOOD / MEDICATION

Food / Drinks

Meds / Supplements	Time	Dose

☐ usual daily medication

Water	Caffeine	Alcohol
☐☐☐☐☐☐☐☐☐☐	x ________	x ________

FOOD ANALYSIS

New food introduced?
☐ Yes ☐ No

Food reintroduction?
☐ Yes ☐ No

Details

MEDICATION ANALYSIS

New med/dose introduced?
☐ Yes ☐ No

Medication stopped?
☐ Yes ☐ No

Details

ACTIVITY ANALYSIS

Heightened exertion levels?
☐ Yes ☐ No

Lowered exertion levels?
☐ Yes ☐ No

Details

SLEEP ANALYSIS

When you woke up this morning, did you feel well-rested?	☐ Yes	☐ No	☐ A bit
Did you snore or stop breathing throughout the night?	☐ Yes	☐ No	☐ Not sure
Roughly how many times did you wake up throughout the night?			

Notes / Suspected Triggers

ENTRY #70 | M T W T F S S | DATE:

HOW ARE YOU *Feeling today?*

Amazing!	Meh
Great	Not good
Good	Terrible!

RATE YOUR PAIN LEVEL

① ② ③ ④ ⑤ ⑥ ⑦ ⑧ ⑨ ⑩

WHAT ABOUT YOUR...?

Mood	① ② ③ ④ ⑤ ⑥ ⑦ ⑧ ⑨ ⑩
Energy Levels	① ② ③ ④ ⑤ ⑥ ⑦ ⑧ ⑨ ⑩
Mental Clarity	① ② ③ ④ ⑤ ⑥ ⑦ ⑧ ⑨ ⑩

PAIN & PHYSICAL SYMPTOMS

Symptom	Severity	am	pm
	① ② ③ ④ ⑤	☐	☐
	① ② ③ ④ ⑤	☐	☐
	① ② ③ ④ ⑤	☐	☐
	① ② ③ ④ ⑤	☐	☐
	① ② ③ ④ ⑤	☐	☐
	① ② ③ ④ ⑤	☐	☐
	① ② ③ ④ ⑤	☐	☐
	① ② ③ ④ ⑤	☐	☐

front *back*

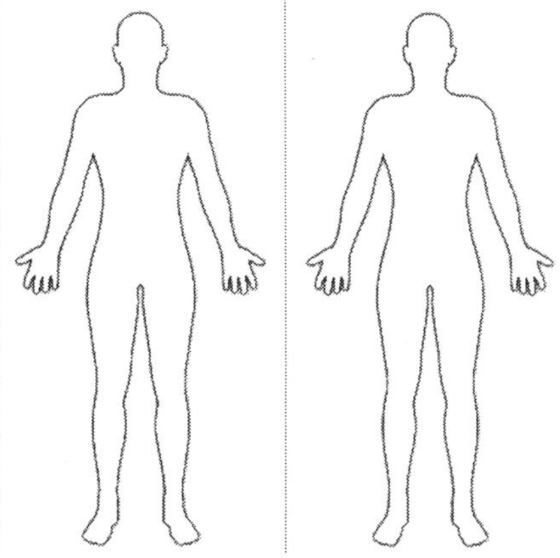

OTHER SYMPTOMS

general

Symptom	Severity	Time	
☐ Fatigue	① ② ③ ④ ⑤	☐ a.m.	☐ p.m.
☐ Lethargy	① ② ③ ④ ⑤	☐ a.m.	☐ p.m.
☐ Malaise	① ② ③ ④ ⑤	☐ a.m.	☐ p.m.
☐ Weakness	① ② ③ ④ ⑤	☐ a.m.	☐ p.m.
☐ Dizziness	① ② ③ ④ ⑤	☐ a.m.	☐ p.m.
☐ Trembling	① ② ③ ④ ⑤	☐ a.m.	☐ p.m.
☐ Twitching	① ② ③ ④ ⑤	☐ a.m.	☐ p.m.
☐ Insomnia	① ② ③ ④ ⑤	☐ a.m.	☐ p.m.

illness

Symptom	Severity	Time	
☐ Nausea	① ② ③ ④ ⑤	☐ a.m.	☐ p.m.
☐ Vomiting	① ② ③ ④ ⑤	☐ a.m.	☐ p.m.
☐ Constipation	① ② ③ ④ ⑤	☐ a.m.	☐ p.m.
☐ Diarrhea	① ② ③ ④ ⑤	☐ a.m.	☐ p.m.
☐ Sore throat	① ② ③ ④ ⑤	☐ a.m.	☐ p.m.
☐ Congestion	① ② ③ ④ ⑤	☐ a.m.	☐ p.m.
☐ Coughing	① ② ③ ④ ⑤	☐ a.m.	☐ p.m.
☐ Acid reflux	① ② ③ ④ ⑤	☐ a.m.	☐ p.m.

psychological

Symptom	Severity	Time	
☐ Anxiety	① ② ③ ④ ⑤	☐ a.m.	☐ p.m.
☐ Depression	① ② ③ ④ ⑤	☐ a.m.	☐ p.m.
☐ Memory loss	① ② ③ ④ ⑤	☐ a.m.	☐ p.m.
☐ Confusion	① ② ③ ④ ⑤	☐ a.m.	☐ p.m.
☐ Poor focus	① ② ③ ④ ⑤	☐ a.m.	☐ p.m.
☐ Mood swings	① ② ③ ④ ⑤	☐ a.m.	☐ p.m.
☐ Suicidal	① ② ③ ④ ⑤	☐ a.m.	☐ p.m.

other

Symptom	Severity	Time	
	① ② ③ ④ ⑤	☐ a.m.	☐ p.m.
	① ② ③ ④ ⑤	☐ a.m.	☐ p.m.
	① ② ③ ④ ⑤	☐ a.m.	☐ p.m.
	① ② ③ ④ ⑤	☐ a.m.	☐ p.m.
	① ② ③ ④ ⑤	☐ a.m.	☐ p.m.
	① ② ③ ④ ⑤	☐ a.m.	☐ p.m.
	① ② ③ ④ ⑤	☐ a.m.	☐ p.m.

SLEEP

hours ________ *quality* ① ② ③ ④ ⑤

STRESS LEVELS

None	Low	Medium	High	Max	@$#%!

WEATHER

☐ Cold ☐ Mild ☐ Hot
☐ Dry ☐ Humid ☐ Wet

Allergen Levels: ________

BM Pressure: ________

EXERCISE

☐ Heck yes, I worked out.
☐ I managed to exercise a bit.
☐ No, I haven't exercised at all.
☐ I did some stuff, and that counts.

DETAILS

FOOD / MEDICATION

Food / Drinks

Meds / Supplements	Time	Dose
☐ usual daily medication		

Water *Caffeine* *Alcohol*

x ________ x ________

FOOD ANALYSIS

New food introduced?

☐ Yes ☐ No

Food reintroduction?

☐ Yes ☐ No

Details

MEDICATION ANALYSIS

New med/dose introduced?

☐ Yes ☐ No

Medication stopped?

☐ Yes ☐ No

Details

ACTIVITY ANALYSIS

Heightened exertion levels?

☐ Yes ☐ No

Lowered exertion levels?

☐ Yes ☐ No

Details

SLEEP ANALYSIS

When you woke up this morning, did you feel well-rested?	☐ Yes	☐ No	☐ A bit
Did you snore or stop breathing throughout the night?	☐ Yes	☐ No	☐ Not sure

Roughly how many times did you wake up throughout the night?

Notes / Suspected Triggers

ENTRY #71 | M T W T F S S | DATE:

HOW ARE YOU *Feeling today?*

Amazing!	Meh
Great	Not good
Good	Terrible!

RATE YOUR PAIN LEVEL

① ② ③ ④ ⑤ ⑥ ⑦ ⑧ ⑨ ⑩

WHAT ABOUT YOUR...?

Mood	① ② ③ ④ ⑤ ⑥ ⑦ ⑧ ⑨ ⑩
Energy Levels	① ② ③ ④ ⑤ ⑥ ⑦ ⑧ ⑨ ⑩
Mental Clarity	① ② ③ ④ ⑤ ⑥ ⑦ ⑧ ⑨ ⑩

PAIN & PHYSICAL SYMPTOMS

Symptom	Severity	am	pm
	① ② ③ ④ ⑤	☐	☐
	① ② ③ ④ ⑤	☐	☐
	① ② ③ ④ ⑤	☐	☐
	① ② ③ ④ ⑤	☐	☐
	① ② ③ ④ ⑤	☐	☐
	① ② ③ ④ ⑤	☐	☐
	① ② ③ ④ ⑤	☐	☐
	① ② ③ ④ ⑤	☐	☐

front *back*

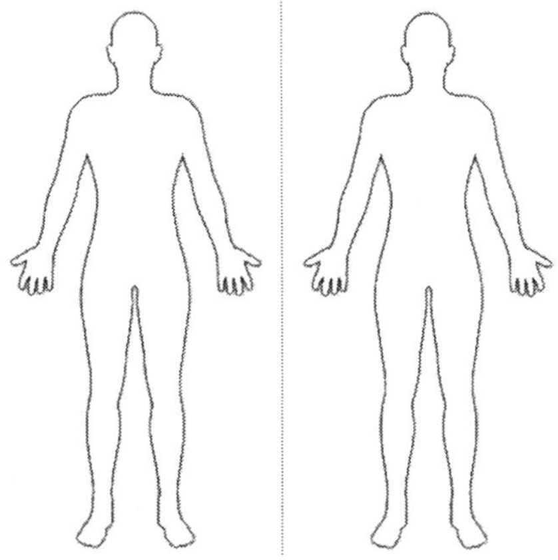

OTHER SYMPTOMS

general

Symptom	Severity	Time	
☐ Fatigue	① ② ③ ④ ⑤	☐ a.m.	☐ p.m.
☐ Lethargy	① ② ③ ④ ⑤	☐ a.m.	☐ p.m.
☐ Malaise	① ② ③ ④ ⑤	☐ a.m.	☐ p.m.
☐ Weakness	① ② ③ ④ ⑤	☐ a.m.	☐ p.m.
☐ Dizziness	① ② ③ ④ ⑤	☐ a.m.	☐ p.m.
☐ Trembling	① ② ③ ④ ⑤	☐ a.m.	☐ p.m.
☐ Twitching	① ② ③ ④ ⑤	☐ a.m.	☐ p.m.
☐ Insomnia	① ② ③ ④ ⑤	☐ a.m.	☐ p.m.

illness

Symptom	Severity	Time	
☐ Nausea	① ② ③ ④ ⑤	☐ a.m.	☐ p.m.
☐ Vomiting	① ② ③ ④ ⑤	☐ a.m.	☐ p.m.
☐ Constipation	① ② ③ ④ ⑤	☐ a.m.	☐ p.m.
☐ Diarrhea	① ② ③ ④ ⑤	☐ a.m.	☐ p.m.
☐ Sore throat	① ② ③ ④ ⑤	☐ a.m.	☐ p.m.
☐ Congestion	① ② ③ ④ ⑤	☐ a.m.	☐ p.m.
☐ Coughing	① ② ③ ④ ⑤	☐ a.m.	☐ p.m.
☐ Acid reflux	① ② ③ ④ ⑤	☐ a.m.	☐ p.m.

psychological

Symptom	Severity	Time	
☐ Anxiety	① ② ③ ④ ⑤	☐ a.m.	☐ p.m.
☐ Depression	① ② ③ ④ ⑤	☐ a.m.	☐ p.m.
☐ Memory loss	① ② ③ ④ ⑤	☐ a.m.	☐ p.m.
☐ Confusion	① ② ③ ④ ⑤	☐ a.m.	☐ p.m.
☐ Poor focus	① ② ③ ④ ⑤	☐ a.m.	☐ p.m.
☐ Mood swings	① ② ③ ④ ⑤	☐ a.m.	☐ p.m.
☐ Suicidal	① ② ③ ④ ⑤	☐ a.m.	☐ p.m.

other

Symptom	Severity	Time	
	① ② ③ ④ ⑤	☐ a.m.	☐ p.m.
	① ② ③ ④ ⑤	☐ a.m.	☐ p.m.
	① ② ③ ④ ⑤	☐ a.m.	☐ p.m.
	① ② ③ ④ ⑤	☐ a.m.	☐ p.m.
	① ② ③ ④ ⑤	☐ a.m.	☐ p.m.
	① ② ③ ④ ⑤	☐ a.m.	☐ p.m.
	① ② ③ ④ ⑤	☐ a.m.	☐ p.m.

SLEEP

hours ________ quality ① ② ③ ④ ⑤

STRESS LEVELS

None	Low	Medium	High	Max	@$#%!

WEATHER

☐ Cold ☐ Mild ☐ Hot
☐ Dry ☐ Humid ☐ Wet

Allergen Levels: ________

BM Pressure: ________

EXERCISE

☐ Heck yes, I worked out.
☐ I managed to exercise a bit.
☐ No, I haven't exercised at all.
☐ I did some stuff, and that counts.

DETAILS

FOOD / MEDICATION

Food / Drinks

Meds / Supplements	Time	Dose

☐ usual daily medication

Water	Caffeine	Alcohol
	x ________	x ________

FOOD ANALYSIS		MEDICATION ANALYSIS		ACTIVITY ANALYSIS	
New food introduced?		New med/dose introduced?		Heightened exertion levels?	
☐ Yes	☐ No	☐ Yes	☐ No	☐ Yes	☐ No
Food reintroduction?		Medication stopped?		Lowered exertion levels?	
☐ Yes	☐ No	☐ Yes	☐ No	☐ Yes	☐ No
Details		Details		Details	

SLEEP ANALYSIS

When you woke up this morning, did you feel well-rested?	☐ Yes	☐ No	☐ A bit
Did you snore or stop breathing throughout the night?	☐ Yes	☐ No	☐ Not sure
Roughly how many times did you wake up throughout the night?			

Notes / Suspected Triggers

ENTRY #72 | M T W T F S S | DATE:

HOW ARE YOU *Feeling today?*

Amazing!	Meh
Great	Not good
Good	Terrible!

RATE YOUR PAIN LEVEL

① ② ③ ④ ⑤ ⑥ ⑦ ⑧ ⑨ ⑩

WHAT ABOUT YOUR...?

Mood	1	2	3	4	5	6	7	8	9	10
Energy Levels	1	2	3	4	5	6	7	8	9	10
Mental Clarity	1	2	3	4	5	6	7	8	9	10

PAIN & PHYSICAL SYMPTOMS

Symptom	Severity	am	pm
	① ② ③ ④ ⑤	☐	☐
	① ② ③ ④ ⑤	☐	☐
	① ② ③ ④ ⑤	☐	☐
	① ② ③ ④ ⑤	☐	☐
	① ② ③ ④ ⑤	☐	☐
	① ② ③ ④ ⑤	☐	☐
	① ② ③ ④ ⑤	☐	☐
	① ② ③ ④ ⑤	☐	☐

front **back**

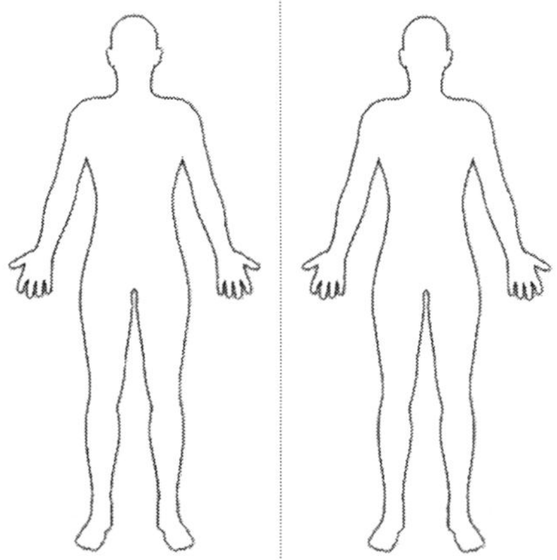

OTHER SYMPTOMS

general

Symptom	Severity	Time	
☐ Fatigue	① ② ③ ④ ⑤	☐ a.m.	☐ p.m.
☐ Lethargy	① ② ③ ④ ⑤	☐ a.m.	☐ p.m.
☐ Malaise	① ② ③ ④ ⑤	☐ a.m.	☐ p.m.
☐ Weakness	① ② ③ ④ ⑤	☐ a.m.	☐ p.m.
☐ Dizziness	① ② ③ ④ ⑤	☐ a.m.	☐ p.m.
☐ Trembling	① ② ③ ④ ⑤	☐ a.m.	☐ p.m.
☐ Twitching	① ② ③ ④ ⑤	☐ a.m.	☐ p.m.
☐ Insomnia	① ② ③ ④ ⑤	☐ a.m.	☐ p.m.

illness

Symptom	Severity	Time	
☐ Nausea	① ② ③ ④ ⑤	☐ a.m.	☐ p.m.
☐ Vomiting	① ② ③ ④ ⑤	☐ a.m.	☐ p.m.
☐ Constipation	① ② ③ ④ ⑤	☐ a.m.	☐ p.m.
☐ Diarrhea	① ② ③ ④ ⑤	☐ a.m.	☐ p.m.
☐ Sore throat	① ② ③ ④ ⑤	☐ a.m.	☐ p.m.
☐ Congestion	① ② ③ ④ ⑤	☐ a.m.	☐ p.m.
☐ Coughing	① ② ③ ④ ⑤	☐ a.m.	☐ p.m.
☐ Acid reflux	① ② ③ ④ ⑤	☐ a.m.	☐ p.m.

psychological

Symptom	Severity	Time	
☐ Anxiety	① ② ③ ④ ⑤	☐ a.m.	☐ p.m.
☐ Depression	① ② ③ ④ ⑤	☐ a.m.	☐ p.m.
☐ Memory loss	① ② ③ ④ ⑤	☐ a.m.	☐ p.m.
☐ Confusion	① ② ③ ④ ⑤	☐ a.m.	☐ p.m.
☐ Poor focus	① ② ③ ④ ⑤	☐ a.m.	☐ p.m.
☐ Mood swings	① ② ③ ④ ⑤	☐ a.m.	☐ p.m.
☐ Suicidal	① ② ③ ④ ⑤	☐ a.m.	☐ p.m.

other

Symptom	Severity	Time	
	① ② ③ ④ ⑤	☐ a.m.	☐ p.m.
	① ② ③ ④ ⑤	☐ a.m.	☐ p.m.
	① ② ③ ④ ⑤	☐ a.m.	☐ p.m.
	① ② ③ ④ ⑤	☐ a.m.	☐ p.m.
	① ② ③ ④ ⑤	☐ a.m.	☐ p.m.
	① ② ③ ④ ⑤	☐ a.m.	☐ p.m.
	① ② ③ ④ ⑤	☐ a.m.	☐ p.m.

SLEEP

hours ______ quality ① ② ③ ④ ⑤

STRESS LEVELS

None	Low	Medium	High	Max	@$#%!

WEATHER

☐ Cold ☐ Mild ☐ Hot
☐ Dry ☐ Humid ☐ Wet

Allergen Levels: ________

BM Pressure: ________

EXERCISE

☐ Heck yes, I worked out.
☐ I managed to exercise a bit.
☐ No, I haven't exercised at all.
☐ I did some stuff, and that counts.

DETAILS

FOOD / MEDICATION

Food / Drinks

Meds / Supplements	Time	Dose

☐ usual daily medication

Water *Caffeine* *Alcohol*

x ________ x ________

FOOD ANALYSIS

New food introduced?

☐ Yes ☐ No

Food reintroduction?

☐ Yes ☐ No

Details

MEDICATION ANALYSIS

New med/dose introduced?

☐ Yes ☐ No

Medication stopped?

☐ Yes ☐ No

Details

ACTIVITY ANALYSIS

Heightened exertion levels?

☐ Yes ☐ No

Lowered exertion levels?

☐ Yes ☐ No

Details

SLEEP ANALYSIS

When you woke up this morning, did you feel well-rested?	☐ Yes	☐ No	☐ A bit
Did you snore or stop breathing throughout the night?	☐ Yes	☐ No	☐ Not sure

Roughly how many times did you wake up throughout the night?

Notes / Suspected Triggers

ENTRY #73 | M T W T F S S | DATE:

HOW ARE YOU *Feeling today?*

RATE YOUR PAIN LEVEL

① ② ③ ④ ⑤ ⑥ ⑦ ⑧ ⑨ ⑩

WHAT ABOUT YOUR...?

Mood	① ② ③ ④ ⑤ ⑥ ⑦ ⑧ ⑨ ⑩
Energy Levels	① ② ③ ④ ⑤ ⑥ ⑦ ⑧ ⑨ ⑩
Mental Clarity	① ② ③ ④ ⑤ ⑥ ⑦ ⑧ ⑨ ⑩

PAIN & PHYSICAL SYMPTOMS

Symptom	Severity	am	pm
	① ② ③ ④ ⑤	☐	☐
	① ② ③ ④ ⑤	☐	☐
	① ② ③ ④ ⑤	☐	☐
	① ② ③ ④ ⑤	☐	☐
	① ② ③ ④ ⑤	☐	☐
	① ② ③ ④ ⑤	☐	☐
	① ② ③ ④ ⑤	☐	☐
	① ② ③ ④ ⑤	☐	☐

front ***back***

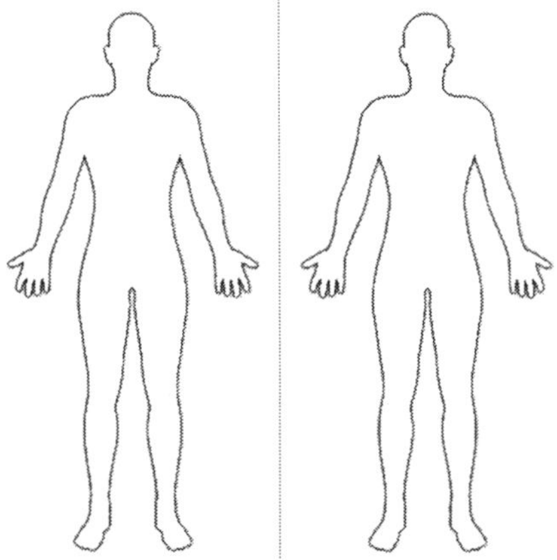

OTHER SYMPTOMS

general

Symptom	Severity	Time	
☐ Fatigue	① ② ③ ④ ⑤	☐ a.m.	☐ p.m.
☐ Lethargy	① ② ③ ④ ⑤	☐ a.m.	☐ p.m.
☐ Malaise	① ② ③ ④ ⑤	☐ a.m.	☐ p.m.
☐ Weakness	① ② ③ ④ ⑤	☐ a.m.	☐ p.m.
☐ Dizziness	① ② ③ ④ ⑤	☐ a.m.	☐ p.m.
☐ Trembling	① ② ③ ④ ⑤	☐ a.m.	☐ p.m.
☐ Twitching	① ② ③ ④ ⑤	☐ a.m.	☐ p.m.
☐ Insomnia	① ② ③ ④ ⑤	☐ a.m.	☐ p.m.

illness

Symptom	Severity	Time	
☐ Nausea	① ② ③ ④ ⑤	☐ a.m.	☐ p.m.
☐ Vomiting	① ② ③ ④ ⑤	☐ a.m.	☐ p.m.
☐ Constipation	① ② ③ ④ ⑤	☐ a.m.	☐ p.m.
☐ Diarrhea	① ② ③ ④ ⑤	☐ a.m.	☐ p.m.
☐ Sore throat	① ② ③ ④ ⑤	☐ a.m.	☐ p.m.
☐ Congestion	① ② ③ ④ ⑤	☐ a.m.	☐ p.m.
☐ Coughing	① ② ③ ④ ⑤	☐ a.m.	☐ p.m.
☐ Acid reflux	① ② ③ ④ ⑤	☐ a.m.	☐ p.m.

psychological

Symptom	Severity	Time	
☐ Anxiety	① ② ③ ④ ⑤	☐ a.m.	☐ p.m.
☐ Depression	① ② ③ ④ ⑤	☐ a.m.	☐ p.m.
☐ Memory loss	① ② ③ ④ ⑤	☐ a.m.	☐ p.m.
☐ Confusion	① ② ③ ④ ⑤	☐ a.m.	☐ p.m.
☐ Poor focus	① ② ③ ④ ⑤	☐ a.m.	☐ p.m.
☐ Mood swings	① ② ③ ④ ⑤	☐ a.m.	☐ p.m.
☐ Suicidal	① ② ③ ④ ⑤	☐ a.m.	☐ p.m.

other

Symptom	Severity	Time	
	① ② ③ ④ ⑤	☐ a.m.	☐ p.m.
	① ② ③ ④ ⑤	☐ a.m.	☐ p.m.
	① ② ③ ④ ⑤	☐ a.m.	☐ p.m.
	① ② ③ ④ ⑤	☐ a.m.	☐ p.m.
	① ② ③ ④ ⑤	☐ a.m.	☐ p.m.
	① ② ③ ④ ⑤	☐ a.m.	☐ p.m.
	① ② ③ ④ ⑤	☐ a.m.	☐ p.m.

SLEEP

hours ________ *quality* ① ② ③ ④ ⑤

STRESS LEVELS

None	Low	Medium	High	Max	@$#%!

WEATHER

☐ Cold ☐ Mild ☐ Hot
☐ Dry ☐ Humid ☐ Wet

Allergen Levels: ________

BM Pressure: ________

EXERCISE

☐ Heck yes, I worked out.
☐ I managed to exercise a bit.
☐ No, I haven't exercised at all.
☐ I did some stuff, and that counts.

DETAILS

FOOD / MEDICATION

Food / Drinks

Meds / Supplements	Time	Dose
☐ usual daily medication		

Water	*Caffeine*	*Alcohol*
	x ________	x ________

FOOD ANALYSIS		MEDICATION ANALYSIS		ACTIVITY ANALYSIS	
New food introduced?		New med/dose introduced?		Heightened exertion levels?	
☐ Yes	☐ No	☐ Yes	☐ No	☐ Yes	☐ No
Food reintroduction?		Medication stopped?		Lowered exertion levels?	
☐ Yes	☐ No	☐ Yes	☐ No	☐ Yes	☐ No
Details		*Details*		*Details*	

SLEEP ANALYSIS

When you woke up this morning, did you feel well-rested?	☐ Yes	☐ No	☐ A bit
Did you snore or stop breathing throughout the night?	☐ Yes	☐ No	☐ Not sure
Roughly how many times did you wake up throughout the night?			

Notes / Suspected Triggers

ENTRY #74 | M T W T F S S | DATE:

HOW ARE YOU *Feeling today?*

Amazing!	Meh
Great	Not good
Good	Terrible!

RATE YOUR PAIN LEVEL

① ② ③ ④ ⑤ ⑥ ⑦ ⑧ ⑨ ⑩

WHAT ABOUT YOUR...?

Mood	① ② ③ ④ ⑤ ⑥ ⑦ ⑧ ⑨ ⑩
Energy Levels	① ② ③ ④ ⑤ ⑥ ⑦ ⑧ ⑨ ⑩
Mental Clarity	① ② ③ ④ ⑤ ⑥ ⑦ ⑧ ⑨ ⑩

PAIN & PHYSICAL SYMPTOMS

Symptom	Severity	am	pm
	① ② ③ ④ ⑤	☐	☐
	① ② ③ ④ ⑤	☐	☐
	① ② ③ ④ ⑤	☐	☐
	① ② ③ ④ ⑤	☐	☐
	① ② ③ ④ ⑤	☐	☐
	① ② ③ ④ ⑤	☐	☐
	① ② ③ ④ ⑤	☐	☐
	① ② ③ ④ ⑤	☐	☐

front *back*

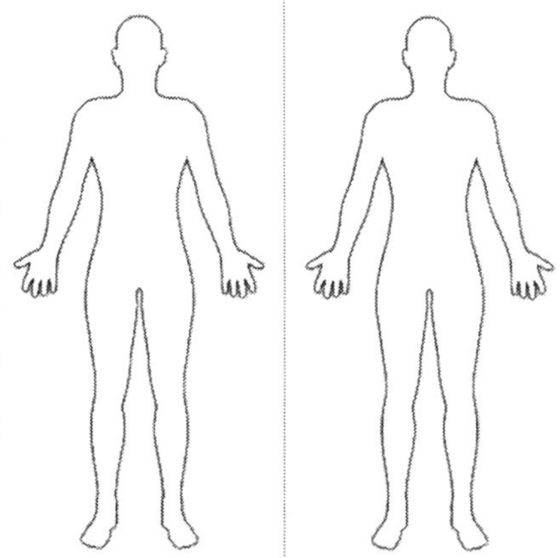

OTHER SYMPTOMS

general

Symptom	Severity	Time	
☐ Fatigue	① ② ③ ④ ⑤	☐ a.m.	☐ p.m.
☐ Lethargy	① ② ③ ④ ⑤	☐ a.m.	☐ p.m.
☐ Malaise	① ② ③ ④ ⑤	☐ a.m.	☐ p.m.
☐ Weakness	① ② ③ ④ ⑤	☐ a.m.	☐ p.m.
☐ Dizziness	① ② ③ ④ ⑤	☐ a.m.	☐ p.m.
☐ Trembling	① ② ③ ④ ⑤	☐ a.m.	☐ p.m.
☐ Twitching	① ② ③ ④ ⑤	☐ a.m.	☐ p.m.
☐ Insomnia	① ② ③ ④ ⑤	☐ a.m.	☐ p.m.

illness

Symptom	Severity	Time	
☐ Nausea	① ② ③ ④ ⑤	☐ a.m.	☐ p.m.
☐ Vomiting	① ② ③ ④ ⑤	☐ a.m.	☐ p.m.
☐ Constipation	① ② ③ ④ ⑤	☐ a.m.	☐ p.m.
☐ Diarrhea	① ② ③ ④ ⑤	☐ a.m.	☐ p.m.
☐ Sore throat	① ② ③ ④ ⑤	☐ a.m.	☐ p.m.
☐ Congestion	① ② ③ ④ ⑤	☐ a.m.	☐ p.m.
☐ Coughing	① ② ③ ④ ⑤	☐ a.m.	☐ p.m.
☐ Acid reflux	① ② ③ ④ ⑤	☐ a.m.	☐ p.m.

psychological

Symptom	Severity	Time	
☐ Anxiety	① ② ③ ④ ⑤	☐ a.m.	☐ p.m.
☐ Depression	① ② ③ ④ ⑤	☐ a.m.	☐ p.m.
☐ Memory loss	① ② ③ ④ ⑤	☐ a.m.	☐ p.m.
☐ Confusion	① ② ③ ④ ⑤	☐ a.m.	☐ p.m.
☐ Poor focus	① ② ③ ④ ⑤	☐ a.m.	☐ p.m.
☐ Mood swings	① ② ③ ④ ⑤	☐ a.m.	☐ p.m.
☐ Suicidal	① ② ③ ④ ⑤	☐ a.m.	☐ p.m.

other

Symptom	Severity	Time	
	① ② ③ ④ ⑤	☐ a.m.	☐ p.m.
	① ② ③ ④ ⑤	☐ a.m.	☐ p.m.
	① ② ③ ④ ⑤	☐ a.m.	☐ p.m.
	① ② ③ ④ ⑤	☐ a.m.	☐ p.m.
	① ② ③ ④ ⑤	☐ a.m.	☐ p.m.
	① ② ③ ④ ⑤	☐ a.m.	☐ p.m.
	① ② ③ ④ ⑤	☐ a.m.	☐ p.m.

SLEEP

hours ________ *quality* (1) (2) (3) (4) (5)

STRESS LEVELS

None	Low	Medium	High	Max	@$#%!

WEATHER

☐ Cold ☐ Mild ☐ Hot
☐ Dry ☐ Humid ☐ Wet

Allergen Levels: ________

BM Pressure: ________

EXERCISE

☐ Heck yes, I worked out.
☐ I managed to exercise a bit.
☐ No, I haven't exercised at all.
☐ I did some stuff, and that counts.

DETAILS

FOOD / MEDICATION

Food / Drinks

Meds / Supplements	Time	Dose
☐ usual daily medication		

Water ☐☐☐☐☐☐☐☐☐☐

Caffeine x ________

Alcohol x ________

FOOD ANALYSIS

New food introduced?
☐ Yes ☐ No

Food reintroduction?
☐ Yes ☐ No

Details

MEDICATION ANALYSIS

New med/dose introduced?
☐ Yes ☐ No

Medication stopped?
☐ Yes ☐ No

Details

ACTIVITY ANALYSIS

Heightened exertion levels?
☐ Yes ☐ No

Lowered exertion levels?
☐ Yes ☐ No

Details

SLEEP ANALYSIS

When you woke up this morning, did you feel well-rested? ☐ Yes ☐ No ☐ A bit

Did you snore or stop breathing throughout the night? ☐ Yes ☐ No ☐ Not sure

Roughly how many times did you wake up throughout the night?

Notes / Suspected Triggers

ENTRY #75 | M T W T F S S | DATE:

HOW ARE YOU *Feeling today?*

Amazing!	Meh

Great	Not good

Good	Terrible!

RATE YOUR PAIN LEVEL

① ② ③ ④ ⑤ ⑥ ⑦ ⑧ ⑨ ⑩

WHAT ABOUT YOUR...?

Mood	① ② ③ ④ ⑤ ⑥ ⑦ ⑧ ⑨ ⑩
Energy Levels	① ② ③ ④ ⑤ ⑥ ⑦ ⑧ ⑨ ⑩
Mental Clarity	① ② ③ ④ ⑤ ⑥ ⑦ ⑧ ⑨ ⑩

PAIN & PHYSICAL SYMPTOMS

Symptom	Severity	am	pm
	① ② ③ ④ ⑤	☐	☐
	① ② ③ ④ ⑤	☐	☐
	① ② ③ ④ ⑤	☐	☐
	① ② ③ ④ ⑤	☐	☐
	① ② ③ ④ ⑤	☐	☐
	① ② ③ ④ ⑤	☐	☐
	① ② ③ ④ ⑤	☐	☐
	① ② ③ ④ ⑤	☐	☐

front ***back***

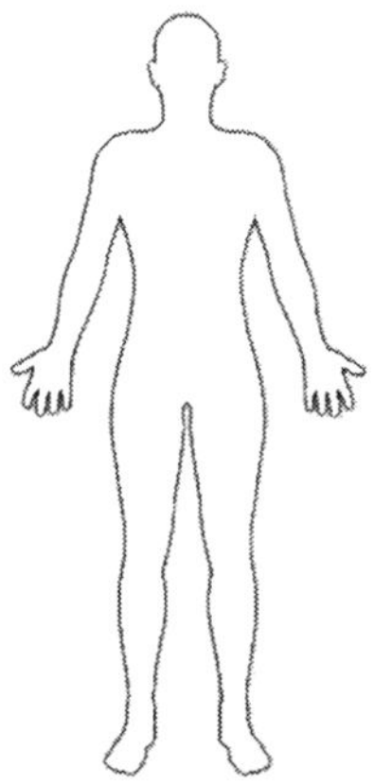
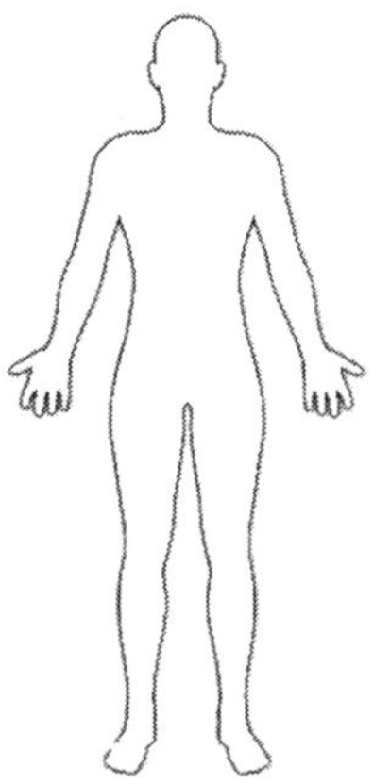

OTHER SYMPTOMS

general

Symptom	Severity	Time	
☐ Fatigue	① ② ③ ④ ⑤	☐ a.m.	☐ p.m.
☐ Lethargy	① ② ③ ④ ⑤	☐ a.m.	☐ p.m.
☐ Malaise	① ② ③ ④ ⑤	☐ a.m.	☐ p.m.
☐ Weakness	① ② ③ ④ ⑤	☐ a.m.	☐ p.m.
☐ Dizziness	① ② ③ ④ ⑤	☐ a.m.	☐ p.m.
☐ Trembling	① ② ③ ④ ⑤	☐ a.m.	☐ p.m.
☐ Twitching	① ② ③ ④ ⑤	☐ a.m.	☐ p.m.
☐ Insomnia	① ② ③ ④ ⑤	☐ a.m.	☐ p.m.

illness

Symptom	Severity	Time	
☐ Nausea	① ② ③ ④ ⑤	☐ a.m.	☐ p.m.
☐ Vomiting	① ② ③ ④ ⑤	☐ a.m.	☐ p.m.
☐ Constipation	① ② ③ ④ ⑤	☐ a.m.	☐ p.m.
☐ Diarrhea	① ② ③ ④ ⑤	☐ a.m.	☐ p.m.
☐ Sore throat	① ② ③ ④ ⑤	☐ a.m.	☐ p.m.
☐ Congestion	① ② ③ ④ ⑤	☐ a.m.	☐ p.m.
☐ Coughing	① ② ③ ④ ⑤	☐ a.m.	☐ p.m.
☐ Acid reflux	① ② ③ ④ ⑤	☐ a.m.	☐ p.m.

psychological

Symptom	Severity	Time	
☐ Anxiety	① ② ③ ④ ⑤	☐ a.m.	☐ p.m.
☐ Depression	① ② ③ ④ ⑤	☐ a.m.	☐ p.m.
☐ Memory loss	① ② ③ ④ ⑤	☐ a.m.	☐ p.m.
☐ Confusion	① ② ③ ④ ⑤	☐ a.m.	☐ p.m.
☐ Poor focus	① ② ③ ④ ⑤	☐ a.m.	☐ p.m.
☐ Mood swings	① ② ③ ④ ⑤	☐ a.m.	☐ p.m.
☐ Suicidal	① ② ③ ④ ⑤	☐ a.m.	☐ p.m.

other

Symptom	Severity	Time	
	① ② ③ ④ ⑤	☐ a.m.	☐ p.m.
	① ② ③ ④ ⑤	☐ a.m.	☐ p.m.
	① ② ③ ④ ⑤	☐ a.m.	☐ p.m.
	① ② ③ ④ ⑤	☐ a.m.	☐ p.m.
	① ② ③ ④ ⑤	☐ a.m.	☐ p.m.
	① ② ③ ④ ⑤	☐ a.m.	☐ p.m.
	① ② ③ ④ ⑤	☐ a.m.	☐ p.m.

SLEEP

hours ________ quality ① ② ③ ④ ⑤

STRESS LEVELS

None	Low	Medium	High	Max	@$#%!

WEATHER

☐ Cold ☐ Mild ☐ Hot
☐ Dry ☐ Humid ☐ Wet

Allergen Levels: ________

BM Pressure: ________

EXERCISE

☐ Heck yes, I worked out.
☐ I managed to exercise a bit.
☐ No, I haven't exercised at all.
☐ I did some stuff, and that counts.

DETAILS

FOOD / MEDICATION

Food / Drinks	Meds / Supplements	Time	Dose

☐ usual daily medication

Water *Caffeine* *Alcohol*

x ________ x ________

FOOD ANALYSIS

New food introduced?

☐ Yes ☐ No

Food reintroduction?

☐ Yes ☐ No

Details

MEDICATION ANALYSIS

New med/dose introduced?

☐ Yes ☐ No

Medication stopped?

☐ Yes ☐ No

Details

ACTIVITY ANALYSIS

Heightened exertion levels?

☐ Yes ☐ No

Lowered exertion levels?

☐ Yes ☐ No

Details

SLEEP ANALYSIS

When you woke up this morning, did you feel well-rested?	☐ Yes	☐ No	☐ A bit
Did you snore or stop breathing throughout the night?	☐ Yes	☐ No	☐ Not sure

Roughly how many times did you wake up throughout the night?

Notes / Suspected Triggers

ENTRY #76 | M T W T F S S | DATE:

HOW ARE YOU *Feeling today?*

Amazing!	Meh
Great	Not good
Good	Terrible!

RATE YOUR PAIN LEVEL

① ② ③ ④ ⑤ ⑥ ⑦ ⑧ ⑨ ⑩

WHAT ABOUT YOUR...?

Mood	① ② ③ ④ ⑤ ⑥ ⑦ ⑧ ⑨ ⑩
Energy Levels	① ② ③ ④ ⑤ ⑥ ⑦ ⑧ ⑨ ⑩
Mental Clarity	① ② ③ ④ ⑤ ⑥ ⑦ ⑧ ⑨ ⑩

PAIN & PHYSICAL SYMPTOMS

Symptom	Severity	am	pm
	① ② ③ ④ ⑤	☐	☐
	① ② ③ ④ ⑤	☐	☐
	① ② ③ ④ ⑤	☐	☐
	① ② ③ ④ ⑤	☐	☐
	① ② ③ ④ ⑤	☐	☐
	① ② ③ ④ ⑤	☐	☐
	① ② ③ ④ ⑤	☐	☐
	① ② ③ ④ ⑤	☐	☐

front *back*

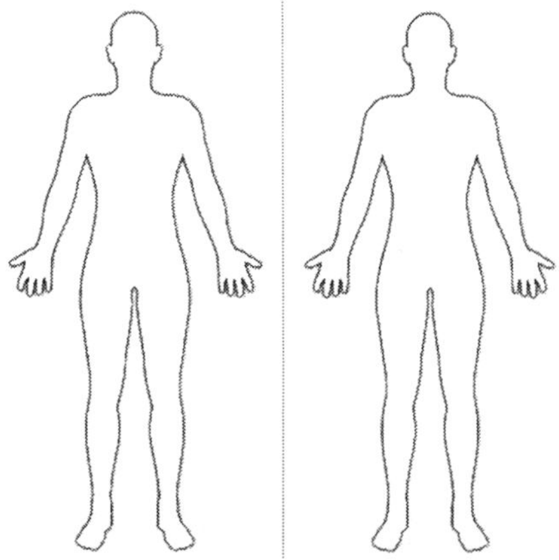

OTHER SYMPTOMS

general

Symptom	Severity	Time	
☐ Fatigue	① ② ③ ④ ⑤	☐ a.m.	☐ p.m.
☐ Lethargy	① ② ③ ④ ⑤	☐ a.m.	☐ p.m.
☐ Malaise	① ② ③ ④ ⑤	☐ a.m.	☐ p.m.
☐ Weakness	① ② ③ ④ ⑤	☐ a.m.	☐ p.m.
☐ Dizziness	① ② ③ ④ ⑤	☐ a.m.	☐ p.m.
☐ Trembling	① ② ③ ④ ⑤	☐ a.m.	☐ p.m.
☐ Twitching	① ② ③ ④ ⑤	☐ a.m.	☐ p.m.
☐ Insomnia	① ② ③ ④ ⑤	☐ a.m.	☐ p.m.

illness

Symptom	Severity	Time	
☐ Nausea	① ② ③ ④ ⑤	☐ a.m.	☐ p.m.
☐ Vomiting	① ② ③ ④ ⑤	☐ a.m.	☐ p.m.
☐ Constipation	① ② ③ ④ ⑤	☐ a.m.	☐ p.m.
☐ Diarrhea	① ② ③ ④ ⑤	☐ a.m.	☐ p.m.
☐ Sore throat	① ② ③ ④ ⑤	☐ a.m.	☐ p.m.
☐ Congestion	① ② ③ ④ ⑤	☐ a.m.	☐ p.m.
☐ Coughing	① ② ③ ④ ⑤	☐ a.m.	☐ p.m.
☐ Acid reflux	① ② ③ ④ ⑤	☐ a.m.	☐ p.m.

psychological

Symptom	Severity	Time	
☐ Anxiety	① ② ③ ④ ⑤	☐ a.m.	☐ p.m.
☐ Depression	① ② ③ ④ ⑤	☐ a.m.	☐ p.m.
☐ Memory loss	① ② ③ ④ ⑤	☐ a.m.	☐ p.m.
☐ Confusion	① ② ③ ④ ⑤	☐ a.m.	☐ p.m.
☐ Poor focus	① ② ③ ④ ⑤	☐ a.m.	☐ p.m.
☐ Mood swings	① ② ③ ④ ⑤	☐ a.m.	☐ p.m.
☐ Suicidal	① ② ③ ④ ⑤	☐ a.m.	☐ p.m.

other

Symptom	Severity	Time	
	① ② ③ ④ ⑤	☐ a.m.	☐ p.m.
	① ② ③ ④ ⑤	☐ a.m.	☐ p.m.
	① ② ③ ④ ⑤	☐ a.m.	☐ p.m.
	① ② ③ ④ ⑤	☐ a.m.	☐ p.m.
	① ② ③ ④ ⑤	☐ a.m.	☐ p.m.
	① ② ③ ④ ⑤	☐ a.m.	☐ p.m.
	① ② ③ ④ ⑤	☐ a.m.	☐ p.m.

SLEEP

hours ______ quality ① ② ③ ④ ⑤

STRESS LEVELS

None	Low	Medium	High	Max	@$#%!

WEATHER

☐ Cold ☐ Mild ☐ Hot
☐ Dry ☐ Humid ☐ Wet

Allergen Levels: ______

BM Pressure: ______

EXERCISE

☐ Heck yes, I worked out.
☐ I managed to exercise a bit.
☐ No, I haven't exercised at all.
☐ I did some stuff, and that counts.

DETAILS

FOOD / MEDICATION

Food / Drinks

Meds / Supplements	Time	Dose

☐ usual daily medication

Water *Caffeine* *Alcohol*

☐☐☐☐☐☐☐☐☐☐ x ______ x ______

FOOD ANALYSIS

New food introduced?

☐ Yes ☐ No

Food reintroduction?

☐ Yes ☐ No

Details

MEDICATION ANALYSIS

New med/dose introduced?

☐ Yes ☐ No

Medication stopped?

☐ Yes ☐ No

Details

ACTIVITY ANALYSIS

Heightened exertion levels?

☐ Yes ☐ No

Lowered exertion levels?

☐ Yes ☐ No

Details

SLEEP ANALYSIS

When you woke up this morning, did you feel well-rested?	☐ Yes	☐ No	☐ A bit
Did you snore or stop breathing throughout the night?	☐ Yes	☐ No	☐ Not sure
Roughly how many times did you wake up throughout the night?			

Notes / Suspected Triggers

ENTRY #77 | M T W T F S S | DATE:

HOW ARE YOU *Feeling today?*

Amazing!	Meh
Great	Not good
Good	Terrible!

RATE YOUR PAIN LEVEL

① ② ③ ④ ⑤ ⑥ ⑦ ⑧ ⑨ ⑩

WHAT ABOUT YOUR...?

Mood	① ② ③ ④ ⑤ ⑥ ⑦ ⑧ ⑨ ⑩
Energy Levels	① ② ③ ④ ⑤ ⑥ ⑦ ⑧ ⑨ ⑩
Mental Clarity	① ② ③ ④ ⑤ ⑥ ⑦ ⑧ ⑨ ⑩

PAIN & PHYSICAL SYMPTOMS

Symptom	Severity	am	pm
	① ② ③ ④ ⑤	☐	☐
	① ② ③ ④ ⑤	☐	☐
	① ② ③ ④ ⑤	☐	☐
	① ② ③ ④ ⑤	☐	☐
	① ② ③ ④ ⑤	☐	☐
	① ② ③ ④ ⑤	☐	☐
	① ② ③ ④ ⑤	☐	☐
	① ② ③ ④ ⑤	☐	☐

front ***back***

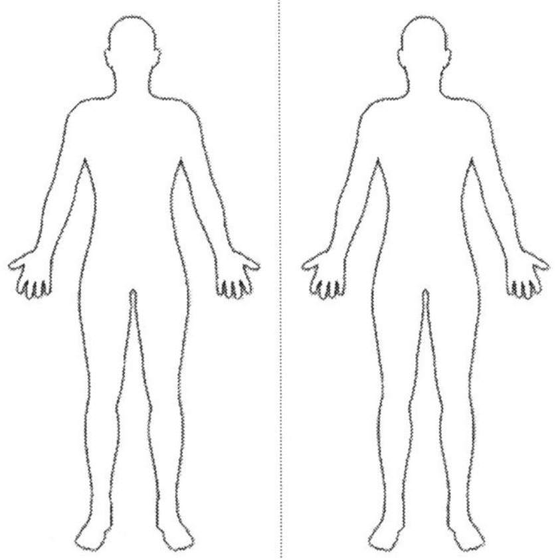

OTHER SYMPTOMS

general

Symptom	Severity	Time	
☐ Fatigue	① ② ③ ④ ⑤	☐ a.m.	☐ p.m.
☐ Lethargy	① ② ③ ④ ⑤	☐ a.m.	☐ p.m.
☐ Malaise	① ② ③ ④ ⑤	☐ a.m.	☐ p.m.
☐ Weakness	① ② ③ ④ ⑤	☐ a.m.	☐ p.m.
☐ Dizziness	① ② ③ ④ ⑤	☐ a.m.	☐ p.m.
☐ Trembling	① ② ③ ④ ⑤	☐ a.m.	☐ p.m.
☐ Twitching	① ② ③ ④ ⑤	☐ a.m.	☐ p.m.
☐ Insomnia	① ② ③ ④ ⑤	☐ a.m.	☐ p.m.

illness

Symptom	Severity	Time	
☐ Nausea	① ② ③ ④ ⑤	☐ a.m.	☐ p.m.
☐ Vomiting	① ② ③ ④ ⑤	☐ a.m.	☐ p.m.
☐ Constipation	① ② ③ ④ ⑤	☐ a.m.	☐ p.m.
☐ Diarrhea	① ② ③ ④ ⑤	☐ a.m.	☐ p.m.
☐ Sore throat	① ② ③ ④ ⑤	☐ a.m.	☐ p.m.
☐ Congestion	① ② ③ ④ ⑤	☐ a.m.	☐ p.m.
☐ Coughing	① ② ③ ④ ⑤	☐ a.m.	☐ p.m.
☐ Acid reflux	① ② ③ ④ ⑤	☐ a.m.	☐ p.m.

psychological

Symptom	Severity	Time	
☐ Anxiety	① ② ③ ④ ⑤	☐ a.m.	☐ p.m.
☐ Depression	① ② ③ ④ ⑤	☐ a.m.	☐ p.m.
☐ Memory loss	① ② ③ ④ ⑤	☐ a.m.	☐ p.m.
☐ Confusion	① ② ③ ④ ⑤	☐ a.m.	☐ p.m.
☐ Poor focus	① ② ③ ④ ⑤	☐ a.m.	☐ p.m.
☐ Mood swings	① ② ③ ④ ⑤	☐ a.m.	☐ p.m.
☐ Suicidal	① ② ③ ④ ⑤	☐ a.m.	☐ p.m.

other

Symptom	Severity	Time	
	① ② ③ ④ ⑤	☐ a.m.	☐ p.m.
	① ② ③ ④ ⑤	☐ a.m.	☐ p.m.
	① ② ③ ④ ⑤	☐ a.m.	☐ p.m.
	① ② ③ ④ ⑤	☐ a.m.	☐ p.m.
	① ② ③ ④ ⑤	☐ a.m.	☐ p.m.
	① ② ③ ④ ⑤	☐ a.m.	☐ p.m.
	① ② ③ ④ ⑤	☐ a.m.	☐ p.m.

SLEEP

hours ________ *quality* ① ② ③ ④ ⑤

STRESS LEVELS

None	Low	Medium	High	Max	@$#%!

WEATHER

☐ Cold ☐ Mild ☐ Hot
☐ Dry ☐ Humid ☐ Wet

Allergen Levels: ________

BM Pressure: ________

EXERCISE

☐ Heck yes, I worked out.
☐ I managed to exercise a bit.
☐ No, I haven't exercised at all.
☐ I did some stuff, and that counts.

DETAILS

FOOD / MEDICATION

Food / Drinks

Meds / Supplements	**Time**	**Dose**

☐ usual daily medication

Water *Caffeine* *Alcohol*

x ________ x ________

FOOD ANALYSIS

New food introduced?

☐ Yes ☐ No

Food reintroduction?

☐ Yes ☐ No

Details

MEDICATION ANALYSIS

New med/dose introduced?

☐ Yes ☐ No

Medication stopped?

☐ Yes ☐ No

Details

ACTIVITY ANALYSIS

Heightened exertion levels?

☐ Yes ☐ No

Lowered exertion levels?

☐ Yes ☐ No

Details

SLEEP ANALYSIS

When you woke up this morning, did you feel well-rested?	☐ Yes	☐ No	☐ A bit
Did you snore or stop breathing throughout the night?	☐ Yes	☐ No	☐ Not sure
Roughly how many times did you wake up throughout the night?			

Notes / Suspected Triggers

ENTRY #78 | M T W T F S S | DATE:

HOW ARE YOU *Feeling today?*

Amazing!	Meh
Great	Not good
Good	Terrible!

RATE YOUR PAIN LEVEL

① ② ③ ④ ⑤ ⑥ ⑦ ⑧ ⑨ ⑩

WHAT ABOUT YOUR...?

Mood	① ② ③ ④ ⑤ ⑥ ⑦ ⑧ ⑨ ⑩
Energy Levels	① ② ③ ④ ⑤ ⑥ ⑦ ⑧ ⑨ ⑩
Mental Clarity	① ② ③ ④ ⑤ ⑥ ⑦ ⑧ ⑨ ⑩

PAIN & PHYSICAL SYMPTOMS

Symptom	Severity	am	pm
	① ② ③ ④ ⑤	☐	☐
	① ② ③ ④ ⑤	☐	☐
	① ② ③ ④ ⑤	☐	☐
	① ② ③ ④ ⑤	☐	☐
	① ② ③ ④ ⑤	☐	☐
	① ② ③ ④ ⑤	☐	☐
	① ② ③ ④ ⑤	☐	☐
	① ② ③ ④ ⑤	☐	☐

front *back*

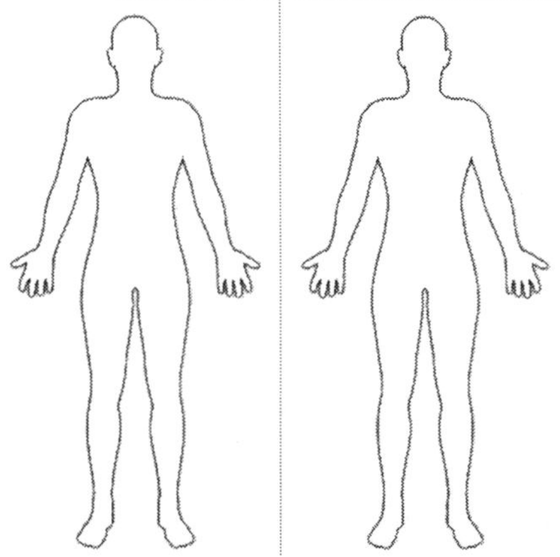

OTHER SYMPTOMS

general

Symptom	Severity	Time	
☐ Fatigue	① ② ③ ④ ⑤	☐ a.m.	☐ p.m.
☐ Lethargy	① ② ③ ④ ⑤	☐ a.m.	☐ p.m.
☐ Malaise	① ② ③ ④ ⑤	☐ a.m.	☐ p.m.
☐ Weakness	① ② ③ ④ ⑤	☐ a.m.	☐ p.m.
☐ Dizziness	① ② ③ ④ ⑤	☐ a.m.	☐ p.m.
☐ Trembling	① ② ③ ④ ⑤	☐ a.m.	☐ p.m.
☐ Twitching	① ② ③ ④ ⑤	☐ a.m.	☐ p.m.
☐ Insomnia	① ② ③ ④ ⑤	☐ a.m.	☐ p.m.

illness

Symptom	Severity	Time	
☐ Nausea	① ② ③ ④ ⑤	☐ a.m.	☐ p.m.
☐ Vomiting	① ② ③ ④ ⑤	☐ a.m.	☐ p.m.
☐ Constipation	① ② ③ ④ ⑤	☐ a.m.	☐ p.m.
☐ Diarrhea	① ② ③ ④ ⑤	☐ a.m.	☐ p.m.
☐ Sore throat	① ② ③ ④ ⑤	☐ a.m.	☐ p.m.
☐ Congestion	① ② ③ ④ ⑤	☐ a.m.	☐ p.m.
☐ Coughing	① ② ③ ④ ⑤	☐ a.m.	☐ p.m.
☐ Acid reflux	① ② ③ ④ ⑤	☐ a.m.	☐ p.m.

psychological

Symptom	Severity	Time	
☐ Anxiety	① ② ③ ④ ⑤	☐ a.m.	☐ p.m.
☐ Depression	① ② ③ ④ ⑤	☐ a.m.	☐ p.m.
☐ Memory loss	① ② ③ ④ ⑤	☐ a.m.	☐ p.m.
☐ Confusion	① ② ③ ④ ⑤	☐ a.m.	☐ p.m.
☐ Poor focus	① ② ③ ④ ⑤	☐ a.m.	☐ p.m.
☐ Mood swings	① ② ③ ④ ⑤	☐ a.m.	☐ p.m.
☐ Suicidal	① ② ③ ④ ⑤	☐ a.m.	☐ p.m.

other

Symptom	Severity	Time	
	① ② ③ ④ ⑤	☐ a.m.	☐ p.m.
	① ② ③ ④ ⑤	☐ a.m.	☐ p.m.
	① ② ③ ④ ⑤	☐ a.m.	☐ p.m.
	① ② ③ ④ ⑤	☐ a.m.	☐ p.m.
	① ② ③ ④ ⑤	☐ a.m.	☐ p.m.
	① ② ③ ④ ⑤	☐ a.m.	☐ p.m.
	① ② ③ ④ ⑤	☐ a.m.	☐ p.m.

SLEEP

hours ________ quality ① ② ③ ④ ⑤

STRESS LEVELS

None	Low	Medium	High	Max	@$#%!

WEATHER

☐ Cold ☐ Mild ☐ Hot
☐ Dry ☐ Humid ☐ Wet

Allergen Levels: ________

BM Pressure: ________

EXERCISE

☐ Heck yes, I worked out.
☐ I managed to exercise a bit.
☐ No, I haven't exercised at all.
☐ I did some stuff, and that counts.

DETAILS

FOOD / MEDICATION

Food / Drinks

Meds / Supplements	Time	Dose
☐ usual daily medication		

Water	Caffeine	Alcohol
	x ________	x ________

FOOD ANALYSIS

New food introduced?
☐ Yes ☐ No

Food reintroduction?
☐ Yes ☐ No

Details

MEDICATION ANALYSIS

New med/dose introduced?
☐ Yes ☐ No

Medication stopped?
☐ Yes ☐ No

Details

ACTIVITY ANALYSIS

Heightened exertion levels?
☐ Yes ☐ No

Lowered exertion levels?
☐ Yes ☐ No

Details

SLEEP ANALYSIS

When you woke up this morning, did you feel well-rested?	☐ Yes	☐ No	☐ A bit
Did you snore or stop breathing throughout the night?	☐ Yes	☐ No	☐ Not sure
Roughly how many times did you wake up throughout the night?			

Notes / Suspected Triggers

ENTRY #79 | M T W T F S S | DATE:

HOW ARE YOU *Feeling today?*

Amazing!	Meh
Great	Not good
Good	Terrible!

RATE YOUR PAIN LEVEL

① ② ③ ④ ⑤ ⑥ ⑦ ⑧ ⑨ ⑩

WHAT ABOUT YOUR...?

Mood	① ② ③ ④ ⑤ ⑥ ⑦ ⑧ ⑨ ⑩
Energy Levels	① ② ③ ④ ⑤ ⑥ ⑦ ⑧ ⑨ ⑩
Mental Clarity	① ② ③ ④ ⑤ ⑥ ⑦ ⑧ ⑨ ⑩

PAIN & PHYSICAL SYMPTOMS

Symptom	Severity	am	pm
	① ② ③ ④ ⑤	☐	☐
	① ② ③ ④ ⑤	☐	☐
	① ② ③ ④ ⑤	☐	☐
	① ② ③ ④ ⑤	☐	☐
	① ② ③ ④ ⑤	☐	☐
	① ② ③ ④ ⑤	☐	☐
	① ② ③ ④ ⑤	☐	☐
	① ② ③ ④ ⑤	☐	☐

front ***back***

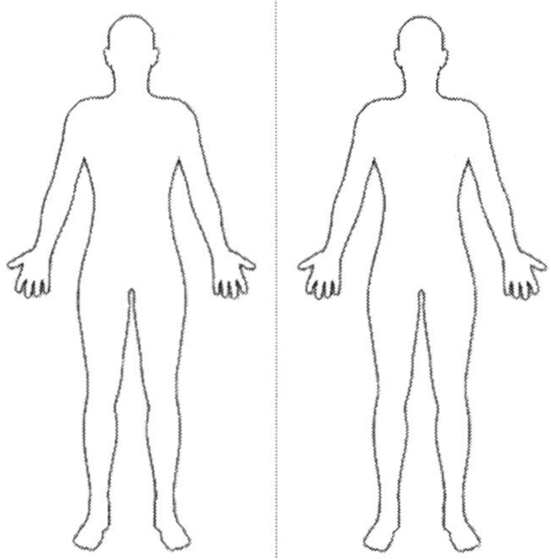

OTHER SYMPTOMS

general

Symptom	Severity	Time	
☐ Fatigue	① ② ③ ④ ⑤	☐ a.m.	☐ p.m.
☐ Lethargy	① ② ③ ④ ⑤	☐ a.m.	☐ p.m.
☐ Malaise	① ② ③ ④ ⑤	☐ a.m.	☐ p.m.
☐ Weakness	① ② ③ ④ ⑤	☐ a.m.	☐ p.m.
☐ Dizziness	① ② ③ ④ ⑤	☐ a.m.	☐ p.m.
☐ Trembling	① ② ③ ④ ⑤	☐ a.m.	☐ p.m.
☐ Twitching	① ② ③ ④ ⑤	☐ a.m.	☐ p.m.
☐ Insomnia	① ② ③ ④ ⑤	☐ a.m.	☐ p.m.

illness

Symptom	Severity	Time	
☐ Nausea	① ② ③ ④ ⑤	☐ a.m.	☐ p.m.
☐ Vomiting	① ② ③ ④ ⑤	☐ a.m.	☐ p.m.
☐ Constipation	① ② ③ ④ ⑤	☐ a.m.	☐ p.m.
☐ Diarrhea	① ② ③ ④ ⑤	☐ a.m.	☐ p.m.
☐ Sore throat	① ② ③ ④ ⑤	☐ a.m.	☐ p.m.
☐ Congestion	① ② ③ ④ ⑤	☐ a.m.	☐ p.m.
☐ Coughing	① ② ③ ④ ⑤	☐ a.m.	☐ p.m.
☐ Acid reflux	① ② ③ ④ ⑤	☐ a.m.	☐ p.m.

psychological

Symptom	Severity	Time	
☐ Anxiety	① ② ③ ④ ⑤	☐ a.m.	☐ p.m.
☐ Depression	① ② ③ ④ ⑤	☐ a.m.	☐ p.m.
☐ Memory loss	① ② ③ ④ ⑤	☐ a.m.	☐ p.m.
☐ Confusion	① ② ③ ④ ⑤	☐ a.m.	☐ p.m.
☐ Poor focus	① ② ③ ④ ⑤	☐ a.m.	☐ p.m.
☐ Mood swings	① ② ③ ④ ⑤	☐ a.m.	☐ p.m.
☐ Suicidal	① ② ③ ④ ⑤	☐ a.m.	☐ p.m.

other

Symptom	Severity	Time	
	① ② ③ ④ ⑤	☐ a.m.	☐ p.m.
	① ② ③ ④ ⑤	☐ a.m.	☐ p.m.
	① ② ③ ④ ⑤	☐ a.m.	☐ p.m.
	① ② ③ ④ ⑤	☐ a.m.	☐ p.m.
	① ② ③ ④ ⑤	☐ a.m.	☐ p.m.
	① ② ③ ④ ⑤	☐ a.m.	☐ p.m.
	① ② ③ ④ ⑤	☐ a.m.	☐ p.m.

SLEEP

hours ________

quality ① ② ③ ④ ⑤

STRESS LEVELS

None	Low	Medium	High	Max	@$#%!

WEATHER

☐ Cold ☐ Mild ☐ Hot

☐ Dry ☐ Humid ☐ Wet

Allergen Levels: ________

BM Pressure: ________

EXERCISE

☐ Heck yes, I worked out.

☐ I managed to exercise a bit.

☐ No, I haven't exercised at all.

☐ I did some stuff, and that counts.

DETAILS

FOOD / MEDICATION

Food / Drinks

Meds / Supplements	Time	Dose

☐ usual daily medication

Water *Caffeine* *Alcohol*

x ________ x ________

FOOD ANALYSIS

New food introduced?

☐ Yes ☐ No

Food reintroduction?

☐ Yes ☐ No

Details

MEDICATION ANALYSIS

New med/dose introduced?

☐ Yes ☐ No

Medication stopped?

☐ Yes ☐ No

Details

ACTIVITY ANALYSIS

Heightened exertion levels?

☐ Yes ☐ No

Lowered exertion levels?

☐ Yes ☐ No

Details

SLEEP ANALYSIS

When you woke up this morning, did you feel well-rested?	☐ Yes	☐ No	☐ A bit
Did you snore or stop breathing throughout the night?	☐ Yes	☐ No	☐ Not sure
Roughly how many times did you wake up throughout the night?			

Notes / Suspected Triggers

ENTRY #80 | M T W T F S S | DATE:

HOW ARE YOU *Feeling today?*

Amazing!	Meh
Great	Not good
Good	Terrible!

RATE YOUR PAIN LEVEL

① ② ③ ④ ⑤ ⑥ ⑦ ⑧ ⑨ ⑩

WHAT ABOUT YOUR...?

Mood	① ② ③ ④ ⑤ ⑥ ⑦ ⑧ ⑨ ⑩
Energy Levels	① ② ③ ④ ⑤ ⑥ ⑦ ⑧ ⑨ ⑩
Mental Clarity	① ② ③ ④ ⑤ ⑥ ⑦ ⑧ ⑨ ⑩

PAIN & PHYSICAL SYMPTOMS

Symptom	Severity	am	pm
	① ② ③ ④ ⑤	☐	☐
	① ② ③ ④ ⑤	☐	☐
	① ② ③ ④ ⑤	☐	☐
	① ② ③ ④ ⑤	☐	☐
	① ② ③ ④ ⑤	☐	☐
	① ② ③ ④ ⑤	☐	☐
	① ② ③ ④ ⑤	☐	☐
	① ② ③ ④ ⑤	☐	☐

front *back*

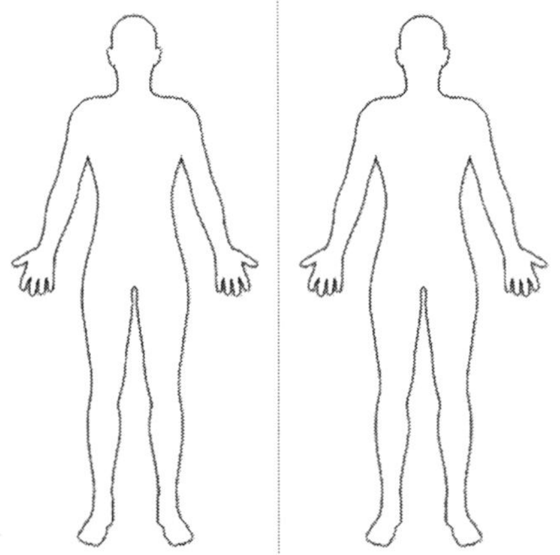

OTHER SYMPTOMS

general

Symptom	Severity	Time	
☐ Fatigue	① ② ③ ④ ⑤	☐ a.m.	☐ p.m.
☐ Lethargy	① ② ③ ④ ⑤	☐ a.m.	☐ p.m.
☐ Malaise	① ② ③ ④ ⑤	☐ a.m.	☐ p.m.
☐ Weakness	① ② ③ ④ ⑤	☐ a.m.	☐ p.m.
☐ Dizziness	① ② ③ ④ ⑤	☐ a.m.	☐ p.m.
☐ Trembling	① ② ③ ④ ⑤	☐ a.m.	☐ p.m.
☐ Twitching	① ② ③ ④ ⑤	☐ a.m.	☐ p.m.
☐ Insomnia	① ② ③ ④ ⑤	☐ a.m.	☐ p.m.

illness

Symptom	Severity	Time	
☐ Nausea	① ② ③ ④ ⑤	☐ a.m.	☐ p.m.
☐ Vomiting	① ② ③ ④ ⑤	☐ a.m.	☐ p.m.
☐ Constipation	① ② ③ ④ ⑤	☐ a.m.	☐ p.m.
☐ Diarrhea	① ② ③ ④ ⑤	☐ a.m.	☐ p.m.
☐ Sore throat	① ② ③ ④ ⑤	☐ a.m.	☐ p.m.
☐ Congestion	① ② ③ ④ ⑤	☐ a.m.	☐ p.m.
☐ Coughing	① ② ③ ④ ⑤	☐ a.m.	☐ p.m.
☐ Acid reflux	① ② ③ ④ ⑤	☐ a.m.	☐ p.m.

psychological

Symptom	Severity	Time	
☐ Anxiety	① ② ③ ④ ⑤	☐ a.m.	☐ p.m.
☐ Depression	① ② ③ ④ ⑤	☐ a.m.	☐ p.m.
☐ Memory loss	① ② ③ ④ ⑤	☐ a.m.	☐ p.m.
☐ Confusion	① ② ③ ④ ⑤	☐ a.m.	☐ p.m.
☐ Poor focus	① ② ③ ④ ⑤	☐ a.m.	☐ p.m.
☐ Mood swings	① ② ③ ④ ⑤	☐ a.m.	☐ p.m.
☐ Suicidal	① ② ③ ④ ⑤	☐ a.m.	☐ p.m.

other

Symptom	Severity	Time	
	① ② ③ ④ ⑤	☐ a.m.	☐ p.m.
	① ② ③ ④ ⑤	☐ a.m.	☐ p.m.
	① ② ③ ④ ⑤	☐ a.m.	☐ p.m.
	① ② ③ ④ ⑤	☐ a.m.	☐ p.m.
	① ② ③ ④ ⑤	☐ a.m.	☐ p.m.
	① ② ③ ④ ⑤	☐ a.m.	☐ p.m.
	① ② ③ ④ ⑤	☐ a.m.	☐ p.m.

SLEEP

hours ________ quality (1) (2) (3) (4) (5)

STRESS LEVELS

None	Low	Medium	High	Max	@$#%!

WEATHER

☐ Cold ☐ Mild ☐ Hot
☐ Dry ☐ Humid ☐ Wet

Allergen Levels: ________

BM Pressure: ________

EXERCISE

☐ Heck yes, I worked out.
☐ I managed to exercise a bit.
☐ No, I haven't exercised at all.
☐ I did some stuff, and that counts.

DETAILS

FOOD / MEDICATION

Food / Drinks

Meds / Supplements	Time	Dose
☐ usual daily medication		

Water *Caffeine* *Alcohol*

x ________ x ________

FOOD ANALYSIS

New food introduced?
☐ Yes ☐ No

Food reintroduction?
☐ Yes ☐ No

Details

MEDICATION ANALYSIS

New med/dose introduced?
☐ Yes ☐ No

Medication stopped?
☐ Yes ☐ No

Details

ACTIVITY ANALYSIS

Heightened exertion levels?
☐ Yes ☐ No

Lowered exertion levels?
☐ Yes ☐ No

Details

SLEEP ANALYSIS

When you woke up this morning, did you feel well-rested?	☐ Yes	☐ No	☐ A bit
Did you snore or stop breathing throughout the night?	☐ Yes	☐ No	☐ Not sure
Roughly how many times did you wake up throughout the night?			

Notes / Suspected Triggers

ENTRY #81 | M T W T F S S | DATE:

HOW ARE YOU *Feeling today?*

Amazing!	Meh
Great	Not good
Good	Terrible!

RATE YOUR PAIN LEVEL

① ② ③ ④ ⑤ ⑥ ⑦ ⑧ ⑨ ⑩

WHAT ABOUT YOUR...?

Mood	① ② ③ ④ ⑤ ⑥ ⑦ ⑧ ⑨ ⑩
Energy Levels	① ② ③ ④ ⑤ ⑥ ⑦ ⑧ ⑨ ⑩
Mental Clarity	① ② ③ ④ ⑤ ⑥ ⑦ ⑧ ⑨ ⑩

PAIN & PHYSICAL SYMPTOMS

Symptom	Severity	am	pm
	① ② ③ ④ ⑤	☐	☐
	① ② ③ ④ ⑤	☐	☐
	① ② ③ ④ ⑤	☐	☐
	① ② ③ ④ ⑤	☐	☐
	① ② ③ ④ ⑤	☐	☐
	① ② ③ ④ ⑤	☐	☐
	① ② ③ ④ ⑤	☐	☐
	① ② ③ ④ ⑤	☐	☐

front *back*

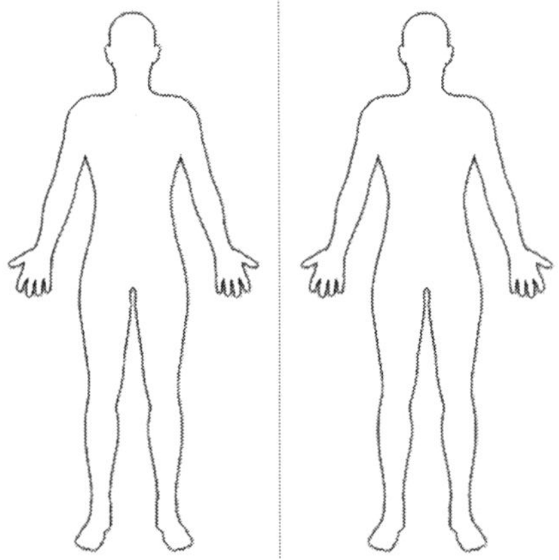

OTHER SYMPTOMS

general

Symptom	Severity	Time	
☐ Fatigue	① ② ③ ④ ⑤	☐ a.m.	☐ p.m.
☐ Lethargy	① ② ③ ④ ⑤	☐ a.m.	☐ p.m.
☐ Malaise	① ② ③ ④ ⑤	☐ a.m.	☐ p.m.
☐ Weakness	① ② ③ ④ ⑤	☐ a.m.	☐ p.m.
☐ Dizziness	① ② ③ ④ ⑤	☐ a.m.	☐ p.m.
☐ Trembling	① ② ③ ④ ⑤	☐ a.m.	☐ p.m.
☐ Twitching	① ② ③ ④ ⑤	☐ a.m.	☐ p.m.
☐ Insomnia	① ② ③ ④ ⑤	☐ a.m.	☐ p.m.

illness

Symptom	Severity	Time	
☐ Nausea	① ② ③ ④ ⑤	☐ a.m.	☐ p.m.
☐ Vomiting	① ② ③ ④ ⑤	☐ a.m.	☐ p.m.
☐ Constipation	① ② ③ ④ ⑤	☐ a.m.	☐ p.m.
☐ Diarrhea	① ② ③ ④ ⑤	☐ a.m.	☐ p.m.
☐ Sore throat	① ② ③ ④ ⑤	☐ a.m.	☐ p.m.
☐ Congestion	① ② ③ ④ ⑤	☐ a.m.	☐ p.m.
☐ Coughing	① ② ③ ④ ⑤	☐ a.m.	☐ p.m.
☐ Acid reflux	① ② ③ ④ ⑤	☐ a.m.	☐ p.m.

psychological

Symptom	Severity	Time	
☐ Anxiety	① ② ③ ④ ⑤	☐ a.m.	☐ p.m.
☐ Depression	① ② ③ ④ ⑤	☐ a.m.	☐ p.m.
☐ Memory loss	① ② ③ ④ ⑤	☐ a.m.	☐ p.m.
☐ Confusion	① ② ③ ④ ⑤	☐ a.m.	☐ p.m.
☐ Poor focus	① ② ③ ④ ⑤	☐ a.m.	☐ p.m.
☐ Mood swings	① ② ③ ④ ⑤	☐ a.m.	☐ p.m.
☐ Suicidal	① ② ③ ④ ⑤	☐ a.m.	☐ p.m.

other

Symptom	Severity	Time	
	① ② ③ ④ ⑤	☐ a.m.	☐ p.m.
	① ② ③ ④ ⑤	☐ a.m.	☐ p.m.
	① ② ③ ④ ⑤	☐ a.m.	☐ p.m.
	① ② ③ ④ ⑤	☐ a.m.	☐ p.m.
	① ② ③ ④ ⑤	☐ a.m.	☐ p.m.
	① ② ③ ④ ⑤	☐ a.m.	☐ p.m.
	① ② ③ ④ ⑤	☐ a.m.	☐ p.m.

SLEEP

hours ________ *quality* ① ② ③ ④ ⑤

STRESS LEVELS

None	Low	Medium	High	Max	@$#%!

WEATHER

☐ Cold ☐ Mild ☐ Hot
☐ Dry ☐ Humid ☐ Wet

Allergen Levels: ________
BM Pressure: ________

EXERCISE

☐ Heck yes, I worked out.
☐ I managed to exercise a bit.
☐ No, I haven't exercised at all.
☐ I did some stuff, and that counts.

DETAILS

FOOD / MEDICATION

Food / Drinks

Meds / Supplements	Time	Dose

☐ usual daily medication

Water *Caffeine* *Alcohol*

x ________ x ________

FOOD ANALYSIS

New food introduced?
☐ Yes ☐ No
Food reintroduction?
☐ Yes ☐ No
Details

MEDICATION ANALYSIS

New med/dose introduced?
☐ Yes ☐ No
Medication stopped?
☐ Yes ☐ No
Details

ACTIVITY ANALYSIS

Heightened exertion levels?
☐ Yes ☐ No
Lowered exertion levels?
☐ Yes ☐ No
Details

SLEEP ANALYSIS

When you woke up this morning, did you feel well-rested?	☐ Yes	☐ No	☐ A bit
Did you snore or stop breathing throughout the night?	☐ Yes	☐ No	☐ Not sure
Roughly how many times did you wake up throughout the night?			

Notes / Suspected Triggers

ENTRY #82 | M T W T F S S | DATE:

HOW ARE YOU *Feeling today?*

Amazing!	Meh
Great	Not good
Good	Terrible!

RATE YOUR PAIN LEVEL

① ② ③ ④ ⑤ ⑥ ⑦ ⑧ ⑨ ⑩

WHAT ABOUT YOUR...?

Mood	① ② ③ ④ ⑤ ⑥ ⑦ ⑧ ⑨ ⑩
Energy Levels	① ② ③ ④ ⑤ ⑥ ⑦ ⑧ ⑨ ⑩
Mental Clarity	① ② ③ ④ ⑤ ⑥ ⑦ ⑧ ⑨ ⑩

PAIN & PHYSICAL SYMPTOMS

Symptom	Severity	am	pm
	① ② ③ ④ ⑤	☐	☐
	① ② ③ ④ ⑤	☐	☐
	① ② ③ ④ ⑤	☐	☐
	① ② ③ ④ ⑤	☐	☐
	① ② ③ ④ ⑤	☐	☐
	① ② ③ ④ ⑤	☐	☐
	① ② ③ ④ ⑤	☐	☐
	① ② ③ ④ ⑤	☐	☐

front

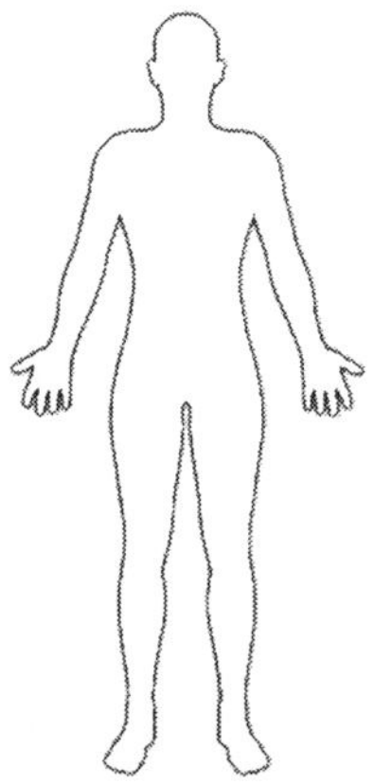

back

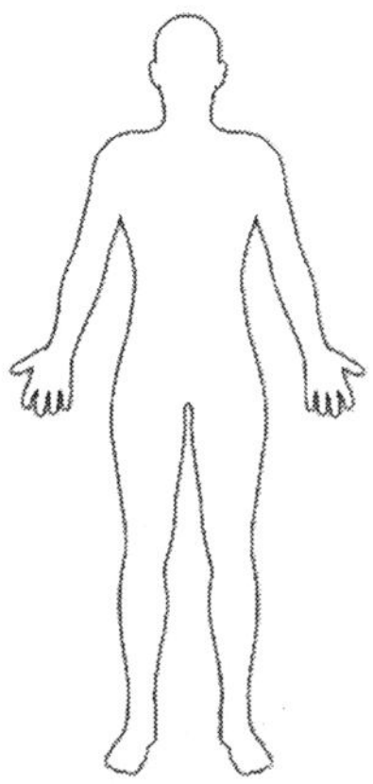

OTHER SYMPTOMS

general

Symptom	Severity	Time	
☐ Fatigue	① ② ③ ④ ⑤	☐ a.m.	☐ p.m.
☐ Lethargy	① ② ③ ④ ⑤	☐ a.m.	☐ p.m.
☐ Malaise	① ② ③ ④ ⑤	☐ a.m.	☐ p.m.
☐ Weakness	① ② ③ ④ ⑤	☐ a.m.	☐ p.m.
☐ Dizziness	① ② ③ ④ ⑤	☐ a.m.	☐ p.m.
☐ Trembling	① ② ③ ④ ⑤	☐ a.m.	☐ p.m.
☐ Twitching	① ② ③ ④ ⑤	☐ a.m.	☐ p.m.
☐ Insomnia	① ② ③ ④ ⑤	☐ a.m.	☐ p.m.

illness

Symptom	Severity	Time	
☐ Nausea	① ② ③ ④ ⑤	☐ a.m.	☐ p.m.
☐ Vomiting	① ② ③ ④ ⑤	☐ a.m.	☐ p.m.
☐ Constipation	① ② ③ ④ ⑤	☐ a.m.	☐ p.m.
☐ Diarrhea	① ② ③ ④ ⑤	☐ a.m.	☐ p.m.
☐ Sore throat	① ② ③ ④ ⑤	☐ a.m.	☐ p.m.
☐ Congestion	① ② ③ ④ ⑤	☐ a.m.	☐ p.m.
☐ Coughing	① ② ③ ④ ⑤	☐ a.m.	☐ p.m.
☐ Acid reflux	① ② ③ ④ ⑤	☐ a.m.	☐ p.m.

psychological

Symptom	Severity	Time	
☐ Anxiety	① ② ③ ④ ⑤	☐ a.m.	☐ p.m.
☐ Depression	① ② ③ ④ ⑤	☐ a.m.	☐ p.m.
☐ Memory loss	① ② ③ ④ ⑤	☐ a.m.	☐ p.m.
☐ Confusion	① ② ③ ④ ⑤	☐ a.m.	☐ p.m.
☐ Poor focus	① ② ③ ④ ⑤	☐ a.m.	☐ p.m.
☐ Mood swings	① ② ③ ④ ⑤	☐ a.m.	☐ p.m.
☐ Suicidal	① ② ③ ④ ⑤	☐ a.m.	☐ p.m.

other

Symptom	Severity	Time	
	① ② ③ ④ ⑤	☐ a.m.	☐ p.m.
	① ② ③ ④ ⑤	☐ a.m.	☐ p.m.
	① ② ③ ④ ⑤	☐ a.m.	☐ p.m.
	① ② ③ ④ ⑤	☐ a.m.	☐ p.m.
	① ② ③ ④ ⑤	☐ a.m.	☐ p.m.
	① ② ③ ④ ⑤	☐ a.m.	☐ p.m.
	① ② ③ ④ ⑤	☐ a.m.	☐ p.m.

SLEEP

hours ________ quality ① ② ③ ④ ⑤

STRESS LEVELS

None	Low	Medium	High	Max	@$#%!

WEATHER

☐ Cold ☐ Mild ☐ Hot
☐ Dry ☐ Humid ☐ Wet

Allergen Levels: ________
BM Pressure: ________

EXERCISE

☐ Heck yes, I worked out.
☐ I managed to exercise a bit.
☐ No, I haven't exercised at all.
☐ I did some stuff, and that counts.

DETAILS

FOOD / MEDICATION

Food / Drinks

Meds / Supplements	Time	Dose
☐ usual daily medication		

Water *Caffeine* *Alcohol*

Caffeine x ________ Alcohol x ________

FOOD ANALYSIS

New food introduced?
☐ Yes ☐ No
Food reintroduction?
☐ Yes ☐ No
Details

MEDICATION ANALYSIS

New med/dose introduced?
☐ Yes ☐ No
Medication stopped?
☐ Yes ☐ No
Details

ACTIVITY ANALYSIS

Heightened exertion levels?
☐ Yes ☐ No
Lowered exertion levels?
☐ Yes ☐ No
Details

SLEEP ANALYSIS

When you woke up this morning, did you feel well-rested?	☐ Yes	☐ No	☐ A bit
Did you snore or stop breathing throughout the night?	☐ Yes	☐ No	☐ Not sure
Roughly how many times did you wake up throughout the night?			

Notes / Suspected Triggers

ENTRY #83 | M T W T F S S | DATE:

HOW ARE YOU *Feeling today?*

Amazing!	Meh
Great	Not good
Good	Terrible!

RATE YOUR PAIN LEVEL

① ② ③ ④ ⑤ ⑥ ⑦ ⑧ ⑨ ⑩

WHAT ABOUT YOUR...?

Mood	① ② ③ ④ ⑤ ⑥ ⑦ ⑧ ⑨ ⑩
Energy Levels	① ② ③ ④ ⑤ ⑥ ⑦ ⑧ ⑨ ⑩
Mental Clarity	① ② ③ ④ ⑤ ⑥ ⑦ ⑧ ⑨ ⑩

PAIN & PHYSICAL SYMPTOMS

Symptom	Severity	am	pm
	① ② ③ ④ ⑤	☐	☐
	① ② ③ ④ ⑤	☐	☐
	① ② ③ ④ ⑤	☐	☐
	① ② ③ ④ ⑤	☐	☐
	① ② ③ ④ ⑤	☐	☐
	① ② ③ ④ ⑤	☐	☐
	① ② ③ ④ ⑤	☐	☐
	① ② ③ ④ ⑤	☐	☐

front ***back***

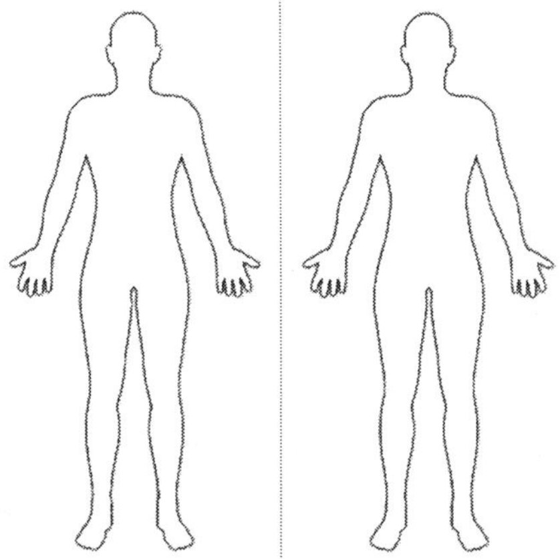

OTHER SYMPTOMS

general

Symptom	Severity	Time	
☐ Fatigue	① ② ③ ④ ⑤	☐ a.m.	☐ p.m.
☐ Lethargy	① ② ③ ④ ⑤	☐ a.m.	☐ p.m.
☐ Malaise	① ② ③ ④ ⑤	☐ a.m.	☐ p.m.
☐ Weakness	① ② ③ ④ ⑤	☐ a.m.	☐ p.m.
☐ Dizziness	① ② ③ ④ ⑤	☐ a.m.	☐ p.m.
☐ Trembling	① ② ③ ④ ⑤	☐ a.m.	☐ p.m.
☐ Twitching	① ② ③ ④ ⑤	☐ a.m.	☐ p.m.
☐ Insomnia	① ② ③ ④ ⑤	☐ a.m.	☐ p.m.

illness

Symptom	Severity	Time	
☐ Nausea	① ② ③ ④ ⑤	☐ a.m.	☐ p.m.
☐ Vomiting	① ② ③ ④ ⑤	☐ a.m.	☐ p.m.
☐ Constipation	① ② ③ ④ ⑤	☐ a.m.	☐ p.m.
☐ Diarrhea	① ② ③ ④ ⑤	☐ a.m.	☐ p.m.
☐ Sore throat	① ② ③ ④ ⑤	☐ a.m.	☐ p.m.
☐ Congestion	① ② ③ ④ ⑤	☐ a.m.	☐ p.m.
☐ Coughing	① ② ③ ④ ⑤	☐ a.m.	☐ p.m.
☐ Acid reflux	① ② ③ ④ ⑤	☐ a.m.	☐ p.m.

psychological

Symptom	Severity	Time	
☐ Anxiety	① ② ③ ④ ⑤	☐ a.m.	☐ p.m.
☐ Depression	① ② ③ ④ ⑤	☐ a.m.	☐ p.m.
☐ Memory loss	① ② ③ ④ ⑤	☐ a.m.	☐ p.m.
☐ Confusion	① ② ③ ④ ⑤	☐ a.m.	☐ p.m.
☐ Poor focus	① ② ③ ④ ⑤	☐ a.m.	☐ p.m.
☐ Mood swings	① ② ③ ④ ⑤	☐ a.m.	☐ p.m.
☐ Suicidal	① ② ③ ④ ⑤	☐ a.m.	☐ p.m.

other

Symptom	Severity	Time	
	① ② ③ ④ ⑤	☐ a.m.	☐ p.m.
	① ② ③ ④ ⑤	☐ a.m.	☐ p.m.
	① ② ③ ④ ⑤	☐ a.m.	☐ p.m.
	① ② ③ ④ ⑤	☐ a.m.	☐ p.m.
	① ② ③ ④ ⑤	☐ a.m.	☐ p.m.
	① ② ③ ④ ⑤	☐ a.m.	☐ p.m.
	① ② ③ ④ ⑤	☐ a.m.	☐ p.m.

SLEEP

hours ________ *quality* ① ② ③ ④ ⑤

STRESS LEVELS

None	Low	Medium	High	Max	@$#%!

WEATHER

☐ Cold ☐ Mild ☐ Hot
☐ Dry ☐ Humid ☐ Wet

Allergen Levels: ________
BM Pressure: ________

EXERCISE

☐ Heck yes, I worked out.
☐ I managed to exercise a bit.
☐ No, I haven't exercised at all.
☐ I did some stuff, and that counts.

DETAILS

FOOD / MEDICATION

Food / Drinks

Meds / Supplements	Time	Dose
☐ usual daily medication		

Water *Caffeine* *Alcohol*

x ________ x ________

FOOD ANALYSIS	
New food introduced?	
☐ Yes	☐ No
Food reintroduction?	
☐ Yes	☐ No
Details	

MEDICATION ANALYSIS	
New med/dose introduced?	
☐ Yes	☐ No
Medication stopped?	
☐ Yes	☐ No
Details	

ACTIVITY ANALYSIS	
Heightened exertion levels?	
☐ Yes	☐ No
Lowered exertion levels?	
☐ Yes	☐ No
Details	

SLEEP ANALYSIS

When you woke up this morning, did you feel well-rested?	☐ Yes	☐ No	☐ A bit
Did you snore or stop breathing throughout the night?	☐ Yes	☐ No	☐ Not sure
Roughly how many times did you wake up throughout the night?			

Notes / Suspected Triggers

ENTRY #84 | M T W T F S S | DATE:

HOW ARE YOU *Feeling today?*

Amazing!	Meh
Great	Not good
Good	Terrible!

RATE YOUR PAIN LEVEL

① ② ③ ④ ⑤ ⑥ ⑦ ⑧ ⑨ ⑩

WHAT ABOUT YOUR...?

Mood	① ② ③ ④ ⑤ ⑥ ⑦ ⑧ ⑨ ⑩
Energy Levels	① ② ③ ④ ⑤ ⑥ ⑦ ⑧ ⑨ ⑩
Mental Clarity	① ② ③ ④ ⑤ ⑥ ⑦ ⑧ ⑨ ⑩

PAIN & PHYSICAL SYMPTOMS

Symptom	Severity	am	pm
	① ② ③ ④ ⑤	☐	☐
	① ② ③ ④ ⑤	☐	☐
	① ② ③ ④ ⑤	☐	☐
	① ② ③ ④ ⑤	☐	☐
	① ② ③ ④ ⑤	☐	☐
	① ② ③ ④ ⑤	☐	☐
	① ② ③ ④ ⑤	☐	☐
	① ② ③ ④ ⑤	☐	☐

front *back*

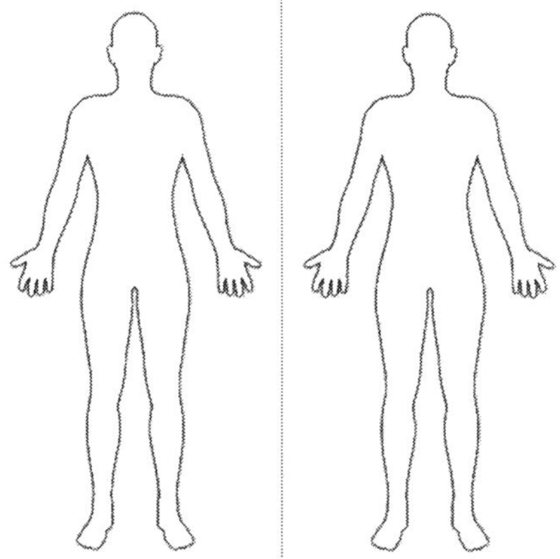

OTHER SYMPTOMS

general

Symptom	Severity	Time	
☐ Fatigue	① ② ③ ④ ⑤	☐ a.m.	☐ p.m.
☐ Lethargy	① ② ③ ④ ⑤	☐ a.m.	☐ p.m.
☐ Malaise	① ② ③ ④ ⑤	☐ a.m.	☐ p.m.
☐ Weakness	① ② ③ ④ ⑤	☐ a.m.	☐ p.m.
☐ Dizziness	① ② ③ ④ ⑤	☐ a.m.	☐ p.m.
☐ Trembling	① ② ③ ④ ⑤	☐ a.m.	☐ p.m.
☐ Twitching	① ② ③ ④ ⑤	☐ a.m.	☐ p.m.
☐ Insomnia	① ② ③ ④ ⑤	☐ a.m.	☐ p.m.

illness

Symptom	Severity	Time	
☐ Nausea	① ② ③ ④ ⑤	☐ a.m.	☐ p.m.
☐ Vomiting	① ② ③ ④ ⑤	☐ a.m.	☐ p.m.
☐ Constipation	① ② ③ ④ ⑤	☐ a.m.	☐ p.m.
☐ Diarrhea	① ② ③ ④ ⑤	☐ a.m.	☐ p.m.
☐ Sore throat	① ② ③ ④ ⑤	☐ a.m.	☐ p.m.
☐ Congestion	① ② ③ ④ ⑤	☐ a.m.	☐ p.m.
☐ Coughing	① ② ③ ④ ⑤	☐ a.m.	☐ p.m.
☐ Acid reflux	① ② ③ ④ ⑤	☐ a.m.	☐ p.m.

psychological

Symptom	Severity	Time	
☐ Anxiety	① ② ③ ④ ⑤	☐ a.m.	☐ p.m.
☐ Depression	① ② ③ ④ ⑤	☐ a.m.	☐ p.m.
☐ Memory loss	① ② ③ ④ ⑤	☐ a.m.	☐ p.m.
☐ Confusion	① ② ③ ④ ⑤	☐ a.m.	☐ p.m.
☐ Poor focus	① ② ③ ④ ⑤	☐ a.m.	☐ p.m.
☐ Mood swings	① ② ③ ④ ⑤	☐ a.m.	☐ p.m.
☐ Suicidal	① ② ③ ④ ⑤	☐ a.m.	☐ p.m.

other

Symptom	Severity	Time	
	① ② ③ ④ ⑤	☐ a.m.	☐ p.m.
	① ② ③ ④ ⑤	☐ a.m.	☐ p.m.
	① ② ③ ④ ⑤	☐ a.m.	☐ p.m.
	① ② ③ ④ ⑤	☐ a.m.	☐ p.m.
	① ② ③ ④ ⑤	☐ a.m.	☐ p.m.
	① ② ③ ④ ⑤	☐ a.m.	☐ p.m.
	① ② ③ ④ ⑤	☐ a.m.	☐ p.m.

SLEEP

hours ________ *quality* ① ② ③ ④ ⑤

STRESS LEVELS

None	Low	Medium	High	Max	@$#%!

WEATHER

☐ Cold ☐ Mild ☐ Hot
☐ Dry ☐ Humid ☐ Wet

Allergen Levels: ________

BM Pressure: ________

EXERCISE

☐ Heck yes, I worked out.
☐ I managed to exercise a bit.
☐ No, I haven't exercised at all.
☐ I did some stuff, and that counts.

DETAILS

FOOD / MEDICATION

Food / Drinks

Meds / Supplements	Time	Dose
☐ usual daily medication		

Water	*Caffeine*	*Alcohol*
	x ________	x ________

FOOD ANALYSIS

New food introduced?
☐ Yes ☐ No

Food reintroduction?
☐ Yes ☐ No

Details

MEDICATION ANALYSIS

New med/dose introduced?
☐ Yes ☐ No

Medication stopped?
☐ Yes ☐ No

Details

ACTIVITY ANALYSIS

Heightened exertion levels?
☐ Yes ☐ No

Lowered exertion levels?
☐ Yes ☐ No

Details

SLEEP ANALYSIS

When you woke up this morning, did you feel well-rested?	☐ Yes	☐ No	☐ A bit
Did you snore or stop breathing throughout the night?	☐ Yes	☐ No	☐ Not sure
Roughly how many times did you wake up throughout the night?			

Notes / Suspected Triggers

ENTRY #85	M T W T F S S	DATE:

HOW ARE YOU *Feeling today?*

Amazing!	Meh
Great	Not good
Good	Terrible!

RATE YOUR PAIN LEVEL

① ② ③ ④ ⑤ ⑥ ⑦ ⑧ ⑨ ⑩

WHAT ABOUT YOUR...?

Mood	① ② ③ ④ ⑤ ⑥ ⑦ ⑧ ⑨ ⑩
Energy Levels	① ② ③ ④ ⑤ ⑥ ⑦ ⑧ ⑨ ⑩
Mental Clarity	① ② ③ ④ ⑤ ⑥ ⑦ ⑧ ⑨ ⑩

PAIN & PHYSICAL SYMPTOMS

Symptom	Severity	am	pm
	① ② ③ ④ ⑤	☐	☐
	① ② ③ ④ ⑤	☐	☐
	① ② ③ ④ ⑤	☐	☐
	① ② ③ ④ ⑤	☐	☐
	① ② ③ ④ ⑤	☐	☐
	① ② ③ ④ ⑤	☐	☐
	① ② ③ ④ ⑤	☐	☐
	① ② ③ ④ ⑤	☐	☐

front

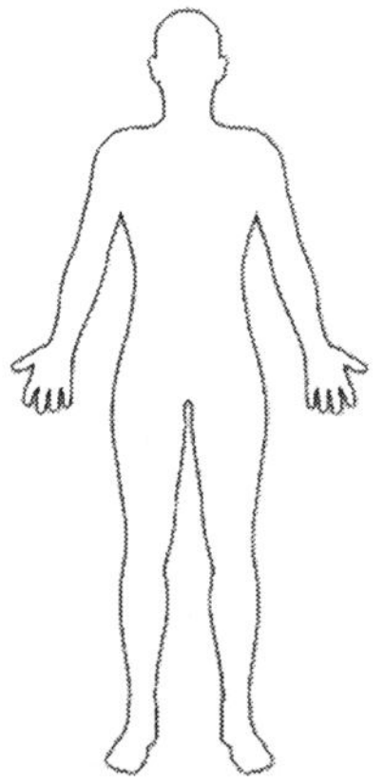

back

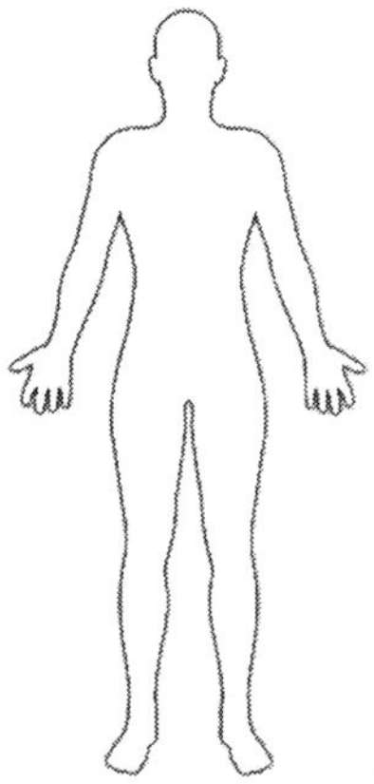

OTHER SYMPTOMS

general

Symptom	Severity	Time	
☐ Fatigue	① ② ③ ④ ⑤	☐ a.m.	☐ p.m.
☐ Lethargy	① ② ③ ④ ⑤	☐ a.m.	☐ p.m.
☐ Malaise	① ② ③ ④ ⑤	☐ a.m.	☐ p.m.
☐ Weakness	① ② ③ ④ ⑤	☐ a.m.	☐ p.m.
☐ Dizziness	① ② ③ ④ ⑤	☐ a.m.	☐ p.m.
☐ Trembling	① ② ③ ④ ⑤	☐ a.m.	☐ p.m.
☐ Twitching	① ② ③ ④ ⑤	☐ a.m.	☐ p.m.
☐ Insomnia	① ② ③ ④ ⑤	☐ a.m.	☐ p.m.

illness

Symptom	Severity	Time	
☐ Nausea	① ② ③ ④ ⑤	☐ a.m.	☐ p.m.
☐ Vomiting	① ② ③ ④ ⑤	☐ a.m.	☐ p.m.
☐ Constipation	① ② ③ ④ ⑤	☐ a.m.	☐ p.m.
☐ Diarrhea	① ② ③ ④ ⑤	☐ a.m.	☐ p.m.
☐ Sore throat	① ② ③ ④ ⑤	☐ a.m.	☐ p.m.
☐ Congestion	① ② ③ ④ ⑤	☐ a.m.	☐ p.m.
☐ Coughing	① ② ③ ④ ⑤	☐ a.m.	☐ p.m.
☐ Acid reflux	① ② ③ ④ ⑤	☐ a.m.	☐ p.m.

psychological

Symptom	Severity	Time	
☐ Anxiety	① ② ③ ④ ⑤	☐ a.m.	☐ p.m.
☐ Depression	① ② ③ ④ ⑤	☐ a.m.	☐ p.m.
☐ Memory loss	① ② ③ ④ ⑤	☐ a.m.	☐ p.m.
☐ Confusion	① ② ③ ④ ⑤	☐ a.m.	☐ p.m.
☐ Poor focus	① ② ③ ④ ⑤	☐ a.m.	☐ p.m.
☐ Mood swings	① ② ③ ④ ⑤	☐ a.m.	☐ p.m.
☐ Suicidal	① ② ③ ④ ⑤	☐ a.m.	☐ p.m.

other

Symptom	Severity	Time	
	① ② ③ ④ ⑤	☐ a.m.	☐ p.m.
	① ② ③ ④ ⑤	☐ a.m.	☐ p.m.
	① ② ③ ④ ⑤	☐ a.m.	☐ p.m.
	① ② ③ ④ ⑤	☐ a.m.	☐ p.m.
	① ② ③ ④ ⑤	☐ a.m.	☐ p.m.
	① ② ③ ④ ⑤	☐ a.m.	☐ p.m.
	① ② ③ ④ ⑤	☐ a.m.	☐ p.m.

SLEEP

hours ________ *quality* ① ② ③ ④ ⑤

STRESS LEVELS

None	Low	Medium	High	Max	@$#%!

WEATHER

☐ Cold ☐ Mild ☐ Hot
☐ Dry ☐ Humid ☐ Wet

Allergen Levels: ________
BM Pressure: ________

EXERCISE

☐ Heck yes, I worked out.
☐ I managed to exercise a bit.
☐ No, I haven't exercised at all.
☐ I did some stuff, and that counts.

DETAILS

FOOD / MEDICATION

Food / Drinks

Meds / Supplements	Time	Dose

☐ usual daily medication

Water *Caffeine* *Alcohol*

x ________ x ________

FOOD ANALYSIS

New food introduced?
☐ Yes ☐ No
Food reintroduction?
☐ Yes ☐ No
Details

MEDICATION ANALYSIS

New med/dose introduced?
☐ Yes ☐ No
Medication stopped?
☐ Yes ☐ No
Details

ACTIVITY ANALYSIS

Heightened exertion levels?
☐ Yes ☐ No
Lowered exertion levels?
☐ Yes ☐ No
Details

SLEEP ANALYSIS

When you woke up this morning, did you feel well-rested?	☐ Yes	☐ No	☐ A bit
Did you snore or stop breathing throughout the night?	☐ Yes	☐ No	☐ Not sure
Roughly how many times did you wake up throughout the night?			

Notes / Suspected Triggers

ENTRY #86 | M T W T F S S | DATE:

HOW ARE YOU *Feeling today?*

Amazing!	Meh
Great	Not good
Good	Terrible!

RATE YOUR PAIN LEVEL

① ② ③ ④ ⑤ ⑥ ⑦ ⑧ ⑨ ⑩

WHAT ABOUT YOUR...?

Mood	① ② ③ ④ ⑤ ⑥ ⑦ ⑧ ⑨ ⑩
Energy Levels	① ② ③ ④ ⑤ ⑥ ⑦ ⑧ ⑨ ⑩
Mental Clarity	① ② ③ ④ ⑤ ⑥ ⑦ ⑧ ⑨ ⑩

PAIN & PHYSICAL SYMPTOMS

Symptom	Severity	am	pm
	① ② ③ ④ ⑤	☐	☐
	① ② ③ ④ ⑤	☐	☐
	① ② ③ ④ ⑤	☐	☐
	① ② ③ ④ ⑤	☐	☐
	① ② ③ ④ ⑤	☐	☐
	① ② ③ ④ ⑤	☐	☐
	① ② ③ ④ ⑤	☐	☐
	① ② ③ ④ ⑤	☐	☐

front

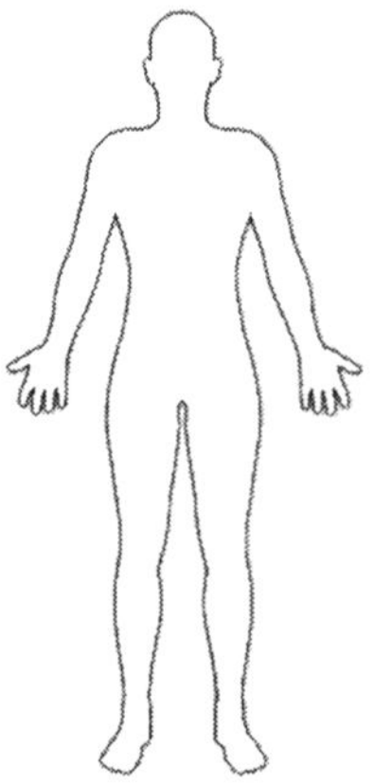

back

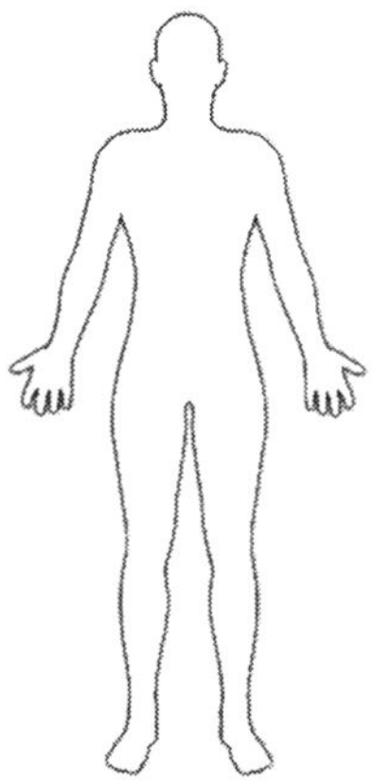

OTHER SYMPTOMS

general

Symptom	Severity	Time	
☐ Fatigue	① ② ③ ④ ⑤	☐ a.m.	☐ p.m.
☐ Lethargy	① ② ③ ④ ⑤	☐ a.m.	☐ p.m.
☐ Malaise	① ② ③ ④ ⑤	☐ a.m.	☐ p.m.
☐ Weakness	① ② ③ ④ ⑤	☐ a.m.	☐ p.m.
☐ Dizziness	① ② ③ ④ ⑤	☐ a.m.	☐ p.m.
☐ Trembling	① ② ③ ④ ⑤	☐ a.m.	☐ p.m.
☐ Twitching	① ② ③ ④ ⑤	☐ a.m.	☐ p.m.
☐ Insomnia	① ② ③ ④ ⑤	☐ a.m.	☐ p.m.

illness

Symptom	Severity	Time	
☐ Nausea	① ② ③ ④ ⑤	☐ a.m.	☐ p.m.
☐ Vomiting	① ② ③ ④ ⑤	☐ a.m.	☐ p.m.
☐ Constipation	① ② ③ ④ ⑤	☐ a.m.	☐ p.m.
☐ Diarrhea	① ② ③ ④ ⑤	☐ a.m.	☐ p.m.
☐ Sore throat	① ② ③ ④ ⑤	☐ a.m.	☐ p.m.
☐ Congestion	① ② ③ ④ ⑤	☐ a.m.	☐ p.m.
☐ Coughing	① ② ③ ④ ⑤	☐ a.m.	☐ p.m.
☐ Acid reflux	① ② ③ ④ ⑤	☐ a.m.	☐ p.m.

psychological

Symptom	Severity	Time	
☐ Anxiety	① ② ③ ④ ⑤	☐ a.m.	☐ p.m.
☐ Depression	① ② ③ ④ ⑤	☐ a.m.	☐ p.m.
☐ Memory loss	① ② ③ ④ ⑤	☐ a.m.	☐ p.m.
☐ Confusion	① ② ③ ④ ⑤	☐ a.m.	☐ p.m.
☐ Poor focus	① ② ③ ④ ⑤	☐ a.m.	☐ p.m.
☐ Mood swings	① ② ③ ④ ⑤	☐ a.m.	☐ p.m.
☐ Suicidal	① ② ③ ④ ⑤	☐ a.m.	☐ p.m.

other

Symptom	Severity	Time	
	① ② ③ ④ ⑤	☐ a.m.	☐ p.m.
	① ② ③ ④ ⑤	☐ a.m.	☐ p.m.
	① ② ③ ④ ⑤	☐ a.m.	☐ p.m.
	① ② ③ ④ ⑤	☐ a.m.	☐ p.m.
	① ② ③ ④ ⑤	☐ a.m.	☐ p.m.
	① ② ③ ④ ⑤	☐ a.m.	☐ p.m.
	① ② ③ ④ ⑤	☐ a.m.	☐ p.m.

SLEEP

hours ________ *quality* ① ② ③ ④ ⑤

STRESS LEVELS

None	Low	Medium	High	Max	@$#%!

WEATHER

☐ Cold ☐ Mild ☐ Hot
☐ Dry ☐ Humid ☐ Wet

Allergen Levels: ________

BM Pressure: ________

EXERCISE

☐ Heck yes, I worked out.
☐ I managed to exercise a bit.
☐ No, I haven't exercised at all.
☐ I did some stuff, and that counts.

DETAILS

FOOD / MEDICATION

Food / Drinks

Meds / Supplements	Time	Dose
☐ usual daily medication		

Water — ☐ ☐ ☐ ☐ ☐ ☐ ☐ ☐ ☐ ☐

Caffeine x ________

Alcohol x ________

FOOD ANALYSIS

New food introduced?
☐ Yes ☐ No

Food reintroduction?
☐ Yes ☐ No

Details

MEDICATION ANALYSIS

New med/dose introduced?
☐ Yes ☐ No

Medication stopped?
☐ Yes ☐ No

Details

ACTIVITY ANALYSIS

Heightened exertion levels?
☐ Yes ☐ No

Lowered exertion levels?
☐ Yes ☐ No

Details

SLEEP ANALYSIS

When you woke up this morning, did you feel well-rested?	☐ Yes	☐ No	☐ A bit
Did you snore or stop breathing throughout the night?	☐ Yes	☐ No	☐ Not sure
Roughly how many times did you wake up throughout the night?			

Notes / Suspected Triggers

ENTRY #87 | M T W T F S S | DATE:

HOW ARE YOU *Feeling today?*

Amazing!	Meh
Great	Not good
Good	Terrible!

RATE YOUR PAIN LEVEL

① ② ③ ④ ⑤ ⑥ ⑦ ⑧ ⑨ ⑩

WHAT ABOUT YOUR...?

Mood	① ② ③ ④ ⑤ ⑥ ⑦ ⑧ ⑨ ⑩
Energy Levels	① ② ③ ④ ⑤ ⑥ ⑦ ⑧ ⑨ ⑩
Mental Clarity	① ② ③ ④ ⑤ ⑥ ⑦ ⑧ ⑨ ⑩

PAIN & PHYSICAL SYMPTOMS

Symptom	Severity	am	pm
	① ② ③ ④ ⑤	☐	☐
	① ② ③ ④ ⑤	☐	☐
	① ② ③ ④ ⑤	☐	☐
	① ② ③ ④ ⑤	☐	☐
	① ② ③ ④ ⑤	☐	☐
	① ② ③ ④ ⑤	☐	☐
	① ② ③ ④ ⑤	☐	☐
	① ② ③ ④ ⑤	☐	☐

front *back*

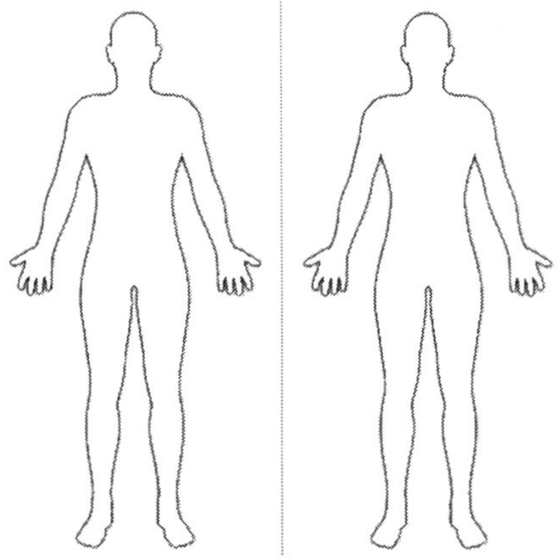

OTHER SYMPTOMS

general

Symptom	Severity	Time	
☐ Fatigue	① ② ③ ④ ⑤	☐ a.m.	☐ p.m.
☐ Lethargy	① ② ③ ④ ⑤	☐ a.m.	☐ p.m.
☐ Malaise	① ② ③ ④ ⑤	☐ a.m.	☐ p.m.
☐ Weakness	① ② ③ ④ ⑤	☐ a.m.	☐ p.m.
☐ Dizziness	① ② ③ ④ ⑤	☐ a.m.	☐ p.m.
☐ Trembling	① ② ③ ④ ⑤	☐ a.m.	☐ p.m.
☐ Twitching	① ② ③ ④ ⑤	☐ a.m.	☐ p.m.
☐ Insomnia	① ② ③ ④ ⑤	☐ a.m.	☐ p.m.

illness

Symptom	Severity	Time	
☐ Nausea	① ② ③ ④ ⑤	☐ a.m.	☐ p.m.
☐ Vomiting	① ② ③ ④ ⑤	☐ a.m.	☐ p.m.
☐ Constipation	① ② ③ ④ ⑤	☐ a.m.	☐ p.m.
☐ Diarrhea	① ② ③ ④ ⑤	☐ a.m.	☐ p.m.
☐ Sore throat	① ② ③ ④ ⑤	☐ a.m.	☐ p.m.
☐ Congestion	① ② ③ ④ ⑤	☐ a.m.	☐ p.m.
☐ Coughing	① ② ③ ④ ⑤	☐ a.m.	☐ p.m.
☐ Acid reflux	① ② ③ ④ ⑤	☐ a.m.	☐ p.m.

psychological

Symptom	Severity	Time	
☐ Anxiety	① ② ③ ④ ⑤	☐ a.m.	☐ p.m.
☐ Depression	① ② ③ ④ ⑤	☐ a.m.	☐ p.m.
☐ Memory loss	① ② ③ ④ ⑤	☐ a.m.	☐ p.m.
☐ Confusion	① ② ③ ④ ⑤	☐ a.m.	☐ p.m.
☐ Poor focus	① ② ③ ④ ⑤	☐ a.m.	☐ p.m.
☐ Mood swings	① ② ③ ④ ⑤	☐ a.m.	☐ p.m.
☐ Suicidal	① ② ③ ④ ⑤	☐ a.m.	☐ p.m.

other

Symptom	Severity	Time	
	① ② ③ ④ ⑤	☐ a.m.	☐ p.m.
	① ② ③ ④ ⑤	☐ a.m.	☐ p.m.
	① ② ③ ④ ⑤	☐ a.m.	☐ p.m.
	① ② ③ ④ ⑤	☐ a.m.	☐ p.m.
	① ② ③ ④ ⑤	☐ a.m.	☐ p.m.
	① ② ③ ④ ⑤	☐ a.m.	☐ p.m.
	① ② ③ ④ ⑤	☐ a.m.	☐ p.m.

SLEEP

hours ________ *quality* ① ② ③ ④ ⑤

STRESS LEVELS

None	Low	Medium	High	Max	@$#%!

WEATHER

☐ Cold ☐ Mild ☐ Hot
☐ Dry ☐ Humid ☐ Wet

Allergen Levels: ________
BM Pressure: ________

EXERCISE

☐ Heck yes, I worked out.
☐ I managed to exercise a bit.
☐ No, I haven't exercised at all.
☐ I did some stuff, and that counts.

DETAILS

FOOD / MEDICATION

Food / Drinks

Meds / Supplements	Time	Dose
☐ usual daily medication		

Water *Caffeine* *Alcohol*

x ________ x ________

FOOD ANALYSIS

New food introduced?
☐ Yes ☐ No
Food reintroduction?
☐ Yes ☐ No
Details

MEDICATION ANALYSIS

New med/dose introduced?
☐ Yes ☐ No
Medication stopped?
☐ Yes ☐ No
Details

ACTIVITY ANALYSIS

Heightened exertion levels?
☐ Yes ☐ No
Lowered exertion levels?
☐ Yes ☐ No
Details

SLEEP ANALYSIS

When you woke up this morning, did you feel well-rested?	☐ Yes	☐ No	☐ A bit
Did you snore or stop breathing throughout the night?	☐ Yes	☐ No	☐ Not sure
Roughly how many times did you wake up throughout the night?			

Notes / Suspected Triggers

ENTRY #88 | M T W T F S S | DATE:

HOW ARE YOU *Feeling today?*

Amazing!	Meh
Great	Not good
Good	Terrible!

RATE YOUR PAIN LEVEL

① ② ③ ④ ⑤ ⑥ ⑦ ⑧ ⑨ ⑩

WHAT ABOUT YOUR...?

Mood	① ② ③ ④ ⑤ ⑥ ⑦ ⑧ ⑨ ⑩
Energy Levels	① ② ③ ④ ⑤ ⑥ ⑦ ⑧ ⑨ ⑩
Mental Clarity	① ② ③ ④ ⑤ ⑥ ⑦ ⑧ ⑨ ⑩

PAIN & PHYSICAL SYMPTOMS

Symptom	Severity	am	pm
	① ② ③ ④ ⑤	☐	☐
	① ② ③ ④ ⑤	☐	☐
	① ② ③ ④ ⑤	☐	☐
	① ② ③ ④ ⑤	☐	☐
	① ② ③ ④ ⑤	☐	☐
	① ② ③ ④ ⑤	☐	☐
	① ② ③ ④ ⑤	☐	☐
	① ② ③ ④ ⑤	☐	☐

front ***back***

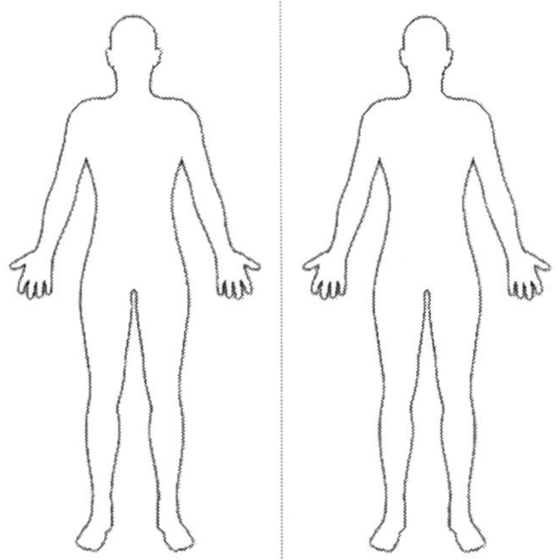

OTHER SYMPTOMS

general

Symptom	Severity	Time	
☐ Fatigue	① ② ③ ④ ⑤	☐ a.m.	☐ p.m.
☐ Lethargy	① ② ③ ④ ⑤	☐ a.m.	☐ p.m.
☐ Malaise	① ② ③ ④ ⑤	☐ a.m.	☐ p.m.
☐ Weakness	① ② ③ ④ ⑤	☐ a.m.	☐ p.m.
☐ Dizziness	① ② ③ ④ ⑤	☐ a.m.	☐ p.m.
☐ Trembling	① ② ③ ④ ⑤	☐ a.m.	☐ p.m.
☐ Twitching	① ② ③ ④ ⑤	☐ a.m.	☐ p.m.
☐ Insomnia	① ② ③ ④ ⑤	☐ a.m.	☐ p.m.

illness

Symptom	Severity	Time	
☐ Nausea	① ② ③ ④ ⑤	☐ a.m.	☐ p.m.
☐ Vomiting	① ② ③ ④ ⑤	☐ a.m.	☐ p.m.
☐ Constipation	① ② ③ ④ ⑤	☐ a.m.	☐ p.m.
☐ Diarrhea	① ② ③ ④ ⑤	☐ a.m.	☐ p.m.
☐ Sore throat	① ② ③ ④ ⑤	☐ a.m.	☐ p.m.
☐ Congestion	① ② ③ ④ ⑤	☐ a.m.	☐ p.m.
☐ Coughing	① ② ③ ④ ⑤	☐ a.m.	☐ p.m.
☐ Acid reflux	① ② ③ ④ ⑤	☐ a.m.	☐ p.m.

psychological

Symptom	Severity	Time	
☐ Anxiety	① ② ③ ④ ⑤	☐ a.m.	☐ p.m.
☐ Depression	① ② ③ ④ ⑤	☐ a.m.	☐ p.m.
☐ Memory loss	① ② ③ ④ ⑤	☐ a.m.	☐ p.m.
☐ Confusion	① ② ③ ④ ⑤	☐ a.m.	☐ p.m.
☐ Poor focus	① ② ③ ④ ⑤	☐ a.m.	☐ p.m.
☐ Mood swings	① ② ③ ④ ⑤	☐ a.m.	☐ p.m.
☐ Suicidal	① ② ③ ④ ⑤	☐ a.m.	☐ p.m.

other

Symptom	Severity	Time	
	① ② ③ ④ ⑤	☐ a.m.	☐ p.m.
	① ② ③ ④ ⑤	☐ a.m.	☐ p.m.
	① ② ③ ④ ⑤	☐ a.m.	☐ p.m.
	① ② ③ ④ ⑤	☐ a.m.	☐ p.m.
	① ② ③ ④ ⑤	☐ a.m.	☐ p.m.
	① ② ③ ④ ⑤	☐ a.m.	☐ p.m.
	① ② ③ ④ ⑤	☐ a.m.	☐ p.m.

SLEEP

hours ________

quality ① ② ③ ④ ⑤

STRESS LEVELS

None	Low	Medium	High	Max	@$#%!

WEATHER

☐ Cold ☐ Mild ☐ Hot

☐ Dry ☐ Humid ☐ Wet

Allergen Levels: ________

BM Pressure: ________

EXERCISE

☐ Heck yes, I worked out.

☐ I managed to exercise a bit.

☐ No, I haven't exercised at all.

☐ I did some stuff, and that counts.

DETAILS

FOOD / MEDICATION

Food / Drinks

Meds / Supplements	Time	Dose

☐ usual daily medication

Water *Caffeine* *Alcohol*

☐☐☐☐☐☐☐☐☐☐

x ________ x ________

FOOD ANALYSIS

New food introduced?

☐ Yes ☐ No

Food reintroduction?

☐ Yes ☐ No

Details

MEDICATION ANALYSIS

New med/dose introduced?

☐ Yes ☐ No

Medication stopped?

☐ Yes ☐ No

Details

ACTIVITY ANALYSIS

Heightened exertion levels?

☐ Yes ☐ No

Lowered exertion levels?

☐ Yes ☐ No

Details

SLEEP ANALYSIS

When you woke up this morning, did you feel well-rested?	☐ Yes	☐ No	☐ A bit
Did you snore or stop breathing throughout the night?	☐ Yes	☐ No	☐ Not sure
Roughly how many times did you wake up throughout the night?			

Notes / Suspected Triggers

ENTRY #89 | M T W T F S S | DATE:

HOW ARE YOU *Feeling today?*

Amazing!	Meh
Great	Not good
Good	Terrible!

RATE YOUR PAIN LEVEL

① ② ③ ④ ⑤ ⑥ ⑦ ⑧ ⑨ ⑩

WHAT ABOUT YOUR...?

Mood	① ② ③ ④ ⑤ ⑥ ⑦ ⑧ ⑨ ⑩
Energy Levels	① ② ③ ④ ⑤ ⑥ ⑦ ⑧ ⑨ ⑩
Mental Clarity	① ② ③ ④ ⑤ ⑥ ⑦ ⑧ ⑨ ⑩

PAIN & PHYSICAL SYMPTOMS

Symptom	Severity	am	pm
	① ② ③ ④ ⑤	☐	☐
	① ② ③ ④ ⑤	☐	☐
	① ② ③ ④ ⑤	☐	☐
	① ② ③ ④ ⑤	☐	☐
	① ② ③ ④ ⑤	☐	☐
	① ② ③ ④ ⑤	☐	☐
	① ② ③ ④ ⑤	☐	☐
	① ② ③ ④ ⑤	☐	☐

front

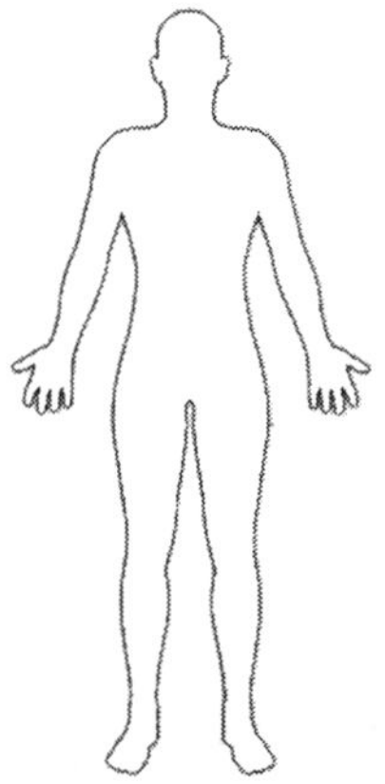

back

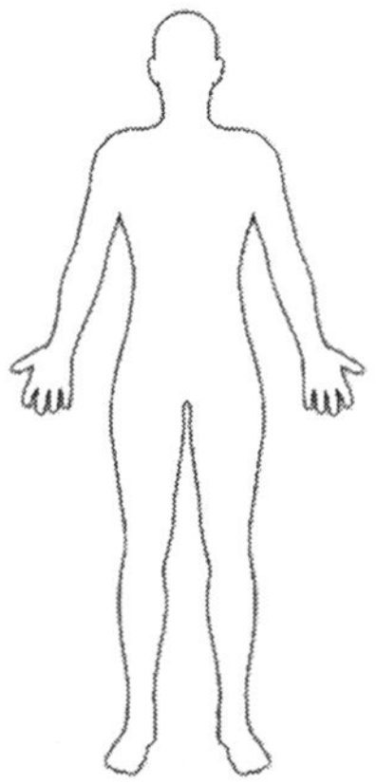

OTHER SYMPTOMS

general

Symptom	Severity	Time	
☐ Fatigue	① ② ③ ④ ⑤	☐ a.m.	☐ p.m.
☐ Lethargy	① ② ③ ④ ⑤	☐ a.m.	☐ p.m.
☐ Malaise	① ② ③ ④ ⑤	☐ a.m.	☐ p.m.
☐ Weakness	① ② ③ ④ ⑤	☐ a.m.	☐ p.m.
☐ Dizziness	① ② ③ ④ ⑤	☐ a.m.	☐ p.m.
☐ Trembling	① ② ③ ④ ⑤	☐ a.m.	☐ p.m.
☐ Twitching	① ② ③ ④ ⑤	☐ a.m.	☐ p.m.
☐ Insomnia	① ② ③ ④ ⑤	☐ a.m.	☐ p.m.

illness

Symptom	Severity	Time	
☐ Nausea	① ② ③ ④ ⑤	☐ a.m.	☐ p.m.
☐ Vomiting	① ② ③ ④ ⑤	☐ a.m.	☐ p.m.
☐ Constipation	① ② ③ ④ ⑤	☐ a.m.	☐ p.m.
☐ Diarrhea	① ② ③ ④ ⑤	☐ a.m.	☐ p.m.
☐ Sore throat	① ② ③ ④ ⑤	☐ a.m.	☐ p.m.
☐ Congestion	① ② ③ ④ ⑤	☐ a.m.	☐ p.m.
☐ Coughing	① ② ③ ④ ⑤	☐ a.m.	☐ p.m.
☐ Acid reflux	① ② ③ ④ ⑤	☐ a.m.	☐ p.m.

psychological

Symptom	Severity	Time	
☐ Anxiety	① ② ③ ④ ⑤	☐ a.m.	☐ p.m.
☐ Depression	① ② ③ ④ ⑤	☐ a.m.	☐ p.m.
☐ Memory loss	① ② ③ ④ ⑤	☐ a.m.	☐ p.m.
☐ Confusion	① ② ③ ④ ⑤	☐ a.m.	☐ p.m.
☐ Poor focus	① ② ③ ④ ⑤	☐ a.m.	☐ p.m.
☐ Mood swings	① ② ③ ④ ⑤	☐ a.m.	☐ p.m.
☐ Suicidal	① ② ③ ④ ⑤	☐ a.m.	☐ p.m.

other

Symptom	Severity	Time	
	① ② ③ ④ ⑤	☐ a.m.	☐ p.m.
	① ② ③ ④ ⑤	☐ a.m.	☐ p.m.
	① ② ③ ④ ⑤	☐ a.m.	☐ p.m.
	① ② ③ ④ ⑤	☐ a.m.	☐ p.m.
	① ② ③ ④ ⑤	☐ a.m.	☐ p.m.
	① ② ③ ④ ⑤	☐ a.m.	☐ p.m.
	① ② ③ ④ ⑤	☐ a.m.	☐ p.m.

SLEEP

hours ________ *quality* ① ② ③ ④ ⑤

STRESS LEVELS

None	Low	Medium	High	Max	@$#%!

WEATHER

☐ Cold ☐ Mild ☐ Hot
☐ Dry ☐ Humid ☐ Wet

Allergen Levels: ________
BM Pressure: ________

EXERCISE

☐ Heck yes, I worked out.
☐ I managed to exercise a bit.
☐ No, I haven't exercised at all.
☐ I did some stuff, and that counts.

DETAILS

FOOD / MEDICATION

Food / Drinks

Meds / Supplements	Time	Dose
☐ usual daily medication		

Water	*Caffeine*	*Alcohol*
	x ________	x ________

FOOD ANALYSIS		MEDICATION ANALYSIS		ACTIVITY ANALYSIS	
New food introduced?		New med/dose introduced?		Heightened exertion levels?	
☐ Yes	☐ No	☐ Yes	☐ No	☐ Yes	☐ No
Food reintroduction?		Medication stopped?		Lowered exertion levels?	
☐ Yes	☐ No	☐ Yes	☐ No	☐ Yes	☐ No
Details		*Details*		*Details*	

SLEEP ANALYSIS

When you woke up this morning, did you feel well-rested?	☐ Yes	☐ No	☐ A bit
Did you snore or stop breathing throughout the night?	☐ Yes	☐ No	☐ Not sure
Roughly how many times did you wake up throughout the night?			

Notes / Suspected Triggers

ENTRY #90 | M T W T F S S | DATE:

HOW ARE YOU *Feeling today?*

Amazing!	Meh
Great	Not good
Good	Terrible!

RATE YOUR PAIN LEVEL

① ② ③ ④ ⑤ ⑥ ⑦ ⑧ ⑨ ⑩

WHAT ABOUT YOUR...?

Mood	① ② ③ ④ ⑤ ⑥ ⑦ ⑧ ⑨ ⑩
Energy Levels	① ② ③ ④ ⑤ ⑥ ⑦ ⑧ ⑨ ⑩
Mental Clarity	① ② ③ ④ ⑤ ⑥ ⑦ ⑧ ⑨ ⑩

PAIN & PHYSICAL SYMPTOMS

Symptom	Severity	am	pm
	① ② ③ ④ ⑤	☐	☐
	① ② ③ ④ ⑤	☐	☐
	① ② ③ ④ ⑤	☐	☐
	① ② ③ ④ ⑤	☐	☐
	① ② ③ ④ ⑤	☐	☐
	① ② ③ ④ ⑤	☐	☐
	① ② ③ ④ ⑤	☐	☐
	① ② ③ ④ ⑤	☐	☐

front *back*

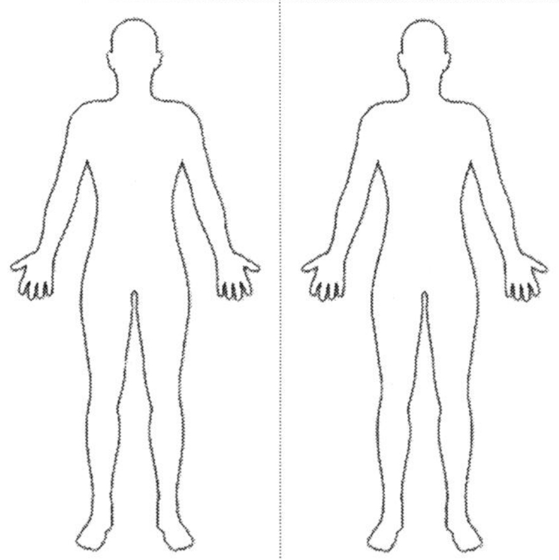

OTHER SYMPTOMS

general

Symptom	Severity	Time	
☐ Fatigue	① ② ③ ④ ⑤	☐ a.m.	☐ p.m.
☐ Lethargy	① ② ③ ④ ⑤	☐ a.m.	☐ p.m.
☐ Malaise	① ② ③ ④ ⑤	☐ a.m.	☐ p.m.
☐ Weakness	① ② ③ ④ ⑤	☐ a.m.	☐ p.m.
☐ Dizziness	① ② ③ ④ ⑤	☐ a.m.	☐ p.m.
☐ Trembling	① ② ③ ④ ⑤	☐ a.m.	☐ p.m.
☐ Twitching	① ② ③ ④ ⑤	☐ a.m.	☐ p.m.
☐ Insomnia	① ② ③ ④ ⑤	☐ a.m.	☐ p.m.

illness

Symptom	Severity	Time	
☐ Nausea	① ② ③ ④ ⑤	☐ a.m.	☐ p.m.
☐ Vomiting	① ② ③ ④ ⑤	☐ a.m.	☐ p.m.
☐ Constipation	① ② ③ ④ ⑤	☐ a.m.	☐ p.m.
☐ Diarrhea	① ② ③ ④ ⑤	☐ a.m.	☐ p.m.
☐ Sore throat	① ② ③ ④ ⑤	☐ a.m.	☐ p.m.
☐ Congestion	① ② ③ ④ ⑤	☐ a.m.	☐ p.m.
☐ Coughing	① ② ③ ④ ⑤	☐ a.m.	☐ p.m.
☐ Acid reflux	① ② ③ ④ ⑤	☐ a.m.	☐ p.m.

psychological

Symptom	Severity	Time	
☐ Anxiety	① ② ③ ④ ⑤	☐ a.m.	☐ p.m.
☐ Depression	① ② ③ ④ ⑤	☐ a.m.	☐ p.m.
☐ Memory loss	① ② ③ ④ ⑤	☐ a.m.	☐ p.m.
☐ Confusion	① ② ③ ④ ⑤	☐ a.m.	☐ p.m.
☐ Poor focus	① ② ③ ④ ⑤	☐ a.m.	☐ p.m.
☐ Mood swings	① ② ③ ④ ⑤	☐ a.m.	☐ p.m.
☐ Suicidal	① ② ③ ④ ⑤	☐ a.m.	☐ p.m.

other

Symptom	Severity	Time	
	① ② ③ ④ ⑤	☐ a.m.	☐ p.m.
	① ② ③ ④ ⑤	☐ a.m.	☐ p.m.
	① ② ③ ④ ⑤	☐ a.m.	☐ p.m.
	① ② ③ ④ ⑤	☐ a.m.	☐ p.m.
	① ② ③ ④ ⑤	☐ a.m.	☐ p.m.
	① ② ③ ④ ⑤	☐ a.m.	☐ p.m.
	① ② ③ ④ ⑤	☐ a.m.	☐ p.m.

SLEEP

hours ________ *quality* ① ② ③ ④ ⑤

STRESS LEVELS

None	Low	Medium	High	Max	@$#%!

WEATHER

☐ Cold ☐ Mild ☐ Hot
☐ Dry ☐ Humid ☐ Wet

Allergen Levels: ________

BM Pressure: ________

EXERCISE

☐ Heck yes, I worked out.
☐ I managed to exercise a bit.
☐ No, I haven't exercised at all.
☐ I did some stuff, and that counts.

DETAILS

FOOD / MEDICATION

Food / Drinks

Meds / Supplements	Time	Dose

☐ usual daily medication

Water *Caffeine* *Alcohol*

x ________ x ________

FOOD ANALYSIS

New food introduced?

☐ Yes ☐ No

Food reintroduction?

☐ Yes ☐ No

Details

MEDICATION ANALYSIS

New med/dose introduced?

☐ Yes ☐ No

Medication stopped?

☐ Yes ☐ No

Details

ACTIVITY ANALYSIS

Heightened exertion levels?

☐ Yes ☐ No

Lowered exertion levels?

☐ Yes ☐ No

Details

SLEEP ANALYSIS

When you woke up this morning, did you feel well-rested? ☐ Yes ☐ No ☐ A bit

Did you snore or stop breathing throughout the night? ☐ Yes ☐ No ☐ Not sure

Roughly how many times did you wake up throughout the night?

Notes / Suspected Triggers

Notes

Printed in Poland
by Amazon Fulfillment
Poland Sp. z o.o., Wrocław
27 August 2023

3571f60c-afa2-4a1d-a016-a8514fcb0a96R01